T0308403

Robert Jones says it well, "The Bible does not merely inform our counseling, ... the Bible drives our counseling." I believe he is exactly correct. The contributors to *Scripture and Counseling* encourage, teach, and show us how this happens as we pursue and develop a robust biblical strategy in ministry to hurting, confused, and broken people. The book is obviously comprehensive! It is also well written. I suspect it will become a standard resource in the field of biblical counseling.

Dr. Daniel L. Akin, President,
Southeastern Baptist Theological Seminary, Wake Forest, NC

What role does the Word of God play in counseling? This is a crucial and often energetically debated question in the church and among counselors. The contributors to *Scripture and Counseling* have carefully, thoughtfully, and helpfully explored both how to think about the Bible in counseling and how to use the Bible in counseling. I commend this significant work to anyone who looks to Scripture to help people make sense of life in a broken world.

Jack Delk, Pastor for Counseling,
Bethlehem Baptist Church, Minneapolis

Because we live in a culture that considers the Bible to be at best irrelevant, or even ridiculous, there has been a growing question even among serious Christians as to its sufficiency, especially for counseling the serious problems of the soul. *Scripture and Counseling* provides the framework for a profitable discussion of this issue and helps us appreciate the richness of God's Word in helping people who are hurting. It purposefully and wisely moves from how counselors' correct beliefs about the Bible directly affect how it will be beneficial to them. Anyone interested in helping people with the Scriptures should read this book.

Dr. John D. Street, President, Association of Certified Biblical Counselors,
Chair, MABC Graduate Program, The Master's College & Seminary

Scripture and Counseling is both theologically robust and pastorally helpful. On its pages you will find a lively discussion that will bring you up to speed on the conversation taking place among contemporary biblical counseling.

J. D. Greear, Pastor, The Summit Church

Scripture and Counseling offers the Christian an apologetic for the Bible's sufficiency for the care of souls and then demonstrates it through common yet challenging disciple-making matters we encounter in a broken world. Every follower of Christ should read this collaborative volume to glean biblical truths for enthusiastic, loving disciple-making within the context of personal ministry. Committed disciple-makers, relying upon the Word of God and the Holy Spirit to transform heart desires for God's glory, will discover the "why and how" of biblical counseling in this excellent work.

Dr. Mark E. Shaw, Pastor and Executive Director of Vision of Hope,
a ministry of Faith Church, Lafayette, IN; author of *The Heart of Addiction*

Scripture and Counseling is not just a book about Scripture, but a book about how to apply Scripture to our lives and in our ministries to others in manner that will lead us to function as God intended, resulting in God's glory and our ultimate good. This will be an extremely helpful tool for people who want to apply the Word of God in their counseling ministry in an efficient and effective manner.

Dr. Nicolas Ellen, Professor of Biblical Counseling,
College of Biblical Studies

Conviction and competence are key ingredients to caring well for the souls of others. All followers of Christ must have a growing conviction that God's Word is sufficient and a growing competence in how to use it to care for one another. By providing a sound theology of Scripture and a thorough approach to using God's Word, *Scripture and Counseling* is an indispensable resource for helping believers grow in both conviction and competence.

Andrew Rogers, Pastor of Soul Care,
College Park Church, Indianapolis

My heart rejoices whenever I hear of a book being published that strengthens our understanding of and commitment to the sufficiency of the Scriptures for personal ministry. This book is relentless in the pursuit of that goal! As a textbook, as a resource, and as a source of inspiration and encouragement in the modern "battle for the Bible," *Scripture and Counseling* will serve and strengthen many generations of Bible students and soul care practitioners.

Dr. Wayne Vanderwier, Executive Director
of Overseas Instruction in Counseling

Scripture and Counseling is a book that every friend and critic of biblical counseling will find challenging and enlightening. Linking counseling and preaching with simplicity and profundity reveals the full effects the ministry of the Word can have upon the body of Christ. The authors demonstrate the wisdom of counseling the Word as being sufficient for life and ministry.

Dr. Thomas Zempel, Pastor-Professor of Counseling,
Colonial Baptist Church, Cary, NC

When it comes to diagnosing and solving life's issues, a biblical counselor is someone who is committed to the sufficiency of God's Word found in the Bible rather than the wisdom of man found in psychology. But what does that mean in practical terms? How would you know the difference? In *Scripture and Counseling*, the authors have masterfully brought this issue, and this much-debated topic in the counseling world to the forefront. The authors' collaborative work and thorough scholarship will lead you, whether you are a pastor, biblical counselor, or psychologist, to settle what you believe and practice in your counseling ministry. This is a must-read.

Dr. Kevin E. Hurt, Senior Pastor,
Grace Bible Church

A BIBLICAL COUNSELING COALITION BOOK

SCRIPTURE AND COUNSELING

GOD'S WORD FOR LIFE IN A BROKEN WORLD

BOB KELLEMEN, GENERAL EDITOR

JEFF FORREY, MANAGING EDITOR

FOREWORD BY R. ALBERT MOHLER JR.

ZONDERVAN

Scripture and Counseling
Copyright © 2014 by Biblical Counseling Coalition

This title is also available as a Zondervan ebook.

Requests for information should be addressed to:
Zondervan, 3900 *Sparks Dr. SE, Grand Rapids, Michigan 49546*

Library of Congress Cataloging-in-Publication Data

Scripture and counseling : God's word for life in a broken world / Bob Kellemen, general editor, Jeffery Forrey, managing editor.
     pages cm
     "A Biblical Counseling Coalition book."
     Includes bibliographical references and index.
     ISBN 978-0-310-51683-5
     1. Counseling—Religious aspects—Christianity. 2. Bible—Psychology. 3. Christian life—Biblical teaching. I. Kellemen, Robert W., editor.
     BR115.C69S37 2014
     253.5—dc23   2014010369

Published in association with the literary agency of Wolgemuth & Associates, Inc.

Cover design: Lucas Art and Design
Cover photography: iStockphoto
Interior design: David Conn

Printed in the United States of America

---

22 23 24 25 26 27 28 29 30 31 32 /TRM/ 22 21 20 19 18 17 16 15 14 13

CONTENTS

FOREWORD

R. ALBERT MOHLER JR.

One of the most revolutionary aspects of the gospel of Jesus Christ is the assumption that our main problem is inside of us and our only hope for rescue comes from without. In matters of counseling, the secular worldview, driven by the engine of therapy, says precisely the opposite—our problem is something outside of us, and the rescue we need is something that comes from within. This is the very antithesis of gospel proclamation. It is impossible to reconcile the doctrine of human depravity with the ethos of self-esteem. It is impossible to mix orthodox theology and secular therapeutic counseling.

Any attempt to reconcile these worldviews with the gospel subverts the gospel intentionally or unintentionally. Mixing secular psychology with the church's theology makes the gospel something it is not. The history of secular counseling bears witness to this fact. Freud told us that our problem is in our subconscious and must be treated by therapy; Jung found the problem in the structures of the unconscious brain; Maslow told us that what we need is self-actualization; Bettelheim told us to get in touch with our stories; and the list goes on. These notions are all contrary to the Christian worldview. Yet one of the great tragedies of our age is that the average Christian bookstore is teeming with literature promoting the agenda of secular psychology. Sadly, much of this literature succeeds in the Christian market by barely camouflaging the secular worldviews it promotes.

This means that the task of biblical counseling must be undertaken with a sense of urgency. We are living in a time of tremendous cultural and theological confusion and this has led to a vast and dangerous infection of the church. Regrettably, many churches have embraced counseling that majors on the therapeutic. Marketable and pragmatic, this form of counseling orbits around the self and is theologically anemic. It lacks the transforming power of the gospel — a gospel that reminds us that the solution to our problems comes from outside ourselves, not from within.

In counseling, as in every area of life, the people of God must take their marching orders from the Word of God, committed to its authority and sufficiency. Believers are called to counsel one another with the rich truth of God's Word in a way consistent with the gospel of Jesus Christ. At the center of this counseling ministry that we have to one another is the church — more specifically local churches marked by the truth, power, and authority of God's Word and of the gospel (Matthew 16:13 – 20). The communion of the saints, ordered by the authority of God's Word, is the center of biblical counseling.

Christ has richly lavished his grace on his church. As we minister, serve, and worship together we receive the vast riches of God's counsel together. Part of the biblical counseling ministry of the church proceeds from the pulpit as church members corporately submit themselves to the Word of God. At other times a more personal ministry of the Word is needed as members counsel one another about specific problems, looking at specific situations in the Scriptures.

The communion of the saints exercises godly counsel through worship, preaching, the ordinances, and other means of grace. The communion of the saints is a communion of godly counsel givers. We are not merely individual Christians, loosely scattered throughout the world. Christians are members of the body of Christ, and our identity is bound up in the community of God's people. As Paul reminds us, "If one member suffers, all suffer together" (1 Corinthians 12:26). Therefore, congregations and churches must be theologically equipped to apply the Word of God to one another's lives. In this way the church is equipped, the church is called, the church is exhorted, the church is encouraged, and the church is made into the likeness of Christ.

As a communion of holy ones, our aim is to conform one another to the image of Christ. In the words of Paul, each member is to work as God has gifted him such that the body "builds itself up in love" (Ephesians 4:16). Words of godly counsel are the natural discourse of a believing congregation. And counseling is part of the natural order of the church, as saints move toward faithfulness and maturity.

Preaching on Ephesians 6:14, Martyn Lloyd-Jones said, "There can be no doubt whatsoever that all the troubles in the church today, and most of the troubles in the world, are due to a departure from the authority of the Bible." The recent history of counseling ministries in evangelical churches has demonstrated the truthfulness of Lloyd-Jones's words. As churches outsource counseling needs to the secular world or adopt the worldview of therapeutic psychology into their own ministries, they damage the church's convictions about the authority and sufficiency of God's Word and belittle the redeeming power of the gospel.

The contributors to this volume are men and women who faithfully uphold the Word of God as the church's only resource for Christ-centered change. I commend their conviction in this Word, a Word that reveals how God has rescued sinners by turning them away from self to the cross and the resurrection of his Son. I am thankful for the *Biblical Counseling Coalition's* commitment to promote counseling that is grounded in sound theology and rooted in the life of the church. And I am even more thankful that the BCC is producing the book that you are now holding in your hands. *Scripture and Counseling: God's Word for Life in a Broken World* is representative of the type of theologically sophisticated and pastorally sensitive counseling literature needed in evangelical churches.

OUR PRAYER
FOR YOU

BOB KELLEMEN

We face a tremendous weakening of confidence in the Bible as central to life. This is true for the pastor ministering to struggling people in the congregation, for the counselor in the counseling office, for the layperson talking with a struggling friend at Starbucks, and for the small group leader unsure of what to say to a hurting group member. *Scripture and Counseling* encourages these individuals — people like you — to regain their *confidence* in God's Word for real-life issues and equips them to grow in their *competence* in using God's Word to tackle the complex issues of life.

Is God's Word profoundly sufficient, necessary, authoritative, and relevant to equip God's people to address specific, complex issues in today's broken world? *Scripture and Counseling* does more than answer with a resounding "Yes!" It communicates a way of *viewing* God's Word to address life in a broken world — a robust *theology* of the personal ministry of the Word. And it presents a way of *using* God's Word to minister to broken people — a practical *methodology* of the personal ministry of the Word.

The "sufficiency of Scripture" has become an oft-debated buzzword in academic circles. However, this issue has vital ramifications well beyond academic debates. The failure to understand, develop, and implement a wise and practical approach to the sufficiency and necessity of God's Word for the personal ministry of the Word has weakened the church's ministry of the Word and the church's impact in the world.

Scripture and Counseling focuses on a positive and practical presentation of scriptural authority, relevancy, necessity, profundity, and sufficiency for daily life. With real-life seriousness it addresses the vital question: How do we *view* and *use* the Bible to help one another to deal biblically with the complex issues of suffering and sin?

Scripture and Counseling does not simply communicate, "Please stop going to the self-help section of Amazon to find answers for your problems." Instead, *Scripture and Counseling* communicates, "Here's why and how to develop a *robust biblical* approach to the personal ministry of the Word."

The subtitle—*God's Word for Life in a Broken World*—guides every chapter contributor. With every word they penned, they have asked, "How can my chapter encourage and equip pastors, small group leaders, biblical counselors, one-another ministers, and spiritual friends to trust God's Word and to use God's Word to minister to broken people?"

Our prayer for you as you read *Scripture and Counseling* is the same as Paul's prayer for the believers in Philippi. Persecuted because of their faith (Phil. 1:29–30), struggling with fears and anxiety (Phil. 1:28; 4:6), experiencing relational conflicts (Phil. 4:2), and battling against temptations toward selfishness (Phil. 2:2–4) and self-sufficiency (Phil. 3:1–11), they needed to hear the same Christ-centered message we need to hear today:

> And it is my prayer that your love may abound more and more, with knowledge and all discernment, so that you may approve what is excellent, and so be pure and blameless for the day of Christ, filled with the fruit of righteousness that comes through Jesus Christ, to the glory and praise of God (Phil. 1:9–11).

We pray that *Scripture and Counseling* will encourage you to trust

God's Word to provide rich insight for living in the midst of even the most difficult times of suffering and the most distressing battles against besetting sins. We pray that *Scripture and Counseling* will provide you with a robust, loving, best-practice guide so you will gain competence in using God's Word to address the real-life issues of people in a broken world. And we pray that the result will be the bride of Christ growing in Christlikeness to the glory and praise of God.

PART I

HOW WE *VIEW* THE BIBLE FOR LIFE IN A BROKEN WORLD

BOB KELLEMEN

In part 1 we want to assist you to develop a robust biblical *view* of Scripture for life and godliness—a biblical *theology* of Scripture for counseling. Throughout part 1, our authors demonstrate the "why" of Scripture for counseling, leading to increased *confidence* in God's Word.

In the introduction, "The Preacher, the Counselor, and the Congregation," the pastoral team of Kevin DeYoung and Pat Quinn develop the relationship between the pulpit ministry of the Word and the personal ministry of the Word. Kevin and Pat demonstrate how confidence and competence in God's Word can and should saturate *every* aspect of ministry.

In chapter 1, "The Richness and Relevance of God's Word," Kevin Carson develops a foundational biblical theology of God's Word for our lives. Kevin helps us to grasp what is at stake, understand the issues, and grow in our confidence in the Bible's comprehensive relevance to life in a broken world.

Paul Tautges and Steve Viars in chapter 2, "Sufficient for Life and Godliness," ask, "If Scripture is the lens through which we view the world, then how does that lens work?" Paul and Steve help us to understand more clearly how God's Word thoroughly equips us for life and ministry.

In chapter 3, "Where Do We Find Truth?," and chapter 4, "What Is

Psychology?," Jeffery Forrey takes us on a journey with several friends who ponder in-depth, real-life questions about the Bible, sources of truth, and the relationship between biblical counseling and psychology. In his two chapters, Jeff helps us to gain an increased wonder at God's revelation—in creation and Scripture. And he helps us to see the importance of understanding the creature through the Creator.

In chapter 5, "Scripture Is Sufficient, but to Do What?," Jeremy Pierre addresses the nature and purpose of Scripture. Jeremy helps us to grow in our confidence in the comprehensive relevancy and necessity of the Scriptures for building a model of people, problems, and change.

Robert Jones in chapter 6, "The Christ-Centeredness of Biblical Counseling," demonstrates how counseling that flows from Scripture is focused on Christ. Robert reminds us that the purpose of Scripture-based counseling is to lead people to adore, commune with, become like, depend upon, and follow Jesus Christ.

In chapter 7, "A Counseling Primer from the Great Cloud of Witnesses," Bob Kellemen traces the story of the relationship between the Bible and counseling throughout church history. Bob helps us to grow in appreciation of the historical legacy of confidence in God's Word to change lives.

Sam Williams in chapter 8, "What about the Body?," explores the implications of scriptural sufficiency given that we are embodied beings. Sam helps us to appreciate the complexity of the mind-body relationship and to think through a biblical theology of the body, of medication, and of mental illness.

In chapter 9, "Caution: Counseling Systems Are Belief Systems," the team of Ernie Baker and Howard Eyrich share with readers the cautions that the apostle Paul shared with his readers in Colossians. Ernie and Howard help us to grow in discernment about the foundations upon which counseling systems are built.

In chapter 10, "The Bible Is Relevant for That?," Bob Kellemen addresses how we *view* the Bible for life in a broken world. Using the issue of sexual abuse, Bob helps us to build a robust, comprehensive way of viewing the Bible in order to develop biblical approaches to life issues.

As you read each chapter in part 1, I encourage you to see them as part of a much larger whole. Though written by a dozen authors, the chapters weave together a story. As the outline contained above indicates, each chapter crafts a specific piece of the puzzle that it is working into place. No one chapter is attempting to say everything about issues related to the Bible's rich sufficiency and robust relevancy for life in a broken world. However, taken together, it is our prayer that the combined chapters in *Scripture and Counseling* may offer you a mosaic of the Bible's authority and necessity for daily life and relationships under the cross.

THE PREACHER, THE COUNSELOR, AND THE CONGREGATION

KEVIN DEYOUNG AND PAT QUINN

At University Reformed Church, where we serve, one of the firm convictions is that the ministry of the preacher and the ministry of the counselor are not different kinds of ministry, but rather the same ministry given in different ways in different settings. Both are fundamentally, thoroughly, and unapologetically Word ministries. One may be more proclamation and monologue, and the other more conversational and dialogue, but the variation in approach and context does not undermine their shared belief in the power of the Word of God to do the work of God in the people of God. What shapes our understanding of pulpit ministry is a strong confidence in the necessity, sufficiency, authority, and relevance of God's Word. The same confidence shapes our understanding of counseling ministry.

The Word of God is necessary. We cannot truly know God or know ourselves unless God speaks. While Christians can learn from the insights of those blessed by common grace and those with gifts of reason and observation, the care of souls requires revelation from the

Maker of souls. We preach and we counsel from the Scriptures not simply because they help us see a few good insights, but because they are the spectacles through which we must see everything.

The Word of God is sufficient. All we need for life and godliness, for salvation and sanctification has been given to us in the Bible. This doesn't mean the Scriptures tell us everything we need to know about everything or that there is a verse somewhere in the Bible that names all our problems. The Bible is not exhaustive. But it is enough. We don't have to turn away from God's Word when we get to the really hard and messy stuff of life. The Bible has something to say to the self-loathing, the self-destructive, and the self-absorbed. We do not need to be afraid to preach and counsel from the Word of God into the darkest places of the human heart.

The Word of God is authoritative. The Christ who is Lord exercises His lordship by means of His Word. To reject His Word is to reject Him. In a day filled with sermonettes for Christianettes, we must not forget that what most distinguished Jesus' preaching from that of the scribes and Pharisees was His authority. The Word gives definitive claims, issues obligatory commands, and makes life-changing promises. All three must be announced with authority. This authority may be spoken in a loud voice or a soft whisper, in a prayer or in a personal note, with an outstretched finger or an open embrace. Authority is not dependent on personality or one's position within the church building. Authority comes from God's Word, and the counselor no less than the preacher must bring this authority to bear on all those encountered, especially on those who swear allegiance to Christ.

God's Word is relevant. Terms change. Science changes. Our experiences change. But the human predicament does not change, the divine remedy does not change, and the truth does not change. This makes the Word of God eternally relevant. Whatever work we can accomplish in the church apart from the Word of God is not the work that matters most. When it comes to matters of heaven and hell, matters of sin and salvation, matters of brokenness and healing, we are powerless in ourselves to effect any of the good change we want to see. This is why we must rely on the unchanging Word of God. If Christ is relevant — and what Christian would dare say He is not — then we can never ignore what He has to say to us. There is less wisdom in our new techniques than we think and more power in God's Word than we imagine.

A GOSPEL-TUNED TAG TEAM

I (Kevin) love the partnership in the Word that I share with Pat. It's encouraging — and unfortunately rare in many churches — to know that what I preach on Sunday will be reinforced by our counseling ministry Monday through Saturday. I don't have to worry that Pat will be working from a different foundation or pursuing a different cure. He's far more gifted than I am at asking questions, assigning homework, leading Bible studies, and gently helping people apply the Word of God to their problems. But though he may be more skilled in his context, he doesn't do anything substantially different from what I do in mine. He talks about faith, repentance, sin, salvation, the gospel, justification, lies, truth, forgiveness, promises, commands, communion with God, and union with Christ — all the same themes I expound from the pulpit week after week.

I'd like to think my preaching makes Pat's counseling easier. He can build on what I teach, use what I preach, and remind people of last week's sermons because when we both work from the Word, we end up saying the same things. I know I've become a better preacher knowing that Pat is such a good counselor. Hearing the questions he asks and the cases he's working on helps me make sure that *my message does not just aim for an announcement of truth, but also for the care of souls*. It's always more effective to preach with real people, real hurts, real struggles, and real temptations in view. Being involved in our counseling ministry forces me to think how this week's text speaks to a teenager with same-sex attraction, or to an older man struggling with bitterness, or to a young couple with no hope for their marriage, or to a confused wife who can't stand her husband. If my sermons don't help with counseling, then I need to rework my approach to preaching. And if a church's counseling is totally unlike, in substance and grounding, faithful expositional preaching, then that church's counseling probably is something other than biblical. The preacher and the counselor working together, teaching the same truths from the same Bible to the same heart conditions, can be a powerfully gospel-tuned tag team.

THE PREACHER AND THE COUNSELOR

I (Pat) have been serving as director of counseling ministries at University Reformed Church since 2009. When Kevin became pastor in 2005, we discovered that we had a mutual love for biblical counseling, and this eventually led to creating a new staff position for me. I have had the privilege of serving with Kevin as an elder, worship leader, teacher, and counselor, and have benefited greatly from his leadership, preaching, and encouragement. Our shared vision for the ministry of the Word has made it a joy to serve together.

Shared Convictions

One of our shared convictions is *a commitment to and confidence in the necessity, sufficiency, authority, and relevancy of Scripture for helping people work through suffering and sin issues in a way that glorifies God and brings spiritual growth — making disciples.* Since one way of defining counseling is "remedial disciple making," this mutual commitment allows us to work together in direct and indirect ways. In my counseling training material I explain:

> While God speaks in many ways, He has spoken finally, decisively, and authoritatively through His Son Jesus Christ as recorded in the Scriptures (authority). While the Bible does not give an exhaustive list of all modern counseling problems and cures, it does provide a comprehensive way of looking at and addressing them (sufficiency and relevance). No other "word," counseling model, or therapeutic technique can effect awakening to the reality of God, deep conviction of what is most deeply wrong with us, complete forgiveness and acceptance, death to the sinful nature, freedom to change, and hope of future perfection (necessity).[1]

23

These shared convictions about Scripture allow us to be, as Kevin wrote, a gospel-tuned tag team to help people change. Here's what this looked like in two counseling cases.

Tag-Team Stories[2]

The first story illustrates how the necessity, sufficiency, authority, and relevancy of Scripture worked with a modern psychiatric problem. The second relates how preacher and counselor worked together to help a troubled couple find grace to restore their marriage.

JAMES

James came for counseling a couple of years ago struggling with extreme obsessive-compulsive disorder (OCD). The first time we met and I reached out to shake his hand, he asked me if I had washed my hands. In addition to this germophobia, James was wrestling with doubts about God and his salvation. As James and I continued to meet, it became increasingly clear that unprocessed sin from his past and the rejection from a recent breakup with a young woman were making him feel unclean, provoking his doubts, and fueling his OCD. This was very disorienting and painful for him. It was a joy to use Scriptures like Hebrews 9:14 to help James better understand how the gospel of grace connected with his inner and outer experience of uncleanness: "How much more will the blood of Christ [the great purifier], who through the eternal Spirit offered himself without blemish to God [through an atoning sacrifice], purify our conscience from dead works [i.e., compulsive hand washings] to serve the living God" (brackets added).

One day James said that while he was tracking with this somewhat, what he was struggling with still seemed much more physical than spiritual. He wasn't totally connecting his OCD with Jesus' purifying sacrifice. This is where a seemingly obscure passage from Leviticus, which Kevin had preached through in 2009, proved an invaluable link between a sense of physical defilement and spiritual cleansing. We looked at Leviticus 15, which is all about laws for bodily discharges (James was especially troubled by these) and God's remedy for physical uncleanness. I pointed out that even these physical issues needed a spiritual sacrifice of atonement (see Lev. 15:13 – 15), thus showing how our inner and outer selves are related and how God has provided a purifying remedy for both. This seemed to click with James and he left encouraged, but little did I realize how this connection between Old Testament ritual laws and New Testament gospel would help set James free from OCD.

A week later James's father copied me on an email to family members about a conversation he and James had the day we met.

> This past Monday, after his session with Pat, I drove him to class. After a silent time of studying for class, James suddenly began sharing with me nonstop about 15 minutes of Scripture references that Pat and he had gone over, most of them focusing on what uncleanness was in the Old Testament and contrasting that with the purity we have before God through the blood of Christ. As we drove, I noticed that James was no longer holding his hands in that awkward way he has for weeks to avoid touching anything. I also noted that James decided to forgo the extensive, elaborate hand washing with Germ-X that he has always done. Since that day, I would have trouble pointing to any unusual behavior whatsoever on James's part — no impossibly long showers, no inability to stop washing hands, etc. James confided in me, "I feel like I have been carrying a heavy burden around with me for years." The changes I have been seeing in him suggest God's lifting of that burden.

While James had much more growing in grace and freedom ahead of him, the immediate relevance and liberating power of Scripture to make a decisive difference in this life-dominating problem is stunning!

FRANK AND CARA

If James's story is about shared *convictions* about Scripture, Frank and Cara's story is about shared *ministry* in helping a couple restore their marriage after unfaithfulness. Kevin once said, tongue in cheek, "Pat, I make the messes (through preaching) and you clean them up (through counseling)." Here's how this worked in this couple's life.

A few years ago Frank and Cara went to church and heard Kevin preach a sermon on sexual purity. Frank recalled, "Almost immediately I felt besieged by guilt from the Holy Spirit about my unfaithfulness.

I've never experienced anything like the following week. I was unable to shake that sermon or that text from my mind." Frank wrestled with whether he should confess to his wife that week. "Through my week of struggle, the consistent message I received from God was this: 'I'm big enough to handle the upheaval in your life that will result from your confession.'" God gave Frank faith to confess honestly and Cara courage to respond graciously, and sometime after this, at their request, we began marriage counseling. What followed was over a year of painful but ultimately glorious ministry of Word and Spirit. While I did most of the counseling overall, Kevin played a major role at the beginning and occasionally he and I met with them together: a couple of times to counsel and encourage and once to share in a marital recommitment ceremony.

Obvious issues to deal with included helping Cara wrestle through disillusionment and the painful process of forgiveness, helping Frank to produce fruit flowing from repentance, helping them rebuild trust, and, most importantly, helping them see and repent of heart and behavior sins that were being exposed through this trial. The grace of God was beautifully evident. Frank showed consistent and brokenhearted repentance, and Cara showed amazing courage, perseverance, and grace. But it was not easy, especially for Cara. There were ups and downs, times of leaping ahead and stumbling back, radiant hope and dark despair, sweet smiles and bitter tears—but always amazing grace. Often I sat back in awe at the power of the Redeemer through His Word to overcome the devastation caused by sin and Satan. Scriptures that relevantly spoke grace and hope to them included the following:

- "For I know the plans I have for you, declares the LORD, plans for welfare [wholeness] and not for evil, to give you a future and a hope" (Jer. 29:11). This helped them see that God was with them, slowly but surely bringing hope out of despair.
- "... because they exchanged the truth about God for a lie and worshiped and served the creature rather than the Creator, who is blessed forever" (Rom. 1:25). Here we explored heart issues of

various God substitutes, cynicism, and unbelief that blindsided and tripped them up.

- "He who did not spare his own Son but gave him up for us all, how will he not also with him graciously give us all things?" (Rom. 8:32). As they rebuilt trust in God and one another, it was important to explore together what "all things" means. We saw that it included the forgiveness of sins, massive hope and strength to suffer well on the way, power to forgive, and the sweet promise of an eternal honeymoon with Jesus in heaven.
- "Fear not, for you will not be ashamed ... for you will forget the shame of your youth.... For your Maker is your husband, the LORD of hosts is his name" (Isa. 54:4–5). The Lord, who is our "husband" and has reconciled us to Himself at great cost, overcomes shame and gives hope for the future.
- The story of the Prodigal Son (Luke 15:11–32). This story (especially Timothy Keller's wonderful treatment of it in *The Prodigal God*)[3] was very helpful in identifying basic flesh patterns for Frank and Cara. Interestingly, they each identified with a different brother in the story.

It has been a privilege for Kevin and me (and others) to walk with Frank and Cara as they trusted and followed God on a hard road. There is more sanctifying work ahead, but their lives are a trophy of God's grace. One of my great joys as a counselor has been to hear Cara say, "I would never have believed God could change my heart this way," and, "I see grace everywhere."

THE COUNSELOR AND THE CONGREGATION

Our vision for the ministry of the Word includes not only shared convictions and ministry between preacher and counselor but also various training venues for the congregation in order to create a culture of one-anothering. We provide exposure to and training in biblical counseling through new member classes, leadership training, and two counselor-training classes. Our goal is to equip members of the congregation to be "disciple-making disciples" in the home, in the church, in the community, and across the world. We hope soon to offer biblical-counseling training to other local gospel-centered churches and to make it a part of our missionary care.

I have had the privilege of training a variety of people who are serving in a variety of ministries. Kristina, a former campus worker, currently finds biblical-counseling training most helpful at home: "As a mom of little ones, I find myself applying biblical-counseling principles most often to my own heart and family. God's Word is powerful, and 'face-to-face ministry of the Word' is happening more often in our home." Kevin has found the training helpful as a college resident director: "Before our class I would go to mentoring meetings without much preparation and with little time spent reflecting afterward to prepare for the next meeting. Learning to take notes and to take time to prepare for my time with students has been fruitful." Mike is a counselor at a local rescue mission: "The ongoing classes on counseling homosexuals were over the top. About this same time, I was asked to counsel two people struggling with same-sex attraction. Because of our study, for the first time I felt compassion for men who wanted to change but didn't know how." What a joy to help equip God's people to minister His life-changing Word in a variety of places—"as far as the curse is found."

CONCLUSION

Preacher, counselor, and congregation all ministering the Word of Life in a broken world—a beautiful vision. Have we arrived? Hardly. Do we have only success stories to report? Of course not. But we have seen enough of the relevance and power of the Word to press on. After all, this is God's vision, not ours: "He gave ... [pastors] and teachers, to equip the saints for the work of ministry, for building up the body of Christ, until we all attain to the unity of the faith and the knowledge of the Son of God" (Eph. 4:11 – 13).

THE RICHNESS
AND RELEVANCE
OF GOD'S WORD

KEVIN CARSON

The Bible is for you, me, and us. As a gift from God, the Bible benefits us (2 Tim. 3:16–17). It also touches life in so many different ways. In fact, simply stated, *the Bible is about what life is about.*

In the pages of the Bible you read the stuff of life, stuff that, since the Garden (Gen. 3:1–24), emanates from life in a broken world. There are births, weddings, children, and deaths. There are times of peace and times of war. There are periods of work and rest. There are heroes and villains. The range of emotions seems endless. There are moments of jubilation and moments of extreme sadness. There are times of hope and times of despair. There are songs of deliverance and songs of lament. There are stories that capture the best and the worst of human beings. You read of love, patience, kindness, and delight as well as hate, impatience, abuse, and sorrow. Just as life brings with it many ups and downs, so also do the pages of the Bible. The Bible is addressed to the living about living.

The Bible is also about *what counseling is about.* We live in a broken world where life is teeming with difficulties, pressures, concerns, and tough circumstances. These pressure-filled situations provide the backdrop for interaction between believers. The Bible speaks about the various situations that fill conversational ministry, whether formal, informal, across a fence, or in a small group—wherever and whatever the circumstance. Some days it is easier to see the connection than others. Consider how the Bible speaks into the following stories:

- Bill and Joan celebrated thirteen years of marriage. One month after their anniversary, Joan noticed that Bill seemed more distant than usual. He stayed increasingly longer and longer at work. When she eventually confronted him regarding his schedule and an increase in text messaging, Bill confessed to a relationship with a woman at work where he was committing marital infidelity.

- Steve and Amanda prayed diligently to get pregnant. After a year of desiring a baby, Amanda finally became pregnant. Together they shared the news with their families and church, prepared the baby's room, and considered names. At the thirty-week OB-GYN visit and ultrasound, they learned there were significant difficulties with the baby. Amanda delivered the baby four weeks later; he lived only hours.

- Jennifer made the college cheerleading squad. All through high school she prepared for just this day. The attention to her weight that started as preparation to make the big jump between high school and college performance levels had morphed into an obsession with her weight and appearance. After collapsing on the field house floor and being rushed to the hospital, the doctor diagnosed her with anorexia nervosa.

- Bryan regretted turning twenty-seven alone. His dream of marriage seemingly withered daily. All the guys with whom he had gone to college were now married and, in Bryan's mind, enjoying all the pleasures of marriage. Bryan confessed to his small group an insatiable addiction to pornography.

- Tom and Marian arrived at church with all five boys in tow. Although married for only seven years, God blessed their home with five boys ages six and under. What seemed like the perfect family at church in actuality was a war zone at home. Tom suffered abuse in his early elementary years and was determined to protect his boys from similar things. As his oldest son inched closer to the age when Tom was abused, his efforts to control and protect angered Marian beyond description.
- Patrick and Donna loved each other. Or maybe not. One day they broadcast the news of their engagement. The next day one or both of them would question if it was really God's will to marry this person. But then, full steam ahead. Or not. Back and forth they went, trying to determine if God really wanted them to get married. Both spoke eloquently of their love for each other; however, both wondered if they were meant to be together.

You have just read six circumstances with varied levels of difficulty. For some, the biblical solution seems easy; for others, not so much. However, the Bible does speak in rich, relevant, and robust ways into each of these life situations. To understand how the Bible connects with each of these and with all other life circumstances, it is necessary to answer two questions:

1. What is unique about the *content* of the Bible?
2. What is unique about the *character* of the Bible?

THE UNIQUE CONTENT OF THE BIBLE

The Bible was written to you and for you as you live life. The words of Scripture—its content—came to the original readers as conversations from God to them about life. Today we get to read and consider the eternal truths embedded in these conversations as opportunities to apply them to life. This cross-generational quality of the Bible highlights the Bible's necessity, relevance, clarity, and profundity. What specifically in the content, then, helps us recognize these qualities in the text?

Your Life Purpose

The Bible is necessary because it provides us with our purpose in life: to glorify God through imitating Jesus. Genesis 1–2 tells the story of God creating the universe and everything in it, including humanity, and describes how perfect it was. The creation of man and woman in the image of God was the crowning moment of the creation week. Genesis records, "God saw everything that he had made, and behold, it was very good" (Gen. 1:31). Pleased with the finished work of creation, God rested.

By the third chapter of the biblical narrative, the perfect turned imperfect, the innocent turned guilty, the sinless turned sinful, and the blessed turned cursed. Adam and Eve sinned (vv. 1–7). Although maintaining the image of God, Adam and Eve no longer shared the perfect quality of that image, for they had fallen. However, God made a promise of a future seed and provided coverings for them that began the process of mankind's redemption (vv. 15, 21). At the apex of human history, Jesus, a shining light, came from heaven to earth to provide redemption by dying for the sins of humanity (Rom. 5:8). Without Jesus, redemption is impossible. From Eden on in the history of humanity, God works for the redemption of people (Rom. 5:1–21). His redeemed people look for the final blessing fully realized in the kingdom and the King (Rev. 21).

GOD'S AGENDA: LIFE CHANGE

As followers of Christ living our lives from day to day, God is actively working toward our good according to His good purposes (Eph. 1:11–12). God is active. Similar to a great orchestration under the direction of a master conductor, God works all circumstances for our good. Paul wrote, "We know that for those who love God all things work together for good, for those who are called according to his purpose" (Rom. 8:28). All things working together means that the orchestration of all life circumstances culminates for our good. All life circumstances include the various life situations mentioned above and every other situation as well. God uses the worst of times and the best of times — both are included in the "all things."

Paul explained the reason God uses all things for our good. "For those whom he foreknew he also predestined to be conformed to the image of his Son, in order that he might be the firstborn among many brothers" (Rom. 8:29). The reason: God's agenda for the believer is to become conformed to the image of Jesus. Although God's plan unfolds in time, it is settled in eternity (notice all the past tense verbs). God plans for us to be like Christ, the perfect prototype. God plans for all His sons and daughters to become similar to His Son — to conform them. Christlikeness is the goal. Events and circumstances orchestrated and ordained by God are the tools He uses to bring about this goal.

GOD'S PROCESS: THE SPIRIT THROUGH THE WORD

God's change process takes place in His children by the Holy Spirit working through God's Word. The Spirit of God transforms the believer as God restores the believer in the image of Christ. Paul also wrote, "And we all, with unveiled face, beholding the glory of the Lord, are being transformed into the same image from one degree of glory to another. For this comes from the Lord who is the Spirit" (2 Cor. 3:18). The believer beholds Christ, the perfect image of the glory of God (John 1:14). The believer sees God's glory best as it is expressed through the pages of the Word.

God uses the Bible through the Spirit's power as He equips His children "for every good work" (2 Tim. 3:17). Paul wrote in Romans, "Do not be conformed to this world, but be transformed by the renewal of your mind, that by testing you may discern what is the will of God, what is good and acceptable and perfect" (Rom. 12:2). The renewal of the believer's mind takes place by the power of the Spirit as the believer reads and meditates on the Scriptures. It is in this process of reading and applying the Scriptures in community with the body of Christ while living life daily that the believer grows into Christlikeness.

YOUR GOAL: TO BE LIKE CHRIST AND BRING GOD GLORY

The Bible *plus* circumstances (Rom. 8:28) provide the believer with the ultimate opportunity to grow and change. It is in these individual, yet essential, moments of life where the follower of Christ chooses between bringing glory to God—which is Christlike—or not (1 Cor. 10:31). It is in these individual moments where the believer chooses to live for something—either for God or self. As the waves of life circumstances continually crash on the shore of life, with each new wave the believer must choose how to respond, what to live for, and whom to live for.

Jesus summarized the choices in each moment of life with precision. He encapsulated the law in two great commandments: "You shall love the Lord your God with all your heart and with all your soul and with all your mind. This is the great and first commandment. And a second is like it: You shall love your neighbor as yourself. On these two commandments depend all the Law and the Prophets" (Matt. 22:37–40; cf. Deut. 6:4–5).

As you face any moment of life, you choose between loving God and your neighbor or loving self. You determine if you are going to live for God in Christ or live for yourself. You decide what is most important to you: Am I going to bring God glory and love Him, or am I going to love myself? You choose whom or what you will love, serve, or worship in this moment of life in a particular circumstance.

IN SUMMARY: THE NECESSITY OF THE BIBLE

Therefore, the Bible is necessary because God calls us to glorify Him by becoming like Christ. It is in the pages of Scripture where we learn who He is, why we need Him, and how to be like Him. When learning about Christ, we learn who we are, what we could be, and what we will be. If there were no Scriptures, there would be no possibility of salvation and the redemption process (Acts 4:12). Furthermore, as those who have received salvation, our love for Christ drives us back to the Scriptures so that we can know Him more. We desire to grow in our intimate knowledge of Christ, and Christ is found in the Bible.

The consistent call to glorify God through becoming like Jesus, who loved God first and foremost and always sought to bring Him glory, insists on the absolute necessity of bringing Scripture to bear in each and every circumstance of life. Not one part of life lived on earth falls outside of the comprehensive nature of the commands given by God to direct us in those circumstances. Thus, the Bible by necessity must speak into each of those circumstances. We need the Bible in order to fulfill God's purpose for our lives.

Our Walk through Life

The Bible provides the parameters for honoring God in the midst of life circumstances. Without the Bible, believers could not understand the extent to which being like Christ changes each aspect of our experience.

JESUS EXPECTS US TO FOLLOW HIM

Before Jesus left the earth, He challenged the disciples, saying to them, "All authority in heaven and on earth has been given to me. Go therefore and make disciples of all nations, baptizing them in the name of the Father and of the Son and of the Holy Spirit, teaching them to observe all that I have commanded you. And behold, I am with you always, to the end of the age" (Matt. 28:18–20). The process Jesus describes is often called discipleship.

Jesus commanded the apostles to make disciples. He invested in the apostles and expected them to reinvest themselves in other Christ followers. After evangelism and Christian baptism, the apostles were to teach the new disciples to observe all that Jesus had commanded. There are two components to Jesus' instruction: (1) to teach and (2) to observe. The apostles were responsible for teaching the new believers whatever Jesus had commanded. This is impossible without the words of Christ serving as the content for that teaching as captured in the

Bible. Furthermore, they were to teach so that future disciples could observe/obey. The apostles taught the next generation of Christ followers the content of what Jesus said and then how to live it out in daily life and relationships, which emphasizes the relevance of the teaching.

This command to carefully obey Jesus' words was not a new idea. Jesus had repeatedly told His disciples that if they loved Him, they would keep His commandments (John 14:15 – 31). Jesus even connected inward abiding in Christ with the outward manifestation of obedience to His commands (John 15:10). Further, the apostle John understood Jesus' lessons and applied Jesus' teaching in his epistle. He wrote, "By this we know that we have come to know him, if we keep his commandments. Whoever says 'I know him' but does not keep his commandments is a liar, and the truth is not in him" (1 John 2:3 – 4). John also connected obedience to Jesus' words with answered prayer, abiding in God, and loving one another (1 John 3:21 – 24). He wrote, "By this we know that we love the children of God, when we love God and obey his commandments. For this is the love of God, that we keep his commandments. And his commandments are not burdensome" (1 John 5:2 – 3). Therefore, John caught that Jesus expected all future disciples to follow carefully in total obedience to what He taught. Jesus knew that the content of what He taught His first disciples would be equally relevant for daily living for all those disciples who followed after them.

Likewise, when Paul gave Timothy instructions on how to be a faithful minister of Jesus Christ, he exhorted him to take the teaching of Christ, which Timothy had learned from Paul, and hold fast to the teachings by the power of the Spirit (2 Tim. 1:13 – 14). Paul wrote, "What you have heard from me in the presence of many witnesses entrust to faithful men who will be able to teach others also" (2 Tim. 2:2). The process is cross-generational. The transmission of truth from one person to another, from one generation to another, produces disciples. The relevancy of the content to daily living makes this process so vital to the discipleship process.

WALKING WORTHY OF OUR CALLING

Paul further emphasized the relevance of the Scriptures in his letter to the Ephesians. Paul commanded the believers in Ephesus to live consistent with the redemption they received in Christ. Paul wrote, "I therefore, a prisoner for the Lord, urge you to walk in a manner worthy of the calling to which you have been called" (Eph. 4:1). Their *calling* refers to their salvation as it had been developed throughout the first three chapters of Ephesians. Their *walking* refers to their lifestyle, which Paul continued to develop throughout the rest of the book. The word *worthy* relates to a scale, so if weight A is equal to weight B, then the weights would be considered "worthy," or equivalent to each other. So Paul taught the Ephesians that they should expect to live life equal to or equivalent to their salvation or redemption.

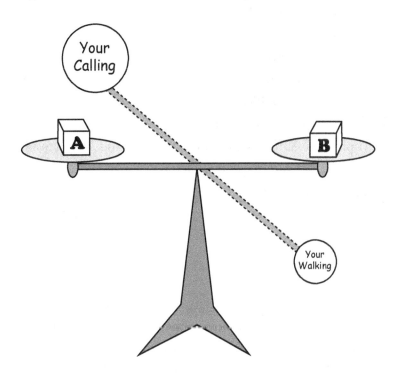

The lifestyle Paul expected is nothing less than the lifestyle that Christ expected from His disciples. Paul referred to this lifestyle as part of God's good work in and through the believer. "For we are his workmanship, created in Christ Jesus for good works, which God prepared beforehand, that we should walk in them" (Eph. 2:10). The practical outcome of redemption in God's plan for an individual believer is to walk in good works — to live the lifestyle God desires.

Paul explained this lifestyle in Ephesians 4–6. There is a significant association throughout this section between understanding the relevancy of truth to be read, understood, and learned and the practical results anticipated in the lifestyle of the believer. There are six discernible connections between life lived and the relevancy of truth to everyday living in a broken world.

1. God's Word affects our communication and communion with others (Eph. 4:1–16). The truth taught by the pastor, when shared by members in conversation, works to both grow and protect the body of Christ. Therefore, it is necessary to know truth and to be able to apply it in relevant ways to congregational living — in all of life.

2. God's Word provides the parameters for living together in Christ (Eph. 4:17–32). As they were to learn and be renewed, Paul expected them to speak truth to one another and apply it to day-by-day living — in all of life.

3. God's Word impacts our love for each other (Eph. 5:1–5). Here believers are commanded to walk in the love of Christ and be an imitator of God. The only way to imitate God is to know Him through His truth. Likewise, the only way to love like Christ is to know and have experienced that kind of love. Both primary commands link back to the relevancy of the truth that is known — for all of life's relationships.

4. God's Word offers help in decision making (Eph. 5:5–14). Paul challenges believers to walk in the character of Christ, which produces practical fruit in living. Christians are to apply the

practical truth to test what is best for honoring God—in every life situation (cf. Phil. 1:9; Col. 2:6–10).

5. God's Word changes our relationships as we walk in the Spirit (Eph. 5:15–6:9). Here Paul instructed those in Christ to know God's Word and apply it consciously to every choice in life. Paul connects walking in the Spirit with being able to live in a God-honoring way as couples (husbands and wives), as families (parents and children), and in the workplace (as employers and employees)—in every life arena.

6. God's Word enables us to be faithful to Christ (Eph. 6:10–20). The final paragraph of instruction in Ephesians commands believers to stand strong in spiritual warfare. Even here, all of the armament relates back to positional truth learned and experienced in Christ and now expected to be applied—in all areas of daily living.

IN SUMMARY: THE RELEVANCE OF THE BIBLE

God's Word is relevant—to all of life. Jesus expects us, as disciples who love Christ and desire to live for Him, to know and obey the truth from the heart. A correlation exists between our personal love of Christ and our knowledge of the Scriptures and our level of active obedience to His commands in daily living. Thankfully, the Bible speaks with clarity and relevance that enables grace-motivated obedience.

Paul wrote to a people in the midst of real struggles and challenged them to speak truth in honest, caring, and practical ways to help each other live consistently with this new life Christ had provided. The Bible delivers to us the necessary relevant instruction, in conjunction with our position in Christ through the gospel, to impact our responses to living life in a broken world. God's Word is not only necessary, it is also relevant to daily living.

Your Wisdom for Life

Necessary. Relevant. *Profound.* The Bible provides us with an unsurpassed depth of insight and knowledge. Various passages help us to understand the richness of biblical wisdom that is imparted to the believer in the pages of Scripture. Christ demonstrated wisdom in walking, talking, and living for God's glory. Only believers in Christ can truly understand the significance of the Bible and live consistent with it (1 Cor. 2:6–16). Without Christ, biblical wisdom does not look attractive and insightful; Christ makes biblical wisdom wise and practical to the believer. Paul rejoiced over the wisdom received in Christ at salvation. Regarding Christ, he wrote, "in whom are hidden all the treasures of wisdom and knowledge" (Col. 2:3). In Christ the believer receives grace that Paul says "he lavished upon us, in all wisdom and insight" (Eph. 1:8). Peter also recognized the wisdom given to the believer in Christ when he penned, "His divine power has granted to us all things that pertain to life and godliness, through the knowledge of him who called us to his own glory and excellence" (2 Peter 1:3). Thus, true wisdom and discernment emanate from our relationship to Christ.

WISDOM PROVIDES KNOWLEDGE AND INSIGHT

A relationship with Christ begins the process of the believer living wisely for Christ. Then, as the believer grows in personal relationship with Christ, the expected result is better discernment in daily living—wisdom for life. Paul made the process clear regarding love. "And it is my prayer that your love may abound more and more, with knowledge and all discernment, so that you may approve what is excellent, and so be pure and blameless for the day of Christ, filled with the fruit of righteousness that comes through Jesus Christ, to the glory and praise of God" (Phil. 1:9–11).

Here Paul connects, in practical terms, the progression of growth with its anticipated results. Paul prayed for their love to abound or increase more and more specifically in knowledge and discernment. *Knowledge* refers to the intimate knowledge of Christ that develops through relationship. Peter O'Brien wrote, "In the Old Testament, as well as in the writings of Paul, knowledge was not a fixed *quantum* but rather something that developed in the life of people as they were obedient."[1] So the believer grows in knowledge. In addition, Paul highlighted all insight. O'Brien explains *all insight* as "the capacity for practical concrete judgment ... insight for *all kinds* of situations as they arise."[2] Similar to how a boat rises with the level of the water, the believer's insight into matters should increase as one's intimate knowledge of Christ grows.

Paul said the purpose for the increase in knowledge and discernment was to test what is excellent. For the believer, the *excellent* are those things that glorify or honor God. The believer now applies their increase in knowledge and discernment to life situations in order to determine what is best in each particular situation, what best brings honor and glory to God. Whereas multiple choices present themselves in any circumstance, the believer makes a decision as to what is *best*. This ability to determine what is best in the context of life highlights the great depth of insight and knowledge provided through the Word to the person in Christ.

WISDOM PROVIDES BETTER UNDERSTANDING

How does the knowledge and insight from the Bible compare to knowledge and insight from other sources? Psalm 119 teaches that the wisdom from the Bible far exceeds other forms of wisdom. Using various terms for the Word of God, the psalmist wrote, "Oh how I love your law! It is my meditation all the day" (v. 97). He identified the fact that he contemplated God's Word continuously. He then explained four benefits from the depth of its knowledge and insight to daily life. The first benefit: "Your commandment makes me wiser than my enemies, for it is ever with me" (v. 98). He recognized that the Bible provided more wisdom to him than that of his adversaries. He continued, "I have more understanding than all my teachers, for your testimonies are my meditation" (v. 99). In comparing the understanding he received from the Bible to the understanding provided to him through formal education, he determined that the Bible provides more of it. The third benefit: "I understand more than the aged, for I keep your precepts" (v. 100). Through his obedience to God's Word, he said it brought him more understanding than life experience. Here, the aged represents the person with many life experiences. The fourth benefit he identified was the ability to do what God wants him to do in his daily living. "I hold back my feet from every evil way, in order to keep your word. I do not turn aside from your rules, for you have taught me" (vv. 101–2). Having learned God's Word, the psalmist stays on the path God desires.

The psalmist rejoiced over God's *superior* wisdom provided through the Word. It is apparent why he started the strophe with: "Oh how I love your law!" (v. 97). God's Word produces a depth of knowledge, insight, and understanding—wisdom—that is better than the wisdom found in the world system, higher education, or experience. He concluded with an explanation of extreme pleasure as he considered the impact of God's Word on his daily life. "How sweet are your words to my taste, sweeter than honey to my mouth! Through your precepts I get understanding; therefore I hate every false way" (Ps. 119:103–4).

WISDOM PROVIDES RESULTS

Wisdom and understanding begin with knowing Christ and are developed through meditation on God's Word. Psalm 1 provides an additional result: life is better. The psalm begins, "Blessed is the man," or "Oh, the happiness of the man!" The psalm identifies what will make a person happy, or blessed. Initially, the psalm warns against associating with the counsel of the world. Then the psalm reads, "But his delight is in the law of the LORD, and on his law he meditates day and night. He is like a tree planted by streams of water that yields its fruit in its season, and its leaf does not wither. In all that he does, he prospers" (Ps. 1:2–3). Similar to Psalm 119, a regular meditation on God's Word throughout the day provides specific benefits. The Bible provides happiness and stability and it prospers the one meditating on it.

IN SUMMARY: THE PROFUNDITY OF THE BIBLE

God's Word is profound. As we face the plethora of daily circumstances, situations, and difficulties, the Bible provides a depth of knowledge and insight that is unsurpassed by any other. In Christ the believer possesses the ability to have true wisdom. Through meditation on God's Word, wisdom gets practical. God's wisdom as it is imparted to us allows us as believers to make excellent choices. The depth of God's wisdom given to us as believers surpasses the knowledge and insight that can be gained from any other source. The result of living life with God's wisdom is happiness as we delight in learning the Word and exercising the depth of knowledge and insight it provides in living life in a broken world.[3]

The Uniqueness of the Content

The Bible is necessary, relevant, and profound. Without the Scriptures, it would be impossible to know our purpose in life or how to live out that purpose. With the Bible, we learn how to walk or live day by day in ways that honor God. The Bible's depth of insight and knowledge provide the wisdom resources needed to choose what is excellent and enjoy a blessed life filled with the best choices.

THE UNIQUE CHARACTER OF THE BIBLE

The Bible not only possesses unique content that connects the biblical text with your life today, the Bible also enjoys a uniqueness of *character*. The Bible comes to the believer through supernatural means, which means we can trust it. The supernatural character of the Bible highlights the Bible's authority, inspiration, infallibility, and inerrancy. What specifically in the character of the Bible allows us to trust it?

The Bible Is God's Word

The distinctive quality of the Bible, which makes it different from any other book ever written, is its divine Author. Although human authors actually penned the Scriptures (2 Peter 1:21), the Bible is God's personal word to humanity. Paul wrote, "All Scripture is breathed out by God" (2 Tim. 3:16). Many refer to this teaching with the term *inspiration*, which basically means this teaching was spoken by God.[4] God supernaturally gave His very words by the Spirit to the authors of Scripture for them to write and for us to have and obey. Therefore, since the Bible is the Word of God, the Bible possesses the authority of God. The Bible is authoritative. As Wayne Grudem states, "To disbelieve or disobey any word of Scripture is to disbelieve or disobey God."[5]

The Bible Is Trustworthy

Two other terms are often considered in referring to the character of the Word of God: *inerrant* and *infallible*. Both terms essentially address whether the Bible has any errors. Is it trustworthy? Can the Bible be trustworthy in some areas such as salvation but not trustworthy in other areas such as history and science? The simple answer is no. The Bible is God's words to humanity; it is without error. John Frame summarizes the issue with: "*Inerrant* means, simply, 'without error.' *Infallible* denies the *possibility* of error.... Scripture is both inerrant and infallible. It is inerrant because it is infallible. There are no errors because there *can be* no errors in the divine speech."[6]

The issue of inerrancy fundamentally comes down to an issue of God's character as it is relayed through the Bible writers. King David testified, "O LORD God, you are God, and your words are true" (2 Sam. 7:28). Paul wrote, "In hope of eternal life, which God, who never lies, promised before the ages began" (Titus 1:2). The writer of Hebrews added that "it is impossible for God to lie" (Heb. 6:18). Therefore, a God who does not lie speaks only words of truth. The psalmist wrote, "The sum of your word is truth, and every one of your righteous rules endures forever" (Ps. 119:160). In Proverbs, Agur added, "Every word of God proves true" (Prov. 30:5). Jesus added to the testimony as to the veracity of Scriptures when he prayed, "Sanctify them in the truth; your word is truth" (John 17:17).

God spoke to humanity in clear ways in the Scripture. Since the Bible is God's words and possesses the authority of God, we can trust it. God created us, redeemed us, and prepared us for good work (Eph. 2:8 – 10). He also left us His Word so we would know Him, know how to honor Him, and know ourselves. As the authoritative, accurate, clear Word of God, we can trust it.

IMPLICATIONS OF THE RICHNESS AND RELEVANCE OF GOD'S WORD

The author of Hebrews, writing his letter of encouragement (13:22) to believers struggling against sin and with suffering, captured powerfully the rich relevance of God's Word. "For the word of God is living and active, sharper than any two-edged sword, piercing to the division of soul and of spirit, of joints and of marrow, and discerning the thoughts and intentions of the heart" (Heb. 4:12).

Yes, the Bible speaks in our lives today. It speaks in ways that fit life in a broken world. The Bible's comprehensive relevance to life, with its unique content and character, provides confidence for the believer in every circumstance. In marriage counseling, it gets us past the "He said … she said" and typical issues of communication, sex, and finances. In moments of great grief, sorrow, and loss, it helps us see past the typical stages of grief. When counseling those with eating disorders, it expands our thinking beyond the behaviors of binge eating, purging, immoderate food diets, restrictions, and body checking. In helping a person struggling with sexual sin, it allows us to see the rest of the story and not get focused on a particular way of acting out. In serving the one struggling with fear, it focuses our attention away from just an object, event, or person. In assisting the one who cannot figure out the future, it provides direction and clarity. And for all, it points to a vibrant walk with God.

The Bible provides the framework from which to offer winsome, robust conversational ministry that gets past the nomenclature of the secular psychotherapies to real dynamic, true, and significant issues of life in Christ. For the counselor, the Bible teaches us about God, people, and problems. It teaches us who God is, what God wants, how God works, and when God acts. Regarding people, it teaches us about the nature of humanity, the root cause of our problems, the necessity of redemption, and the grace and power provided to us through Christ. Considering problems, the Bible provides the worldview, the lens, the categories of thinking, and the wisdom necessary to live life in a broken world.

God has spoken to you, me, and us. Because He has spoken, we can have absolute confidence that regardless of the situations we face in counseling or in our own lives, we know God has something for us. God has a word. He has provided help to see us through the circumstance. We also know that whatever God has said, it is deeper than just the surface level. God is doing more than just wanting us to change a thought or a behavior; God wants to change us in the midst of the circumstance. As believers we enjoy the peace of God because we see the bigger landscape of what God is doing. God's plan is about the redemption process — to bring God glory by becoming more like Christ. Confidence. Purpose. Direction. Relevance. Wisdom. That's God's Word.

CHAPTER 2

SUFFICIENT FOR LIFE
AND GODLINESS

PAUL TAUTGES AND STEVE VIARS

We who counsel, in whatever place and form God has called us, spend significant time with people whose lives, by their own admission, are badly broken. We listen to stories of marriages on the brink of divorce or accounts of childhood abuse that are too horrific to describe here. People reveal to us the addictive behaviors that result in job loss, financial ruin, and the destruction of relationships. Couples speak about relentless drama from extended family members, and children tell of parents whose chronic anger and alcohol abuse control every aspect of their lives. Many of our counselees simply weep in the midst of their brokenness—and we weep with them.

Thankfully, God's Word is no stranger to brokenness. King David lamented, "I have been forgotten like one who is dead; I have become like a broken vessel" (Ps. 31:12). Variations of the same theme are repeated every day around the world to men and women who counsel others. Engaging people in love and wisdom is much more than an academic exercise for us. As followers of Jesus, we weep when others weep (John 11:35; Rom. 12:15). We minister to broken people in a broken world. We often sound, look, and feel like the prophet Jeremiah when he said, "For the brokenness of the daughter of my people I am broken; I mourn, dismay has taken hold of me" (Jer. 8:21 NASB). As we mourn, we share our counselees' hurts and seek to find ways to help them achieve a real sense of healing and wholeness.

That is where the topic of counseling may actually take on a more disturbing ring, because Scripture speaks about the possibility of counselors addressing the hurts of others in ways that actually *do more harm than good*. In the days of Jeremiah, God condemned spiritual counselors who "healed the wound of my people lightly, saying, 'Peace, peace,' when there is no peace" (Jer. 6:14). The last thing a hurting soul needs is a superficial response. True healing requires answers that speak to the fundamental issues of the heart with a balance of grace and truth.

For this reason, having the right source of truth in the counseling room makes a huge difference. Jeremiah explained the reason some people-helpers in his day were offering superficial answers: "My people have committed two evils: / They have forsaken Me, / The fountain of living waters, / To hew for themselves cisterns, / Broken cisterns, / That can hold no water" (Jer. 2:13 NASB).

Words such as these strike appropriate concern and caution into the hearts of those of us who counsel. We practically tremble when we think of serving a broken person with answers that are equally broken. The words of James are always near: "Not many of you should become teachers, my brothers, for you know that we who teach will be judged with greater strictness" (James 3:1).

This leads biblical counselors to be profoundly thankful for the sufficient resources of heaven. We look first to Scripture itself for an explanation of the nature of the revelation that God has provided to address the brokenness of His fallen creation. Alongside the apostle Peter, we marvel that "his divine power has granted to us all things that pertain to life and godliness, through the knowledge of him who called us to his own glory and excellence, by which he has granted to us his precious and very great promises, so that through them you may become partakers of the divine nature, having escaped from the corruption that is in the world because of sinful desire" (2 Peter 1:3–4).

This chapter echoes Peter's confidence by expounding four key passages of Scripture that reveal the sufficiency of God's revelation for all that we are required to believe and the manner in which we are called to live as followers of Jesus Christ. These stones in the foundation of a sound doctrine of the Scriptures display the Word of God as the desirable law, the direct trainer, the divine scalpel, and the definitive authority for Christian living.

THE DESIRABLE LAW: PSALM 19:7–11

In Psalm 19, the choirmaster David exalts the revelation of God. The first six verses, which describe how God's created works reveal His majesty, wisdom, and power, begin this way: "The heavens declare the glory of God, and the sky above proclaims his handiwork. Day to day pours out speech, and night to night reveals knowledge" (vv. 1–2). As a result, this glorious revelation leaves every person accountable to the Creator and, thereby, without excuse (Rom. 1:20). In addition, and more specifically, the psalm explains how Scripture reveals aspects of God's character and will that are not revealed by nature. Nine qualities of Scripture are presented to convince us that God's revelation leads us to a relationship with Him and contains the truth necessary to subsequently transform us from the inside out, beginning in the deepest recesses of our very being—our soul.

Scripture Restores the Soul

The words of God contain the power to restore lost souls back to God. "The law of the LORD is perfect, reviving the soul" (Ps. 19:7). When employed by the Holy Spirit, the Scriptures are the life-giving power of God to produce faith (Rom. 10:17) and to save those who believe in Christ (Rom. 1:16). As a result, redeemed sinners are restored to a friendly relationship with God. Believers then learn to walk by faith, according to the Scriptures, as divine words nourish and strengthen them in the inner person. This is a profound mystery. How God breathes spiritual life into a spiritual corpse, by means of the Scriptures, will never be fully understood. Nevertheless, from the very beginning, words have been the means by which God has brought forth life (Heb. 11:3).

Scripture Makes Simple-Minded People Wise

The words of God are His self-testimony; they bear witness of Him and, as a result, make "wise the simple" (Ps. 19:7). The Hebrew word translated "simple" means open-minded. In other words, simple people are so open-minded so as to believe anything and everything without consideration of truth; they are naive. The Word has the ability to move us from foolishness to wisdom since Scripture reveals to us the glory of Jesus Christ, who is our wisdom (1 Cor. 1:30). When we listen to Him and obey His Word, we increasingly grow in wisdom. In Christ, the promises of Lady Wisdom in Proverbs come to fruition (Prov. 1:20–23).

Scripture Brings Joy to the Heart

The words of God implant joy within the saddened heart. Whether our grief is caused by the suffering that accompanies life in a broken world or is the consequence of our own sinful choices, we may turn to the precepts of the Lord, which "are right, rejoicing the heart" (Ps. 19:8). Even when "severely afflicted," we find the Scriptures to be "the joy of [our] heart" (Ps. 119:107, 111). Jesus explained to His disciples that the reason He taught the Father's commandments to them was so that His joy would be in them and that their joy may "be full" (John 15:11). Therefore, *we affirm that Scripture has the ability to sanctify our hearts' affections.*

Scripture Enlightens the Eyes of the Heart

The words of God, empowered by the Holy Spirit, supernaturally open spiritual eyes that are blinded by the effects of humanity's fall. Scripture is pure, "unmixed with evil,"[1] and it enlightens the eyes of the mind and heart so that believers are able to be responsive to God (Ps. 19:8).

The gospel of John records the healing of a man who was born blind. As significant as it was for this blind man to receive physical sight, the infinitely more valuable sight he received was the gift of eyes to see Jesus for who He really was — the Lord and Savior of needy sinners (John 9:27–33). The gospel is the light of the glory of Jesus Christ (2 Cor. 4:6). Only this gospel can pierce the minds that are blinded by "the god of this world" in order that they may see the beauty of the person and work of Christ (2 Cor. 4:4), which alone has the power "to open their eyes, so that they may turn from darkness to light and from the power of Satan to God" (Acts 26:18).

Scripture Endures Forever

The words of God will never die or become irrelevant; they are "pure" and "enduring forever" (Ps. 19:8–9). Man's theories will come and go, like withering grass and fading flowers, but "the word of our God will stand forever" (Isa. 40:8). The undying Scriptures, by which we "have been born again," are not "perishable seed but ... imperishable ... the living and abiding word of God" (1 Peter 1:22–23).

Scripture Sanctifies the Life

The words of God lead us toward a life of godliness as we submit to the good path they lay out before us, since "the rules of the LORD are true, and righteous altogether" (Ps. 19:9). Jesus told His disciples that they were "already ... clean *because of the word*" that He had spoken to them (John 15:3, emphasis added). He also prayed to the Father for the apostles and for all those who would believe through their witness: "Sanctify them in the truth; your word is truth" (John 17:17). It is by means of our obedience to Scripture that we mature in the application of our salvation (1 Peter 2:2).

Scripture Defines the Value of Its Own Treasure

The words of God are more valuable and, therefore, "more to be desired ... than gold, even much fine gold; sweeter also than honey and drippings of the honeycomb" (Ps. 19:10). To the believer—whose soul has been revived by its gospel and whose life is being transformed from its inward-working power—Scripture is our most prized earthly possession. It alone defines success and prosperity in God's terms, rather than by the world's values and expectations. Joshua testified of this when, as Israel's new leader, he made it clear that life after Moses would continue to be defined by meditation on, and obedience to, the revelation of God: "This Book of the Law shall not depart from your mouth, but you shall meditate on it day and night, so that you may be careful to do according to all that is written in it. For then you will make your way prosperous, and then you will have good success" (Josh. 1:8).

Scripture Warns Us of the Consequences of Disobeying God

The words of God, by both precept and illustration, warn of the consequences of sin and foolishness. By the rules of Scripture we are "warned" (Ps. 19:11). For example, its precepts command, "You shall not commit adultery" (Ex. 20:14), and warn young men (and old, of course) to stay far away from the immoral woman, "for her house sinks down to death" (Prov. 2:18). However, by means of illustration, Scripture also invites us to enter the devastated world of King David whose heart never ceased to grieve the consequences of adultery from the moment he violated Bathsheba until he was placed in the royal tomb. Nathan's horrific prophecy unfolded just as God had said (2 Sam. 12:10–12).

Scripture Promises Reward to Those Who Obey

The words of God, in like manner, also promise "great reward" to those who align their heart and life to its standard (Ps. 19:11). Out of the pain of his scarred life, ruined family, and humiliated kingdom, King David's dying words to his son Solomon become an immortal challenge to the rest of us to "keep the charge of the LORD your God, walking in his ways and keeping his statutes, his commandments, his rules, and his testimonies" in order that we "may prosper in all that [we] do and wherever [we] turn" (1 Kings 2:3). The closing book of the Bible affirms the same promise to those who obey God's Word: "Blessed is the one who reads aloud the words of this prophecy, and blessed are those who hear, and *who keep* what is written in it, for the time is near" (Rev. 1:3, emphasis added).

These nine qualities of Scripture display its full-orbed sufficiency to not only explain what walking with God in a broken world may entail but also to empower us to live according to His revealed will. This unchanging revelation of God prevails as a secure lighthouse on the sea of humanity's ever-changing theories.

THE DIRECT TRAINER: 2 TIMOTHY 3:10–17

A second central text presents the Scriptures as our sufficient life-trainer. The apostle Paul declared to his young protégé Timothy that the Scriptures are "breathed out by God" (2 Tim. 3:16), which is a more helpful translation than "inspired." Rather than the writers of Scripture being *in*spired to write, it is the Holy Spirit who *ex*haled the mind of God in written form.[2] Wayne Grudem wrote:

> Since it is writings that are said to be "breathed out," this breathing must be understood as a metaphor for speaking the words of Scripture. This verse states in brief form what was evident in many passages in the Old Testament: the Old Testament writings are regarded as God's Word in written form. For every word of the Old Testament, God is the one who spoke (and still speaks) it, although God used human agents to write these words down.[3]

Since the Scriptures are breathed out by God, they are "profitable," meaning they are useful and beneficial for life and godliness. Biblical instruction is "excellent and profitable for people" (Titus 3:8). The usefulness of the Scriptures is demonstrated by four of its life-training functions: "All Scripture is breathed out by God and profitable for teaching, for reproof, for correction, and for training in righteousness, that the man of God may be complete, equipped for every good work" (2 Tim. 3:16–17).

Scripture Teaches Us What We Must Believe

First, the Scriptures teach what we are required to believe about God, ourselves, and the Redeemer. "Teaching" refers to doctrine, but never merely doctrine divorced from life. Paul's exhortation to Timothy maintains this indispensable connection: "Keep a close watch on yourself and on the teaching" (1 Tim. 4:16). We must take great care to pay attention to our lives as well as our theology. As a result, we will be able to teach the way of Christ not only in word but also by example.

Scripture Reproves Us When We Err

Second, the Scriptures convict us when we sin. They are beneficial in their "reproof" since they accurately point out when and where we have stepped off of God's good path of obedience. As rebuke is necessary, there is no more effective tool than the Word of God. The Holy Spirit uses His own writings to reprove us and prompt us toward repentance. The personal one-another ministry of the Word occasionally requires this, one example being the occasion in which God required the apostle Paul to oppose Peter "to his face" because, by his hypocritical living, Peter was not "in step with the truth of the gospel" (see Gal. 2:11 – 14).

Scripture Directs Us Back to the Straight Course

Third, the Scriptures do not merely reprove us, they also freely offer the good news of how Jesus Christ changes our lives when we submit to Him. The word translated "correction" means "setting up straight."[4] God's Word not only convicts and reproves our disobedience, it also teaches us how to get back on the right track so that we may become useful vessels fit for the Master.

Another illustration of how the words of God may be used in a corrective manner is the ministry of Nathan to David (2 Sam. 12:1 – 15). The biblical text explains that "the LORD sent Nathan to David" for the purpose of reproving him for committing adultery with Bathsheba and murdering her husband. The Holy Spirit guided Nathan to choose his words carefully. As a result, Nathan told David a short story about a rich man who stole a poor man's solitary lamb. Once David's anger was kindled against the rich man's sin and a longing for justice was ignited in his heart, Nathan declared, "You are the man!" (2 Sam. 12:7). In response to this heart-wrenching confrontation, David said to Nathan, "I have sinned against the LORD" (v. 13). Thus we see how the words of God, delivered to a fellow sinner, brought forth the fruit of reproof— correction and repentance.

Scripture Trains Us in Righteous Living

Fourth, the Scriptures are useful for "training," for educating believers with Scripture. Richard Trench says the following about the Greek word *paideia* in relation to *epanorthosis*, "correction":

> *Paideia* is one of those words to which Christianity gave a deeper meaning.... For the Greek, *paideia* simply meant "education." But those who had learned that "foolishness is bound up in the heart" both "of a child" and of man and that "the rod of correction will drive it far from him" (Prov. 22:15 [NKJV]) gave *paideia* an additional meaning. All effectual instruction for sinful mankind includes and implies chastening, or "correction," in which there must be *epanorthosis*. *Epanorthosis*, which occurs only once in the New Testament, is closely related to *paideia* in 2 Timothy 3:16.[5]

The purpose of this training ministry of the Word is for believers to be "[competent], equipped for every good work" (2 Tim. 3:17). *Synonyms of the New Testament* says, "*Artios* [competent] refers not only to the presence of all the parts that are necessary for completeness but also to the further adaptation and aptitude of these parts for their designed purpose. Paul says that the man of God should be furnished with all that is necessary to carry out his appointed work (2 Timothy 3:17)."[6]

The Scriptures are adequate equipment for the work of teaching, reproving, correcting, and training—for the work of discipleship, which includes counseling. As we faithfully use the words of God to counsel one another, we are "equipped for every good work."

THE DIVINE SCALPEL: HEBREWS 4:12 – 13

The third core text demonstrating the sufficiency of Scripture is Hebrews 4:12 – 13. Here we learn of the power of Scripture to perform surgery where true change begins — in the invisible, immaterial heart. Hebrews 4:12 begins with the little word "for." "*For* the word of God is living and active, sharper than any two-edged sword, piercing to the division of soul and of spirit, of joints and of marrow, and discerning the thoughts and intentions of the heart." *For* is a connecting word that takes us back to the previous verses where we learn of Jesus, the Living Word, who is our spiritual rest. In other words, by faith in His finished work on Calvary we enter our Sabbath, where we rest from the works of human achievement as the basis of acceptance with God. However, like the Israelites in the days of Moses and Joshua, believers must guard their hearts from a spirit of unbelief by remaining "diligent to enter that rest, so that no one will fall, through following the same example of disobedience" (Heb. 4:11, NASB). Accountability comes to all who hear the Word of God, as they did.

These readers had heard enough of God's Word to know what He required of them, yet they remained on the edge of unbelief. If they failed to appropriate the spiritual rest found only in Christ, they were in danger of becoming immune to the truth and, consequently, untouchable. This danger is as real today as it was then. Therefore, the warning must be heeded. Thus Hebrews 4:12 presents the solution to this problem: submitting to the authority of Christ by submitting to the authority of His words. Here we are given five characteristics of the Word of God, which further testify to its sufficiency for the ministry of counseling.

The Bible Is a Divine Book

First, Scripture is "the Word of God." It is divine. In its very first words, God is revealed as the One who speaks. He spoke the universe into existence (Gen. 1); He spoke to Adam in the Garden of Eden (Gen. 2); He spoke to the fathers of His chosen nation (Gen. 12; 15; 31); and

He spoke to that nation through His prophets. Ultimately, He spoke to the world through His Son, the divine speech in human form (John 1:1 – 14; Heb. 1:2). God chose to record the revelation of His Son in written form in the text of the Scriptures, the Word of God. Since the Bible is a divine book, it speaks with divine authority.

The Bible Is a Living Book

Second, the Scriptures are able to transform the inner person because the Scriptures are alive. The word "living," from the Greek verb meaning "to live," is in the present tense and, therefore, can be translated "constantly actively alive." Because it is the voice of Jesus Christ—the Living Word—the Bible never rests. It is always working. A. W. Tozer said it well: "It is the present Voice which makes the written Word all-powerful. Otherwise it would lie locked in slumber within the covers of a book."[7] Being alive, it is also life-giving. It is able to save the soul. Thus, James exhorts us to "in humility receive the word implanted, which is able to save your souls" (James 1:21, NASB).

The Bible Is an Energizing Book

Third, Scripture is productive. "Active" comes from the word from which we get "energy." While the Bible is constantly actively alive, it is also productive. Scripture is the Holy Spirit's instrument for producing spiritual results. God instilled this confidence in the prophet Isaiah, that, when preached, the words of God would accomplish the purpose for which God sent them (Isa. 55:9 – 11). This is equally true in the personal ministry of the Word. When Scripture is employed for the work of counseling, it is like spiritual rain being poured out on God's people, and the result is growth and fruitfulness.

The Bible Is a Penetrating Book

Fourth, Scripture pierces the heart and conscience. The adjective "sharper" originates from the root *temno*, meaning "to cut."[8] The Word has cutting power; it is incisively penetrating. As a two-edged sword pierces through body parts, so the Word of God pierces through the innermost person. This piercing work is what took place in the hearts of his Jewish audience during Peter's preaching at Pentecost. They were "cut to the heart" and brought to repentance (Acts 2:37).

The piercing words of God twist and turn to expose whatever is in our hearts so that we may repent. It is the scalpel used by the Divine Surgeon to expose cancerous sin that must be dealt with in order to gain spiritual health. Biblical counselors, therefore, must let the Word of God do its cutting and healing work. We must always speak the truth in love, but we must always speak the truth. Our counseling must be Word saturated so that the Spirit's tool will be readily available for Him to minister to the deepest hurts and needs of our broken condition.

The Bible Is a Discerning Book

Fifth, the Bible is a "discerning" book. The Greek word is *kritikos*, from which we get "critical." This is the only occurrence of this adjective, but the root *kritays* is used throughout the New Testament of God as Judge and of men when they act like judges (Heb. 12:23; James 4:11). Scripture analyzes and sifts through our inner being, exposing "the thoughts and intentions of the heart" (Heb 4:12). It weighs out the reflections of our mind and the affections of our heart in order to show us what we truly worship and, therefore, serve.

As we offer faithful counsel to others, we use the "sword of the Spirit" (Eph. 6:17), which is the Word of God, "to destroy strongholds. We destroy arguments and every lofty opinion raised against the knowledge of God, and take every thought captive to obey Christ" (2 Cor. 10:4–5). "Strongholds" are false ways of thinking, philosophies of the world that hold people captive. Knowing the Scriptures enables us to take foolish speculations captive to correction. A. W. Pink correctly noted, "There is only one safeguard against error, and that is to be established in the faith; and for that, there has to be prayerful and diligent study, and a receiving with meekness the engrafted Word of

God."[9] As we faithfully employ the Scriptures in counseling, we train others to discern the wrong ways of thinking, which have become fortresses for sin in their lives, so that their minds can be renewed and their lives transformed by the Holy Spirit (Rom. 12:2).

THE DEFINITIVE AUTHORITY: 2 PETER 1:16 – 21

In the fourth central passage we come full circle to where we began — to the divine source of the "precious and very great promises" of God from whom we have received "all things that pertain to life and godliness, through the knowledge of him who called us to his own glory and excellence" (2 Peter 1:3 – 4). The Holy Spirit is the divine Author by whom the Scriptures were inspired, or breathed out, by God. This revelation of God, which explains the gracious provision of new life in Christ, is sufficient and authoritative for our lives. In 2 Peter 1:16 – 21, the apostle Peter put forth the sufficiency of the Scriptures by exalting Jesus Christ and His words above human fables and experiences.

Peter asserted, "For we did not follow cleverly devised myths when we made known to you the power and coming of our Lord Jesus Christ" (2 Peter 1:16). The apostles were eyewitnesses of the earthly ministry of Christ and, therefore, knew the Savior's power firsthand (see also 1 John 2:1 – 3). Yet their faith was not in their experience, but in the written words of God. By virtue of its inspiration, Scripture, "the prophetic word more fully confirmed" (2 Pet. 1:19), is made more sure, more reliable than even the most enthralling spiritual experience — even the one they had on the Mount of Transfiguration. Although Peter, James, and John heard the very voice of the Father "borne from heaven, for we were with him on the holy mountain" (2 Peter 1:18), their confidence was in the Scriptures, not in their emotional experience.

The basis of the apostles' confidence was the Holy Spirit's revelation of God, which was preserved as He "carried along" the minds of the authors of Scripture so that the content of what they wrote was truly from God. "For no prophecy was ever produced by the will of man, but men spoke from God" (2 Peter 1:21). Therefore, those who "pay attention" to Scripture, rather than becoming self-appointed critics of it, "do well" (2 Peter 1:19). Charles Spurgeon had this to say:

> If we doubt God's Word about one thing, we shall have small confidence in it upon another thing. Sincere faith in God must treat all God's Word alike; for the faith which accepts one word of God and rejects another is evidently not faith in God, but faith in our own judgment, faith in our own taste.... Let us hold fast, tenaciously, doggedly, with a death grip, to the truth of the inspiration of God's Word.... Everything in the railway service depends on the accuracy of the signals: when these are wrong, life will be sacrificed. On the road to heaven we need unerring signals, or the catastrophe will be far more terrible.[10]

What God wants us to know about living for Him, He has revealed in words, which are recorded for us as Scripture. The authoritative revelation of God in the Scriptures is sufficient to lead us to Jesus Christ, our Lord and Redeemer, and train us in all things pertaining to life and godliness.

BROKENNESS RESTORED

The Bible's testimony concerning its own sufficiency forms the basis of our confidence in its unique authority for the personal one-another ministry of counseling. However, we are not alone in our assertion. In 1646 the authors of the Westminster Confession of Faith summarized their understanding of the Bible's teaching concerning the sufficiency of Scripture this way:

> The whole counsel of God concerning all things necessary for His own glory, man's salvation, faith and life, is either expressly set down in Scripture, or by good and necessary consequence may be deduced from Scripture: unto which nothing at any time is to be added, whether by new revelations of the Spirit, or traditions of men. Nevertheless, we acknowledge the inward illumination of the Spirit of God to be necessary for the saving understanding of such things as are revealed in the Word: and that there are some circumstances concerning the worship of God, and government of the Church,

common to human actions and societies, which are to be ordered by the light of nature, and Christian prudence, according to the general rules of the Word, which are always to be observed.[11]

As biblical counselors, we echo the confidence of these faithful men, and we are equally, and profoundly, thankful for the provision that God has given to us in His Word.

In Christ and in His sufficient Word, we have access to divine resources as we gently and skillfully help broken people experience His freedom, forgiveness, and grace. Watching the Holy Spirit use His Word to magnify Jesus in the lives of those whom we counsel is a marvelous privilege. Our prayer is that, since we offer counsel from the spring of living water that is healthy and whole, our Redeemer God will be pleased to restore broken lives for His glory and the good of others.

CHAPTER 3

WHERE DO WE FIND TRUTH?

JEFFERY FORREY

When Brad, Tyler, and Mark met for lunch, they were not expecting to get into a heavy discussion. The three friends had periodically met at Burger King ever since they graduated from college. Their lives took different paths once they graduated, but their common faith in Christ brought them together for mutual encouragement.

On this particular afternoon Mark was excited about a small group that he was attending at his church. They had met two times so far, and Mark shared with his friends what he was learning. The person who was leading this small group was a biblical counselor who worked at a counseling ministry in the neighboring community. The counselor, Matt, had been invited to lead interested people from Mark's church in using the Bible to help fellow Christians with problems.

"That sounds interesting, Mark," Tyler said. "So what are you talking about in this small group?"

"We've been talking about why the Bible is suited for helping people with their problems."

"Is this guy a psychologist or something?" Brad asked.

"He says he studied psychology in college, but he studied counseling at some seminary, but I don't remember where. Maybe on the East Coast."

"You going to get psychoanalyzed?" Brad said, snickering.

"No, no. Matt doesn't think that psychoanalysis is appropriate in biblical counseling. He says the Bible gives us what we need to help people with counseling problems to respond in Christlike ways."

Tyler's interest was piqued. "Is he one of those guys who is against psychology?"

"No, he's never said anything like that in our meetings."

Tyler pressed a little further. "OK, but what about all the stuff psychologists have learned? My pastor says we need to learn from God's general revelation as well as the Bible. We just can't ignore science, even though we are Christians."

"Well, I'm not sure what Matt would say. I'll have to ask."

ENTER MATT

Later the three friends were able to meet with Matt at the BK. "Hi, guys. It's good to meet you."

In response to a question from Tyler, Matt tells them a little about himself. "I am a full-time biblical counselor. I work with a network of churches in my community, helping the pastors with cases they do not know how to handle. I became interested in biblical counseling while I was in college. I never planned to become a biblical counselor, but God used a number of experiences to shift my career goals. I found that a lot of my friends felt comfortable enough to share their personal struggles with me. I was willing to listen as they told me about what was bothering them. When they would ask for advice, most of the time I just shared what I had read in the Bible or what I'd heard from Christian leaders. Since a lot of these people were Christians, they were willing to consider what I told them and they thought it was helpful. I was a little nervous about giving advice, so I'd go to our campus Fellowship staff advisers and ask questions about what the Bible says regarding the types of problems my friends struggled with. They would guide me, and I used their counsel from Scripture to help my friends. After three years of these types of experiences, I was asked by one of those advisers what I wanted to do with my life once I graduated from college. I had been thinking about graduate studies in psychology, and he asked if I'd ever considered seminary. I said, 'Nope.' So he told me why he thought it would be good to get a firm biblical and theological foundation before studying something like psychology at a university. As I prayed about it, I could see the wisdom in his suggestion, so I applied to seminary after college. That's how it all started.

"Mark told me about the conversation you guys had a while ago. When it comes to a Christian response to psychology, it's common to hear appeals to 'all truth is God's truth, wherever it is found' or about learning from both the 'book of God's Word' and the 'book of God's world.' When I think about these things, I always find it helpful to begin by defining our terms—what do we mean by the words we use? So let's take a term that is commonly used in these conversations—*general revelation*. What is general revelation?"

WHAT IS "GENERAL REVELATION"?

Matt told a story. "During the summer between my freshman and junior years of college, I was a camp counselor in upstate Pennsylvania. During the week-long staff orientation, I was a roommate to another college student who grew up under the streetlights of Washington, DC. One evening we were outside and my roommate glanced up at the clear sky. Much to my surprise, he fell back against the hill we were standing on. 'Look at that!' he said.

" 'What?' I asked.

" 'The sky! I've never seen so many stars! Praise the Lord Almighty!'

"Having grown up in a rural area of the state, I had lost the wonder that my roommate experienced. Yet his response to the star-studded night sky was certainly more fitting because he was struck not only by the stars but by our Creator who placed them there. And we know his reaction was not unique.

"When he was a shepherd, David obviously had many opportunities to gaze up at the night sky. He also was amazed at what he saw in the sky. And he too was led to acknowledge our Creator." Matt opened a small Bible and read from Psalm 19:

> The heavens declare the glory of God,
>   and the sky above proclaims his handiwork.
> Day to day pours out speech,
>   and night to night reveals knowledge.
> There is no speech, nor are there words,
>   whose voice is not heard.
> Their voice goes out through all the earth,
>   and their words to the end of the world.
> In them he has set a tent for the sun,
>   which comes out like a bridegroom leaving his chamber,
>   and, like a strong man, runs its course with joy.
> Its rising is from the end of the heavens,
>   and its circuit to the end of them,
>   and there is nothing hidden from its heat.
>
> Psalm 19:1 – 6

Then Matt explained the point of his story. "The 'speech of the heavens' which 'opens up an awareness and knowledge of God'[1] is what theologians have come to call *general* (or *natural*) *revelation*. There are two crucial characteristics of this general revelation: First, the design of the creation testifies specifically to the God of Scripture and not to a god of someone's imagination. Second, *everyone* is confronted by the one true and living God through what He has made. This seems to be the point of mentioning 'there is nothing hidden from [the] heat' of the sun. Anyone exposed to the sun — a particularly spectacular part of creation that everyone sees — is exposed to the knowledge of the Creator's existence.

"The apostle Paul also affirmed the unmistakable clarity of God's revelation through what He made. Paul wrote in Romans 1:18 – 20:

> For the wrath of God is revealed from heaven against all ungodliness and unrighteousness of men, who by their unrighteousness suppress the truth.

For what can be known about God is plain to them, because God has shown it to them. For his invisible attributes, namely, his eternal power and divine nature, have been clearly perceived, ever since the creation of the world, in the things that have been made. So they are without excuse.

"Like David, Paul said that God's existence is detectable by the way He constructed the universe. Notice that it is not merely possible to conclude God's existence from observing creation; it is a *fact* of human experience. At some level everyone—atheists and agnostics included—knows God exists. This has been true 'ever since the creation of the world.' Even more sobering is the judgment of God on those who choose to dismiss this revelation: 'They are without excuse. For although they knew God, they did not glorify him as God or give thanks to him' [Romans 1:20–21]."

Brad said, "If you think about it, in addition to being surrounded by creation, we're *part of it*. What difference does that make?"

"Great question," Matt responded between bites of his burger. "We experience the general revelation of God even in isolation from 'nature.' Paul raises this point in Romans 2:14–15: 'When Gentiles, who do not have the law, by nature do what the law requires, they are a law to themselves, even though they do not have the law. They show that the work of the law is written on their hearts, while their conscience also bears witness, and their conflicting thoughts accuse or even excuse them.' Our conscience, designed to reflect the character of God, is part of being made in God's image. Although the conscience can be 'seared' [1 Timothy 4:2], its existence adds to the testimony of the natural world."

"OK, my head's spinning a bit here, Matt," Mark said after a sip of his drink. "Can you summarize all of this so far?"

"Sure. Maybe that cold drink has given you a brain freeze." Matt laughed. "General revelation is knowledge specifically about God's existence and our accountability to Him. It is extensive in scope, and it is an inescapable aspect of human experience. Also, general revelation has been fulfilling its purpose effectively ever since the completion of God's work on the sixth day of the creation week."

HOW SHOULD CHRISTIANS UNDERSTAND THE ROLE OF SCIENCE?

"Here's how this relates to the role of science in our lives. As I mentioned a few minutes ago, psychology permeates Western culture, and this observation is part of a larger reality: the natural and social sciences (biology, chemistry, physics, psychology, sociology, etc.) have become the primary lens through which we understand ourselves, the world around us, and our role in it. Paul Hiebert, a former missionary and anthropologist, explained it like this:

> So long as we use science in our everyday lives—in the form of electricity, automobiles, computers [etc.]—scientific assumptions will influence our theology. The same is true as we draw upon the social sciences.... It will not do to simply pick a few pieces of scientific thought and incorporate them into our Christian thought. If we wish to draw upon our scientific insights, we must face head on the question of how science itself relates to biblical truth.[2]

"I think he's right. For our purposes, then, how biblical counselors think about psychology is really part of this larger question about the role science plays in our lives as the people of God."

"I can vouch for that," Tyler said. "I know some Christians who distrust science because most of what we hear from scientists presupposes an atheistic, materialistic view of the universe. For those scientists, God is not viewed as necessary for understanding people or nature."

"Good point, Tyler," Matt agreed. "Scientists did not need God to map the human genome, or to learn how to predict hurricanes, or to send an unmanned probe to Mars. So Christians are faced with the question: Why bother using God or theology to make sense of the world or our lives? The bottom-line answer to this question is: Because this is God's world, and we exist for His purposes. From a biblical point of view, scientific research must fit within these parameters."

"That makes sense," Brad said. "So how can we pull this off?"

Matt opened his Bible. "To explain that, we need to look at Genesis 1:28. Adam and Eve were given the responsibility to 'multiply ... fill the earth ... subdue it, and have dominion' over the earth and the creatures occupying its various realms. There is a direct connection between humanity as God's image [Genesis 1:26–27] and the responsibility to 'fill the earth and subdue it.' Humanity was created to rule over the earth in imitation of God, who rules over the universe. This is humanity's dominion mandate.

"According to Genesis 2:15–16, God placed Adam in the Garden of Eden 'to work it and keep it'—and to enjoy it. In Genesis 2:15 the dominion mandate of Genesis 1:28 is applied to the initial work of dominion. Adam's responsibility to 'work and keep/guard'[3] in the Garden adds further detail to the mandate in 1:28, to 'subdue [the earth].' Working the ground so that it produces *particular* plants is now added to the initial command, 'rule over the fish … the birds … and … every living creature that moves on the ground' (1:28 NIV).[4] Representing the Creator as 'ruler' involves a responsibility to *develop* the potential of the earth God made. Also, to 'keep' or 'guard' the Garden suggests that part of Adam and Eve's responsibility as 'rulers' was to *protect* as well as develop what had been entrusted to their care.

"Recognizing in Genesis 1:28 the beginnings of civilization or human culture, some theologians have called humanity's dominion mandate the 'Cultural Mandate.' Albert Wolters described the six days of creation in Genesis 1:3–25 as 'a finishing and furnishing of an originally unfinished and empty earth.' Human beings now work together in organized societies around the world to continue 'finishing and furnishing the world.'"[5]

Looking at his friends, Mark smiled and said, "Matt, I think I've had my second brain freeze. Summary, please!"

"Sure," Matt said. "The Cultural Mandate is a fourfold commission. It's a populating activity, a subduing activity, a developing activity, and a preserving activity. However, having said that, one wonders, how are human beings supposed to know how to fulfill these tasks? God made it possible for humanity to learn how to fulfill the Cultural Mandate because of two fundamental truths: First, *God is actively sustaining all of the creatures and the processes we observe in creation.* Looking again at his Bible, Matt read several passages.

You are the LORD, you alone. You have made heaven, the heaven of heavens, with all their host, the earth and all that is on it, the seas and all that is in them; and you preserve all of them.

Nehemiah 9:6

You make springs gush forth in the valleys ... they give drink to every beast of the field.... You cause the grass to grow for the livestock and plants for man to cultivate, that he may bring forth food from the earth.... O LORD, how manifold are your works! In wisdom have you made them all; the earth is full of your creatures.... These [creatures] all look to you, to give them their food in due season. When you give it to them, they gather it up.... When you hide your face, they are dismayed; when you take away their breath, they die and return to their dust.

Psalm 104:10–11, 14, 24, 27–29

For to the snow [God] says, "Fall on the earth.".... By the breath of God ice is given.... He loads the thick cloud with moisture; the clouds scatter his lightning. They turn around and around by his guidance, to accomplish all that he commands them on the face of the habitable world. Whether for correction or for his land or for love, he causes it to happen.

Job 37:6, 10–13

"So help us out here, Matt, how do those verses relate?" Brad asked.

"The biblical writers were not completely ignorant of what we would consider natural processes. They simply understood that the processes were the regular way in which God sustains order in His world," Matt said. "Theologians call God's ongoing work of sustaining creation and directing what happens in creation His work of *providence*.

"And here's the second fundamental truth related to the Creation Mandate: *God has promised that the patterns that give order and regularity to life on earth will continue until Jesus returns to establish a 'new creation.'* After the flood in Noah's lifetime, God promised, 'I will never again curse the ground because of man.... Neither will I ever again strike down every living creature as I have done. While the earth remains, seedtime and harvest, cold and heat, summer and winter, day and night, shall not cease' [Genesis 8:21–22]. Then God presented this promise in the form of a covenant: 'And God said, "This is the sign of the covenant that I make between me and you and every living creature that is with you ...: I have set my bow in the cloud, and it shall be a sign of the covenant between me and the earth"' [Genesis 9:12–13]. This 'Covenant of Preservation' established God's commitment to preserve the created order, in accordance with his purposes for it.[6]

"This preservation promise is important because it maintains the natural laws and other observable patterns in creation that make scientific research possible. So, although the *mechanics* (the how-tos) of fulfilling the Cultural Mandate are not developed in Scripture, they can be discovered by people through careful scientific research. *Scientific research, from a biblical perspective, is a part of the Cultural Mandate made possible by God's Covenant of Preservation.*"

"OK," Tyler said, "so scientific research does have a proper role in a Christian way of thinking, but what about general revelation?"

CAN SCIENTIFIC CLAIMS BE REGARDED AS "GENERAL REVELATION"?

Matt said, "Yes, now we can ask whether scientific claims are identical to general revelation. It's natural to ask why Christians wouldn't accept the insights from psychology, given that they accept insights from other fields of study: medicine, engineering, physics, etc. And if all truth is God's truth, and we have a holy obligation to honor truth wherever it is found, then aren't we being shortsighted to ignore psychology in building our models of Christian counseling?"

"That's kind of like the question my pastor is asking, right?" Tyler said.

"Yes it is," Matt responded. "I really respect your pastor for asking it. True to the underlying premise that 'all truth is God's truth,' Christians involved in psychology and counseling have sometimes appealed to general, or natural, revelation to justify their conclusion that psychological insights need to be used in building a model of Christian counseling. Their reasoning tends to follow these lines, as presented by Gary Collins:

All truth as God's truth has equal warrant, whether truth from nature or Scripture. Therefore, the truths of psychology (general revelation) are neither contradictory nor contrary to revealed truth (special revelation) but are integrative in a harmonious whole.[7]

"In this way of thinking, people equate scientific discoveries with general revelation. However, in doing this, they've also redefined 'general revelation.' General revelation is no longer about God, but about creation. But in that case, it's not clear how Paul's statements about general revelation can be true. Paul taught that general revelation was complete and effective 'ever since the creation of the world.' Furthermore, what was true of general revelation for the apostle was also true for David (who lived centuries before Paul).

"So, here's my summary. In the Bible, general revelation as given is complete. It is *not* a matter of progressive discovery the way scientific research is. In addition, general revelation impresses itself upon the human consciousness. Having been made in God's image and having been born into His world means that general revelation is an immediate and automatic aspect of people's lives. We are always 'without excuse' before our Creator."

"My turn to see if I'm understanding what you're saying," Brad said after swallowing the first bite of his dessert. "There are important *differences* between general revelation and scientific research—but that does not diminish the importance of scientific research. Scientific research is important because the Bible does not provide comprehensive information about all the topics people might investigate, such as putting a probe into orbit around the earth, preventing the spread of a virus, or building a bridge. How's that?"

"Great," Matt responded. "Even though the Bible is the standard for identifying truth, not all truth is found in the Bible. Scientific inquiry is properly concerned with discovering the *mechanics* of how to fulfill the task God gave humanity to 'fill the earth and subdue it' for His glory. Scientific research—even research done within the boundaries of biblical truth—is *not itself revelation*, and therefore, it must *not* be viewed as having the same purpose or authority as revelation."

HOW DOES HUMAN DEPRAVITY AFFECT SCIENTIFIC INQUIRY?

Tyler asked, "So, what difference does it make that some people who 'observe' all this 'stuff' in creation are saved and some are not? That has to matter, right?"

"Mark, you have some sharp friends," Matt said. "Good question, Tyler. Although scientific discoveries cannot be equated with general revelation, they can be *reminders* of general revelation. Depending on a person's relationship with Christ, these reminders of general revelation may prompt adoration and wonder, like David experienced, or they can incite suppression, like Paul wrote about.

"The fall of humanity had far-ranging consequences. Separation from God, alienation from others, and death are a few of those consequences. In addition, especially in Paul's epistles, other results of the fall are revealed: 'darkened in their understanding' [Ephesians 4:18], 'futile in their thinking' [Romans 1:21], a 'hardness of heart' [Ephesians 4:18], and the 'mind on the flesh' [Romans 8:6].

"By virtue of being sinners, people are naturally inclined to ignore or rebel against God in their thinking. Apart from God's grace, they develop a worldview in opposition to God's general and special revelation. They live as if God doesn't matter—even though in their hearts, at some level, they *do* know they are accountable to Him. And it's not as if people apart from Christ have fairly considered God's revelation and decided to choose against it because of its inferior merits. In line with their own perceived autonomy, when confronted with the claims of Christ, they evaluate it as 'foolishness'—which is, ironically, God's *own* evaluation of our fallen mind-set [1 Corinthians 1:18–25]. They exchange the truth of God for a lie, and in their unsaved state the lie seems like the best possible way of looking at life. They are 'blinded' by the 'god of this world,' Satan [2 Corinthians 4:4]."

"So an atheistic worldview affects everything people do in their lives, including scientific pursuits," Mark said in summary.

"Exactly," Matt said. "Within an atheistic worldview, God is considered unnecessary for understanding the creation, and from that premise comes the conclusion that 'God does not exist.' General revelation is *suppressed*; special revelation is *dismissed*."

"So if non-Christians thumb their noses at God, how can they possibly contribute to the Cultural Mandate?" Tyler asked.

"There's one fundamental influence that allows for their productive involvement with the Cultural Mandate, including scientific research," Matt responded. "God restrains the effects of their depravity, allowing them to understand and apply, to some degree, the mechanics of providence. This kindness shown to all sinners without exception is called God's *common grace*. Common grace, though beneficial in its overall effects, does not eliminate the effects of sin on the mind.[8] Even though common grace paves the way for civility in a secular society and for advances in technology, it is not sufficient to change non-Christians' fundamental nature. Even the most tolerant non-Christians, when confronted with the gospel, will rebel against God decisively—apart from the Holy Spirit's work in their hearts [1 Corinthians 2:6–16].

"Acts 14:8–18 illustrates the effect that non-Christians' 'darkened' minds have on their interpretation of the phenomena they observe, whether natural or supernatural. In this story, Paul heals a man who had been crippled since birth. When the townspeople witness the miracle, they immediately assume that Paul and Barnabas are the Greek gods Zeus and Hermes, and they start to worship them. This greatly distresses Paul and Barnabas, and they try to convince the people that they are mere mortals and that the people should be worshiping the one true and living God instead. Paul teaches the Lystrans that the Creator is the one who gave them the rains and the crops that have kept them alive. Luke comments that even saying this barely kept the people from sacrificing to the missionaries.

"These experiences of Paul and Barnabas in Lystra demonstrate how the 'darkened' minds of nonbelievers distort their interpretations of what they see in order to 'suppress the truth,' despite God's clear witness and His kindness shown to them. Here is a primary reason that scientific inquiry cannot simply be equated with general revelation. One can study profitably the mechanics of the created order (how God maintains what happens regularly in creation) without acknowledging the existence of the Lord (which is the point of general revelation). Yet if someone does study the regularities of the created order *with a humble and amazed recognition of the Lord's power, wisdom, and ingenuity*, then the outcome of scientific research merges with the goal of general revelation. Otherwise, the scientists' interpretations of what they observe will be subject to varying degrees of distortion as they 'by their unrighteousness suppress the truth' [Romans 1:18]."

Matt invited the group to move the meeting to his church, which they did. Gathered around a table in Matt's office, Matt started drawing a graph dealing with creation and God. "There's a rough parallel that exists between the order of God's creative acts on the earth recorded in Genesis 1 and the degree of interpretive distortion in non-Christian scientists' conclusions from their research.

"Consider the sequence in Genesis 1," Matt suggested, as he drew the following:

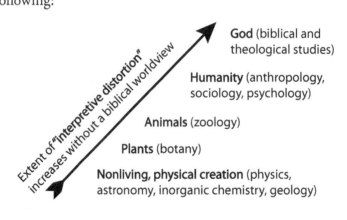

God (biblical and theological studies)

Humanity (anthropology, sociology, psychology)

Animals (zoology)

Plants (botany)

Nonliving, physical creation (physics, astronomy, inorganic chemistry, geology)

Extent of "interpretive distortion" increases without a biblical worldview

"As scientific inquiry proceeds from a focus on the nonliving, physical creation toward a focus on plants and animals and then toward a focus on humanity," Matt said, "there is an increasing risk of interpretive distortion, because at each level scientists are *getting closer to clearer representations of the living God*. And as scientists ask questions regarding the purpose, the use, or the origins of creation, they are asking questions that reveal more explicitly their fundamental worldview assumptions. From a Christian point of view, such questions can be answered only from the Scriptures. Although Christians as well as non-Christians can make valid observations of patterns in the created order, non-Christians' unbiblical worldviews will predispose them to interpret what they observe in a manner that denies the reality of God's existence and humanity's accountability to Him."

HOW DOES REDEMPTION AFFECT SCIENTIFIC INQUIRY?

"So the unregenerate observer," Tyler said, "is at a distinct disadvantage, especially when interpreting creation. You have a fallen image bearer studying a fallen creation. That's at least two strikes against him or her. What about the believer?"

"Another great question," Matt said as he leaned back in his chair. "Fortunately God's amazing grace extends as 'far as the curse is found.'[9] In His plan of redemption, He has provided His people with the resources they need to participate in the Cultural Mandate for His glory once again. Through faith in Christ and our union with Him by the Holy Spirit, as Christians we have been blessed with 'the mind of Christ,' according to 1 Corinthians 2:16. As Christians we do not need to think from the viewpoint of 'the mind [of] the flesh' [Romans 8:6], although we must interact with others who do as they also pursue the Cultural Mandate.

"Consequently, for Christians involved in scientific research — especially those involved in psychology — discernment must be exercised in order to honor the Lord in their work.

THE MEETING ENDS

"Hey, guys, I've got a counseling appointment coming up. I'd be glad to talk again about all of this—"

"If you have one more minute, can you give us a quick summary?" Brad asked.

Smiling, Matt agreed. "Here goes. Even in a fallen world that is subject to decay, the glory of God is evident. God has not left Himself without a testimony of goodness and grace designed to prompt an attitude of awe, appreciation, and the type of apprehension that leads to repentance. As Christians involved in the study of creation, we have a high and exciting calling. We're in a unique position to contribute to the fulfillment of humanity's Cultural Mandate while being 'salt and light' among our nonbelieving peers. We can be actively engaged in the reinterpretation of atheistic scientists' conclusions, progressively 'redeeming' an understanding of creation that gives due attention to its Creator. This is a challenging exercise, especially in the social and behavioral sciences, because of the effects of the fall on our understanding. But, by virtue of the Holy Spirit's ministry in our lives, our involvement in these areas of study can become 'a sacrifice of praise' offered to the Lord in sync with the rest of creation."

CHAPTER 4

WHAT IS PSYCHOLOGY?

JEFFERY FORREY

Matt settled into his seat at Burger King. "Sorry I'm late guys. I had a session that had to go overtime. I was excited to hear from you. What's up?"

Tyler jumped in right away. "My pastor and I were talking, and I tried to explain some of the stuff we talked about at our last meeting. I found out that he has a master's in organizational psychology. Apparently he was called into ministry after he had begun training for a different career. Anyway, he was talking about different things we learn from psychological research. I only ever took one introductory psychology course in college, and truthfully, I was not very interested in the course."

"Yeah, I remember bone-dry lectures that sucked the life out of psychology for me too," Matt responded.

"But now, since my conversations with Pastor Phil and you, I've started to think more about this stuff. What Pastor Phil was sharing with me about the benefits of psychological research seems reasonable, so I am wondering what might we take from psychological research and what should we be cautious about?"

"Well, I don't know if I can answer all of your questions in just one lunch meeting, but maybe we can get started and follow up later."

"OK."

WHAT IS PSYCHOLOGY?

"Simply put, psychology today is usually defined as the scientific study of behavior and mental processes," Matt said. "Behavior, of course, is what is observable by others. 'Mental processes' refers to all those aspects of human experience that occur inside us and that others cannot know about unless we reveal them: thoughts, emotions, perceptions, dreams, and so on.

"Because of the complexities of human experience, psychology itself has evolved into numerous specialties, each attempting to understand certain aspects of our experiences. For example, physiological psychologists study the body's role in producing behavior and mental processes. Developmental psychologists study how behavior and mental processes develop over the course of a life span. Social psychologists study how relationships and groups affect behavior and mental processes. There are dozens of specialties within psychology."

"But how can this stuff be studied *scientifically?*" Mark interjected. "I mean, you can study the brain because it's like a 'thing' you can touch."

"Nice image to go with a burger, dude!" (Brad always had a sensitive stomach!)

"Sorry, but you know what I mean. You can't touch or see a 'thought' or a 'dream.'"

"True, Mark. However, by using tools like questionnaires or interviews, attitudes and thoughts can become like empirical data—what I mean is they can become data that can be treated in the same way as observable data. Of course, there are obvious limitations. People can report such inner experiences falsely or inadequately. But no scientific researcher can escape having to insure the adequacy or accuracy of the data."

"Matt, can we as Christians legitimately use psychological research?" Tyler asked.

"Possibly, yes, but it really depends on what question you're asking, what purpose some research project supposedly serves, how well the research was done, and the extent to which the research purpose can be defended as part of a biblical view of people."

Mark chimed in, "Wait a minute, Matt. I don't think I caught half of what you just said. Could you back up a bit?"

Matt chuckled. "Sure."

WHAT DOES THE BIBLE SAY ABOUT PEOPLE?

"I suppose we should back up and start with the fundamental difference between the assumptions of secular psychological researchers and the biblical view of people. In the Bible, there are two basic descriptors of people that have no place in the thinking of secular psychologists. The first is that humans are made in the image of God, which we've talked about before.[1] We are designed by God to be like God for God's purposes.

"The second idea is summed up in the word *heart*. The biblical writers use this word as a comprehensive descriptor of what goes on inside people. The 'heart' is the *moral and motivational control center of the person*. All of a person's decisions, emotional reactions, behaviors, speech — everything in the person's lifestyle — comes out of the heart. In some passages, the writer describes the *condition* of the heart as determining what is seen in a person's life. For example, Ezekiel wrote that God promised to remove the 'heart of stone' from his people and replace them with 'a heart of flesh' [Ezekiel 36:26]. A 'heart of stone' is a heart that is insensitive to the Spirit and Word of God, which was the problem with the Israelites. That is why they kept returning to idolatry and eventually were sent into exile. But God promised that in the future he would give His people hearts of flesh. Flesh, in contrast to stone, is sensitive — so having hearts of flesh means the people will be responsive to the Spirit and the Word of the Lord. God says, 'I will put my Spirit within you, and cause you to walk in my statutes and ... obey my rules' [Ezekiel 36:27], which will correspond perfectly with hearts of flesh.

"In other passages the writers describe the *contents* of the heart as determining a person's lifestyle choices. In Luke 6, Jesus is quoted as saying that a person brings evil out of the evil stored in his heart—or he brings good out of the good stored in his heart. The mouth speaks out of the overflow of the heart [Luke 6:45].

"To say that the 'heart' is the motivational control center means that the content or condition of the heart prompts the desires, standards, and goals behind a person's lifestyle choices in word, thought, or deed. To say that the heart is the moral control center of the person means that it is always responsive to God. Remember our discussion of general revelation? Not only are we surrounded by creation that declares the glory of God, we are also *part of that declaration*, and even more, *we are designed to be the clearest expression of it.* 'Morality' is simply a measure of our responsiveness to our Creator.

Mark said, "In the Bible, then, people are always connected to God. I mean, we're made in the image of God, and our hearts are always responding to God. Right?"

"Yeah. I can see that," Tyler said, "but what does that have to do with my question about psychology?"

"If 'image of God' and the 'heart' are essential to understanding people, and secular psychologists do not think in these terms, then that puts them at a loss to properly interpret their research data."

"Then we *can't* really learn from psychologists. Is that what you're saying, Matt?" Brad's comment is offered tentatively.

WHAT ARE THE PURPOSES FOR PSYCHOLOGICAL RESEARCH?

"Actually, this only means that there are limitations to what psychological research can do. The more we understand the limitations, the more discerning we will be when we hear claims by psychologists in the media. Remember that one of the things I said earlier was that we need to consider the proposed purposes for any psychological research project. In general, there are four purposes that energize secular psychological research: One is description—the goal psychologists have when something is first discovered or theorized. Another is explanation—suggesting the causes for something. A third is prediction—trying to determine when something will occur. And all these purposes set the stage for the last purpose, modification—ultimately trying to help people overcome problems or experience a happier and more fulfilled life."[2]

"But some of those purposes can't be fulfilled, can they?" Brad asked. "Like explanation, right? If they don't know about the 'heart,' how can they explain the causes of behavior?"

"Yes, Brad, there are clear limitations to secular psychological research," Matt said. "In the case of explanation as a goal, secular psychologists might correctly identify some of the factors that affect behavior. But those factors must all be understood in relation to what the Bible reveals about the heart. For example, we hear that if you have a parent who struggles with alcohol abuse, you are at an increased risk for also abusing alcohol. That statistical observation might mean any of the following:

1. It could imply that there might be a genetic contribution to the experience of alcohol abuse.
2. It could imply that younger generations are taught to respond to life's trials through their parents' example of alcohol abuse.
3. It could imply that both of these are true.

"Sometimes Christians get nervous about such claims because it seems to whittle down personal responsibility. But it doesn't if both genes and parenting are contributing factors and these are ultimately processed and responded to with the heart. What about the other purposes?"

"Description seems simple enough for anyone to do," Tyler offered.

"For the most part, you're right. Anyone with intact senses can make potentially valid observations. I remember when my son was nine years old, I happened to see a little book on 'understanding your nine-year-old.' The book was produced by a well-respected child-development research group, so I checked it out. I was shocked to see how closely the authors' description of the typical nine-year-old matched my particular child. It was uncanny when I read about how nine-year-olds become more time conscious than they had been earlier in their lives. My son had asked for an alarm clock for his birthday. Even in the summer, he was in the habit of setting his alarm for 6:00, getting up, reading his little devotional, and letting the dog outside. When I asked him why he wanted to get up so early in the summer, he said he wanted to make sure he got everything done that he needed to do so he had more time to play. I was amazed to see the authors' description played out in my own house. Unfortunately, he lost that time-consciousness sometime between nine and fourteen!"

"I think I lost that trait too," Mark said. "I think prediction would seem reasonable as a research goal if it is based on lots of observations."

"Yes," Matt said. "But human experiences are really complex. There are many variables that affect our decisions and behaviors, our emotional reactions. There is also the possibility of God's intervention in someone's life. That cannot be predicted!"

Brad jumped in with a comment about control or change of behavior. "I would think control of behavior is not feasible."

"Well, I'd put it this way: Only God has the authority to tell us what our lives should look like. If a counselor is going to give people advice, that counselor automatically presumes to know what direction the counselee's life should take. Even the explicitly stated goal of "not imposing values on a counselee" is based on this very presumption if the counselee is encouraged to live up to *his* potential, pursue *her* own dreams, or do what's best for *her* without directing that person to the Lord. God will judge everything we do in our lives, whether good or evil [Ecclesiastes 12:14; 2 Corinthians 5:9 – 10]. Since counseling is always about lifestyle alterations, it is always something that should be God-centered, at least if that counsel is given in a Christian context."

Tyler had been quiet during this part of the conversation, listening, eating, and slurping his soda. He said, "So we can incorporate psychology into our lives as long as it does not contradict Scripture? Is that what I'm hearing you say, Matt?"

HOW IS BIBLICAL COUNSELING DIFFERENT FROM SECULAR PSYCHOTHERAPY?

"As you probably can tell, this issue is complex—more so than I think a lot of people realize. So I'd like to clarify a couple of points. First, we have been talking about 'psychology' this afternoon. Psychology is much broader than 'psychotherapy' or 'counseling.' 'Psychotherapy' is a part of the broader discipline of psychology, and it is based on secular research and theories about personality traits, motivation, processes of change, and so forth. What I do as a 'biblical counselor' is different in that my goal is really to help fulfill the Great Commission Jesus gave to His disciples: 'Go … and make disciples … baptizing … [and] teaching them to observe all that I have commanded' [Matthew 28:19–20]. I see biblical counseling as a part of discipleship. And the purpose of discipleship is to help people grow in a relationship with Jesus, learning what it means to obey Him, imitate Him, and glorify Him. Biblical counselors do that in the wake of trials or temptations that overwhelm people. My goal, ultimately, is not happiness for my counselee, but, rather, holiness. My understanding of human nature, my goals for counseling, and my methods in counseling must be derived from my study of God's Word. 'Derived from Scripture,' means *defensible from what the Bible says about human nature and about sanctification.* Does that distinction make sense?"

All three friends agreed, "Yes."

HOW MIGHT SECULAR PSYCHOLOGICAL RESEARCH RELATE TO BIBLICAL COUNSELING?

Matt said, "Having established that difference between secular counseling and biblical counseling, I can clarify how *other* areas of psychological research relate to biblical counselors' understanding of human experiences and lifestyle changes. There is a precedent in the Bible for studying people empirically (that is, by observing them or talking to them): the book of Proverbs. Think about the type of content in Proverbs. Can you recall any specific verses?"

Tyler said, "Yes, one verse I've used a lot is, 'A soft answer turns away wrath, but a harsh word stirs up anger' [Proverbs 15:1]."

Mark added, "I've recently memorized Proverbs 10:19, 'When words are many, transgression is not lacking, but whoever restrains his lips is prudent.'"

"Great, guys. Now, what kinds of sentences are those verses?"

Brad wasn't sure what Matt wanted to know. "Do you mean like commands or statements of fact?"

"Yes, I do."

"I guess they're statements of fact. They aren't commands."

"Yes, Brad, that is correct. Most of the verses in Proverbs are declarative sentences; they are descriptions of what typically occurs in people's lives and relationships. Such observations can be made by anyone with intact sensory abilities, as we've said. Therefore, it should not be surprising to find out that there are similarities between the biblical book of Proverbs and proverbial literatures from other ancient Near Eastern cultures (such as Egypt). I was reading a book recently that gave examples of these similarities. If I remember correctly, one ancient Egyptian proverb says, 'As for the scribe who is experienced in his office, he will find himself worthy to be a courtier.' That is very similar to one of the biblical proverbs." Matt uses his Bible app to look up Proverbs 22:29: 'Do you see any truly competent workers? They will serve kings rather than ordinary people' (NLT).[3]

"In both Egyptian and biblical proverbs, such observations were recorded in order to help readers navigate through life more effectively and efficiently. However, in the book of Proverbs, there are presuppositions that move its observations of human experience into a category different from similar pagan literature.

"The book of Proverbs ties its observations of typical human experiences to God's *wisdom*, which, in turn, is tied to a proper relationship with Him." Using his Bible app again, Matt looked up some more verses from Proverbs. "Proverbs 1:7 says, 'The fear of the LORD is the beginning of knowledge; fools despise wisdom and instruction.' Proverbs 9:10 is very similar: 'The fear of the LORD is the beginning of wisdom, and the knowledge of the Holy One is insight.' In these verses 'fear of the Lord' is the proper type of relationship to have with God. 'Wisdom' means having the skills needed to live life well in God's world, in line with His will. God dispenses His wisdom to His people. Listen to Proverbs 2:6–10 (emphasis added):

> For the LORD *gives wisdom*;
>> from his mouth come knowledge and understanding;
> he stores up sound wisdom *for the upright*;
>> he is a shield to those who walk in integrity,
> guarding the paths of justice
>> and watching over the way of his saints.
> Then *you will understand righteousness and justice*
>> *and equity, every good path*;
> *for wisdom will come into your heart*,
>> *and knowledge will be pleasant to your soul.*

"You might remember that the last time we talked, I talked about God's 'providence,' His ongoing work of sustaining and directing everything that happens in creation. The patterns in human experience that are so often the subject of the verses in Proverbs are part of God's providence. That's why they are offered for readers. To be wise, we ought to take into consideration what typically occurs in people's experiences, because that is taking God's providence into consideration in our decision making. 'A man's steps are from the Lord; how then can man understand his way?' [Proverbs 20:24]."

"Matt, what's the 'fear of the Lord'? It's like respect, isn't it?"

"Brad, I would say it's better described as a combination of:

- Awe — jaw-dropping, breath-taking amazement of who God is.
- Apprehension — not wanting to offend this holy, awesome God.
- Appreciation — for the mercy, grace, and love He shows us even though we don't deserve it."

Tyler once again tests his understanding of what Matt is saying. "OK, Matt, you've said that wisdom is knowing how to live in God's world."

"Yes."

"You've said that Proverbs connects being wise to fearing the Lord. But there are examples of the same types of insights found in other proverbs like some found in Egyptian sources."

"Yes."

"We were talking about psychological research. What does this have to do with that?"

"Scientific research," Matt said, "is really just a more sophisticated and structured form of making observations and drawing conclusions—activities which we do regularly throughout our lives. You don't need to be a trained scientist to live life well, but you still need to be able to make observations of patterns (or learn from what others have observed) and draw conclusions about how to use that information in decision making. That's what the writers of the biblical proverbs did. So then, scientific research is part of humanity growing in the wisdom needed to fulfill God's purposes in life. Done well, some psychological research can potentially contribute to that wisdom as long as it is interpreted in the light of biblical teaching about human nature and is applied in the fear of the Lord. Of course, all of this amounts to *reinterpreting* the secular psychologists' conclusions, because the psychologists would not agree with what you've done with them."

"Matt, you've talked a lot about Proverbs and wisdom. What about Jesus?"

"Thanks for that question, Mark. Because wisdom is tied to a proper relationship with the Lord, in the New Testament, wisdom is necessarily tied to a saving relationship with Christ. Paul says Jesus is the 'wisdom of God' for us [1 Corinthians 1:24, 30]. In him are 'hidden all the treasures of wisdom and knowledge' [Colossians 2:3]—not because nonbelievers can't learn about how to make reasonable choices in life, but because only through Christ can God-honoring choices in life be made [Colossians 2:6–8]. There are people who are able to make workable decisions in life that lead to generally desired outcomes, and yet they do so without regard for the will of God. From a human observer's point of view, they can look successful in life. From God's point of view, they are headed for destruction. James called this 'wisdom that ... is earthly, unspiritual, demonic' [James 3:15]; Paul called it the 'wisdom of this age' [1 Corinthians 2:6]. Only through a relationship with Jesus can we have what James called 'wisdom from above' [James 3:17], which Paul called the 'wisdom of God' and 'wisdom ... taught by the Spirit' [1 Corinthians 1:21; 2:13].

"Well, guys, I have to be thinking about getting back to the office. I've appreciated this time with you. Tyler, I was wondering, is there anything I can do to wrap up our conversation for you?"

"I guess not—oh, wait a minute. Could you offer us any guidelines on how to interact with secular psychological claims? That way if we hear or read something from a psychologist, we are in a better position to discern if it's valuable."

"Let me pull up my website. I have a chart on there that might be helpful. You can download it later if you'd like."

	Definitions	Assumptions	Evidence & Logic	Claims & Counterclaims
Secular Perspective	What definitions of the relevant terms does the author use?	What assumptions (about reality, truth, etc.) are implied by the authors' argumentation?	What evidence and logic does the author offer in support of the conclusions? Are there any fallacies?	What conclusions does the author have about the topic? What are the competing counter-claims *made by fellow non-Christians*? (Seek them out!)
Biblical Perspective	If the terminology (or concept) is used in the Bible, how do the definitions **differ**?	How do they **differ** from the assumptions that the biblical authors hold?	How might the evidence be understood **differently** from a biblical perspective?	How do the claims *and* the counterclaims **differ** from conclusions that might be reached using the Bible?

"Let me give you some quick comments on this chart. First, notice that any secular book, article, or webpage should be understood *on its own terms* before it is critiqued. It does no good to critique someone's point of view if it is not even understood! 'If one gives an answer before he hears, it is his folly and shame' [Proverbs 18:13]. Second, notice that in the questions in the Biblical Perspective row, I bolded the words *differ* and *differently*. I did that to emphasize that discernment in the Christian life largely involves seeing the difference between a biblical and a nonbiblical point of view on topics. Not seeing how the secular point of view deviates from a biblical point of view leads to being 'conformed to this world,' according to Romans 12:2. If this happens, we Christians fail to be 'salt and light' in the world [Matthew 5:13 – 16].

"Under Definitions, it's important to remember how secular writers and biblical writers might define their key terms very differently. Under Assumptions, I am reminding people that a secular worldview has very different starting assumptions about reality, truth, morality, human purpose, spirituality, and so on. Under Evidence & Logic, I wanted to remind people to look at the type of evidence being used to support the writer's point of view: Is it relevant? Is it adequate? Is it accurate? The validity of the reasoning offered by the author to interpret the evidence also needs to be evaluated. Under Claims & Counterclaims, I have found it valuable to look for other secular writers who disagree with the writer I am currently reading. If I do not know much about the topic, then seeing the points on which the 'experts' disagree will help me see potential problems that would have escaped me otherwise."

Tyler thought about what Matt showed him and decided to ask, "Matt, could we meet again to discuss an example of how you'd use this chart?"

"Sure."

"Thanks, Matt. We'll be in touch"

AN EXAMPLE OF INTERACTING WITH SECULAR PSYCHOLOGICAL LITERATURE

The following week Mark, Brad, and Tyler met with Matt at his office.

"Welcome guys! I came up with an example that I thought might be helpful to illustrate the process I go through when I read secular psychology literature. The example comes from the writings of Dr. John Gottman. Have any of you heard of him?"

All three men shook their heads.

"For a significant part of his career, he worked for the University of Washington in Seattle. For several decades he has studied the dynamics of marital conflict and marital counseling. He's written several books that have been popular, like *The Relationship Cure*, which I have here with me.[4] In his books, Dr. Gottman writes about several different risk factors in marriages that, if they are not addressed, bring couples closer to divorce.

"One of the reasons his research intrigues me is because he has tried to be as comprehensive as he could be in analyzing marital conflict. He established a studio apartment equipped with video cameras, motion sensors in the chairs, and a one-way mirror for live observations of couples who agree to spend twenty-four hours in the studio apartment. They are 'harnessed' with devices to monitor various measures of stress, such as sweating and heart rate. They are asked, while staying in the apartment, to discuss topics about which there have been disagreements. Their interactions are watched live by trained observers as well as recorded for later examination. After collecting these data on hundreds of couples at all stages of married life, Dr. Gottman has come to confident conclusions about what factors create a stable and happy marriage and what factors erode a marriage."

"How could anyone feel normal with the cameras and all the equipment they're hooked up to?" Brad asked incredulously.

"After a while, Gottman says, they get so involved in the conversation that they soon ignore all the data collection devices. In any case, here is one of his findings. He says that one of the biggest surprises of his professional life came after he and his colleagues were able to set up the 'Love Lab' in 1990 (his specially equipped studio apartment). At the time many psychologists thought that the key to good relationships was self-disclosure: revealing one's most guarded, personal thoughts and experiences to another person. He expected to see lots of such behaviors in the Love Lab, but after viewing hundreds of hours of videotape, he says he found very few examples of such disclosures. 'There were few heart-to-heart exchanges about broken dreams, hidden fears, or unfulfilled sexual desires.'[5]

"Instead, even with couples who scored high on surveys of marital satisfaction, the couples' conversations were more likely to be about mortgage rates, breakfast cereals, and baseball games. At first he was quite discouraged. But the longer he viewed the tapes with students, the thought occurred that 'Maybe it's not the depth of intimacy in conversations that matters. Maybe it doesn't even matter whether couples agree or disagree. Maybe the important thing is *how* these people pay attention to each other, no matter what they're talking about or doing.'[6]

"Gottman lists three basic ways of responding to bids for emotional connection:

- (a) Turning toward the bidder: responding positively, showing interest in what the person has said.[7] This response tells the bidder, 'I hear you'; 'I'm interested in you'; 'I'd like to help you.'[8]
- (b) Turning against the bidder: responding belligerently, argumentatively, sarcastically.[9] Sometimes the response is not as overtly hostile as this. Contradictory responses fall under this category too. For example, a wife asks, "Would you like a tangerine?" And her husband responds, "That's not a tangerine. It's an orange." Although the one who turns against a bidder might not realize the extent of the damage this kind of pattern can have on the relationship, it still damages, because

it communicates: 'I don't respect you'; 'I want to hurt you'; 'I want to drive you away.'[10]

- (c) Turning away from the bidder: ignoring the bid, acting pre-occupied,[11] or interrupting the bid (by offering a response on a totally different topic).[12]

"Gottman says both turning away from bids and turning against bids are detrimental to relationships, but in his experience, the 'turning away' response pattern signals a quicker end for the relationship than the 'turning against' pattern.[13] He writes:

> A bidder's reaction to turning away is typically much different than to an outward attack (turning against); in the latter case, the bidder may feel so enraged that he or she is energized by the interaction. In contrast, when someone turns away from a bid, the bidder loses confidence and self-esteem. In our observational studies, we see how people almost seem to "crumple" when their partners turn away.[14]
> Feeling discouraged once their bids for connection have been rejected or ignored, people rarely re-bid. I was surprised to find that even in satisfied relationships—where you might expect people to confront one another about behavior that upsets them—couples hardly ever repeat a failed bid. It's as if something inside the bidder says, "Why bother? It's no use." And if this hopeless attitude becomes dominant, there's less bidding, less opportunity for connection.[15]

"OK, gentlemen. What do you think?"

Tyler started the dialogue: "It all sounds reasonable. I didn't hear anything I necessarily disagreed with."

Matt pushed him a little further, "*Why* does it sound reasonable? Given that you approach life from a Christian perspective and Dr. Gottman does not, how do you think your reasons for agreeing with these conclusions differ from his own?"

Although Tyler was not sure how to respond, Mark offered some help. "I think we could say that what Gottman calls 'turning away' and 'turning toward' violate passages of Scripture, although I'm not sure where they are."

"Let me help you there, Mark." Matt used his Bible app to find some verses that Mark might have in mind. "One passage we could turn to is Ephesians 4:29, 'Let no corrupting talk come out of your mouths, but only such as is good for building up, as fits the occasion, that it may give grace to those who hear.' *Corrupting talk* tears others down. Since Gottman's goal is to preserve marriages, and communication is necessary for a marriage to exist, he would agree that language that tears down a spouse is unwise. In fact, he does write about how dangerous unchecked criticism and contempt are for relationships. But what is different about Paul's thinking is that Ephesians 4:29 is one of several examples the apostle gives of promoting harmony among Christians, because that is part of living a life 'worthy of the calling you have received' (Ephesians 4:1 NIV). That calling—to be part of Christ's community—is founded on the death of Jesus, by which he '[tore] down the dividing wall of hostility' that separates God from people and that separates the people saved by his grace (Ephesians 2:14–22). Paul is practical in his counsel, but he is not merely pragmatic. His concern is not merely with what works, which is Dr. Gottman's concern; his concern is with 'the praise of [God's] glorious grace' (Ephesians 1:6, 12).

"Notice how the apostle's way of reasoning elevates the practical counsel he gives above any self-serving motivation. But we need to go even further. Paul's reasoning not only counters selfishness, it focuses attention on 'things that are above ... for ... your life is hidden with Christ in God' (Colossians 3:2–3). Dr. Gottman is against selfishness too, but he does not motivate couples to look to Christ, seated at the right hand of God. Biblical counselors should never be content to give a feuding Christian couple four—or forty—rules of communication without also connecting those guidelines to life in Christ. Otherwise, what's going on is 'marriage enrichment,' not discipleship. Don't get me wrong, marriage enrichment is far better than divorce for our society. But biblical counselors serve their Savior, not the larger society. Anything else come to mind?"

Brad chimed in, "The Bible does say something about the problem of 'hope deferred.' Is that what Gottman was writing about with 'turning away' from people bidding for attention?"

"Yes, Gottman's comment on that point was interesting. 'Turning away' deflates one's motivation to pursue the relationship further, presumably because it shatters the person's confidence and sense of worth. The passage you're thinking of is Proverbs 13:12, 'Hope deferred makes the heart sick, but a desire fulfilled is a tree of life.' Then there's Proverbs 18:14 as well: 'A man's spirit will endure sickness, but a crushed spirit who can bear?' I would say that Gottman has merely observed in his research, by God's common grace, what these proverbs had already affirmed long ago.

"One other thing to keep in mind as we interact with Dr. Gottman's research is the difference in definitions for marriage. Marriage in the Bible is not merely a social contract. It is, as Jay Adams describes it so well, a 'Covenant of Companionship.'[16] The covenant has both a horizontal element (spouses are bound together for life) and a vertical element (their commitment to one another is protected by a vow to God). Sound marriages enrich spouses' lives and strengthen communities, but well beyond that, they serve God's purposes for humanity. Therefore, Christians' thinking about marriage should not exclude the vertical element."

Being mindful of the time, Mark said, "Thanks, Matt, for taking all this time with us."

"You're welcome. I've thoroughly enjoyed these conversations. Perhaps we could sum up what we've been talking about recently in this way: Secular psychologists can make potentially valid descriptions of human experiences, and they can raise questions to spur our thinking. However, they cannot offer complete explanations for those experiences, nor can they offer prescriptions for living."

CHAPTER 5

SCRIPTURE IS
SUFFICIENT,
BUT TO DO WHAT?

JEREMY PIERRE

Let's get one thing clear right off the bat: The Bible does not tell you everything you need to know for your seventy- or eighty-year journey in this world. Extrabiblical knowledge is necessary to function as a human being. You learn how to read facial expressions, to understand cause and effect, and to predict the likelihood of future events without the Bible. You establish basic cognitive categories, acquire complex linguistic systems, and condition yourself to like certain things for breakfast before you read your first word of Scripture. In short, I've dedicated this opening paragraph to the task of pointing out the obvious: You rely extensively on sources of knowledge outside what is revealed in Scripture. This reliance is a good thing because God designed you that way.

But extrabiblical knowledge is not sufficient for you to know who you are or why you do what you do. God designed you to need *Him* to tell you about *His* world so that you can understand your own observations of it. Scripture is both necessary and sufficient for giving you a framework for understanding every aspect of your life, all eighty years of it.

FUNCTIONS OF SUFFICIENCY

When we say Scripture is sufficient for understanding human life, what exactly are we saying it's sufficient for? We can answer this in three complementary ways, each answer focusing on different *functions* that Scripture is sufficient to accomplish. All three answers deserve our full attention, but we will focus on the last one as the most pertinent to our present concern of how Scripture is sufficient to form a comprehensive psychology.

1. Scripture is sufficient *to teach* something—that is, everything necessary for doctrine and salvation. This function often gets first attention in various systematic theologies.[1] The *formal principle* of the Reformation, *sola scriptura*, championed that Scripture alone is the source and standard of the Christian faith. No official church doctrine or external interpretation is necessary to know God. Scripture interprets itself and needs no outside voice to make its message understood.

Furthermore, the *material aspect* of Scripture is sufficient to reveal the entirety of what people need to know about God, themselves, salvation, and everything that pertains to the Christian faith.[2] This function of sufficiency aligns with the Bible's own testimony about itself (2 Tim. 3:15–17; 2 Peter 1:3–4). The point here is that Scripture needs nothing else to teach everything necessary for right belief about God and salvation.

2. Scripture is sufficient *to do* something—that is, everything necessary for people to receive/know God through the gospel of Jesus Christ. As the concerns of the Reformation era have given way to more modern, and eventually postmodern, concerns, the very possibility of meaning being conveyed through language has itself been undermined. Evangelical scholars have defended their ground on the sufficiency of Scripture by pointing out that God's words are not mere empty containers of potential meaning, but performative actions. In other words, when God speaks in the Bible, He *does* something.[3] And His words are the sufficient means through which the Holy Spirit's actions take

place. This function of sufficiency also aligns with the Bible's own testimony about itself (Isa. 55:10–11; James 1:18; 1 Peter 1:23). British pastor-theologian Timothy Ward states it succinctly for us: "Because of the ways in which God has chosen to relate himself to Scripture, Scripture is sufficient as the means by which God continues to present himself to us such that we can know him, repeating through Scripture the covenant promise he has brought to fulfillment in Jesus Christ."[4]

This view of the Bible's sufficiency to *do* something is really nothing new, even if the theory has been applied in more complex ways to the nature of language. About the performative action of God through Scripture, John Owen said a long time ago, "Scripture is sufficient unto the end for which it was designed — that is, sufficient to generate, cherish, increase, and preserve faith, and love, and reverence, with holy obedience in them, in such a way and manner as will assuredly bring them unto the end of all supernatural revelation in the enjoyment of God."[5] The point here is that Scripture needs nothing else to accomplish the redemption, transformation, and completion of humanity through the gospel of Jesus Christ.

3. Scripture is sufficient *to see* something — that is, all of creation from a God-ordained perspective. As the first two points establish, Scripture is sufficient to teach us all we need to know God and to do all that is necessary to unite us to Him through the gospel. This third point is a necessary consequence of the first two: We also *see* things differently. Scripture is the sufficient means by which we understand extrabiblical information in its ultimate sense. God has given us everything we need to form a God-oriented (and therefore an exclusively *true*) perspective of everything we study.

SUFFICIENCY AND AUTHORITY

Perhaps that parenthetical addition in the last sentence seemed a bit much. Yet I would like to demonstrate that the close relationship between the sufficiency and the authority of Scripture compels us to it.

The authority of Scripture, most simply said, means that God's words hold mastery over our words about any topic. John Frame makes a pertinent point:

> Since God created and governs all things, he is the original interpreter of creation, the one who understands the world and all its depths—not only its *material nature*, but also its *ultimate meaning and purpose*. God, therefore, has the ultimate viewpoint on the world—the broadest, deepest understanding of it. His word about himself or about the world, therefore, is more credible than any other word or any other means of knowing. It obligates belief, trust, and obedience.[6]

God knows the material nature of all things exhaustively, completely, and accurately. He has perfect encyclopedic knowledge of all topics. He also knows the ultimate meaning and purpose of all things, the ends for which they were designed. He has perfect *telic* (purpose-related) knowledge of all things. And as the ultimate authority, God speaks to us in ways that demand our submission to His perspective. "*Everything* in Scripture comes to us as authoritative communication. Pervasively, Scripture claims our thoughts and decisions."[7] For our purposes, we could say that human beings owe a certain loyalty of perspective to God's Word.

This insight brings us a bit closer to linking the authority of God's Word with its sufficiency. We have already established the obvious fact that Scripture does not tell us everything there is to know about the world—or about human life, for that matter. God's exhaustive knowledge of the world's *material nature* is not contained in Scripture. We do not know how the sun's unquenchable combustion sustains itself or how the human soul precisely corresponds to neurological function. Nor is God's exhaustive knowledge of the *ultimate meaning and purpose* contained in Scripture. God is doing countless things in the world of which we are unaware. He does not reveal His specific purposes in the rise and fall of the nations or why He allows depressive episodes to overwhelm some and not others. Yet it is precisely because Scripture does not contain everything God *could* say that we must pay careful attention to what He *has* said — it reveals what He intends to be the priorities of our knowledge.

Encyclopedic and Emphatic Authority

Though not exhaustive, every word of Scripture *accurately reflects* God's infinite knowledge of both material nature and the ultimate purpose of creation, and God selected each word to communicate what He wants our attention drawn toward. God's Word has more than just *encyclopedic* authority, meaning that on every topic the Bible addresses, it does so with the ultimate authority of God Himself. It also has *emphatic* authority, meaning that whatever God draws our attention to as primary ought to capture our primary attention. In short, sufficiency is not just a matter of the specific information contained in the Bible (encyclopedic), but of how those divine words demand a priority of perspective on information *not* contained in the Bible (emphatic).[8]

This emphatic authority of Scripture is basically synonymous with the third function of sufficiency, which is *to see* all of creation from a God-ordained perspective. Scripture is sufficient to convey the main concerns of God regarding the human experience, and these serve as the authoritative framework by which we interpret all information on that subject. To put it differently, Scripture is all we need to understand God's ultimate design of and purpose for human beings. All other information we gain about human life, be it developmental, cognitive, neurological, or otherwise, is necessarily interpreted in light of God's primary concerns. In one sense, emphasis is everything.

Let me see if I can illustrate the importance of emphasis in shaping a worldview. Imagine a grandfather full of stories about his days growing up in Chicago during the Great Depression. He tells these stories for a purpose: he wishes to shape his grandchildren in certain ways. So he tells of having to split a single egg with his brother or watching his prissy sister wear boy clothes to collect scrap metal. But his favorite story is the night he heard his mother crying and crept into the living room to see her crumpled on the floor. His father, who was not a very affectionate man, silently lifted her from the ground, smoothed her housedress, and put his arms around her. Why does the grandpa tell these stories? No doubt he repeats ad nauseam the lesson he wants to frame his grandchildren's perspective of life: "No matter how bad it gets, never let each other give up."

But even if a grandchild can repeat every detail, he could still misuse these stories in at least two ways. The first way is the more obvious one: he could ignore the stories, not allowing the grandfather's concerns to shape his own. The grandchild, after all, lives a life of affluence and is unable to relate to the experience of hunger or uncertainty, and so he figures those stories are irrelevant and bygone. By doing this, the grandchild concludes that other sources of knowledge—particularly his present experience—are more reliable.

The second way is less obvious, but no less disruptive to the grandfather's purposes: the grandchild could change the emphasis of the stories. As he hears the stories, he sees that his grandpa is now living in a nice home with a two-car garage and reinterprets the details. "No matter how bad it gets, things will always get better." Based on knowledge he observed outside the story, he modified the emphasis of the story and used it in a way the grandpa did not intend. So the details of the story now shape the grandchild's perspective of life in a way that does not match the reason the grandpa told them in the first place. In fact, the grandpa would very much disagree with the grandchild's conclusion. If he learned anything in the Great Depression, it was that it's *not* guaranteed to get better, but showing grit in the face of difficulty is the best way to help others do the same.

To emphasize the wrong thing is to misunderstand the story, even if you know every detail. A grandchild can recognize the historic factuality of everything the grandfather says, thus acknowledging its encyclopedic authority. But he can ignore or change the primary concerns of the grandfather in telling those details, thus ignoring its emphatic authority.[9]

We do this with Scripture when we recognize its truthfulness and authoritative power to speak accurately on whatever topic it addresses, but then either ignore or change what it emphasizes about the human experience. As Frame said, God is *the* original interpreter of creation who understands the world and all its depths. And God the first interpreter lays out His priority of perspective. We could say it this way: As we come to believe what God says in Scripture about people (e.g., that they are covenantal beings who function in ways that reflect God's personhood), we do not just shuffle that belief into the file of beliefs we already have (e.g., that people need eight hours of sleep on average per night or that personhood is formed over the course of particular developmental stages). Rather, the beliefs we derive from Scripture serve as the authoritative system of organization that distinguishes both the truthfulness and the priority of all other beliefs.

In summary, it is not sufficient to acknowledge that Scripture is authoritative about every topic it addresses. A person can do this and still have an entirely lopsided view of any number of things. We are also required to acknowledge that Scripture sets the agenda for what we focus on. God's interpretation of reality demands that our interpretation follow suit.[10]

Emphatic Authority and Psychology

Beliefs about people gained throughout life, whether by casual or more scientific observation, are automatically subordinated, prioritized, and ordered according to some interpretive framework, whether a person is aware of the framework or not. We can have no truly independent beliefs. And the framework is self-perpetuating since whatever our control beliefs are will determine the questions we ask and the eventual direction our psychology heads.

Applying this to the sufficiency of Scripture for psychology, we could say that Scripture is sufficient for *framing the priority of attention regarding the human experience as occurring covenantally before God.* The Bible's perspective of people is that they were created as His image to reflect Him in their design and function as they relate to Him and to one another. At a basic theological level, these are God's concerns that should emphatically shape our psychology.

We could call the beliefs about humanity derived from Scripture *control beliefs*—a sort of *theistic matrix* that serves as the framework for all beliefs. This theistic matrix must authoritatively control all the smaller matrices of belief we have about everything pertaining to the human experience.[11] Theologian Richard Lints spells this out well:

> Our interpretive matrix should be the interpretive matrix of the Scriptures. It should make sense of the past and the present and the future in the same manner that the Scriptures do. In order to do this, a theological framework cannot simply mine the Scriptures looking for answers to a set of specific questions that arise uniquely in the modern era. It should seek out the questions that the Scriptures are asking, for these remain the questions that are important for understanding the past and present and future.[12]

It boils down to the question of *who gets to set the agenda*. Will it be the concerns that arise from our cultural context or those that arise from the worldview of the Bible? An example outside of the field of psychology is instructive on this point: Liberation theologians approach God's Word with certain concerns—namely, class deprivation and economic oppression. Their consideration of sin and salvation are therefore framed by these concerns: sin is largely understood as social injustice, and salvation is liberation of the poor. But, as Grant Osborne points out, this is to contextualize in precisely the wrong direction. God's revealed Word is the final arbiter of truth over all sets of cultural expectations and concerns.[13]

Psychological theorists may think they are safe from transgressing the same boundaries as liberation theologians since they are not trying to do theology. They may believe that having a different starting point for psychological discourse is not stepping on God's toes. But such a belief does not take seriously enough God's jurisdictional claim over the study of human experience. *The study of human experience is theological to the core*, since we are made like God to respond to Him. So we must insist that contemporary questions about humanity do not start our exploration of psychology. The Bible sets the agenda for the questions we ask and the answers we seek, and contemporary concerns are reoriented appropriately.

The interpretive framework Scripture provides fills two primary functions regarding extrabiblical knowledge. The first function is constructive and aligns with the main point we have been making: Scripture makes it possible to organize the information provided us through natural revelation according to God's priorities. Because of the doctrines of the image of God and of common grace, we may generally rely on humankind's ability to make accurate observations about reality, including our own psychological experience. Contrary to postmodern despair of knowledge, we believe that people can attain genuine knowledge through their native faculties; we simply recognize that the knowledge is organized by previous noetic structures (belief system).[14] This is why we argue for the importance of submitting those structures continuously to the concerns of the Bible.

The second function is corrective; it guards against the error we are prone to by being sinfully inclined away from God's priorities and concerns. As sinners, we love our own way and interpret facts based on our own perspectives that either ignore or alter God's (Rom. 1:19–23; 1 Cor. 1:20–25). Put simply, there is a world of difference between *general revelation* and *our interpretation* of general revelation. We will misuse the knowledge we gain apart from submission to Scripture's priorities.

All that I have been laying out is expressed in both the theory and the practice of counseling. We will now consider both.

OUR THEORETICAL VIEW
OF THE HUMAN EXPERIENCE

The ongoing conversation about the sufficiency of Scripture in forming a psychology is not happening on the floor of the American Psychological Association annual meeting. It occurs amidst people who care about the Bible and want to follow Christ in the present cultural context. And among this group, as David Powlison helpfully points out, two distinct—and ultimately incompatible—approaches to Scripture have arisen. They differ primarily in their "organizing centers," which is the same thing as saying their control beliefs. The first approach considers *external psychological theory as necessary* to a complete view of human experience, and the second considers *Scripture sufficient to construct* such a view.

The first approach understands secular psychologies as necessary to constitute a complete view of the human experience. The observations that psychologists make from various secular theories make a *vital external* contribution to a biblical psychology.[15] Such a view attempts to honor the encyclopedic authority of the Bible—whatever topic the Bible speaks on, it does so with authority. It's just that those topics are not plentiful, at least as far as psychology is concerned. And so progress in a comprehensive view of human experience is a matter of expanding research of external theories; and the Bible is seen as an encyclopedia of static and rather limited subject matter.

This approach does not adequately acknowledge the *emphatic* authority of Scripture. It does not allow the doctrine of Scripture to control the priorities, emphases, and interests of its research. Instead, its agenda of concern is set by worldviews that do not have God as the source, center, or goal of human experience.[16] These folks love the Bible; the problem is, they miss how radically world defining and perspective controlling it can and must be. What God is primarily concerned about regarding people should be what they are primarily concerned about regarding people. Perhaps they need to believe that God's concerns are never petty, narrow, or irrelevant to human suffering and dysfunction, no matter how complex.

And, on closer inspection, we find that this approach ends up not adequately acknowledging the Bible's *encyclopedic* authority either. The supposedly *limited set* of religious topics the Bible addresses—sin and salvation, for instance—are actually meta-categories that gloriously overflow with human drama. Sin is not just simple conscious action, but reckless, self-oriented disposition. Salvation is more than insurance for some future judgment day, but a complex blossoming of the soul toward God and others. And we have not even mentioned the Bible's hard gaze into the complexities of human suffering, its piercing insight into interpersonal dynamics, or its dramatic description of human experience. This approach certainly attempts to be biblical, but an inadequate understanding of what authority entails leaves those who follow this approach with a pretty insufficient Bible.

The second approach views the Bible as containing *comprehensive internal* resources sufficient for constructing a model of psychology. Modern psychologies may inform, but they do not play a constitutive role in the formation of our gaze into human experience. The concerns of God in Scripture — doctrine — control the emphatic direction, the questions posed, and the solutions offered in addressing human dysfunction in the most comprehensive manner. Powlison explains, "We best study human psychology not by submitting ourselves to the world's deviant psychologies but by looking at the world through the gaze of our own systematic biblical understanding."[17]

What we see is heavily dependent on the questions we ask, and the questions we ask are dependent on our control beliefs. To say that various secular psychologies make a *vital external* contribution is to allow their emphases and concerns to set the direction and limits of our gaze at the human experience. Powlison's piercing description of these consequences is worth a lengthy quote:

> However unwittingly, Christians allow conceptual categories from personality theory or self-help or medicine, the authority of the latest research study, the well-socialized and tacit assumptions of the mental health professional, and the necessities of licensure and accreditation to permeate thought and practice. All of this works in concert to unnerve faith. The Bible becomes an ancillary and supportive text, a source of proof-texts in the worst sense. Christian faith and biblical citation are pressed to rationalize *ideas intrinsically alien to the mind of God.* Only when our first priority is first will we truly think and act in ways that transform our culture, those we counsel, and ourselves.[18]

The danger of a non-sufficiency view of Scripture is that it introduces ideas intrinsically alien to the mind of God as major premises of a model that claims to be biblical. Instead, we should let grandpa tell us the meaning of his own story, and thus the meaning of ours.

So, regarding our theoretical view of human experience, I will attempt as succinct an answer as possible to the question "Sufficient for what?"

Scripture is sufficient to frame the entirety of both human experience and the context in which that experience occurs according to God's essential purpose for people to reflect His personhood by means of the gospel of Jesus Christ.

Let's unpack this a bit. What I mean by *human experience* and *the context in which that experience occurs* is that God sees the intricacies of a person's internal experience as well as the incalculable contextual factors that influence that experience—whether social, historical, linguistic, cultural, physiological, situational, or any other categorical term we want to use.[19]

God knows the human experience. He knows the breadth of the soul's functions, how those functions interrelate and how they function optimally. He knows the experiential dynamics that lead to certain clusters of dysfunction; He knows how those dysfunctions are expressed neurologically; and He knows how those neurological patterns entrench a person into seemingly unalterable tendencies.

God also knows the context of human experience. He knows the powerful influence of caretakers, the scarring effect of traumatic experiences, how a person's native linguistic system forms lifelong cognitive categories, how cultural expectations shape a person's perspective of self, how genes influence neurological development to create certain predispositions, and how poverty (or wealth, for that matter) influences a person's expectations of the world.

God knows all these things a lot better than we ever will, no matter how precise our means of measurement get. And He *still* chose to reveal in the ancient text of Scripture His main concerns about the human experience in precisely the way He did. And that main concern is His *essential purpose for people to reflect His personhood by means of the gospel of Jesus Christ.* The gospel of Jesus Christ is the interpretive center of Scripture,[20] and a person's relation to that gospel is the primary concern of the Bible's psychology.

OUR PRACTICAL WORK WITH PEOPLE

Where the rubber meets the road is in the counseling room. How does a Christian counselor actually *use* Scripture? Quoting from it does not guarantee that a counselor is honoring its sufficiency for the task. We must practically submit to its emphatic authority, not just its encyclopedic authority. In *practice*, emphasis becomes vital.

Horton explains, "It is possible to hold a high view of biblical authority and sufficiency in theory while yielding a magisterial role in practice to sociology, politics, marketing, psychology, and other cultural authorities."[21] So perhaps a good set of self-directed questions for a counselor to test his or her understanding of sufficiency would be: In my interactions with people in counseling, are God's primary concerns regarding the human experience *my* primary concerns regarding *my counselees'* experience? Or is my primary approach a set of concerns from outside research, with explicitly biblical matters being supplemental?

Practically speaking for Christian counselors, it's a matter of emphasis. Two counselors with similar theological convictions (and similar familiarity with various psychological models) can conduct a counseling session in entirely different ways. They can both discuss the same topics in the course of a given counseling session, but subordinate those topics differently, resulting in an entirely different experience for the counselee. Let me illustrate this grammatically. Consider the following sentences, both of which contain the same information, but are subordinated differently.

- While it's true that Isaiah Smith grew up in a culture that condoned slavery, he is responsible for owning and mistreating his slaves.
- While it's true that Isaiah Smith is responsible for owning and mistreating his slaves, he grew up in a culture that condoned slavery.

The difference in emphasis makes us end up with two very different points. Both sentences acknowledge the truth value of both concepts in the pairing, but they assemble them differently, resulting in completely different sentence functions. The first sentence functions to condemn Isaiah Smith's actions, and the second functions to explain them. Let's try a set of examples that strike a little closer to home:

- While it's true that developmental and psychosocial realities have shaped who you are today, Scripture addresses you as a moral agent who actively responds to life in covenantal ways.
- While it's true that Scripture addresses you as a moral agent actively responding in covenantal ways, developmental and psychosocial realities have shaped who you are today.

Christian counselors need to take an honest look at which of these two sentences more accurately reflects what occurs in their counseling rooms. Better yet, we should *regularly* assess this, since no one's position guarantees they are avoiding concerns foreign to Scripture as a constitutive part of their approach.

Let's consider an example. A former marine experiences traumatic episodes long after he is safely back on his home soil. He has frequent nightmares, finds himself angry at authority and hateful of civilians, and cannot sit with his back toward the door in any room. The latest DSM (*Diagnostic and Statistical Manual of Mental Disorders*) would give us a fairly accurate description of the types of experiences he's having and label it post-traumatic stress disorder (PTSD). This extrabiblical information is descriptively helpful, and it even seems to explain something the Bible does not. Scripture, after all, does not contain specific answers of causation for these specific dynamics. But upon closer consideration, neither does the DSM. It may describe the observable dynamic, but it does not explain it. In other words, it describes a *symptom cluster*, but it addresses neither its ultimate cause nor its ultimate meaning.

Basing a therapeutic approach on the diagnostic criteria of PTSD will not address the deep things of human life as God sees them. The fear so deeply entrenched that it comes over the ex-marine involuntarily demands a deeper explanation — a theological one. People were not made to die, and the abrupt ending of life in death is foreign to our design. This young marine not only lived under the immediate threat of death for months but also witnessed it firsthand and dealt it out himself, viewing it through the scope of his gun. He was led into battle by imperfect and often self-inclined authority figures, all in defense of an American ideal he saw the threadbare edges of when rolling through someone else's homeland in a Humvee. His are life-meaning questions, edge-of-reality questions, basic-moral-fabric questions. Why is death so terrible? And why can't I get over it? For him, there's no going home; he's been disillusioned of his past securities.

And only the gospel of Jesus Christ — in its broadest, fullest sense — can offer an adequate answer to the ultimate cause and meaning of his fear and anger, of his grief and insecurity. And only Jesus can reveal to him the promised destiny of that place of ultimate security, where city gates are doorless because even the idea of "enemy" will have passed away. And it is that hope that will change his soul in the meantime.

Practically speaking, God's perspective of this young man's trouble should frame ours. The observations of others are helpful in their own right, but the constitutive framework has been laid out for us in a Bible that is more than sufficient to explain human experience.

CHAPTER 6

THE CHRIST-CENTEREDNESS OF BIBLICAL COUNSELING

ROBERT JONES

What makes biblical counseling biblical? The most obvious answer lies in how biblical counselors view the Bible. We believe that Scripture forms our counseling theory and practice. The Bible does not merely *inform* our counseling, as if it were simply one source of truth among several. Instead, the Bible *drives* our counseling. A biblical counseling approach does not arise from elsewhere, only to be supported or supplemented by Scripture. The Bible both creates and propels our approach.

If this is true, then two implications follow: Our counseling will reflect the Bible's central theme—God's redemptive work in Jesus Christ. And it will reflect the Bible's central ministry vision—to bring Jesus to needy people and to help them know, love, and follow Him.

This chapter aims to show that any form of counseling worthy of the name "biblical" must highlight the Bible's central figure, Jesus. Counseling that is truly biblical must be "*Christ*-ian." It must be Christ-*driven*, in the sense of "having a compulsive or urgent quality (e.g., a *driven* sense of obligation)" and "propelled or motivated by something (e.g., results-*driven*)."[1] True biblical counseling is fixed on Jesus and propelled by Him.

Consider Colossians 1:28 – 29, in which the apostle Paul summarizes his ministry. "He is the one we proclaim, admonishing and teaching everyone with all wisdom, so that we may present everyone fully mature in Christ. To this end I strenuously contend with all the energy Christ so powerfully works in me."*

Notice the comprehensive, Christ-centered aspects of Paul's work:

- His central task is plain: to proclaim *Jesus Christ*.
- His method is simple, not mystical or magical: to *admonish* and *teach* with wisdom (two verbs that describe not only the public ministry of God's Word but also the private ministry, e.g., counseling).
- His target audience is comprehensive: to minister to *everyone*, not just corporately but individually.
- His desired outcome is stellar: to present everyone *fully mature* in Christ.
- His urgent effort is stirring: to *strenuously contend*.
- His power source is inexhaustible: he is empowered with *Christ's energy*.

In other words, Jesus is the content, the goal, and the power source for Paul.

A few verses later, Paul focuses again on Jesus as the centerpiece of his ministry, "Christ, in whom are hidden all the treasures of wisdom and knowledge" (Col. 2:2 – 3). Paul then warns of the dangers of man-made philosophies that compete with Jesus. "See to it that no one takes you captive through hollow and deceptive *philosophy*, which depends on human tradition and the basic principles of this world rather than on Christ" (Col. 2:8, emphasis added). Paul builds his ministry on Jesus,

---

* All Scripture quotations in this chapter are from the *Holy Bible, New International Version* (1984).

not on the philosophies, theologies, psychologies, therapies, or religions of this passing world. The passage excludes attempts to syncretize or integrate Jesus with other belief systems. Why? Paul explains, "For in Christ all the fullness of the Deity lives in bodily form, and in Christ you have been brought to fullness. He is the head over every power and authority" (Col. 2:9–10).

Elsewhere Paul summarizes his ministry in similar Christ-centered terms: "When I came to you, I did not come with eloquence or human wisdom as I proclaimed to you the testimony about God. For I resolved to know nothing while I was with you except Jesus Christ and him crucified" (1 Cor. 2:1–2). "My dear children, for whom I am again in the pains of childbirth until Christ is formed in you" (Gal. 4:19–20). Indeed, Jesus is the foundation and the fountain of Paul's ministry.

What does Christ-centered counseling look like? How can we make our counseling more Christ-driven? I would suggest five marks.[2]

MARK #1: JESUS' TEACHING AS OUR FINAL UNDERSTANDING OF SCRIPTURE

The Bible can be a confusing book, difficult to understand for many people. How do the Old and New Testaments connect? Why don't Christians obey the laws in Leviticus or offer animal sacrifices? The answer is that Jesus has come, fulfilling the Old Testament. As our supreme Lawgiver and Prophet, the teaching by Him and His apostles has become the final Word from God, enabling us to interpret the whole Bible in a coherent way.

Jesus understood this. Consider His provocative words to the Jewish leaders: "You study the Scriptures diligently because you think that in them you have eternal life. These are the very Scriptures that testify about me, yet you refuse to come to me to have life" (John 5:39–40). He is the central point of their Hebrew Scriptures. The whole Old Testament points to Jesus.

We see this pictured on the Mount of Transfiguration in the way

God the Father supremely highlighted Jesus. Mark 9:2–4 records the scene: "After six days Jesus took Peter, James and John with him and led them up a high mountain, where they were all alone. There he was transfigured before them. His clothes became dazzling white, whiter than anyone in the world could bleach them. And there appeared before them Elijah and Moses, who were talking with Jesus."

Moses (the Old Testament lawgiver) and Elijah (arguably God's greatest Old Testament prophet) apparently represent the Law and the Prophets. When Peter suggests building three shelters to honor Jesus, Moses, and Elijah—effectively placing Jesus on par with the Law and the Prophets—God the Father intervenes: "Then a cloud appeared and covered them, and a voice came from the cloud: 'This is my Son, whom I love. Listen to him!'" (Mark 9:7). The Father's voice exalts Jesus as not only the final Prophet and Lawgiver but the superior One, whose voice everyone must now follow. The scene ends with Moses and Elijah disappearing. Jesus alone remains.

Or consider our Lord's words to two of His followers who expressed doubts concerning the reports of His resurrection: "He said to them, 'How foolish you are, and how slow to believe all that the prophets have spoken! Did not the Messiah have to suffer these things and then enter his glory?' And beginning with Moses and all the Prophets, he explained to them what was said in all the Scriptures concerning himself" (Luke 24:25–27; see also vv. 44–45). For Jesus, the whole of the Bible is about Him.

Hebrews 1 also announced the finality of the Son-revelation over against all previous revelations from God. "In the past God spoke to our ancestors through the prophets at many times and in various ways, but in these last days he has spoken to us by his Son, whom he appointed heir of all things, and through whom also he made the universe" (Heb. 1:1–2). The writer then exalts the Son as "the radiance of God's glory and the exact representation of his being" (1:3) and the one who is superior to the angels, the mediators of the old covenant (Heb. 1:4; 2:2; Deut. 33:2; Acts 7:53; Gal. 3:19).

What does this Christ-centered way of reading our Bible mean for a Christian counselor? It means that we can, and should, use our entire Bibles to bring Jesus to counselees — to help them know Jesus initially and follow Him continually.

For example, as we point people to the great stories of Godly men and women in Genesis, we can embed those characters in the larger picture of God's redemptive story. We must not settle for Abraham as merely a model of righteousness. We see him (and all his flaws) as part of God's bigger plan to preserve His people and bring forth the Messiah. Abraham was a man of faith who looked forward to the fulfillment of God's promises, a fulfillment we have already begun to experience in Jesus' first coming, but not yet fully experienced, as we too await God's final consummation.

When we take people to the Psalms, we can realize that the psalmists' sufferings sometimes point us toward Jesus' sufferings for us. Even the psalms that cry out to God to judge the wicked become encouragements to those who have been mistreated, because they remind us that God one day will make all things right.

When we guide our counselees from the book of Proverbs, we must not dispense verses like tidbits of wise advice from *Poor Richard's Almanac*. Proverbs pictures the way Jesus the ultimate Man of wisdom walked as our example, the way He enables us now to walk, and the way we one day will walk on the new earth.

MARK #2: JESUS AS OUR PERFECT EXAMPLE OF GODLY HUMANITY

In describing the mark of a true Christian, the apostle John expresses a bottom line, "This is how we know we are in him: Whoever claims to live in him must live as Jesus did" (1 John 2:5–6). Living like Jesus lived evidences true Christian conversion and provides the perfect standard for how our counselees should live. We have a definite model of flawless love, joy, and peace to hold before our counselees.

In an address to the faculty and students of the University Psychiatric Clinic in Vienna, Jay Adams summarized the disunity across the
field of psychotherapy. He noted the lack of any objective standard to
assess health versus disorder.

> You may say that society is the standard, or you may say pragmatically that
> what works is the standard, or that the counselee is the standard; but when
> you finally boil it all down and strip off the externals, what you have left is
> this: the individual psychotherapist determines the standard. The problem
> of subjectivity is enormous. [3]

The proposed solution?

> There has to be a standard, and a model that conforms to it, so that we can
> both know and see what a human being should be like. We have to have
> a picture of what a human should look like if we're going to try to change
> people. Where are we going to get such a picture?[4]

Referring to those who practice Christ-centered biblical counseling,
Adams answered:

> They say that human beings should look like Jesus Christ! They say that the
> Bible not only gives a description of what a person should be like in abstract
> terms but that Jesus Christ is the model of such a person in terms of action
> and speech. Indeed, in contrast to the psychotherapeutic confusion, it has
> been most powerfully demonstrated in America that a true consensus can be
> developed when there is such a standard.[5]

In other words, Christ-centered counseling is not counselor-centered
(seeking to conform people into *our* desired image) or client-centered
(seeking to conform people into *their* desired image). *It is Person-
centered with a capital* P. We point people to a Person who is external
to us and to them, seeking to conform them into the objective image
of Jesus.

For example, in helping people learn to speak in godly ways, biblical
counselors often point their counselees to passages like Ephesians 4:29;
Proverbs 12:18; or 15:1 — epistles that command or wisdom literature
that describes godly speech. But we often bypass the biblical snapshots
of Jesus, the one prophetically described as "the most excellent of men,"

whose "lips have been anointed with grace" (Ps. 45:2). If the temple guards were indeed correct — "No one ever spoke the way this man does" (John 7:46) — then we have much left to mine out from Jesus' model.

What kind of words did Jesus speak? Consider five categories seen in the Gospels that flesh out the principles we find in the Epistles and Wisdom Literature. Our Lord spoke words that

- sustained and refreshed weary, burdened hearts (Isa. 50:4; Matt. 11:28–29);
- comforted grieving hearts (Luke 7:13; John 11:23; in both cases, we see timely, compassionate speech followed by loving actions);
- rebuked and humbled proud hearts (Matt. 16:22–23; 23:1–39; Mark 10:13–16; Rev. 2–3);
- instructed ignorant hearts (Isa. 11:2; John 3:1–21; 4:4–26);
- assured doubting or distressed hearts (Matt. 12:19–20; John 14–16, e.g., 14:27).

What would our marriage counseling look like if we directed couples to reflect on Jesus' speech and to ask Him to transform their communication by the power of the same Spirit who controlled Him?

Or consider how to help people who suffer mistreatment. How often do we consider the Gospels' passion narratives? Surely the way Jesus dealt with His arrest, trials, beatings, and crucifixion can instruct and embolden our sinned-against counselees to persevere in godliness. The apostle Peter understood this. In his first epistle, Peter sets before his suffering readers our Lord's example: "To this you were called, because Christ suffered for you, leaving you an example, that you should follow in his steps. 'He committed no sin, and no deceit was found in his mouth.' When they hurled their insults at him, he did not retaliate; when he suffered, he made no threats. Instead, he entrusted himself to him who judges justly" (1 Peter 2:21–23).

Tom was an angry husband, frustrated with his wife's failures as a homemaker and mother, and adept at justifying his temper tantrums.

After another major tirade, they agreed to meet with me. I heard their respective accounts of the fight, and I asked to speak privately with Tom. We looked together at the above passage. We observed the severity of Jesus' suffering—a totally innocent man victimized by intense verbal and physical abuse. Yet He did not respond sinfully—no cursing, no revenge, and no retaliation. Instead, Jesus trusted God the righteous Judge, and He entrusted Himself and His perpetrators into God's hands. He prayed for His enemies, forgave the repentant thief, cared for His mother, and absorbed God's wrath for all our sins.

As I shared this, Tom nodded in assent. Then he uttered these words, "All that is fine, Bob, but I'm not Jesus." So I looked at Tom and replied, "Tom, you are too good of a Bible student to use that excuse." (Tom had been a Bible-study leader at his previous church.) "You are missing the explicit point of the passage. Look at verse 21: 'To this you were called.' Tom, Jesus' godly response to mistreatment is for you 'an example, that you should follow in his steps.' Peter's point is not biographical; he is not writing an essay about Jesus. He is telling his readers (and you and me) how to respond to abuse in Christlike ways. I'm not defending your wife's failures. I'm asking you to follow Jesus, repent of your sinful anger, ask God and your wife to forgive you, and press on with fresh love and obedience to the Lord."

Of course, we could point to the example of Jesus in many other areas in the Gospels—His emotions, His response to authorities, His patience when people were slow to understand, etc. Biblical counselors committed to being more Christ-centered can turn to the example of Jesus to set before their counselees.

MARK #3: JESUS' CROSS AND RESURRECTION AS OUR MOTIVATION FOR GROWTH AND CHANGE

Among the ways that biblical counseling differs from other forms of counseling is our unqualified reliance on a specific, real time-and-space event — the death and resurrection of an actual historical Person, Jesus the Redeemer. Other forms of counseling ultimately depend on a philosophical viewpoint that leads counselees to act; our approach depends on the actions of Another. His epoch-changing work has provided us today with the foundational dynamic we need for true change.

The apostle Paul unpacks this dynamic in 2 Corinthians 5:14 – 15. What propelled him forward as an energetic apostle despite those who called him a fool? Reflecting on the life-changing impact of God's love in Christ, Paul answers, "For Christ's love compels us, because we are convinced that one died for all, and therefore all died. And he died for all, that those who live should no longer live for themselves but for him who died for them and was raised again" (2 Cor. 5:14 – 15).

Christ-centered biblical counselors direct their counselees to live for Him — to grow and change in practical ways — for a very specific reason: because God in love has sent His own Son to die and be raised for them. Commenting on this passage, J. Murray Harris concludes, "Here, then, is clear evidence of the Christocentric focus of Pauline ethics. Christian conduct is motivated and determined by Christ."[6]

What does this look like in counseling? It means bringing Jesus to counselees by using the Scriptures, inviting them to trust in Him in fresh ways, and urging them to live for the One who died and rose for them. It means reviewing God's love for them and Jesus' death and resurrection for them, and then exploring what it means to live as died-for and raised-for people. The fact that someone *needed* to die for us reminds us of our sinfulness and helplessness; the fact that Jesus *did* die for us reminds us that He loves us. And the fact that Jesus rose from the dead assures us that the Father accepted His sacrifice and that Jesus is a living and active Savior who is with us by His Spirit to help us to follow Him.

Why is this important? Because it is God's grace in Christ that "teaches us to say 'No' to ungodliness and worldly passions, and to live self-controlled, upright and godly lives in this present age" (Titus 2:12). The truth of God's love seen in Christ's death and resurrection for us motivates us to put off sin and put on righteousness. This Jesus "gave himself for us to redeem us from all wickedness and to purify for himself a people that are his very own, eager to do what is good" (v. 14). The goal of Christ's death and resurrection was to redeem us from sin and make us doers of good works. The gospel trains us to live for the Lord who died and rose for us.

Consider a practical Christ-centered suggestion. In encouraging husbands and wives to live out their marital roles, we might explain a passage like Ephesians 5:22–33. We might ask each spouse to memorize, meditate on, and put into practice verse 22 (for wives) and verse 25 (for husbands). But a biblical counselor concerned to make his counseling more Christ-centered might add another step, a step that recognizes the gospel context in which the Spirit embedded these commands. We can ask them to concurrently read, meditate on, and reflect on Ephesians 1:1–14, a passage that like a refreshing waterfall showers us with descriptions of God's salvation blessings. Counselees can list ten truths from these verses about what God in Christ has given them or done for them and then reflect prayerfully on how these spiritual riches can motivate them to carry out their Ephesians 5 marital duties.

What does this mean for counselees facing sin patterns that are difficult to break? Based on Matthew 5–7 (the Sermon on the Mount), we can guide those we counsel to humble themselves before God (5:3–12), to see that their sinful behavior begins in their hearts (5:21–30), to radically amputate all occasions/excuses for sin (5:29–30), to seek God's kingdom above other pursuits (6:33), to ask, seek, and knock for the Father's help (7:7–12), and to be doers not mere hearers of Christ's words (7:24–27).

While these truths are helpful for those who struggle with sinful habits, they miss some vital realities of the gospel. Why? Because the gospel of Matthew doesn't start with the commands of Matthew 5–7. It begins with Matthew 1–4, chapters that picture a glorious Savior.

In Matthew 1, we gaze at Jesus as the Son of Abraham and the Son of David (vv. 1–17), the One who has fulfilled the promises of the Abrahamic and Davidic covenants. We learn that He is Jesus, who will save His people from their sins, and Immanuel, God with us (vv. 21 – 23). In Matthew 2 we see Jesus as God's Son being rescued out of Egypt, fulfilling the Exodus motif (vv. 13 – 15), and portrayed as a lowly, humble "Nazarene" (vv. 21 – 23). In Matthew 3 He humbles Himself to be baptized by John (vv. 13 – 15) and is then immediately endowed with God's Spirit and declared to be God's special, beloved Son, well pleasing to the Father (vv. 16 – 17).

When we turn to Matthew 4, we see Him overcoming a threefold, satanic temptation in the desert. He defeats the devil by God's Spirit and God's Word as He declares three times, "It is written." This is good news for the one caught in a pattern of sin. But there's more here. Jesus, the ultimate Son of God, succeeded where Israel, the previous son of God (Ex. 4:22), failed. While Israel faltered in unbelief during its forty-year desert temptation, Jesus flourished in faith as He overcame His concentrated forty-day desert temptation (Matt. 4:1 – 11). Matthew then displays Jesus as the one who brings light and hope to everyone, including the Gentiles (vv. 15 – 16), the one who brings the kingdom (vv. 17, 23), and the one who heals diseases and casts out demons (vv. 23 – 25).

How then does Matthew 1 – 4 affect the way we might apply Matthew 5 – 7 to the person struggling with sinful habits? It impacts how we look at the Lord who calls us to change. He is the bringer of grace, the kingdom, and hope. He has already fulfilled God's law on our behalf, earning a righteousness that we could not. He promises His forgiveness, His presence, His victory, and His power to help us obey Matthew 5 – 7.

Let me add a personal observation as one who has studied biblical counseling for thirty years. Against various forms of pietism, our movement recovered and championed the doctrine of progressive sanctification. But I don't think we have been as clear on doctrines like definitive (or initial) sanctification, justification, adoption, and union with Christ (including Christian identity) — doctrines that are foundational to progressive sanctification and any call to grow and change. Thankfully, in more recent years, biblical counselors have stressed how the Bible's "indicatives" (the facts of what God has done, is doing, and will do) precede and empower the Bible's "imperatives" (the commands to be and do what God wants us to be and do). God grounds His call for us to change in His own changing work for us and in us. Biblical counselors must skillfully teach both, in their proper flow and balance. As we call people to practical obedience and Christian maturity, we must help them see God's grace in Jesus, the assurance of complete forgiveness, our sonship in Christ, and fresh gospel-compelled motivations to live purposefully for our crucified, risen Redeemer.

MARK #4: JESUS' PRESENCE AND POWER AS THE SOURCE OF SPIRITUAL STRENGTH AND HELP

Counselees seeking biblical counseling can quickly become discouraged when they see the depth and breadth of the Bible. "How can I possibly follow this Book? How can I grasp and implement the multitude of Bible commands? The Bible addresses so many areas of my life. There are so many principles, demands, and applications. I feel so overwhelmed."

The good news is that the God who commands is the God who supplies. Do we need to learn contentment in hard situations? Let Paul's testimony inspire and motivate us:

> I am not saying this because I am in need, for I have learned to be content whatever the circumstances. I know what it is to be in need, and I know what it is to have plenty. I have learned the secret of being content in any and every situation, whether well fed or hungry, whether living in plenty or in want.
>
> Philippians 4:11–12

How can this happen? How did Paul learn contentment? Paul continues in verse 13, "I can do all this through him who gives me strength." Rather than serving as an isolated verse plucked out of midair to promise extraordinary feats of miraculous power, verse 13 flows from the immediate context. Jesus Christ gives Paul the power to walk contentedly with the Lord despite hardships.

Do we need divine help to handle a difficult task? Maybe it involves a conflict with a roommate, spouse, or coworker. Although we know that God wants us to pursue peace, we feel weak, alone, and helpless. Notice Paul's testimony as he faced a threatening situation: "At my first defense, no one came to my support, but everyone deserted me. May it not be held against them. But the Lord stood at my side and gave me strength" (2 Tim. 4:16–17). By faith Paul saw and felt Jesus' supernatural strength next to him—"the Lord stood at my side and gave me strength"—through the indwelling Holy Spirit.

Do we need assurance that God has not abandoned us, even when we have failed Him? Again, it is the risen Christ who provides us with such confidence: "Because Jesus lives forever, he has a permanent priesthood. Therefore he is able to save completely those who come to God through him, because he always lives to intercede for them" (Heb. 7:24–25).

Christ-centered counselors hold forth the risen Jesus and His intercessory work as part of a Christian counselee's confidence in Christian living.

What actions might encourage our counselees to depend on Jesus' present-day presence and daily enabling power? Prayer. As we begin a session, we can help our counselees—and us—by consciously invoking Jesus' presence. We can ask Him to meet with us and have His way in each of our hearts. As we close a session, we can ask Jesus to go with our counselees as they return to their problem-filled world. And in assigning Bible-study homework, we can add a final step: to talk with God about the insights and conclusions they have gained from their study. One way we grow in our relationship with Christ is by sharing with Him in prayer our innermost thoughts, struggles, and joys.

For example, we might give counselees a Bible study on worry that invites them to look up several passages. But we can also include this as the last part of their assignment: "Write a prayer to the Lord in which you acknowledge His presence and promises as you seek His face to help you deal with a present fear or worry." If we assign them a book chapter or booklet on some aspect of sexual sin, we can ask them to mark their reading or to write on a separate sheet of paper the top three or four insights. But how about adding a final ingredient: "Write a prayer in which you ask God to deepen your love for Him and to help you pursue purity in your mind and body."

Why is this so important? As Paul Tripp so helpfully reminds us, "We do not offer people a system of redemption, a set of insights and principles. We offer people a Redeemer."[7] The Biblical Counseling Coalition's Confessional Statement concurs:

> We point people to a person, Jesus our Redeemer, and not to a program, theory, or experience. We place our trust in the transforming power of the Redeemer as the only hope to change people's hearts, not in any human system of change. People need a personal and dynamic relationship with Jesus, not a system of self-salvation, self-management, or self-actualization (John 14:6). Wise counselors seek to lead struggling, hurting, sinning, and confused people to the hope, resources, strength, and life that are available only in Christ.[8]

Biblical counseling connects people to an actual Person who transforms them.

MARK #5: JESUS' RETURN AS OUR ULTIMATE HOPE FOR ALL OUR COUNSELING PROBLEMS

When Christ-centered biblical counselors say that the "Bible has the answers to all our problems," what do we mean? Do we mean that if we read, believe, and do all that the Bible says, then all our personal problems and relationship problems in this life will be fixed?

No. While the Bible addresses every type of problem under the sun (see Ecclesiastes and Proverbs for an amazing span of topics!), there are problems that cannot and will not be solved apart from Christ's return.

Those who have been traumatized in their childhood might continue to struggle with some level of fear throughout their adult years. Those who have been sexually active in sinful ways might continue to struggle with measures of lust. Those who are inclined toward depression might continue to battle various degrees of depression. Only the second coming of Christ and the work of the triune God in His final stages of redemption will fix all our human problems. While the Bible predicts and guarantees these ultimate answers and encourages us to bank our hopes on those answers, the Bible itself doesn't bring those future changes. Only Jesus can.

What does Jesus promise one day to do that will bring those final fixes? First, our Lord promises us a perfect heart. There is relief on the way for every counselee who experiences ongoing frustration over remaining sin and frequent failures. As the apostle John foresees, "Dear friends, now we are children of God, and what we will be has not yet been made known. But we know that when Christ appears, we shall be like him, for we shall see him as he is" (1 John 3:2). The flesh-versus-Spirit internal civil war will end one day when Jesus returns for us. But there is a vital corollary to draw from this text. When Jesus appears, we shall be like Him, but not a moment before then. Until Christ returns, we will not be fully like Him, no matter how many biblical counseling sessions we provide our counselees and no matter how diligent their efforts. Only the second coming will solve all our problems.

Second, our Lord promises us a perfect body. Speaking of the resurrection body that will replace our decaying bodies, Paul writes, "The body that is sown is perishable, it is raised imperishable; it is sown in dishonor, it is raised in glory; it is sown in weakness, it is raised in power; it is sown a natural body, it is raised a spiritual body" (1 Cor. 15:42–44). That body will be like Christ's glorious, resurrection body (1 Cor. 15:45–49; see also 2 Cor. 5). Can you imagine that? No more arthritis, cancer, or heart disease. No more physical disabilities, dementia, or brain injuries. While the Adamic curse introduced bodily decay and death, Jesus' first coming began the process to reverse the curse. One day soon He will return to complete it.

Third, our Lord promises us a perfect place, the new heaven and new earth. For counselees who suffer ongoing personal mistreatment and other forms of suffering endemic to this fallen world, the apostle Peter reminds us of God's promise, "But in keeping with his promise we are looking forward to a new heaven and a new earth, where righteousness dwells" (2 Peter 3:13). And the apostle John envisions the fulfillment. After the destruction of the devil and all who followed him (Rev. 20:10) and the sight of the new heaven and earth emerging (Rev. 21:1–2), John hears God's loud voice from the throne declaring,

> "Look! God's dwelling place is now among the people, and he will dwell with them. They will be his people, and God himself will be with them and be their God. He will wipe every tear from their eyes. There will be no more death or mourning or crying or pain, for the old order of things has passed away."
>
> Revelation 21:3–4 (NIV, 2011)

Until Christ returns, our biblical counseling will continually be limited by our fallen world. Until then, our counselees will leave our office each time to face an imperfect, sin-cursed place. Come quickly, Lord Jesus!

CONCLUSION

One of the beauties of the biblical counseling movement is the diversity of styles, personalities, techniques, and gifts that mark individual counselors. But what we all have in common is a shared view of the supremacy of Jesus Christ and the goal of our counseling ministry — to see Jesus increasingly formed in those we serve. As John Piper observes:

> All counseling issues involve the exaltation or the denigration of Jesus Christ. Either our attitudes and feelings and behaviors are making much or making little of Christ. We were created to make much of Christ. There is no true success in counseling if a person becomes socially functional without conscious dependence on and delight in Jesus Christ.[9]

True biblical counseling, therefore, is eminently Christ-centered in at least the five ways we considered: His teaching forms our final understanding of Scripture as we minister that Word to people. His own life offers an engaging picture of perfect humanity. His cross and resurrection stimulate us to grow and change. His presence with us by His Spirit provides the power we need to love and follow Him. And His promised return brings assurance that one day the Redeemer will fix and purify all things, even the things (like us!) that remain broken and sinful until that day. May God help each of us to use our Bibles and our own deepening love for our Savior to radiate Christ and to bring Him skillfully and lovingly to those we counsel.

CHAPTER 7

A COUNSELING PRIMER FROM THE GREAT CLOUD OF WITNESSES

BOB KELLEMEN

When I was in seminary, intense discussions erupted between students who identified themselves as committed to the "sufficiency of Scriptures" for counseling and students who identified themselves as committed to an "integration approach to counseling." It seemed to me that these terms were being used with little definition or precision and that the discussion seemed lacking in historical context.

I kept thinking, *Surely the church has always been about the business of compassionately and wisely helping hurting and hardened people to deal with suffering and sin.* I kept asking myself and others, "Couldn't we learn much from the great cloud of witnesses who preceded us that we could apply to ministry today? Wouldn't probing the wisdom of the ancient path be beneficial for our current discussion?" This led to a three-decade treasure hunt into the history of the personal ministry of the Word as practiced by our Christian forebears in the faith.[1]

My treasure hunt was motivated in part by G. K. Chesterton's insight that history and tradition are democracy extended through time. History gives "votes to the most obscure of all classes, our ancestors. It is the *democracy of the dead.*" It refuses to submit to the small and arrogant elite "who merely happen to be walking around."[2]

THE FORGOTTEN ART

From the time of the early church until the rise of modern psychology, pastoral work was synonymous with biblical soul care — the Scripture-directed, prayer-shaped ministry that is devoted to persons singly or in groups, in settings sacred and profane.[3] Since then, for many, the practice of pastoral care has become a forgotten art. Modern pastoral caregivers seem ignorant of the contributions of the church in the areas of biblical soul care.[4]

Thomas Oden explains that too often we conceptualize personal ministry models without the aid of the historic voices of the church.

> The preaching and counseling pastor needs to know that current pastoral care stands in a tradition of two millennia of reflection on the tasks of soul care. The richness of the classic Christian pastoral tradition remains pertinent to ministry today. The laity have a right to competent, historically grounded pastoral care. The pastor has a right to the texts that teach how pastors have understood their work over the centuries. *Modern chauvinism has falsely taught us a theory of moral inferiority: that new ideas are intrinsically superior, and old patterns inferior.* This attitude has robbed the laity of the pastoral care they deserve, and the ministry of the texts that can best inform the recovery of pastoral identity.... Long before psychology was a distinct profession, pastors engaged in activities that required psychological wisdom. Pastors have always struggled for the health of persons and the life of souls.[5]

Some Christians seem willing to listen only to their own voice or the voice of contemporaries. Pastor and church historian Wayne Oates notes that Protestants, in particular, "tend to start over from scratch every three or four generations." Therefore, we do not adequately consolidate the communal wisdom of the centuries because of our "antipathy for tradition." As a result, we "have accrued less capital" in the form of proverbs, manuals of mutual ministry, and a theology of body life.[6] Oden summarizes the results well: "Christians have usually been losers when they have neglected the consensual writers of their own history and tradition."[7]

Church historians William Clebsch and Charles Jaekle present a convincing explanation for our lack of contact with the history of Christian mutual care.

> Faced with an urgency for some system by which to conceptualize the human condition and to deal with the modern grandeurs and terrors of the human spirit, theoreticians of the cure of souls have too readily adopted the leading academic psychologies. Having no pastoral theology to inform our psychology or even to identify the cure of souls as a mode of human helping, we have allowed psychoanalytic thought, for example, to dominate the vocabulary of the spirit.[8]

Today's crying needs drown out yesterday's relevant answers. Why? We lack a sufficient awareness of the victorious ways in which people have faced life issues in bygone centuries through trust in God's Word. We have lost our historical awareness of how the church has practiced the personal ministry of the Word.

Remembering the Forgotten Art

John McNeil, perhaps the past century's preeminent historian of soul care, summarizes the evidence for the historical practice of the personal ministry of the Word.

> Lying deep in the experience and culture of the early Christian communities were the twin tasks of mutual edification (*aedifictio mutua*) and fraternal correction (*correptio fraterna*). In numerous passages (Rom. 14:19; 15:14; Col. 3:16; 1 Thess. 5:11; 5:14; 2 Thess. 3:15; just to list a few) we cannot fail to see the apostle Paul's design to create an atmosphere in which the intimate exchange of spiritual help, the mutual guidance of souls, would be a normal feature of Christian behavior.[9]

Where McNeil focuses on mutual lay care, pastor and church historian Charles Kemp highlights pastoral care.

> There has apparently never been a time or place where individuals did not seek out religious leaders for personal help for: sustaining comfort, guidance and counsel, reconciliation through forgiveness and assurance, and healing or spiritual health. The process can be traced from the Old Testament to Christ and the Apostles in the New Testament to the early Church to the medieval Church to the Reformation and up to our own day.[10]

With eloquence befitting the beauty of historical pastoral care, Clebsch and Jaekle reveal something of the breadth of pastoral ministry through personal care.

> The Christian ministry of the cure of souls, or pastoral care, has been exercised on innumerable occasions and in every conceivable human circumstance, as it has aimed to relieve a plethora of perplexities besetting persons of every class and condition and mentality. Pastors rude and barely plucked from paganism, pastors sophisticated in the theory and practice of their profession, and pastors at every stage of adeptness between these extremes, have sought and wrought to help troubled people overcome their troubles. To view pastoral care in historical perspective is to survey a vast endeavor, to appreciate a noble profession, and to receive a grand tradition.[11]

E. Brooks Holifield, in his classic study of American pastoral care, speaks about the extensive personal ministry of pastors.

> The Christian clergy has been a talkative lot. *But for almost twenty centuries they have spent more time listening to people than preaching to them.* As early as the second century, they began to write letters and treatises instructing one another about spiritual direction and consolation, repentance and discipline, grief and growth. They designated their task as "cure of souls," and *so voluminous were their prescriptions that by the seventeenth century it was difficult to find an original cure for a wounded spirit.*[12]

To emphasize his point, Holifield notes that when Thomas Fuller published *The Cause and Cure of a Wounded Conscience*, he apologized both for adding yet another book to the overcrowded field of pastoral care and for quoting so extensively from previous soul care writers. However, what was true in the seventeenth century changed dramatically by the nineteenth century. Oden notes:

> It is well known that classic Protestant evangelical teachers made frequent and informed references to the ancient Christian pastoral writers. Calvin was exceptionally well grounded in Augustine, but was also thoroughly familiar with the texts of Cyprian, Tertullian, John Chrysostom, Ambrose, Jerome, Leo, and Gregory the Great. *Not until the late nineteenth century did the study of ancient pastoral writers atrophy among Protestant pastors.*[13]

Oden studied the frequency of references to the classical pastoral tradition in the works of seven nineteenth-century pastoral care writers, representing six denominations. He found more than 150 references to ten classical pastoral writers: Cyprian, Tertullian, John Chrysostom, Augustine, Gregory the Great, Martin Luther, John Calvin, Richard Baxter, George Herbert, and Jeremy Taylor. Turning to the twentieth century, Oden examined seven pastoral care writers. Not one of these authors referenced a single work from the classical pastoral care tradition. Where, then, were these writers turning for authoritative sources in pastoral care and counseling? Oden found 330 references in these modern writings to Freud, Jung, Rogers, Fromm, Sullivan, and Berne.[14] *Over eighteen hundred years of wisdom and instruction on pastoral care and counseling had disappeared.*

Abducted and Abdicated

This chapter thus far points to a common problem and a common cause: caring for the soul through the personal ministry of the Word has been abducted by secular thinking because we have abdicated our spiritual heritage. Past generations of Christians built their approach to people-helping on a spiritual theology—the rich application of Scripture's understanding of people, problems, and solutions to real-life struggles and concerns. Pastors saw counseling as a subset of practical pastoral theology. One result of neglecting this area has been to leave the church almost totally dependent on secular models for human growth.

Over a half century ago, church historian Seward Hiltner perceived that "we lack in pastoral theology a sense of identification with our pastoral roots and heritage. Unless such identification is present, it will be difficult to develop a systematic pastoral theology for our day."[15] He presented a solution to this lack of pastoral heritage: "This situation demands that we inquire into some significant orders of shepherding data from the past as well as from the present.... If we should find matters of importance in past practice and theory that are being neglected in modern work, then we should have to judge critically the modern."[16]

We now direct our attention to just such an endeavor—a brief historical survey of biblical soul care. We'll explore the question, "*Throughout church history, how have God's people viewed and used God's Word for helping hurting and hardened people to find the healing hope of Christ's grace through the personal ministry of the Word?*"

IN THE BEGINNING WAS THE WORD

If we are to examine the history of the personal ministry of the Word, we have to start where church history began—with God's Word. The historical background to Paul's letter to the Colossians and the historical purpose behind Paul's words to the believers at Colossae make Colossians a pertinent place to begin our historical survey.

The Christians in Colossae were facing suffering—condemnation from Satan (Col. 1:22), judgment by others (Col. 2:16), interpersonal grievances and struggles (Col. 3:13, 15), and family discord (Col. 3:19–21). They were also battling sinful temptations—sexual immorality, impurity, lust, evil desires, greed, anger, rage, malice, slander, and lying (Col. 3:5–9). In today's world, these are the types of life issues that cause us to grab our smartphone and schedule a counseling appointment.

In Paul's world, these were also the type of life issues that caused people to visit first-century soul experts.[17] Paul forged Colossians 2 in the heart of active controversy regarding which source of wisdom could address perplexing life issues.[18] Like today, first-century Christians engaged in heated debate about where they could find wisdom for life in a broken world.[19]

Paul steps onto the debate platform in Colossians 2 to point people to Christ's all-sufficient wisdom because in Him "are hidden all the treasures of wisdom and knowledge" (v. 3).* What's the context for Paul's reference to Christ's wisdom? It's the same context that brings

---

* All Scripture quotations in this chapter are from the *Holy Bible, New International Version* (1984).

folks to counseling sessions today: relationship *with God*, that they would be mature in Christ; and relationships *with one another*, that they would be united in love; and inner life issues, that they would be encouraged in heart (Col. 1:28; 2:2).

What's the motivation behind Paul's emphasis on Christ's all-sufficient wisdom? He is concerned that this flock will turn to the world's pseudo-wisdom instead of to the wisdom of the Word. "I tell you this so that no one may deceive you by fine-sounding arguments" (Col. 2:4). "See to it that no one takes you captive through hollow and deceptive *philosophy*, which depends on human tradition and the basic principles of this world rather than on Christ" (Col. 2:8, emphasis added).

Ancient Philosophy and Modern Psychology Cover the Same Terrain

Here's the word that confuses us—*philosophy*. We hear that word and we assume it means some abstract, esoteric, academic reasoning about theoretical issues unrelated to real life. That's not how Paul uses the word or how Paul's readers understood the word *philosophy*.

Philosophy in Paul's day focused on diagnosing and healing diseases of the soul produced by false beliefs and mishandled desires that were cured by expert talk based on a systematic theory of human well-being.[20] Clearly, *ancient philosophy and modern psychology cover the same terrain.*[21] In fact, ancient philosophy, modern psychology, *and* gospel-centered counseling all cover the same terrain—but with a very different source of wisdom. Paul's first-century caution to beware of deceptive philosophy is also *Paul's twenty-first-century caution for us to beware of deceptive theoretical psychology that depends on human wisdom and not on Christ's all-sufficient wisdom.*

These "expert talkers" of Paul's day claimed they were elite thinkers who possessed superior insight necessary for overcoming suffering and defeating sin. They argued that without their advanced teaching, progressive wisdom, and special knowledge, no one could handle life maturely.[22] Paul's shepherd's heart was angered by such elitism. Twice in Colossians 1:28 he repeated that Christ's wisdom is for *everyone*. His message, F. F. Bruce wrote, was that "there is no part of Christian teaching that is to be reserved for a spiritual elite. All the truth of God is for all the people of God."[23]

William Hendriksen paraphrased the message the false counselors of Paul's day were sharing with the Colossians: "Are you putting up a tremendous but losing battle against the temptations of your evil nature? We can help you. Faith in Christ, though fine as far as it goes, is not sufficient, for Christ is not a *complete* Savior."[24] Bruce described it as a "syncretism" (blending, mixing) of Jewish religious ritual with Hellenistic philosophy of living that was fine with adding in elements of Christianity.[25] Paul's shepherd's concern was alarmed by this message of "*Christ + human wisdom.*" It is as if he is saying in Colossians 2:1–9, "*Strangely, we seem prepared to learn how to live from almost anyone but Christ!*"

That's exactly what these first-century counselors were touting—how to live the good life out of a good heart for the good of society.[26] Though their models of the good life and their theories about how to achieve it varied (just as today we have hundreds of counseling models and theories), these first-century soul physicians all sought to help people to live a flourishing life where they could fulfill their unique purpose by making a meaningful contribution to society. And they sought to accomplish this goal by *talk therapy*—using human reasoning, argumentation, dialogue, discourse, instruction, confrontation, and reproof to change their counselees' beliefs and behaviors.[27] Truly, there is nothing new under the sun.

Beware!

Ever since Genesis 3, we have faced two competing sources of wisdom about people, problems, and solutions. Paul provided wise counsel on how to respond. In fact, Paul's counsel about counseling in Colossians 2:4 would have been excellent guidance for Eve. "Don't be deceived by fine-sounding arguments!" Paul pictured these first-century counselors as communicators, teachers, and debaters who wooed and wowed people with style that lacked substance. They deceived or beguiled people (like Satan does) through false reasoning—human reason apart from divine revelation. They had an appealing sales pitch with an appalling product.

Paul was so concerned that he told the Colossians, "Beware!" He was saying, "Wake up! Pay attention. Danger! Danger! Don't be duped or caught off guard." That would have been excellent counsel for Adam when he failed to guard the garden. Paul used military language when he warned them against being taken captive—carried away as booty in the spoils of war. He described the weapons of warfare as hollow philosophy—human reasonings that are empty, proud, and lacking content and worth for real-life change. They are also deceptive—designed to trick or con, to entice through a pleasant illusion.

Paul was so fiercely against such counsel because it is according to human tradition and the basic principles of the world and not according to Christ. This is once again military language—"basic principles" was a term used of military units organized for warfare in columns. The term became used for *foundational systems of belief on which people patterned their lives.* Paul was saying, "Don't be duped by the enemy or your allegiance will be stolen by secular, sin-distorted human reasoning used to try to cure souls. Don't even think of following people who are separated from the life of God because they can teach you only how to live life separated from God."

A SHORT STORY OF THE LONG HISTORY OF "BIBLICAL PSYCHOLOGY"[28]

To be clear, Paul's caution was not about medical science or descriptive research. He was not speaking to or against those categories. Paul's caution was against building a *theory* of people, problems, solutions, and people-helping based on the world's wisdom—on *secular theoretical psychology/philosophy.* In contrast to that, Paul was insisting on a "biblical psychology."

I understand that some readers become nervous when they see a term like *biblical psychology*, so let's define it carefully.

Biblical psychology interprets the Scriptures to discern how human nature in God's image has been shaped by Creation (people), Fall (problems), and Redemption (solutions) and applies that wisdom to care for souls in a Christlike and Christ-centered way (people-helping).[29]

Or, as professor of theology Wayne Rollins defined it, biblical psychology is "the study of the biblical perspective on the origin, nature, pathology, health, and destiny of the human psyche or soul."[30]

Is biblical psychology the ancestor or the offspring of secular psychology? Which came first? Franz Delitzsch, in his landmark work *A System of Biblical Psychology*, noted in 1855 that "biblical psychology is no science of yesterday. It is one of the oldest sciences of the church."[31] Sigmund Freud, the founder of modern talk therapy, was born *one year after* this quote. Wilhelm Wundt, considered by many to be the founder of modern research psychology, did not establish his first psychological laboratory *for another twenty-three years*.[32]

Delitzsch's work includes an introductory chapter on the history of biblical psychology. He notes that the oldest written sources for biblical psychology outside the New Testament are Tertullian's *De Anima* (*On the Soul*), a work by Melito the bishop of Sardis, and Irenaeus's work *Against Heresies* 2.33.5. After surveying a theology of the soul from Justin Martyr up to his own time, Delitzsch concluded, "The ancient church had a psychological literature that claims respect no less for its extent than for its substance."[33]

Rollins noted that "psychology was studied and practiced long before it was named."[34] The use of the term *psychology* made its first documented appearance at the beginning of the Reformation. In 1530 Martin Luther's coworker Philipp Melanchthon discussed the term in his *Commentarius de Anima* (*Commentary on the Soul*). Here he differentiated psychology as the biblical study of the human soul from pneumatology, the biblical study of the Holy Spirit. By the time Delitzsch penned the first edition of his psychological work (1855), the term *psychology* enjoyed common currency throughout Europe and America.

What Has Athens to Do with Jerusalem?

As we have seen, though the term *psychology* arises in the sixteenth century, the Christian study and care of the soul is ancient. The notion that there are two distinct fields of inquiry—psychology and theology—which require "integration" would have been inconceivable to thinkers like Tertullian, Gregory, and Luther. For them, theology as the "queen of the sciences" encompassed all knowledge, especially wisdom about the nature of human beings. They would have seen their "biblical psychology" as a subset of the theological categories of anthropology (creation/people), hamartiology (fall/problems), soteriology (redemption/solutions), and practical/pastoral/spiritual theology (people-helping/care of souls).

Anyone examining the history of pastoral care soon finds that the Bible has always been the church's central source for matters of the soul. Oden wrote:

> There is no Christian pastoral care in any period of its history without Scripture, without the law and gospel, without the prophetic and apostolic witness through which God's own care is made known. The practice of pastoral care, according to the classical tradition, does not proceed as if it were an independent psychological wisdom, or as if pastoral wisdom were to be achieved apart from the previous study of Scripture and the immediate personal address of Scripture.[35]

The role that Scripture plays in providing wisdom for living was stated powerfully in the Westminster Confession. It did not deny a natural knowledge of the inner life, but viewed that knowledge as corrupted and incomplete without God's own self-disclosure.

> Although the light of nature, and the works of creation and providence, do so far manifest the goodness, wisdom, and power of God, as to leave men inexcusable; yet are they not sufficient to give that knowledge of God; and of his will, which is necessary unto salvation; therefore it pleased the Lord, at sundry times, and in divers manners, to reveal himself, and to declare

that his will unto his Church; and afterwards, for the better preserving and propagation of the truth, and for the more sure establishment and comfort of the Church against the corruption of the flesh, and the malice of Satan, and of the world, to commit the same wholly unto writing; which maketh the holy Scripture to be more necessary; these former ways of God revealing his will unto his people being now ceased.[36]

Cyril of Jerusalem (c. AD 313–386) epitomized this belief: "We must not deliver anything whatsoever, without the sacred Scriptures, nor let ourselves be misled by mere probability, or by marshaling arguments. And do not simply credit me, when I tell you these things, unless you get proof from the Holy Scriptures of the things set forth by me."[37]

Aligning himself with Paul's view in Colossians, Tertullian of Carthage (AD 150–220), declared a clear opposition between divine revelation and human speculation. It was in his work *Prescription against Heretics* that Tertullian first asked in rhetorical indignation, "What indeed has Athens to do with Jerusalem?"[38] "Athens" refers to the Platonic Academy and by extension represents all Greek philosophy (psychology). "Jerusalem" represents the teachings of Jesus and the apostles. Tertullian rejected the study of nonbiblical, non-apostolic sources to supplement or even interpret that witness to truth that transcends all human inquiry and investigation. He "was pessimistic about the human mind's ability to avoid idolatry and dangerous syncretism."[39]

His "prescription" against all heresies was for Christians to avoid attempting to rationalize Christian beliefs using Greek philosophical categories and concepts alien to biblical truth. He wrote, "To know nothing in opposition to the rule of faith is to know all things."[40] Tertullian was using hyperbole to drive home his point that the most important knowledge is that consistent with and in conformity to the Word of God.[41]

Tertullian developed his biblical understanding of the soul in his classic work *De Anima*, which Delitzsch called "the first Christian psychology."[42] In this work, Tertullian not only proposes a Christian view of the soul, but again confronts secular views which he deemed to be inconsistent with the Word of God. Delitzsch describes it as the first ecclesiastical attempt to supersede the two great classical secular statements on the soul—Plato's *Phaedo* and Aristotle's *De Anima*.

In the Beginning Was Theology

A consistent theme woven throughout the history of Christian soul care is its biblical, theological, and Christological foundation. Clement of Alexander summarizes the Christ-centered, gospel-driven focus of the soul caregiver: "Awaiting the favorable opportunity, he corrects evil, diagnoses the causes of inordinate passion, extracts the roots of unreasonable lusts, advises what we should avoid, and *applies all the remedies of salvation* to those who are sick."[43]

Gregory I (c. AD 540–604) is considered by both Protestant and Catholic historians as the leading pastoral theologian during the first millennium of the Western church. His *Book of Pastoral Rule* was the textbook for the next thousand years, respected and quoted by many, including Martin Luther.

A major premise of Gregory's pastoral care was not the integration of philosophy and Scripture, but the "integration" of truth and life by applying Scripture wisely to each person's life. "Gregory the Great," Oden wrote, "reflected practically upon how the pastor's counsel can be adopted to each personal situation, yet still maintain the unity of apostolic teaching."[44] In his *Pastoral Care*, Gregory advised that "Discourse should be adapted to the character of the hearers, so as to be suited to the individual in his respective needs.... Hence, every teacher, in order to edify all in the one virtue of charity, must touch the hearts of his hearers *by using one and the same doctrine, but not by giving to all one and the same exhortation.*"[45]

Martin Luther, though known primarily as a Reformer, was also a master pastor. Robert Kolb explains that the core of Luther's ministry involved "applying the living voice of the Gospel to people's lives."[46] Note how Luther related faith in Christ to the afflicted and downcast.

There is only one article and rule of theology, and this is true faith or trust in Christ. All other articles flow into and out of this one; without it the others are meaningless. The devil has tried from the very beginning to deride this article and to put his own wisdom in its place. However, this article has a good savor for all who are afflicted, downcast, troubled, and tempted, and these are the ones who understand the gospel.[47]

Luther built this particular application of the gospel on the broader theological foundation known as a "theological anthropology."[48] It is the study of the nature of humanity as created by God, depraved by the fall, and restored by redemption in Christ. In Luther's eyes, the Bible did not present a study of the nature of humanity as an end in itself. Rather, the Bible describes humanity in relationship to Deity. Luther's pastoral care developed from a *coram Deo* psychology which *studied the creature in light of and in relationship to the Creator.*[49]

Holifield summarizes the historic tradition of soul care with the phrase "in the beginning was theology" because physicians of the soul have "always understood themselves to be theologians."[50] He especially highlighted how the Reformed and Puritan tradition of pastoral care was theologically grounded. He traced from Martin Luther to John Calvin to William Perkins to Richard Sibbes to William Ames to Richard Baxter and Jonathan Edwards the common focus on developing a biblical theology of the heart, a biblical understanding of idolatry of the heart, and a biblical understanding of the process of personal heart change.[51]

The Birth and Growth of Modern Biblical Psychology

Martin Luther's protégé Philipp Melanchthon was virtually the father of the modern term *psychology*.[52] He was the first to use the term in an academic setting, employing it in his lectures in 1530 and, as mentioned, in his *Commentarius De Anima* (1540). Melanchthon, like Tertullian, built his model of psychology on the Bible and measured the truth of classical psychology by the light and standard of biblical revelation.

Casper Bartholinus was one of the first authors to use the term *psychology* in the title of a work on the study of the soul — *Guide to a True*

Psychology from the Sacred Writings (1619). Bartholinus was a teacher of medicine and theology at the University of Copenhagen. In the introduction to his work, he stated that his objective was to develop a biblical psychology, that is, a true doctrine of the human soul. He identified Genesis 2:7 as the foundation of a true biblical psychology, with its portrait of humanity, formed from the dust of the ground by God, who breathed life into his nostrils, making him a living being. Bartholinus quoted the passage in Latin, then provided an exegesis of the Hebrew original. He demonstrated the commitment of Reformation psychology to a biblically based doctrine over against the natural anthropology and psychology of Aristotle and Plato.[53]

The Reformers passed the mantle of biblical psychology to the Puritans, whose soul-care manuals provide a rich treasure trove of insights into the personal ministry of the Word. Richard Baxter's *The Reformed Pastor* is one exemplar of many.[54] "Baxter had recourse to biblical models and precedents in defining the task of the pastor as counselor for the soul, analogous to the physician who cares for the body."[55] He exhorted his fellow pastors that they "must be ready to give advice to inquirers who come to us with cases of conscience.... A minister is not to be merely a public preacher, but to be known as a counselor for their souls, as the physician is for their bodies."[56]

Timothy Keller explains that the Puritans were committed to the functional authority of the Scripture. For them it was the comprehensive manual for dealing with all problems of the heart. From the Word, they developed a sophisticated and sensitive system of diagnosis for personal problems.[57]

Biblical psychology was ushered into the modern era by the man to whom Delitzsch ascribes the title "the father of modern biblical psychology," the German theologian Magnus Friedrich Roos.[58] His groundbreaking work *Fundamenta Psychologiæ ex Sacra Scriptura Collecta* (1769, *Outlines of Psychology Drawn from the Holy Scriptures*) sparked renewed interest in the subject in German theology. Roos was the first person in the modern era to attempt a comprehensive exegesis of terms and contexts relating to biblical psychology from the Scriptures. He treated the subject lexicographically, analyzing key psychological terms such as *psyche, pneuma,* and *kardia.*

In developing his biblical theology, Roos rejected the idea of fitting the sacred writers into the dogmas of philosophy. He used the Bible "not as a mere test of truth already found, but as a source of truth still undiscovered."[59]

Johann T. Beck wrote his *Outlines of Biblical Psychology* in 1843, borrowing heavily from the work of M. F. Roos. It was translated into English from the original German in 1877. Delitzsch describes this as the first attempt to reduce biblical psychology to a scientific form and to promote the claim that biblical psychology has "an independent existence in the organism of entire theology."[60]

Franz Delitzsch (1813 – 90), whom we have already met, wrote his *A System of Biblical Psychology* in 1855. He was a professor of Hebrew and Old Testament at the University of Leipzig and a master of Hebrew, Arabic, Syriac, Samaritan, Persian, Greek, and Latin texts. Faithful to his pietistic upbringing, he maintained his focus on the text's timeless meaning for the soul. His objective in writing *A System of Biblical Psychology* was to answer a question of personal importance to him, namely, how the human soul relates to the phenomena of spirit and matter. He understood biblical psychology to be "a scientific representation of the doctrine of Scripture on the psychical constitution of man as it was created, and the ways in which this constitution has been affected by sin and redemption. There is such a doctrine in Scripture."[61] Over against detractors who argued that Scripture no more provides an objective psychology than it does a cosmology, Delitzsch replied that Scripture says "infinitely more about man's soul and spirit than about Orion and the Plelades."[62] He contended that we can find a generally harmonized anthropology and psychology presupposed in all of Scripture, aimed at providing a picture of the "psychical constitution" of the human soul, of the illnesses and sins that beset it, and of ways to cure it (salvation/redemption).[63]

With an eye to his profession as theologian, scholar, and church leader, Delitzsch defended the inclusion of psychology within the ranks of critical biblical research. He saw biblical psychology as a God-given capacity "granted to the human soul of raising itself above itself by self-investigation."[64] The Bible offers the reader a description of the natural condition of the self and proffers a vision of the new humanity to which it is called in Christ.

In this vein, Delitzsch asked, "What is biblical psychology?" He answered, "It is psychology which has to offer to dogmatics the knowledge that is required for the understanding of the human essential constitution of the God-man." It is "the restoration of the true human nature."[65] The goal of biblical psychology thus involves not only description and analysis, but diagnosis and a protocol of treatment.

CONCLUSION

When we hear terms like "the modern biblical counseling movement" and "the sufficiency of Scripture," two very distinct images may come to mind. One image portrays biblical counseling and confidence in the sufficiency of Scripture as interlopers—something new and novel, of recent origin and development. Another, more historically accurate image—as we have seen—sees modern biblical counseling's trust in the rich relevance of God's Word as a *continuation* of biblical one-another ministry practiced in the Scriptures and throughout two thousand years of church history. Long before the advent of modern secular psychology and long before the launch of the modern biblical counseling movement, God's people trusted God's Word as the authoritative, robust, and sufficient source of wisdom for living in a fallen and broken world.

What we call "biblical counseling" has been known by many names throughout church history: pastoral care, pastoral counseling, soul care, cure of souls, spiritual direction, spiritual friendship, one-another ministry, discipleship. The common denominator in the historic practice of the personal ministry of the Word has been examining God's Word to develop a comprehensive understanding of people, problems, and solutions and relating those truths compassionately and relevantly to people's lives in the form of soul care. As I surmised thirty years ago, history attests that *the church has always been about the business of viewing and using God's Word to compassionately and wisely help hurting and hardened people to deal with suffering and sin.*

CHAPTER 8

WHAT ABOUT THE BODY?

SAM WILLIAMS

The Word became flesh. It is nearly incredible to contemplate the descent of an omnicompetent Being, who created and sustains everything in the universe, pinpointing Himself in the velvet skin of a baby weighing just a few pounds, and is unable to feed Himself or walk or talk.

It is just as remarkable that this supernatural, extraordinarily holy being would not only become flesh but would also choose to reside within our bodies of flesh. Nevertheless, that is the story and it is the new covenant: God would come someday and not just dwell with us but also dwell within us. In many ways, the Christian faith and its practice are *about the body.*

The body was not a minor key in the ministry of Paul, who urged the Roman Christians, "Present your bodies as a living sacrifice, holy and acceptable to God, which is your spiritual worship" (Rom. 12:1). Paul took the role of his own body in ministry seriously, saying, "I discipline my body and keep it under control, lest after preaching to others I myself should be disqualified" (1 Cor. 9:27). There is some gravity here: It is possible to preach the gospel, to minister the Word of God to others, and then disqualify yourself—not the message but yourself—by what you do or don't do with your body. Paul believes that what you do with your body counts, not a little bit, but a lot. In these passages, it is clear that the body is not peripheral to the Christian life.

It is obvious that the persons we minister to are not angels—mere spirit beings—and yet it seems that the lion's share of Christian ministry addresses the spiritual and mental part of our being but neglects the role of the body. What are the implications for pastoral ministry and biblical counseling of this belief that we are both soul *and body?*

All Christian ministry must, by necessity, deal with the body. What this chapter aims to do is outline a biblical theology of the body—what does the body have to do with God, and what does God have to do with the body—and then examine practical implications for ministry, especially counseling. How do we minister to *embodied* souls? How much and what type of attention *should* be paid to the body in our Christian ministries and biblical counseling? Then, two common and often controversial questions will be addressed in this chapter. What is the role of the body in what are commonly understood as emotional or mental problems or mental disorders? And what about medication for these problems?

A BRIEF THEOLOGY OF THE BODY

Good is the flesh that the Word has become,
   good is the birthing, the milk in the breast,
   good is the feeding, caressing and rest,
   good is the body for knowing the world,
Good is the flesh that the Word has become.
Good is the body for knowing the world,
   sensing the sunlight, the tug of the ground,
   feeling, perceiving, within and around,
   good is the body, from cradle to grave,
Good is the flesh that the Word has become.
Good is the body, from cradle to grave,
   growing and ageing, arousing, impaired,
   happy in clothing, or lovingly bared,
   good is the pleasure of God in our flesh,
Good is the flesh that the Word has become.
Good is the pleasure of God in our flesh,

longing in all, as in Jesus, to dwell,
glad of embracing, and tasting, and smell,
good is the body, for good and for God,
Good is the flesh that the Word has become.*

God is a spirit being who created us in like manner, as spiritual beings, but also, in His wisdom, with bodies as the means/instruments through which we accomplish His mission on earth. With our material bodies we serve God, exercise dominion over the rest of the material world, and love other embodied persons.

Most conservative evangelical Bible scholars and theologians, as well as most of historic orthodox Christianity, have embraced what philosophers call *substance dualism*. This simply means that we are composed of an immaterial soul or spirit and a material body. Human persons are simultaneously supernatural and natural beings, composed of two parts, or essences (*substance* is the philosophical term), that exist in a constantly interacting unity, but an essential duality. We are one functionally, but two essentially. A human person is an embodied spirit being made in the very image and likeness of God.

The body cannot be reduced to spirit, and the spirit or soul cannot be reduced to body. For this reason, neither biological reductionism (that all activities of the person can be reduced to materialistic explanations — we are just our brains) nor hyper-spiritual Gnosticism (that the body is secondary or evil or unnecessary) make good biblical sense. Each of these two parts of the person has its own integrity. However, even though body and soul are different things (substances or essences), they are made for each other and it is their union that makes us human beings. Theologian John Cooper calls this *holistic dualism*, which is a helpful phrase that means people are two-part beings, but these two parts are not intended to function separately, but instead interact intimately and continuously as one.[2] Therefore, we should be careful with

---

* "Good Is the Flesh" by Brian Wren, © 1989, 1996 by Hope Publishing Co., Carol Stream, IL 60188. All rights reserved. Used by permission.

questions like "Is that a spiritual problem or a physical problem?" that tend to force us into simplistic responses.

The apostle Paul found similar problems in the Corinthian church of the first century, where they had absorbed Greek perspectives (especially those of the philosopher Plato) about the body, to the extent that their beliefs and attitudes toward their bodies were far from biblical. They believed their bodies were merely temporary containers for their immortal souls, and that the physical matters of life were inferior. Real Christianity was about the spiritual things. They mistakenly had come to believe that they did not need to be too concerned about what they did with their body.

Paul reminded them what their bodies were for by asking, "Or do you not know that your body is a temple of the Holy Spirit within you, whom you have from God? You are not your own" (1 Cor. 6:19). Paul's point here is that God no longer dwells in the tabernacle and the ark or in Solomon's temple. "You are the temple," he says. The body is God's dwelling place. Paul concludes with a reminder about the cost of their redemption and the implication for their bodies. "For you were bought with a price. So glorify God in your body" (1 Cor. 6:20).

The body is one of the places where God chooses to dwell—first in the incarnation of His Son, then not just with but *in* every person who follows this Son. Wherever God chooses to be present, that place is holy—in other words, the human body is designed and set apart for divine purposes. What we do with our body matters, not a little bit but a lot. Therefore, biblical counseling takes into account the role of the body in all of life, including its effects upon our soul, our spiritual lives. The good news is that redemption and sanctification apply to the whole person—the body as well as the soul.

BODY STEWARDSHIP: CARING FOR THE BODY

As material beings in a material world, our bodies' biological clocks are synchronized for this particular world in a solar system with alternating phases of light and darkness in twenty-four-hour cycles. A regularly practiced circadian rhythm of sleep, meals, work, exercise, and social life provides a kind of harmony that tempers mood, facilitates good thinking, and provides a context for wise choices. Some counselees may ignore or rebel against the biological and environmental clocks that God has given us, but they cannot be reset or redesigned. There is a psychological cost associated with poor stewardship of the body: brittle moods, difficulty attending and concentrating, lack of energy, sometimes anxiety or depression, and on occasion for some people even psychosis.

Many counseling issues require that counselors address how their counselees care for their bodies — sleeping, eating, and exercise are health issues, sometimes very significant in their spiritual and psychological effects. Christian maturity comes up short when there is no training and discipline, no proper nurturing and care for the body.

Multiple studies have shown the psychological and biological benefits of exercise: stabilizing moods, reducing anxiety and depression, improving intellectual performance, increasing energy, improving sleep and appetite, and improving the health and resilience of the body.[3]

A healthy diet can also improve emotional and cognitive functioning. People feel and think better, for both biological and psychological reasons, when they are eating to live rather than living to eat, or starving themselves, or overdosing on junk food. Excessive sugar or caffeine intake can exacerbate or even cause emotional instability.

The cost of neglecting or abusing the body is even more significant for people with frequent mood problems. Sensible stewardship in this area can make a big difference. Restoration of regular and reliable sleep patterns facilitates mood stability in people with roller-coaster mood swings. In addition, regularizing meal times, work schedules, exercise periods, and times for socializing and recreation can be a powerful stabilizing force for their emotions.[4]

MENTAL DISORDERS

The Bible affirms that we are both natural and supernatural beings, and that the material body and the immaterial soul affect each other. Moreover, since all creation has been infected with sin, our bodies age, get sick and diseased, and eventually die. Both sin and Satan afflict our body as well as our soul/spirit/heart. As a consequence of the fall, and as an implication of the doctrine of sin, some of our problems in life are a result of body problems. The brain in particular plays a crucial role in every part of our lives, mediating thoughts, emotions, and behaviors and functioning as a kind of CEO for the whole body. To assert the body's involvement in spiritual or mental matters is rather obvious. Most of us have experienced the effect of the body on the soul after a period of insomnia or when going a day without eating.

Finally, there are a variety of biological causes of mood or mind dysfunction: medication side effects, drug abuse, neurological disorders including those related to aging, metabolic and endocrinologic abnormalities, cardiovascular problems, and others. It is important to be aware of these possibilities and not presume all difficulties are psychological, moral, or spiritual in origin. It is best to be cautious, referring to a competent physician whenever there is reasonable suspicion of a medical problem. Ed Welch lists characteristics that raise the likelihood of a biological origin for mood problems:

1. The counselee is over forty years old; and
2. there is no previous history of mood disorder; and
3. there have been no recent traumas, stressors, or major changes in lifestyle; or
4. the counselee is taking multiple medications.[5]

Since most counselors and pastors are not specialists in the body, it is important to develop relationships with physicians in a variety of specialties, especially a primary care physician and a psychiatrist, preferably Christian. Of course, physicians vary in diagnostic skill, style of prescribing medicines, attentiveness and availability to the counselee and counselor, and spiritual sensitivity, but finding competent, wise, and caring physicians to work with can make a big difference.

It is often difficult, and sometimes impossible, to sort out exactly what comes from the body and what comes from the soul, what is biological and what is spiritual or mental. Further complicating this constant interaction of body and soul are recent findings about the effects of life experiences on not just the functioning but also the structure of the brain (neuroplasticity), especially through powerful childhood experiences when the brain is developing rapidly, but also by means of psychological trauma or habitual behavior such as addiction. Brain and experience constantly interact and influence one another. Both the brain and our past experiences play a significant role in our spiritual or mental health.

What is still controversial in the mental health field is the precise role that the brain plays in mental disorders. Older theories that mental disorders, like depression or anxiety, result from simple neurochemical imbalances have been replaced by much more sophisticated theories that posit the problem in impaired cell plasticity and signal processing within and among the brain's approximately 100 billion neurons. What is more clear, although also not fully understood or specified, is that there is a significant degree of heritability for some disorders, especially the more severe mental disorders such as schizophrenia, bipolar disorder, and autism. Of course, that we genetically inherit particular weaknesses and strengths is not in itself a very controversial assertion.

What Is a Mental Disorder?

Specifying what is and is not a mental disorder has long been and is still a matter of debate among mental health professionals.[6] There are anti-psychiatry and libertarian critics who oppose the very concept of mental disorder because it may be (and has been, for example, in China and the former Soviet Union) used to wield political control. Others are concerned that to call something a mental disorder eliminates human responsibility. Some criticize the concept because of its tendency to dehumanize patients and pathologize their identity.

Another common concern, among academics in particular, is that the concept of mental disorder lacks scientific and medical validity. Joel Paris, in his book *The Intelligent Clinician's Guide to the DSM-5*, writes, "Psychiatry has to put off science-based definitions of mental disorders to a future time when it knows more."[7] Another rather surprising critique of the most recent version of the American Psychiatric Association's diagnostic manual came from Tom Insel, director of the National Institute of Mental Health, claiming that the new manual is seriously flawed because it was not based on any objective laboratory measures.[8]

In spite of the medical and scientific sound of the term *mental disorder*, its definition and validation have defied experts and lack a resounding consensus. Perhaps this is what we should expect as we try to nail down what is going on at the intersection of the brain (which is the most complex arrangement of matter in the known natural world) and the supernatural mind or soul (wherein we are created in the image and likeness of God).

With so much quibbling and concern, is it legitimate to conceptualize people in this fashion? Is this concept helpful or redeemable? What follows are a few answers that can help us negotiate this slippery slope.

Let's start by leveling the playing field on God's terms. Ecclesiastes 9:3 says, "The hearts of the children of man are full of evil, and madness ["insanity" in some translations] is in their hearts while they live." I remember the first "insane" person I met. I was ten years old and spent the day with my father on one of his construction sites, the Arizona state mental hospital, where he had befriended one of the patients. I was immediately struck by how "weird" he was — his strange mannerisms and clothing, especially the ten watches on his right arm. I thought, okay, so this is insanity, clinical craziness. And yet, when we think about it further, who is more disordered: that man with the watches or the man who leaves his wife and kids for his twenty-five-year-old secretary? Our moral and spiritual insanities are surely more malignant than paranoid schizophrenia or bipolar disorder.

God is an equal opportunity diagnostician: He declares everybody (and every soul) insane. We all have mental problems. In one, very biblical, sense we can say yes to the observations of psychologists and psychiatrists that people are disordered. There is something wrong with all of us and in every part of our being. On God's terms and outside of His grace, we are pervasively disordered: our minds are darkened, our emotions run wild, our motives are self-serving, our desires are evil, and our choices are all too often absolutely insane. From this perspective, *we might choose to rehabilitate the concept instead of rejecting it altogether.* How would a biblical psychology that reckons with the pervasive effects of sin upon both the natural body and the supernatural soul define *mental disorder*?

Our understanding of the fall and the massive effects of sin lead us to expect disease and disorder in every aspect of our lives. From our perspective, all pathology, including psychopathology, is a result of the effects of sin on the human body and soul. The DSM-5 is at one level an impressive list of these effects, categorizing, defining, and describing problems that people struggle with.

The list of mental disorders in the DSM-5 is a detailed description of the primary symptoms that characterize people with particular mental, behavioral, and emotional difficulties. For persons who are trained in diagnosis and careful about the process, it provides one reliable way *to categorize and communicate* about the types of problems a person is struggling with. It can be helpful in drawing attention to the different types of problems that people deal with and in delineating typical challenges inherent within these disorders. It can be one component in understanding a person and their problems.

And yet, how to understand the cause of these disorders is still up for debate. It is important to remember that most of the diagnoses in the DSM-5 are only descriptions, not explanations that aim to specify the root cause of the problem. They are diagnoses like hypertension or hypoglycemia, which merely describe symptoms but do not explicate their cause.

Furthermore, that which makes us distinctively human, our spiritual and moral facets, is neglected by secular definitions of mental order, disorder, and reordering. Thus, the secular concept of mental disorder is not a thorough description of—nor does it provide an explanation for—people's problems. A more thorough biblical psychology must factor God (and subsequently the moral and spiritual valence of each symptom) back into the equation if we are interested in a diagnosis that is consistent with our worldview.[9]

Finally, regardless of our opinions about the concept of mental disorder, it is the *lingua franca* in most of the Western world. It is worthwhile for us to be familiar with the primary diagnostic categories in the DSM-5, for it is the language of physicians and mental health professionals and, therefore, of many church members and counselees.

DIFFERENTIATING BETWEEN MEDICAL, MENTAL, AND MORAL/SPIRITUAL PROBLEMS

At this point there are no commonly accepted medical or psychological tests to detect the brain dysfunction that may play a significant role in some mental disorders. Even though genetics research does indicate a significant biological component in some mental disorders, these findings do not tell us the precise cause of particular disorders. Furthermore, even when there is reason to suspect that there may be significant brain dysfunction, such a recognition would not negate the moral or spiritual challenges that person might be facing, since we are always both biological and spiritual beings. Ed Welch helpfully observes, "Psychiatric problems are always spiritual problems and sometimes physical problems."[10]

It is reasonable and biblical to acknowledge biological conditions as real and sometimes very powerful influences in what people do, think, or feel. Of course, to recognize that something is *influential* is not equivalent to asserting that it is *determinative*. Situational factors, such as a disordered brain or an abusive or traumatic environment, can be powerful life influences and yet still not bear the burden of explanation for a person's life. Such a recognition actually retains the dignity of every person, since each one is designed as an image or likeness of God. Superficial, deterministic explanations dehumanize people, rendering them as automatons rather than persons with the dignity and honor ascribed to us in Psalm 8.

Help for people with mental disorders should be comprehensive, going "as far as the curse is found," thus reckoning with disorder in both soul and body. Pastor and professor Jeremy Pierre explains:

> We should not approach human problems with the false dichotomy: Is this problem spiritual or physical? Rather we should consider how the physical is affecting the spiritual, and vice-versa. Thinking in this vein prevents the counselor from concluding that a problem is physical while ignoring spiritual influences, and vice-versa.... We must not mix up addressing sin's effects with addressing sin itself.[11]

And yet there are times when we must make some measure of differentiation between what is physically broken and what is morally wrong. Doing so is not always simple and not always the most important place to start, but sometimes God's glory and Christian love mean we must try to sort these things out. Scripture, careful observation, and conversation can help us distinguish between disease and sin in many instances. The following questions can help in this process:

1. Does the Bible explicitly address this particular problem? Does this issue belong more on the spectrum of righteous versus sinful, or on a spectrum of strength versus weakness?
2. Does this problem seem to occur independent of environmental, relational, and spiritual contingencies? Does the problem begin or persist regardless of their particular situation?

For example, a person diagnosed with bipolar disorder may experience unpredictable periods of mania wherein they stay awake all night, they talk rapidly and excessively, their thoughts race, and they develop delusions or hallucinations. These symptoms are not explicitly moral matters as much as they are a component of manic mood dysregulation. Short of medication, reducing stimulation, and keeping the person safe, there is not much that can be done about these symptoms. On the other hand, a person may also spend inordinate amounts of money unwisely, drive recklessly, and become sexually promiscuous. Even though bipolar disorder may be biologically driven, these symptoms are moral matters and therefore the person should be warned against such sinful excesses, encouraged to repent and receive forgiveness, and connected to friends and family who can help them keep their mania from leading them into sin.

Another example would be a person diagnosed with anxiety disorder who worries about their health, money, and the approval of others. These would be important topics to discuss with the person in counseling, examining their difficulty trusting God's provision and love for them and finding areas in which they can learn to turn more consistently away from anxiety toward a greater confidence in God's sovereign grace. On the other hand, the same person may suffer panic attacks that are unbidden, that strike for no apparent reason even though they may be growing in their trust in and obedience to Christ. Practical advice about managing panic attacks (reminding themselves that this is only a panic attack, that it won't last long, and that even though they can't immediately control what is going on in their body, they can still trust Christ with their heart), along with how to suffer with and toward Christ are the more appropriate forms of counsel in this instance. Paul's reminder in 2 Corinthians 4:16 may fit here: "So we do not lose heart. Though our outer self is wasting away, our inner self is being renewed day by day."

THE MEDICATION QUESTION

In thinking about the potential role of medication, a good starting point is to avoid the extremes where there tend to be strong opinions but little fair-minded, thoughtful, and biblical reflection. One extreme, on the far left end of the spectrum, essentially says, "Blame it on the brain. Pass the medicine, please." Recently, following a new wave of research on the adolescent brain, a major conservative denomination seminary professor wrote, "Teens do think differently, and *the true source of their behavior is their brain.* This helps explain why your teen can be hugging you one minute and screaming, 'I hate you,' the next" (emphasis added).[12] According to Jesus, however, it is "out of the abundance of the heart his mouth speaks" (Luke 6:45). The brain may be sick or diseased, but the Bible says that our hearts are the source of our actions, words, thoughts, intentions, beliefs, attitudes, desires, and delights (Prov. 4:23; Matt. 12:34; Mark 7:21–23). Our bodies certainly affect us—and yet the Bible says it is our hearts that are the source of our lives.

The other extreme to be avoided regarding medication is at the far right end of the spectrum. It says something like this: "Thou shalt not take Prozac." It is essentially a legalism, an imposition of a personal opinion as if it is a divine command. Proverbs 30:6 warns, "Do not add to [God's] words, lest he rebuke you and you be found a liar." Since all creation is infected with sin, including our bodies and brains, it is reasonable and biblical to acknowledge the possibility that some problems may to some extent be rooted in or significantly affected by a diseased or dysfunctioning body.

So how shall we approach medication? It is often the case in life and in medicine that when there is limited clarity on the precise cause of the problem or the cure, our response, as stated by Ed Welch in his book, should be, "The medication question is a wisdom question."[13] Should this or that person take medicine? The best first answer is, "I don't know." Part of the reason for such an answer is that most of the time, unless you are a trained and licensed physician, the medication question is not yours to answer. The answer belongs to the person first and the physician second. When asked about your opinion, a good second answer is, "Let's talk about it, think about it, pray about it, and ask that God would grant you wisdom. Maybe I can help as you think about this."

In addition, there may be times when you want to consider medication as a part of someone's care. Let me suggest some basic guidelines to help determine when it is appropriate to refer someone for an evaluation for medication.

- A starting point, when psychotropic medication should be considered, is when non-medication approaches (competent biblical counseling, consistent effort to change, and prayer) have not resulted in the remission of significant symptoms.
- And these symptoms (anxiety, depression, acute and intense suffering, hallucinations or delusions, obsessions or compulsions) are impairing the person's capacity to function and fulfill their primary roles and responsibilities, that is, as parent, spouse, or student, or in their vocation.
- Or symptoms are so severe the person cannot cognitively process (attend, focus, and concentrate upon, understand, and interact rationally with) biblical truth.
- Or symptoms are so severe that the functioning of the body is significantly impaired (sleep, appetite, severe fatigue).
- Or the counselee is dangerous to self or others (suicidal, homicidal, at imminent risk of harm to self or others).
- Or when symptoms result from organic/medical causes (i.e., dementia, autism, Parkinson's disease) and safer non-medication approaches have not resulted in sufficient symptom remission.

Biblical counselors realize that their role is to seek wisdom and provide guidance, and to consult with competent and caring physicians. It is not to prescribe or discontinue medicine. There are many mysteries and variables that surround the medication question, so it is important to be careful with our personal opinions about psychotropic medication.

Sensible psychotropic medication can be one of God's common

graces, mediated by science and doctors and technology, helpfully reducing symptoms and suffering. It can be helpful to varying degrees, depending on the patient and the prescriber. Medicine can facilitate cognitive, emotional, and behavioral change—which is good—but can't change the human heart—which is eternally significant. Psychotropic medications are not salvific or even a cure for the disorders whose symptoms they may alleviate. When medications are working, they are functioning much like aspirin or insulin—helpfully reducing symptoms, but not dealing with the spiritual or biological sources.

Standing before our holy and loving God, every one of us is in desperate need of a cure. And because of the power and wisdom and love of God in Jesus, there is one. Robert Jones's attitude regarding medication for depression should be applied broadly, "Depressed people need Jesus and His gospel provisions, whatever the cause of their depression and whether or not they take medication."[14] Biblical counseling brings very good news: The Lord Jesus Christ assumed a full human nature in order (someday) to redeem all of human nature, bodies and souls. The incarnation and resurrection of Christ is God's promise of full and final redemption not only of our souls but also of whatever may be broken in our bodies or brains.

CHAPTER 9

CAUTION: COUNSELING SYSTEMS ARE BELIEF SYSTEMS

ERNIE BAKER AND HOWARD EYRICH

At a speaking opportunity in a local church, I had the privilege of meeting a psychologist who was responsible for all of the counseling of her state's death row inmates. After the Sunday school hour, she told me she enjoyed the presentation on biblical counseling and then shared about her responsibilities. I was impressed with her care for people and with her interest in biblical counseling. She then raised an issue that was causing her much concern. "I've been attending this church for months and keep offering to help with counseling, but no one will take me up on my offer. I feel like I'm being held at arm's length. Can you help me understand this?" I didn't know all the background, but knowing this church's view of Scripture, I could guess some of the issues.

We met after the morning service, and I heard about her decades of service and experience. She struck me as a woman with a wealth of practical wisdom for dealing with people. So why would her church have concerns? What was the issue? She just wanted to help people. But I was surmising that the church was concerned that what they believe about people, problems, and the Scriptures may not be compatible with her views.

Knowing that there are different theories about why we have the problems we do and that varying counseling systems have arisen from these theories, I asked her what her approach was to counseling. She explained that she had two master's degrees and had been trained in an Adlerian counseling approach as well as in family systems counseling.[1]

I then began to explain that there are many philosophical issues related to these counseling systems. In particular, I noted that they are really *belief systems*. Every counseling system has a view of the nature of the problem and what solution naturally follows. As I unfolded my thinking, she caught on quickly and began to fill in the blanks with her training and told me what she was taught. It became very evident to her that her counseling systems were philosophies, and she began to see why her church might be concerned that her belief system might be contrary to a biblical belief system about people. Both she and the church were interested in answering questions such as "Why do humans have problems?" "How do we help people with their problems?" Her church leaders were concerned that the answers to those questions be derived from Scripture.

I was also able to explain to her that her church and biblical counseling are both concerned about mixing biblical truth with secular theories of people and that this mixture of belief systems is called *syncretism*. Syncretism is not new; it is "the amalgamation or attempted amalgamation of different religions, cultures, or schools of thought."[2] It often flourished in the history of Israel. For example, we read in 2 Kings 1:2–3:

> Now Ahaziah fell through the lattice in his upper chamber in Samaria, and lay sick; so he sent messengers, telling them, "Go, inquire of Baal-zebub, the god of Ekron, whether I shall recover from this sickness." But the angel of the LORD said to Elijah the Tishbite, "Arise, go up to meet the messengers of the king of Samaria, and say to them, 'Is it because there is no God in Israel that you are going to inquire of Baal-zebub, the god of Ekron?'"

In Luke 11:18, Jesus indicated that Beelzebul (different spelling, same character) is in fact Satan. Hence, this king of Israel (God's representative in a theocracy) was consorting with Satan to discern his end rather than the God of Israel. That is raw syncretism.

Syncretism is also evident in the Prophetic Books. A clear example is when the true God warned Judah about syncretism through Zephaniah. We read how they were worshiping the stars, Baal, and Milcom *and also* swearing allegiance to the LORD:

> "I [God] will stretch out my hand against Judah and against all the inhabitants of Jerusalem; and I will cut off from this place the remnant of Baal and the name of the idolatrous priests along with the priests, those who bow down on the roofs to the host of the heavens, those who bow down and swear to the LORD and yet swear by Milcom, those who have turned back from following the LORD, who do not seek the LORD or inquire of him."
>
> Zephaniah 1:4–6

It is clear from these examples that the Lord does not think highly of this mixture of beliefs. But why bring up this issue in a book on the authority of Scripture in counseling? We will demonstrate that the subject matter of counseling theories significantly overlaps with the subject matter of theology.[3] Thus, *counseling systems, by their very nature, are really philosophical belief systems.* If this is true, then we must be on high alert for the danger of syncretism.

For a Christian, psychology is one of the most difficult fields of study in which to keep one's bearings. Hence, it is vitally important for the Christian to have a very tightly woven theology as the framework for the study of psychology. Christians seem to fall into two categories in their view of the relationship between psychological theory and theology. Some view these disciplines as parallel; they perceive them to be two unrelated disciplines. Others view them as disciplines that mutually inform each other; they are perceived as disciplines that can be integrated.

A tightly woven biblical theology takes a third view. This view perceives theology as the governing framework by which *psychology as theory building* must be understood and interpreted. This view does not invalidate psychology as a legitimate field of study. However, it recognizes that the presuppositional underpinnings of secular psychology are out of sync with biblical theology and hence provide interpretations of reality (and therefore, often prescriptions) that are consequently also out of sync with the Scriptures.

David Powlison cogently stated the value of studying psychology. He noted that he studied psychology and the history of psychiatry because biblical counseling takes place in contemporary culture and is utterly framed and surrounded by psychiatry. He provided a number of illustrations as to how the knowledge gained in his study provided the opportunity to more precisely understand counselees and address issues biblically.[4]

The apostle Paul at Mars Hill portrayed this for us. He drew upon the philosophical thinking (until the turn of the nineteenth century psychology was a subset of philosophy, and until the Enlightenment philosophy was a subset of religion) of the Athenians. Some in Athens had drawn the conclusion that there was something more to life than they had come to understand and, therefore, had created the category of "the unknown god" as a potential way to explain this *more-to-life* category.

Paul took their provocative conclusion as the starting point for the proclamation of Truth. Later, in Colossians 1–2, however, the same apostle warned us not to become contaminated by "philosophy and empty deceit" in our attempts to understand life (Col. 2:8). At first glance, it might appear that Paul was contradicting himself. But such is not the case. He was not using their theory ("philosophy and empty deceit") as a basis to explain their behavior, but rather to demolish it. He was saying, "You recognize there is more to life than you can explain, so let me introduce you to reality that is known only through revelation."

CONTEXTUAL OBSERVATIONS AND INTERPRETATIONS

Our contextual observations from Colossians will lead us to the question, "How does Paul's teaching apply to us today?" Then we will ask, "How do we implement this application in our counseling?"

Contextual Observation #1: Proto-Gnosticism and Syncretism

Evangelical scholarship is in general agreement that the Colossian church was being infected by proto-Gnosticism.[5] Gnostics came to embrace three errors regarding Christ: He was not creator; He was not God incarnate; and He was not enough to enable the Christian to live a full life. A basic knowledge of Christian theology is all that is required to recognize that these three errors strike at the very heart of the person and work of Christ. The first two chapters of Colossians challenge this proto-Gnosticism (sometimes called the "Colossian heresy").

The Colossian heresy highlighted grasping superior knowledge obtained through a complex system of asceticism, legalism, and mysticism, all of which they wanted to combine with belief in Christ — resulting in syncretism. The participation of the Colossians in this system is precisely what Paul questioned when he wrote:

> If with Christ you died to the elemental spirits of the world, why, as if you were still alive in the world, do you submit to regulations — "Do not handle, Do not taste, Do not touch" (referring to things that all perish as they are used) — according to human precepts and teachings? These have indeed an appearance of wisdom in promoting self-made religion and asceticism and severity to the body, but they are of no value in stopping the indulgence of the flesh.
>
> Colossians 2:20–23

Elemental spirits (stoicheion) may have two different meanings. Some scholars understand this term to refer to spiritual powers or cosmic spirits, while others understand the phrase to refer to the ceremonial worship precepts common to Jews and Gentiles.[6] Given the context, the latter seems to be the more plausible explanation. Hence, Paul was questioning why the Colossian Christians are engaging in a syncretistic approach by reincorporating less than biblical concepts into their understanding of life.

Paul described the real danger of this syncretistic approach in Colossians 2:23. These explanations have the aura of wisdom, but in reality they are of little value in changing the course of life. They appear to provide correctives, which in the Colossian context came through *self-made religion*, ascetic practices, and severe bodily discipline practiced by the proto-Gnostic heretical teachers. The Christians who were practicing proto-Gnosticism were following the lead of Adam and Eve in that they set themselves up as the arbitrators between the counsel of God ("You shall not eat") and the counsel of the serpent ("You shall not surely die") — they coupled following Christ with ascetic practices to effect wholeness. In a similar way, modern-day Christians must be cautious about overshadowing or overpowering biblical anthropology with *psychological speculations — or theory building.*

Contextual Observation #2: Paul's Word-Saturated and Christ-Focused Ministry

METHODOLOGY AND GOALS

In Colossians 1:28, Paul outlined his ministry method and goal. "Him we proclaim, warning everyone and teaching everyone with all wisdom, that we may present everyone mature in Christ." We can summarize Paul's ministry methodology as *the proclamation of Christ in all His fullness.*

This ministry methodology has three dimensions. The first component is admonishment from the Greek word *nouthesis*. This is that word that Jay Adams used in his development of nouthetic counseling. Adams explained that the word has three aspects: (1) it infers a problem; (2) this problem is to be addressed verbally; and (3) this verbal address is to be engaged in love.[7]

The second dimension of Paul's ministry methodology is formal teaching of all the implications of the person of Christ. This second dimension is tempered by the third dimension — all *wisdom*, that is, skillful application.

Three times in Colossians 1:28 Paul said "everyone." Whatever the problem any person may have should be addressed in this manner. As the apostle noted elsewhere (e.g., 1 Thess. 5:14), admonition and teaching is coupled with comforting, support, and patience, with each to be implemented appropriately with diverse individuals. This does not mean that the biblical counselor disregards the ever-growing knowledge base regarding the intricacies of how God designed humanity. Precisely the opposite is true. It means that counselor accesses the knowledge of both hard and soft science, but it is always subject to the authority of Scripture, and its application must always be theologically informed and ethical.

The goal of Paul's ministry is all-encompassing: "present everyone mature in Christ." Paul was concerned about how the Colossian Christians were addressing life issues. His goal was to enable them to be mature in every dimension of life.

Contextual Observation #3: Warnings to Remain Rooted in Christ

In Colossians 2:4, Paul reiterates that his purpose in writing to them is that "no one may delude you with plausible arguments." He continues in Colossians 2:7, reminding them that they were rooted (taught the basic knowledge) and further instructed in the infinitely wise Christ (Heb. 4:15), resulting in the establishing of their faith. And then, in the remainder of Colossians 2, Paul issues three stern warnings.

In Colossians 2:8, "See to it" has the implied tone of a coach telling players not to allow the opposing player to make their often-executed play. Paul was saying, "Do not allow that insidious thinking to deceive you into adopting these elementary principles that are inconsistent with your faith in Christ, who is the very fullness of Deity." He added further warnings in Colossians 2:16–22, where he told the Colossians, in essence, "Don't let anyone stand as the judge of your thinking. Stand your ground as to the validity of your Christian methodology. Don't let anyone defraud you of your prize of being humble and depending on God's methods and goals for life and counseling."

There is no profession in which it is more difficult to discern and avoid "elementary principles" from overshadowing and/or overpowering biblical truth than in counseling. For example, without a finely tuned theology and biblical anthropology, the humanistic thinking that undergirds teaching on self-esteem or poor self-image will seep into Christian thinking. Self, rather than Christ, ends up sitting on the throne of a life.

Contextual Observation #4: Sharpen Our Focus for Living

Paul next described four foundational principles for sharpening our focus that make syncretism obsolete (Col. 3:1–4). Colossians 3:1 provides his first focus: *Keep seeking answers from a sovereign and loving Lord.* The Colossian Christians were being confronted with questions of their identity (who they were) and how to change. The pre-Gnostics were propounding both the questions and the answers. Paul reminded the believers to seek the answers from above.

In its quest for meaning, our society generates questions for which we do not always immediately have answers. Sometimes it takes struggling with the questions for us to ferret out an appropriate biblical approach. For example, how to minister to someone struggling with anorexia was a troubling question for biblical counseling forty years ago. We were surrounded by worldly wisdom that was not working all that well. But as a corporate body we kept seeking answers from above, and today we have gained greater understanding and wisdom.

Paul shared his second focus in Colossians 3:2: *Connect your affections to higher values.* The word for "affections" in the original is inclusive of thinking and feeling, hence we offer this translation. *Higher values* is from a word simply meaning above, high, heavenward. So Paul instructed the Colossians to look to God and His revelation for answers, not to human conclusions.

In a contemporary example of this principle, the broader counseling community has been steeped in the importance of self-esteem and methods of obtaining it. However, biblical counseling, following Paul's lead, concluded from the study of Scripture that this goal and the methods for obtaining it are inconsistent with a Christian approach to life. Instead of adapting the self-esteem movement into biblical counseling, we have discerned other issues at work in the lives of those diagnosed with low self-esteem. Helping counselees cultivate the many-splendored dimensions of their identity in Christ addresses the low self-esteem presentation problem at the *heart* level with a *gospel-centered* approach.

Colossians 3:3 offers Paul's third focus: *Remember your union with Christ.* I (Howard) recently finished reading the work by Stuart Scott and Heath Lambert on counseling the hard cases.[8] A frequent theme in this book is the methodology of leading the counselee to the cross and the understanding of our co-crucifixion with Christ. We died with Him. He died for sin, and we died to sin. He was resurrected, and we were resurrected with Him (Rom. 6:1–11). So Paul told us that our lives are hidden with Christ in God. As a result, we are free to choose to live for God's glory rather than our own desires. This freedom is exercised through the enabling power of the indwelling Holy Spirit (1 Thess. 4:1–8).

Paul shared his fourth focus in Colossians 3:4: *Anticipate the eternal and maintain an eternal perspective.* Nothing can dull the attraction of sin more than the glories of heaven. Even as believers, we seldom contemplate the reality of heaven. But that is what Paul was inciting in the Colossian believers. The syncretistic explanations for the realities of living in this world lose their appeal when considered in the light of eternity.

COUNSELING SYSTEMS ARE PHILOSOPHICAL BELIEF SYSTEMS

So what does Paul's warning have to do with the evangelical world and psychological theory building in particular? As has been hinted at through some of the applications, we believe that incorporating the conclusions of secular psychologies concerning the problems of people with a biblical perspective can result in syncretism. Though well-meaning and sincere, this practice can be naive from a theological, practical, and relational perspective about why people have the problems they do.

Many have recognized the philosophical and religious nature of the psychologies, including psychologists themselves. For example, psychologist Paul Vitz quotes Carl Jung as writing, "Patients force the psychotherapist into the role of priest, and expect and demand that he shall free them from distress. That is why we psychotherapists must occupy ourselves with problems which strictly speaking *belong to the Theologian.*"[9]

During a recent sabbatical I (Ernie) did a significant amount of reading on the current state of the psychologies and what the most-used therapies are. My perception was confirmed that Cognitive Behavioral Therapy (CBT) has huge popularity. Knowing that I would be writing this chapter, I was especially interested to learn that CBT and Buddhism are very similar in their approaches to addressing life's problems. I discovered this relationship in a delightfully informative book on the current state of psychiatry, the drug industry, and alternative approaches to counseling. The author, Yale psychiatry professor Charles Barber, wrote out of a concern about the amount of drugs Americans are putting into their systems to deal with personal problems. He noted:

> Even Aaron Beck has gotten into the Buddhist act. Or perhaps the Dalai Lama has gotten into the cognitive-behavioral act.... Aaron Beck held a public dialogue at the International Congress of Cognitive Psychotherapy in Sweden in 2005. Afterward, Beck posted on the University of Pennsylvania Web site ... "From my readings and discussions with His Holiness and other Buddhists, I am struck with the notion that Buddhism is the philosophy and psychology closest to cognitive therapy and vice versa."[10]

Is CBT just neutral? Doesn't this at least raise some suspicions about taking CBT and baptizing it into Christianity?

Why does this matter? We have already seen that Scripture warns us about being carried away by false philosophies; therefore, it matters because Scripture, meaning the Lord, says it matters. But it also matters because mixing belief systems creates a hybrid belief system that waters down both. This means, practically, that the full authority and beautiful wisdom of Scripture is not unleashed on the problems of people.

EVALUATING BELIEF SYSTEMS

In this section we will use religious terminology to describe belief systems and, in particular, counseling systems. We will see that counseling systems are based on some *source of authority*. Counseling systems also seek to identify human nature and why humans have problems — there is some view of *sin*. These theories also then propose a solution to the perceived dilemma of humanity. In other words, there is a view of *salvation*. It makes sense, then, that there has to be a *methodology* to carry out the view of what the solution is. We will use the theological term *sanctification* here. Counseling systems also have *support systems*. There are those who promote this perspective on counseling and schools that teach its methodology. Lastly, these theories do *apologetics* to defend their belief systems and show the weaknesses of others. Much like Barber does in his book, here we'll use the term *sparring*.[11]

Source of Authority

It has been interesting through the years to see that the psychological and psychiatric world uses the term "bible" to describe the DSM (*Diagnostic and Statistical Manual of Mental Disorders*). As of this writing, the latest and most controversial edition has just been released. One of my students recently told me of an ad he had seen for the new DSM-5. It was in a psychology magazine, and at first glance, he thought they were actually advertising a Bible. The picture showed a beautiful book opened up with big letters stating that the latest edition of the "bible" of psychiatry was now available.

I realize that the term "bible" here is just being used in a generic sense describing a book that gives instruction and is recognized as an authority; it is not being used pejoratively against *the Bible*. That's my point though. Every counseling system has someone or something that gets quoted and is the basis of diagnosis. Sometimes it is the theorist's observations based on experience, sometimes it is a scientific study,[12] or sometimes it is a combination of both.

It ought to be obvious that the basis of authority in Christianity is God's Word—the Bible. But too often other things become the authority. It is easy for the opinions of people to override what God has written. Christians have always been considered "people of the Book." It is to be the primary source for defining our reality since it tells us what the Creator says is reality. Shouldn't He know best what is happening in human souls since He is the Creator?

John MacArthur stated this perspective well: "If there is one word that best describes the Christian worldview, it is *truth*.... Scripture alone teaches us how to perceive the world in a way that accurately corresponds with reality.... The theories and philosophies of men are constantly in flux.... In a very real sense, when it comes to human wisdom the only constant is change."[13]

This doesn't mean we ignore the theories and philosophies of men. It means that we keep them in their proper place. This doesn't mean we don't learn from science, but we have a realistic perspective on science and interpret scientific findings through the lens of Scripture, giving Scripture the primary place.

Sin

Humans have problems. It is not cynical to see another person and ask yourself, "I wonder what his issues are?" That's just reality, and we all know it. There is something *really* wrong with humanity. Secular psychologies recognize this, as Carl Rogers explained, "I am very well aware of the incredible amount of destructive, cruel, malevolent behavior in today's world—from the threats of war to the senseless violence in the streets—I do not find that this evil is inherent in human nature."[14]

Rogers then went on to state why he believes we have problems. "It is cultural influences which are the major factor in our evil behaviors.... I see members of the human species as *essentially* [emphasis in the original] constructive in their fundamental nature but damaged by their experiences."[15]

Rogers's view of humanity (his anthropology) was the starting point for then developing a system to help people with problems (a therapeutic approach). But he didn't see the source of the problems as being the same as what Scripture says is the ultimate source of our problem.

Other systems propose alternative answers to the question of what is wrong with us. Some might say needs aren't being met. Others would say the problem comes from a wounded inner child or that it's just a personality quirk.

From a Christian worldview, sin is the ultimate source of problems. The events described in Genesis 3 impacted everything, and we are all still living with a "Genesis 3 hangover." While we believe there are secondary "causes," like biology or past experiences, we must always remember that what happened in Genesis 3 has permeated everything about life.

Sin is the primary or first cause of everything and has reshaped the human heart (the biblical term for the inner person) to have a distorted view of the world. This is obvious even in the dramatic narrative we call "the fall." The fall displays distorted emotions and divisive relationships. It introduces words and concepts like *fear, shame, guilt,* and *hiding.* The fall permeates my biology and influences the way I respond to life. Scripture says I live out of my heart (Prov. 4:23), and my heart, now influenced by sin, creatively reinterprets environmental influences. Both nature and nurture are impacted by our fall into sin.

If a counseling system is not clear regarding the root cause of the problem, then its interpretation of humanity will be decidedly skewed. Believing in sin against God and its influence on the heart as the primary first cause of behavior makes sense of the world with all of its pain and personal problems. It is a central ingredient in a model that makes the best sense of the data.

Salvation

It may be shocking to some that some psychologies have acknowledged that their proposed solution should be viewed as a form of *salvation.* For example, Jolande Jacobi, one of Carl Jung's students, wrote the following about his system:

Jungian psychotherapy is ... a way of healing and a way of salvation. It has the power to cure.... In addition it knows the way and has the means to lead the individual to his 'salvation,' to the knowledge and fulfillment of his personality which have always been the aim of spiritual striving.... Apart from its medical aspect, Jungian psychotherapy is thus a system of education and *spiritual guidance*.[16]

God's Word provides a deeper solution. It is one that changes hearts, not just thinking. In fact, Scripture says that the Savior came to open blinded eyes and to set captives free. Christ came to save us for all eternity, but Scripture also says that this Good Shepherd is in the soul restoration business (Ps. 23:3).

Sanctification (Methodologies)

It naturally follows then that every counseling system has its own methodologies for effecting change. For Skinner's behaviorism, it was reprogramming through positive and negative reinforcement. For the biblical counseling approach, change builds on a comprehensive biblical theology that leads to the doctrine of progressive sanctification. Biblical counseling endeavors to think deeply about how worship-filled, grace-motivated, Spirit-dependent obedience changes the orientation of the heart toward Christlikeness.

This beautiful, humbling, awe-inspiring, and robustly practical doctrine of progressive sanctification teaches us that the Lord saved us to change us into His image (2 Cor. 3:18). The image of God in us is being restored through the power of the gospel (Col. 3:10). We are being made normal out of an abnormal condition, and Jesus Christ Himself is the template of normality.

Support Systems

You would expect then that various individuals and organizations take up the cause of the various counseling perspectives, and this is exactly what happens. Even though it is typical to mix counseling theories and methodologies (an eclectic approach), in actual practice universities and mental health clinics have preferences for the theories and methodologies they teach. There are also massive organizations that promote the mental health field, like the National Institute of Mental Health, the American Psychiatric Association, the American Psychological Association, and local clinics and support groups that use the preferred theories in their practices.

We are blessed, though, to be part of an amazing organism — the church — that God gave for the purpose of learning His Word and ministering to each other and the world. In particular, the New Testament revolves around local bodies that are to use Scripture to care for one another as they reach out to the world with the liberating and life-changing gospel.

Sparring (Apologetics)

It has intrigued us through the years to read how counseling systems defend themselves and seek to promote their supposed superiority to others. Just as Charles Barber's book seeks to show the immense weaknesses of a drug-only therapy, he also argues for the superiority of other approaches like CBT. He is doing apologetics.

The book you are reading right now is an apologetic for the superiority of the living Word of God as the lens through which we perceive and examine counseling. So, for the sake of apologetics, let us propose that Scripture can be used to do what psychology states it is about:

Psychology is the science that seeks to understand behavior and mental processes and to apply that understanding in the service of human welfare.... As a group, the world's half-million psychologists are interested in all the behaviors and mental processes that make you who you are and make other people who they are in every culture around the world.[17]

We believe that Scripture-based counseling does this and even more. The Scriptures speak abundantly about human behavior both in direct teaching and in narrative form. The implications of the precepts taught about human nature and the stories that illustrate it cannot be exhausted.

The Bible is also a sure guide to understanding thinking. Words for describing the thought life abound, like "mind," "heart," and others. Scripture even addresses how to change our thinking (Rom. 12:1–2; Phil. 4:8).

Scripture goes deeper than this definition of psychology because God's Word talks about the desires and devotion of the heart. It helps us understand where our devotion is to be and where our desires often lead us (Rom. 13:14).

This book is about what biblical counseling believes about Scripture's authority in the counseling world and clarifies what we mean by the term *sufficiency*. Allow us to add our voice briefly to the arguments for the sufficiency of Scripture in counseling. If these S's (source of authority, Scripture, sin, salvation, sanctification/methodologies, support systems, and sparring/doing apologetics) are what make up a belief system, then it is clear that Christians have a *complete belief system for counseling*. By complete, we mean that we have a comprehensive framework for a counseling approach and that it is the interpretive grid to understand other belief systems. Therefore, we don't need to combine our framework for understanding people, problems, and solutions with the framework of other systems.

Like any counseling system, it "provide(s) an organizing structure that confirms how the world works."[18] These words came from Charles Barber talking about the "Stages of Change" and "Motivational Interviewing" models. As I (Ernie) read this, I was thinking, *If that's how a counseling system can be described, then I certainly have one in Scripture.*

WHEN IT IS NOT SYNCRETISM

Now that we have clarified that counseling systems have to do with beliefs, let's consider briefly what can still legitimately be used from other systems. For example, we would conclude it is not syncretism to learn about psychological research. To say that is syncretism would be like saying it is syncretism to learn geology. There are worldview issues with psychology and geology, but they are still academic disciplines.

We can learn useful *descriptive* information from the secular psychologies as they research humans. It is wise to acknowledge these findings, but *always also to assess them biblically.*

It is not syncretism to acknowledge scientific research that does not violate biblical *Truth.* For example, it would not be syncretism to acknowledge that hypothyroidism may be a cause of some depression. Wisdom would tell me that I should know this.

It is not syncretism to learn from helpful methodologies. For example, if a secular counselor has learned through experience how good questions are worded and how bad questions are worded, I can learn from that experience. On the one hand, I need to keep my radar active so that I don't buy into the philosophy behind why those questions are being asked (the framework of that system). On the other hand, learning how to ask questions from another system is not as much of a core issue as incorporating their answer to the question, "Why do people do what they do?" The answer to that question would be in competition with a biblical framework.[19]

A GRID FOR KNOWING
WHERE DANGER LURKS

How would we know then when we are in danger of being "taken captive" by false philosophies, as Paul warned? The following questions are just a sampling of the theological questions that could provide a protective grid.

- Would this system make the counselee the central person of life and hinder the centrality of Christ? Who is on the throne?
- Does this theory or practice reinforce selfism — hindering the dying to self and loving God and others? Who or what is being loved?
- How could this theory detract from the power of the gospel to change lives? Where is the power to change?
- Would this theory rob Scripture of being the primary lens

through which to understand the issues of life? What are the eyeglasses to bring life into focus?

- Would this counseling system rob the church of its authority? Who has the authority?
- Does this theory acknowledge humans as image bearers or as evolved animals? What are humans?
- Does this system believe humans are infected with a sin nature or that they are born as a blank slate? What's wrong with us?

Though they may not be worded to capture all the nuances of various situations, notice that these are *theological* questions. Hence, knowledge of theology is essential since, as noted previously, counseling theories are theological by their very nature.

CONCLUSION

If this chapter (and this book) has prompted some concerns about the syncretistic influence of secular psychology, what practical steps could you take in response? First, studying systematic theology would provide a grid to interpret what you are hearing from the secular psychologies. As you read systematic theology, ask yourself how this compares with what you were taught about humans and their problems in psychology classes.

Second, using each element of the definition of psychology cited above, study Scripture and ask how the themes and details of Scripture fulfill each element of the definition.

Lastly, use the six S's as a way to evaluate psychological theories to understand what that belief system is truly promoting.

Even though this has been a warning chapter, we hope that you are not just challenged to be careful, but also that you are encouraged with the completeness of Scripture to provide a model for the personal problems of people. We invite you to join us in our quest to see the church regain its confidence in the rich, robust, relevant, and relational resources of Scripture for dealing with the complexities of life in a broken world.

CHAPTER 10

THE BIBLE IS RELEVANT FOR THAT?

BOB KELLEMEN

I met with Ashley and her husband, Nate, the day after their twin sons' eleventh birthday. With tears streaming down her face, Ashley shared that twenty-five years earlier, not long after *her* eleventh birthday, a relative began sexually abusing her.

Those who knew Ashley would have been shocked. She grew up in a Christian home, was active at church as an adult, served as a leader in the women's ministry, and was always "pleasant."

Ashley's self-description was poignant. "Yes, I'm the good girl from the good home. The good mom, the good wife. But nobody knows the ugliness I feel inside. Nobody knows how I've pretended and denied all these years. I just can't keep faking it any longer. I'm a mess — depressed to the point that at times I've thought of harming myself. Always fearful and anxious — terrified I'll displease someone. Terrified someone will find out what an empty but evil thing I am ..."

As Ashley's voice trailed off, Nate asked me, "Pastor Bob, can you *help*? Does the Bible offer any *hope* for my wife?"[1]

How you or I respond to Ashley's soul struggles and to Nate's life questions depends on how we answer at least two other fundamental questions about how we *view* and *use* the Bible:

177

- *Truth questions:* "Where do we find wisdom for life in a broken world? How do we *view* God's Word for the personal ministry of the Word?"
- *Life questions:* "How are we to relate truth to life, Scripture to soul? How do we *use* God's Word accurately, compassionately, and competently in the personal ministry of the Word?"

These two questions and the next two chapters serve as a bridge between the two sections of *Scripture and Counseling* as they cover both *viewing* and *using* the Bible for life in a broken world. This chapter and chapter 11 present (1) a robust approach for *viewing* the Bible to develop a biblical model for addressing life issues, and (2) a relational approach to *using* the Bible to apply a biblical model for addressing life issues. They each use the issue of sexual abuse to illustrate the relevancy of Scripture for counseling concerns.

TOWARD A BIBLICAL THEOLOGY OF BIBLICAL COUNSELING

Nate's questions are fair questions, especially since some within the church, when facing difficult issues such as sexual abuse, sadly either offer shallow answers or quickly refer. We sometimes avoid biblical theology for deep soul issues because we really are not convinced that the Bible is *profoundly* relevant, and because we really do not feel competent to discern how to apply the Bible to *significant* life issues. We need a biblical way to *view* and *use* the Bible for biblical counseling that shows, "Yes, the Bible is relevant for *that*."

Nate and Ashley want to know, "Does the Bible truly offer richly relevant counsel for life in a broken world?" You and I want to know, "Does Christianity, the gospel, God's Word offer hope and healing for those who have experienced something as horrendous as sexual abuse?"

Much of the current debate in biblical counseling and Christian psychology revolves around the integration issue. Should or should not Christians integrate secular psychological theory into their theology and methodology of biblical counseling and Christian psychology? Obviously, this is a vital issue—or we would not have written *Scripture and Counseling*. However, these two chapters steer in another important direction. It is essential that those who say, "Do not use secular psychological theory to diagnose and treat matters of the soul," also say, "Here's how to develop a biblical theology to diagnose matters of the soul and how to develop a biblical counseling approach to treat matters of the soul."

This is a different "integration" issue. This one integrates *biblical truth and daily life*. It shows how to relate Christ's changeless truth to our changing times.

Counsel for Soul Issues

For those convinced that the Bible provides counsel for significant soul issues, the next question is, "In what form are those answers provided?"

When dear folks like Ashley and Nate courageously share their raw concerns with other believers, I've noticed that we tend to respond in one of three typical ways. First, some *refer*. The stereotype goes something like this: "I'm a committed Christian. I want to help you with your struggle. However, we have to understand that while the Bible provides insight for our 'spiritual lives,' God never intended that we use His Word to address 'emotional and mental' struggles. For relevant help for those issues, we need outside experts." There's confidence in God, but with a corresponding conviction that for "non-spiritual issues," God's Word is not the most appropriate resource.

Second, some follow a *sprinkling* approach. The stereotype goes something like this: "I'm a committed Christian. I want to help you with your struggles. To the insights I've gleaned from the world's wisdom about your issue, I'll add Christian concern, prayer, and biblical principles where they seem pertinent." There's confidence in God's Word as important in helping hurting people, but its application lacks an understanding of the vital, comprehensive, and authoritative nature of God's Word for life in a broken world.

Third, some follow the *concordance* approach. The stereotype goes something like this: "I'm a committed Christian. I want to help you with your struggle. You have a problem. I'll use my Bible concordance to find God's answer." Some have called this the "one-problem, one-verse, one-solution" approach. There's confidence in the Bible, but its application lacks an understanding of the complexity of life and of the rich nature of God's Word.

In each case, I have purposefully prefaced my comments with "The stereotype ..." Life and counseling are infinitely more complex than three paragraphs can encapsulate. Further, it is *not* my intent to promote an "us against them" or a "good guys/bad guys" mind-set. Rather than accuse or antagonize, I hope to invite, encourage, and equip.

Instead of just saying, "Don't do it *that* way," I desire to increase our *confidence* in God's Word for life in a broken world and increase our *competence* in applying Christ's changeless truth to change lives. I believe that we follow other approaches (like *refer, sprinkle,* and *concordance*) and turn to other sources because (1) no one has equipped us to understand the richness and robustness of God's sufficient Word for life in a broken world—helping us to develop *confidence* in how we *view* the Bible for real life; and (2) no one has equipped us to apply God's authoritative Truth to life relevantly and relationally—helping us to develop the *competence* to *use* God's words for real-life issues.

From Scripture to Soul Care

My prayer is that these next two chapters will further equip us to view and use the Bible in a "fourth way"—the *gospel narrative way.* If we are to view the Bible accurately and use the Bible competently, then we must understand the Bible's story the way God tells it. And God tells His story and ours as the *drama of redemption.* It is a *gospel narrative of relationship.*

God begins by telling the story of relationship initiated in Genesis 1–2 and relationship rejected in Genesis 3. After those first three chapters, the rest of the Bible tells the story of God wooing us back by grace to His holy and loving arms, all the while fighting the Evil One who wants to seduce us away from our first love.

Ever since Genesis 3, *life is a battle for our love*—the ageless question of who captures our heart—Christ or Satan. In *Soul Physicians*, I encapsulated all of life as "a war and a wedding."[2] I've heard others describe it picturesquely as "Slay the dragon; marry the damsel." The Bible calls it "the gospel."

Our counseling is sterile and dead if we see the Bible as an academic textbook or even as a textbook for counseling. But if we *view* and *use* the Bible as the story—the gospel-centered drama—of the battle to win our hearts, then our one-another ministry comes alive.

The Bible presents a grand narrative in which God is both the Author and the Hero, with the story climaxing in Christ. A gospel-centered approach to the Bible focuses less on the stories and more on *the Story*, less on the heroes and more on *the Hero*.

The Bible provides relational wisdom for significant soul issues in a *gospel narrative form*. This requires that we view the Scriptures and life through the biblical lens of Christ's gospel of grace and through the biblical grid of creation, fall, redemption, and consummation (see below). This grand narrative perspective provides the framework we use to conceptualize problems using biblical wisdom principles that apply the gospel of grace to the complexity of real and raw life lived in a fallen and broken world.

We need a process that teaches us how to do biblical exegesis *for biblical counseling*. How do we view and use the Bible to help people to grow in grace, to help people in the progressive sanctification process, to help people to deal biblically with issues of suffering and sin? Figure 10.1 overviews a process that moves us toward answering this vital question.

As you read figure 10.1, don't panic. Yes, it is complex—because life is complex. Yes, it is involved and detailed—because studying Scripture deeply takes thought, time, and effort.

Think of this as learning how to fish rather than being given a fish. Unfortunately, many times when it comes to Scripture and counseling, we're not taught how to fish (instead, we are taught the *refer, sprinkle,* and *concordance* approaches). Other times we're just given a fish — some helpful book that presents the author's approach to relating Scripture to a counseling concern. However, *we never get to peek behind the curtain to see how the author moved step-by-step from Scripture to the life issue.*

In these two chapters, I want to pull back the curtain and invite you into the *process* of *moving from Scripture to soul care.* To keep this complex, involved journey practical, we're going to use the outline (fig. 10.1) as a guide or map to discover the richness of God's Word when applied wisely to difficult life issues such as sexual abuse recovery.

I want to walk with you through a detailed approach where we start with a counseling issue, engage the Scriptures dynamically concerning that issue, and then move into the life of our counselees with biblical wisdom and love. My prayer for you is Paul's prayer for you. "This is my prayer: that your love may abound more and more in knowledge and depth of insight, so that you may be able to discern what is best and may be pure and blameless for the day of Christ ... to the glory and praise of God" (Phil. 1:9 – 11).*

FIGURE 10.1.
TOWARD A BIBLICAL THEOLOGY OF BIBLICAL COUNSELING
How Do We View and Use (Study and Apply) the Bible to Help People in a Broken World?

I. Clarify the life issue for biblical study: What area of concern are we studying?
   A. Probe life labels related to this life issue.
   B. Ponder biblical categories that potentially overlap with this life issue.
      1. Theology of life categories: Creation/Fall/Redemption/ Consummation (CFRC)

---

* All Scripture quotations in this chapter are from the *Holy Bible, New International Version* (1984).

    2. Theology of image-bearers categories: Relational, Rational, Volitional, Emotional, and Physical (RRVEP)

    3. Methodology of biblical counseling categories: Sustaining, Healing, Reconciling, and Guiding (SHRG)

II. Focus our scriptural study using gospel-colored lenses: What is the theme and trajectory of the Bible?

III. Explore the Scriptures by taking our real-life questions to God's Word: How do we accurately relate God's truth to our lives?

  A. Redemptive narrative theology: What's the big picture?—Context

  B. Academic theology: What?—Content/categories

    1. Systematic theology

    2. Biblical theology

    3. Exegetical theology

    4. Lexical theology

    5. Textual theology

  C. Spiritual theology: So what?—Connections

  D. Practical/pastoral theology: What now?—Competence

IV. Examine past and current biblical research on this life issue: How do we humbly respect the wisdom of others?

  A. Historical theology: What then?—Contributions of predecessors

  B. Current theology: Who else?—Contributions of contemporaries

V. Evaluate descriptive research regarding this life area: How do we use research as a catalyst for deep thinking?

  A. What does the descriptive research say about this life issue?

  B. Analyze this data in light of your biblical interpretations

VI. Synthesize our findings: How do we develop a relevant working model of biblical counseling for life issues?

  A. Develop a biblical counseling theology of this life issue: a creation, fall, redemption, and consummation biblical counseling diagnosis

  B. Develop a biblical counseling methodology for this life issue: a biblical counseling intervention/soul care treatment plan

I still remember the first time I counseled someone who had been sexually abused. I knew the Bible was relevant, but I did not understand how to relate God's Word to sexual abuse recovery. It was three decades ago, and I could not find solidly biblical materials. I was determined to understand what the Scriptures said about sexual abuse, the damage done to the soul, and the healing hope offered by the gospel. But where would I start? Basically I had to reinvent the wheel in terms of developing a step-by-step approach to examining the Bible for this specific biblical counseling issue. After thirty years of tweaking, modifying, and maturing my approach, *I want to keep you from having to reinvent the wheel.*

Having said that, I understand that I have *not* cornered the market on the wheel! This section's header reads: *toward* a biblical theology of biblical counseling. In 1981 Walter Kaiser penned his now classic work *Toward an Exegetical Theology.*[3] By using the word *toward*, Kaiser humbly acknowledged that his was not the final word, but one initial attempt at developing an exegetical model of theology. I am suggesting the same: the approach I'm proposing is my current best attempt at *one* model for studying and applying the Bible to help people to grow in grace. It is neither the *final* model nor *the* model.

THE HERMENEUTICAL SPIRAL
FOR BIBLICAL COUNSELING

I've embedded in figure 10.1 and developed further in figure 10.2 what students of the Bible call "the hermeneutical spiral." It refers to the idea that we understand a specific text within the context of the whole of the Bible, and that we understand the whole of the Bible with reference to the individual texts. We can interpret neither the individual passages nor the whole of the Bible without reference to each other.

The hermeneutical spiral developed in this chapter and in chapter 11 uses the works of leaders in the field such as Grant Osborne, Anthony Thiselton, and Kevin Vanhoozer, among others, and translates their perspectives to the field of biblical counseling.[4] Figure 10.2 outlines one model for using one formulation of the hermeneutical spiral for biblical counseling.

FIGURE 10.2.
THE HERMENEUTICAL SPIRAL FOR BIBLICAL COUNSELING

Redemptive narrative theology: Framework and focus—theme and trajectory

"What's the big picture?" Context—redemptive movement

Academic theology: Foundation—information/knowledge

"What?" Content and conviction—truth

    Systematic theology

    Biblical theology

    Exegetical theology

    Lexical theology

    Textual theology

Spiritual theology: Formation—transformation/wisdom

"So what?" Connection, categories, and constructs—relevance

Practical/pastoral theology: Friendship—application/love

"What now?" Competence, care, and cure—relationship

Historical theology: Forebears—validation/confirmation

"What then?" Church history and contributions of predecessors

"Who else?" Current theology and contributions of contemporaries

As you explore figures 10.1 and 10.2, realize that because of the nature of communication, any model has to be presented using a somewhat linear method. While the outline and development of this model will be organized step-by-step in linear fashion, the *order* is less important than the overall process. You could jump in at almost any point in the hermeneutical spiral. You could choose for practical reasons to start at different points in the outline. You could and should move back and forth within the process; it is *not* a straitjacket.

CLARIFY THE LIFE ISSUE FOR BIBLICAL STUDY: WHAT AREA OF CONCERN ARE WE STUDYING?

Imagine that Nate has just asked you, "Can you help? Does the Bible offer any hope for my wife?" After your initial meeting with Ashley and Nate, you're deeply motivated to study the Bible for a biblical counseling approach to sexual abuse. You assume, of course, that your first "step" must be to open your Bible. Anything less or different, some would suppose, would be less than biblical.

However, there is a *logical preliminary* starting point even before building the *theological* foundation. Obviously, before examining something biblically, we must ponder, *"What is it that I am examining biblically?"* In this preliminary stage, we're seeking to identify our area of concern. We're beginning to label and focus our research—trying to develop our awareness of the type of specific life issues and questions that we are bringing to the text of Scripture. Of course, because the process is a spiral, the preliminary categories we developed will be deepened, stretched, altered, strengthened, and challenged at each "step" in the ongoing process.

Probe Life Labels Related to This Life Issue

So as we begin to mentally respond to Nate's question, we use the language and categories of real life as lived today as we attempt to label our area of biblical counseling research. Are we studying sexual abuse? Depression? Anxiety? Idolatry of the heart? Addiction/enslavement/besetting sin? Forgiveness? Reconciliation?

WHAT QUESTIONS DO WE NEED TO ADDRESS?

With Ashley, we are focused on the life issue of sexual abuse recovery. We will want to ask ourselves every question about sexual abuse and recovery that comes to mind. Brainstorming is invaluable. Examples are limitless.

How is sexual abuse defined? What does recovery look like? How does sexual abuse impact the body? The soul? What does sexual abuse do to issues of trust? How does it relate to shame? Self-hatred? How does sexual abuse impact one's sense of femininity? Masculinity? What is sexuality? What is gender? What is masculinity? Femininity? What difference does it make if the sexual abuse was same-sex abuse? What categories explain the sinful motivation of the abuser? What difference does the gospel make? How does forgiveness play a part? Confrontation? Restitution? Reconciliation?

IN CHURCH HISTORY, WHO HAS EXAMINED THIS AND WHAT ISSUES DID THEY ADDRESS?

Later in the process, under historical theology, we will look for answers—for past wisdom that we can relate to life today. For now, we are exploring more for basic awareness. We are not alone. Even issues like sexual abuse have been dealt with by that great cloud of past witnesses.[5] We record what questions they asked and add their insightful probings to ours.

IN CURRENT BIBLICAL COUNSELING, WHO IS EXPLORING THIS AND WHAT ISSUES ARE THEY ADDRESSING?

Later we will probe the works of others for their answers. For now, we are still trying to raise our awareness. My own experience and encouragement is to "be brief" at this stage. While we want to increase our awareness of the type of questions to bring to the text of Scripture, we don't want to be unduly influenced by the theory and practice of others.

IN SECULAR PSYCHOLOGY, WHO IS RESEARCHING THIS AND WHAT QUESTIONS ARE THEY ADDRESSING?

Some might suggest that we should avoid this stage. However, biblical counselors have long believed that there can be a potential catalytic impact when we assess the research being done and weigh the questions being raised in the world of psychology. We don't have to ask the same questions or speak the same "psychologized" language. The research performed and questions raised can drive us back to Scripture with our real and raw questions.

WHAT EXPERIENCE, IF ANY, DO I HAVE COUNSELING WITH THIS ISSUE, AND WHAT QUESTIONS HAS MY COUNSELING RAISED THAT I WILL WANT TO EXPLORE?

We never place human experience parallel to biblical truth. However, Solomon clearly used his life experiences in writing Proverbs and Ecclesiastes (under the Spirit's inspiration). He brought his life lived under the sun to the Son of God and asked hard questions and offered practical counsel. We can do the same. When we do so with an issue like sexual abuse, some of the questions we may raise, with the hope of them being answered in later "stages" of our study, might include: "Why is sexual abuse so powerfully painful?" "Why are the emotions so intense?" "Why is forgiveness so difficult?" "Why is silence and secrecy often the response?" "What happens in the female and male soul when sexual abuse occurs?" "Is sexual abuse just body abuse, or is it more soul abuse and gender abuse?"

WHAT EXPERIENCE, IF ANY, DO I HAVE DEALING WITH THIS PERSONALLY, AND WHAT QUESTIONS HAS MY EXPERIENCE RAISED THAT I WILL WANT TO EXPLORE?

If we have experienced sexual abuse, we can bring our soul questions to our journey into what God's Word says about sexual abuse. Even if we have not experienced sexual abuse, we can still ponder the impact of emotional abuse, verbal abuse, physical abuse, mental abuse, and spiritual abuse upon our own soul (this is not to suggest that any of these types of abuse are identical to sexual abuse). And if we have not experienced sexual abuse ourselves, we can still potentially ponder the impact of sexual abuse on family members and friends. Such ponderings assist us to bring pertinent, relevant, real-life questions to the text of Scripture.

Ponder Biblical Categories That Potentially Overlap with This Life Issue

The point of probing life labels is to help us to move from a merely academic approach to the issue of sexual abuse to a real-life approach. It also helps us to move from a mere one-verse, one-problem, one-solution mentality. Pondering life categories begins to create in our minds the awareness of the depth of issues, the complexity of life, and the richness of the Scriptures.

The questions we raised can now arm us with life categories that we can *begin to bring to the text*—still in a preliminary way. At this time the point is *not* to answer all our questions. The point is to *raise* further questions—to deepen our understanding of the type of issues that we will want to examine through narrative, academic, spiritual, practical, and historical theology.

WHAT EXAMPLES OF A SIMILAR TOPIC DO WE FIND IN THE SCRIPTURES?

Armed with our life categories related to sexual abuse, we can begin to "browse" Scripture. What passages address issues like sex, sexuality, masculinity, gender, rape, incest, sexual abuse (and all the other life categories you collated)? For example, we could list all the "texts of terror" passages in Genesis where men used and abused women (Gen. 12:10–20; 16:1–16; 19:4–11, 30–38; 20:1–18; 21:8–21; 26:7–11; 34:1–31; 38:1–30). We could list Amnon's rape of his half-sister Tamar (2 Sam. 13:1–39). These passages and many others become sources for our academic theology study.

WHERE DO WE FIND SIMILAR CATEGORIES, ISSUES, CONCEPTS, AND CONSTRUCTS IN THE SCRIPTURES?

Sometimes specific passages may not seem to address "sexual abuse." However, Genesis 1–3 surely addresses gender, maleness, femaleness, male-female relationships, and much more, showing both God's original design and the impact of human depravity upon each of these areas. Even concepts such as being naked and unashamed, and then concepts such as being afraid because of nakedness and the resultant hiding are all vital to the development of a theology of sexual abuse recovery.

WHAT WISDOM PRINCIPLES ADDRESS SIMILAR CATEGORIES, ISSUES, CONCEPTS, AND CONSTRUCTS?

One way to categorize biblical counseling questions is to use:

- Theology of life categories: Creation, Fall, Redemption, and Consummation (CFRC)[6]
- Theology of image-bearers categories: Relational (Spiritual, Social, Self-Aware), Rational, Volitional, Emotional, and Physical Beings (RRVEP)[7]
- Methodology of biblical counseling categories: Sustaining, Healing, Reconciling, and Guiding (SHRG)[8]

The rest of this chapter and all of chapter 11 will illustrate how we can use these categories as we study the Bible for biblical counseling. Our task in this stage is to raise questions so we develop biblically astute concepts and real-life wisdom categories that we can take to God's Word.

THEOLOGY OF LIFE CATEGORIES

Consider some examples of prompting questions for sexual abuse that we might develop under the theology of life categories:

- *Ponder creation/people: "How did God originally design us to function in this area?"* As sexual beings? As gendered beings? As males? As females? What does it mean to be naked and unashamed? What is soul shalom (peace)? Sexual shalom? Where in Scripture are these questions addressed?
- *Ponder fall/problems: "How has sin marred our functioning in this area?"* As sexual beings? As gendered beings? As males? As females? What is shame? Nakedness? Hiding? Self-covering? Why are there so many texts of terror in Genesis—what is God trying to tell us about the impact of sin upon sex, sexuality, and relationships?
- *Ponder redemption/solutions: "How has redemption provided us victory in this area?"* How does the gospel speak into this issue? How does new life in Christ and our new identity in Christ relate to

this issue? What is the process of movement toward mature biblical maleness? Femaleness? Forgiveness? Moving from shame to shalom? Confrontation? Reconciliation? Justice? Where in Scripture are these questions addressed?

- *Ponder consummation: "What impact does Christ's final triumph over sin and suffering have in this area now?"* What tears, sorrow, pain, and mourning will be wiped away in that great day? What hope does everlasting life hold for us? How can the truth that our greatest sorrows will be swallowed up relate to sexual abuse today?

THEOLOGY OF IMAGE-BEARERS CATEGORIES
Consider some examples of exploratory questions for sexual abuse that we might develop under the theology of image-bearers categories:

- *Ponder relational (spiritual, social, self-aware) beings: "What does the Bible teach about relational beings in this area?"* How do godly affections (creation), false lovers/broken cisterns (fall), and grace-inspired worship (redemption) relate to the issue of sexual abuse? How did God design our longings, desires, thirsts, and affections? How does sexual abuse mar our longings, desires, thirsts, and affections? How does our redemption in Christ help us to put off ungodly and put on godly longings, desires, thirsts, and affections in response to sexual abuse?
  - ✓ *Ponder relational spiritual beings: "What does the Bible teach about spiritual beings in this area?"* How does sexual abuse impact a person's image of God as Father? Image of Christ? Image of the Spirit? Longings for God? Prayer life? Application of Scripture?
  - ✓ *Ponder relational social beings: "What does the Bible teach about social beings in this area?"* How does sexual abuse impact a person's social relationships — to the abuser, to non-abusers, to members of the same sex, to members of the opposite sex?
  - ✓ *Ponder relational self-aware beings: "What does the Bible teach*

about self-aware beings in this area?" How does sexual abuse impact one's sense of self? One's identity in Christ? One's Christ-esteem and Christ-image? One's sense of shame/shalom? One's sense of guilt/worth/blame? One's gender identity?

- *Ponder rational beings: "What does the Bible teach about rational beings in this area?"* How do people respond to sexual abuse with godly mind-sets (creation), foolish mind-sets (fall), or wise mind-sets (redemption)? What images of God, others, self, and of life develop in the core of the mind as a result of sexual abuse and how can they be renewed by the gospel? What ideas/beliefs/convictions about life develop in the core of the mind as a result of sexual abuse, and how can they be renewed through the gospel?

- *Ponder volitional beings: "What does the Bible teach about volitional beings in this area?"* How do people respond to sexual abuse with godly purposes (creation), self-centered purposes (fall), or other-centered purposes (redemption)? What ungodly styles of relating, goals, motives/motivations, purposes, behaviors, actions, and interactions develop as a result of sexual abuse, and how are they renewed through salvation? How are they rehabituated through grace-based means of growth such as spiritual disciplines, soul care, spiritual direction, and spiritual friendship?

- *Ponder emotional beings: "What does the Bible teach about emotional beings in this area?"* How do people respond to abuse with godly mood states (creation), ungoverned mood states (fall), or Christ-submitted mood states (redemption)? What ungodly ways of handling emotions (and which emotions) typically develop as a result of sexual abuse? How can emotions be comforted by the Father, be soothed in Christ, and be transformed by the Spirit?

- *Ponder physical beings: "What does the Bible teach about physical beings in this area?"* How is God's original design for the mind/body connection distorted by sexual abuse? How can sexual abuse victims learn once again to yield themselves body and soul to God as an act of worship?

METHODOLOGY OF BIBLICAL COUNSELING CATEGORIES

Consider some examples of prompting questions for sexual abuse that we might develop under the methodology of biblical counseling categories:

- *Ponder sustaining: "In this area, what would it look like to sustain someone and help that person understand that it's normal to hurt?"* What is the excruciating "hurt" of sexual abuse? How does the gospel bring comfort to the sexual abuse victim? How does the Christ of the cross bring comfort to the abuse victim? How does the Spirit comfort the agony and shame of sexual abuse? How do I empathize with the pain of sexual abuse?

- *Ponder healing: "In this area, what would it look like to offer Christ's healing encouragement to someone and to help that person to realize that it's possible to hope?"* What is "healing," "recovery," and "transformation" from sexual abuse? What does it look like as a relational, rational, volitional, emotional, physical being? How does Christ's gospel of grace speak into the pain of abuse? How can I bring biblical encouragement without being trite? How do spiritual eyes and/or faith eyes look at and reinterpret sexual abuse from God's perspective?

- *Ponder reconciling: "In this area, what would it look like to bring Christ's reconciling grace to someone and help that person address the horrors of sin with the wonders of forgiveness?"* How can I help the sexual abuse victim apply the gospel to their abuse? What is God's attitude toward the abuser? What does that mean? Look like? What are sinful responses to sexual abuse (*not* being guilty of being abused, but *potentially responding to* the abuse in unbiblical ways)? How do I expose sinful responses without "victimizing the victim"? What does forgiveness of the abuser look like? How is it different from forgetting? What role should restitution and justice play?

- *Ponder guiding: "In this area, what would it look like to guide someone and help that person to know that it's supernatural to mature?"*

How does our new identity in Christ as saints and sons/daughters impact the change/growth/healing process? For a sexual abuse victim, what is spiritual maturity as a relational, rational, volitional, emotional, and physical being? What spiritual processes can help the sexual abuse victim tap into Christ's resurrection power to become more like Jesus?

FOCUS OUR SCRIPTURAL STUDY USING GOSPEL-COLORED LENSES: WHAT IS THE THEME AND TRAJECTORY OF THE BIBLE?

Picture where we are in our journey. Ashley and Nate asked us if the Bible has answers for Ashley's sexual abuse — does it offer hope? We know it does because we know the Bible is not only sufficient, it is relevant. As we've taken our real-life questions about sexual abuse to the Bible, we've seen the richness of Scripture.

But we can't go back to Ashley and Nate with only deep questions. We are seeking gospel-centered wisdom for life. We know that in Christ are hidden all the treasures of wisdom and knowledge (Col. 2:3) and we will identify signposts on that treasure hunt in chapter 11. Before we do that, we need to view the Christ-centered "lay of the land" from Paul in Colossians.

Paul's Gospel Lenses for Relating Truth to Life

If Philippians 1:9–11 is Paul's prayer for the biblical counselor, then Colossians 1:3–14 is Paul's pattern for developing a gospel-centered approach to biblical counseling. As Paul wrote to the believers in Colossae, their situation mirrors ours. They were saints — "God's holy people" (Col. 1:2). They were also sons and daughters of "God our Father" (Col. 1:2). Though forgiven and welcomed home by God through Christ (Col. 1:13, 22), they were facing suffering — condemnation from Satan (Col. 1:22), judgment by others (Col. 2:16), interpersonal grievances and struggles (Col. 3:13, 15), and family discord (Col. 3:19–21). They also battled the same temptations to sin that we face — sexual immorality, impurity, lust, evil desires, greed, anger, rage, malice, slander, and lying (Col. 3:5 – 9).

Paul's mission was to relate gospel truth to the Colossians' relationship: *with God* — that they would be mature in Christ, *with one another* — that they would be united in love, and *with themselves* — that they would be encouraged in heart (Col. 1:28; 2:2). Paul modeled for us counseling that sees God's Word as relational and relevant to life in our broken world.

Paul also modeled for us counseling that is gospel-centered and Christ-focused. Instead of allowing the pressure to provide a quick answer to drive him to simplistic solutions, Paul went "big picture" by focusing on the larger story — the *largest* story — "Christ in you, the hope of glory" (Col. 1:27). Rather than offering smaller story "steps" or "keys," Paul invited his Colossian friends to journey with him so "they may have the full riches of complete understanding, in order that they may know the mystery of God, namely, Christ, in whom are hidden all the treasures of wisdom and knowledge" (Col. 2:2 – 3).

The Good News as the Epicenter of the Good Book

Paul's purpose in responding to the real-life concerns of the Colossian believers was to call them back to the supremacy and sufficiency of Christ, the gospel, Scripture, and Christianity for salvation *and for life today*. He did so by helping them and us to understand the gospel narrative — the drama of redemption.

To the Colossians, struggling to know how to live well and wisely, Paul opened the curtain to the main movement in the drama of redemption — victory, resurrection. Then Paul pointed the spotlight on the main character in the drama of redemption — *Christ*. He rejoiced with the Colossians that they had "faith in Christ Jesus" (Col. 1:4). He pointed their attention to the life, death, and resurrection of Christ, reminding them that they had embraced "the true message of the gospel that has come to you. In the same way, the gospel is bearing fruit and growing throughout the whole world—just as it has been doing among you since the day you heard it and truly understood God's grace" (Col. 1:5–6).

The epicenter of the book of God—the Gospels—is nothing less than a *victory narrative*. Gospels were a common literary form in the ancient Near East during the time of Christ. Whenever a great king won a major victory, he commissioned the writing of a gospel—a vivid retelling of the good news of the vanquished enemy and the victorious king. This glorious good news was told again and again, often from multiple points of views, to exalt the king and encourage his people.

Paul said, "You want to know about change? About victory? Listen to the gospel announcement of Christ's victory! And I'm not talking only about past victory over sin, as amazing as that is. I'm also talking about *ongoing* victory in our *daily* battles as we face suffering and struggle against sin." That is why Paul reminded them—as *believers*—that this gospel was *continuing* to bear fruit and grow "just as it *has been doing among you since the day you heard it and truly understood [it]*" (Col. 1:6, emphasis added).

Paul was *not* in any way minimizing, nor am I, the *eternal* significance of the gospel. In Christ "we have redemption, the forgiveness of sins" (Col. 1:14). In Christ we have been reconciled to God (Col. 1:22). Paul *was* teaching them and us that counsel that is truly biblical is built on *applying the gospel to everyday life*. That's the foundational message that Ashley and Nate need to hear.

A gospel-centered focus is less a "stage" in the process and more a "mind-set" or "viewpoint" that must color every other stage. The central point of the Bible is not to provide an exhaustive list of counseling answers. However, the central theme and trajectory of the Bible—the gospel—does provide a robust, authoritative, and sufficient foundation for counseling because Christ's gospel of grace is our only hope as we face sin and suffering.

WHERE WE'VE BEEN AND WHERE WE'RE HEADED

Embracing Christ doesn't stop a fallen world from falling on us—we still face suffering. And embracing Christ doesn't yet end our battle against the world, the flesh, and the devil—we still wrestle against sin. So how do we learn to relate the gospel to life? How *does* theology relate to biblical counseling? How do we develop a comprehensive and compassionate biblical model for an issue like sexual abuse? We'll address those questions and more in chapter 11, "The Rich Relevance of God's Word."

HOW WE *USE* THE BIBLE FOR LIFE IN A BROKEN WORLD

BOB KELLEMEN

In part 2 of *Scripture and Counseling*, we want to assist you to develop a robust biblical *use* of Scripture in the actual one-another process. Our authors demonstrate in part 2 the "how to" of the sufficiency of Scripture—leading to increased *competence* in the ancient art of the personal ministry of the Word—whether it is called biblical counseling, one-another ministry, spiritual friendship, soul care, spiritual direction, pastoral care, or small group facilitation.

We begin with chapter 11, "The Rich Relevance of God's Word," where Bob Kellemen demonstrates how to use the hermeneutical spiral *for* biblical counseling by applying it to the issue of sexual abuse recovery. He helps us to learn a robust, specific, comprehensive, practical map for *using* the Bible to apply a biblical model for addressing life issues—including the hard cases.

Garrett Higbee, in chapter 12, "The Practicality of the Bible for Becoming a Church of Biblical Counseling," presents a biblical theology of biblical counseling in the local church. Building on the foundation of Christ and His gospel of grace, Garrett provides a four-floor blueprint for one-another ministry in the local church.

Garrett continues his practical theology theme in chapter 13, "Uncommon Community: Biblical Counseling in Small Groups." He helps us to see how Scripture's sufficiency and relevancy can and should saturate every aspect of church life so that our churches are places *of* biblical counseling and *of* small groups.

In chapter 14, "Speaking the Truth in Love," the coauthoring team of Jonathan Holmes and Lilly Park show that the Bible not only has a theology of people, problems, and solutions, it also provides a robust, comprehensive, and practical theology of the counseling/one-another relationships. Jonathan and Lilly help us to learn how to provide *Scripture and soul* in our ministry to one another.

Brad Hambrick, in chapter 15, "The Competency of the Biblical Counselor," explores how the sufficiency of Scripture relates to the competency of the counselor. Brad will help us to identify layers of competency and specific callings of the biblical counselor.

Chapters 16–20 form a section within a section as each chapter uses a counseling issue to illustrate the Bible's rich relevance to life in our broken world. Jeremy Lelek begins this section in chapter 16, "Relating Truth to Life: Gospel-Centered Counseling for Depression," where he uses the issue of depression to illustrate numerous ways to use the Scriptures robustly in counseling.

Next, John Henderson, in chapter 17, "Using Biblical Narrative in the Personal Ministry of the Word," considers the issue of anxiety to illustrate various ways to use the genre of biblical narrative in the counseling/one-another ministry process. Then Deepak Reju, in chapter 18, "Using Wisdom Literature in the Personal Ministry of the Word," addresses the issue of marital counseling to illustrate several ways to use the genre of biblical wisdom literature in the counseling/one-another ministry process.

In chapter 19, "Using the Gospels in the Personal Ministry of the Word," Rob Green examines the issue of parent-child conflict to illustrate many ways to use the genre of the Gospels in the counseling/one-another ministry process. Heath Lambert follows up in chapter 20, "Using the Epistles in the Personal Ministry of the Word," by pondering the issue of OCD (obsessive-compulsive disorder) to illustrate numerous ways to use the genre of the biblical epistles in the counseling/one-another ministry process.

Randy Patten, in the conclusion, "Lessons Learned through

Counseling Experience," notes that we often learn best by using Scriptures *in* counseling. From his decades of biblical counseling experience, Randy highlights four central categories in scriptural counseling: the nature of spiritual ministry, counseling methodology, developing skill as a biblical counselor, and training and supervising counselors.

CHAPTER 11

THE RICH RELEVANCE
OF GOD'S WORD

BOB KELLEMEN

How would the apostle Paul counsel Ashley and Nate? How might he respond to their questions about hope and finding answers for Ashley's sexual abuse?

Perhaps we picture Paul stoically pondering their questions, fingertip tapping his temple. Nothing could be further from the truth as Paul himself describes it. In his desire to care for troubled souls, Paul struggles to the point of weariness, labors to the point of exhaustion, and agonizes like an Olympic wrestler. The whole time he's clinging to Christ's supernatural power working mightily within him (Col. 1:29 – 2:1). Paul models counseling that is passionate and compassionate, other-centered and Christ-dependent. That's an essential reminder in the midst of two chapters where we're wading through heady stuff like "exegesis" and "academic theology."

Or maybe we picture Paul swiftly rattling off "four principles for overcoming sexual abuse." No. When people asked Paul, "Where do we turn for wisdom for life?" he responded with an infinite answer in one word: *"Christ!"* It was this Christ-centered worldview that led the Biblical Counseling Coalition to explain gospel-centered counseling as:

We point people to a person, Jesus our Redeemer, and not to a program, theory, or experience. We place our trust in the transforming power of the Redeemer as the only hope to change people's hearts, not in any human system of change. People need a personal and dynamic relationship with Jesus, not a system of self-salvation, self-management, or self-actualization. Wise counselors seek to lead struggling, hurting, sinning, and confused people to the hope, resources, strength, and life that are available only in Christ.[*]

Pie in the sky? Too heavenly minded to be of any earthly good? That's what the Colossians were being told. And it's what the world tells us today. The gospel might be good for "spiritual stuff," for heaven, but for life today you need Christ + the gospel + Scripture + Christianity + the world's wisdom.

Paul, like John, counters this deficient worldview by pointing people to the all-sufficient Christ who not only offers the amazing grace of eternal life but also the amazing grace of life lived to the fullest—*today* (John 10:10). This Jesus does not make the false promise of a trouble-free life, but the hopeful promise of peace in the midst of a troubled and troubling world (John 16:33).

Having grounded the Colossians in the gospel, Paul keeps praying for them. His prayer in Colossians 1:9–14 provides a gospel-centered pattern for translating God's truth into wisdom for relational living:

- *Academic theology:* "Fill[ed] ... with the knowledge of his will" (Col. 1:9).[1] This is the "What?" question. The Word provides our comprehensive framework for answering life's questions.
- *Spiritual theology:* "Through all the wisdom and understanding that the Spirit gives" (v. 9). This is the "So what?" question. We learn to discern from God's Word the implications of truth for life—insights for living like Christ and for Christ in a fallen world.
- *Practical/pastoral theology:* "So that you may live a life worthy of the Lord" (v. 10). This is the "What now?" question. Yes, sanctification includes "getting used to our salvation." But it also

---

[*]   All Scripture quotations in this chapter are from the *Holy Bible, New International Version* (1984).

involves "applying our salvation" in our daily walk so our lives ascribe worth to our Lord.

✓ *Our walk and works:* "Bearing fruit in every good work" (v. 10). Part of biblical counseling is helping people to be fruitful in their gospel walk. We help people explore how they can wisely love others in the midst of life's trials and temptations.

✓ *Our worship:* "Growing in the knowledge of God" (v. 10). Another aspect of biblical counseling is helping people to worship well. We help people explore how they can wisely love God in gratitude for His grace.

EXPLORE THE SCRIPTURES BY TAKING REAL-LIFE QUESTIONS TO GOD'S WORD

As we apply this biblical pattern to Ashley's life, to her sexual abuse, we start by caring deeply and listening wisely. Then we take her questions and ours to God's Word, and we orient our eyes with the corrective lens of a redemptive narrative focus (see chapter 10). Now we're ready to accurately relate God's truth to Ashley's life.

Academic Theology: Foundation—Information/ Knowledge (The "What?" Question)

There is no "magic" to the order in which these types of theology are presented or studied. In reality, they can and should be blended. With academic theology, some might contend for systematic theology to follow after biblical, exegetical, and lexical theology. I won't quibble—as long as each component is valued for its contribution to the development of a theology of biblical counseling.

SYSTEMATIC THEOLOGY

Systematic theology involves the orderly arrangement of everything the Bible has to say about a given topic. For instance, with the doctrine of the Holy Spirit (pneumatology), systematic theology traces God's inspired teaching on the Spirit from Genesis 1:2 (the Spirit hovering over the waters) to Revelation 22:17 (the Spirit inviting all who are thirsty to come drink from the water of life), and everything in between.

With sexual abuse recovery, we explore this issue systematically throughout the Scriptures, organizing God's teaching on this life issue. We use all the categories we collated and all the questions we probed, pondered, and raised (in chapter 10) — taking them to God's Word. By taking this systematic biblical approach, we begin to saturate our minds with the Bible's perspective on this issue. We trace God's thinking on sexual abuse from cover to cover. In this way, when we counsel Ashley, we are looking at her life and her struggles through God's eyes.

Some of the many systematic theology questions that we might ask, *and now seek to answer*, include these:

What is the Bible's mood regarding sexual abuse? How does it relate to the Bible's overarching gospel theme? What is God saying about human sinfulness and need for grace through so many "texts of terror"? How does the author regard sexual abuse? The characters? God? How did God design us to function as gendered beings?

How did God design us to function sexually? How has sin marred our maleness and femaleness? What impact does redemption have on sexual abuse recovery? How do we function as relational (spiritual, social, self-aware), rational, volitional, emotional, and physical beings relative to sexual abuse recovery? In the Bible, how are people who have been sexually abused sustained, healed, reconciled, and guided?

Another strength of the systematic theology perspective for biblical counseling is the ability to trace themes across the breadth of Scripture. Not every passage of Scripture screams "text of terror!" Or "sexual abuse!" However, a great deal of Scripture, examined systematically, addresses life issues relative to sexual abuse. For example, in examining sexual abuse concepts systematically, we might explore the entire Bible's teaching on issues such as the following:

Shame. Shalom. Maleness. Femaleness. Male/female relation-
ship. Same-sex attraction. Gender. Sexuality. Voice/voicelessness.
Power/powerlessness. Forgiveness. Restitution. Reconciliation.
Confrontation. Grace. Healing. Sense of self. Longings and
affections. Self-sufficiency. Hiding. Self-protection. Comfort.
Image of God. Putting off/on.

BIBLICAL THEOLOGY

Biblical theology involves exploring a theme, topic, issue, or question
as developed in one biblical book, or by one biblical author, or even
chronologically through the history of the text. With pneumatology, we
might study all of John's writings on the Spirit—moving from John's
gospel to 1, 2, and 3 John and to Revelation. What theology of the
Spirit does John present?

With sexual abuse recovery, we bring all our questions and concepts related to this life issue to one biblical book or author. We might
study only Genesis, or we might study all five books of the Pentateuch
(authored by Moses). If studying Genesis, the texts of terror where
women are raped, abused, or controlled could be powerful passages for
us to examine. And we could explore throughout Genesis concepts previously mentioned: gender, shame, shalom, maleness, femaleness, etc.

The essential purpose with biblical theology and biblical counseling
issues is to saturate our minds with *the text in context*. Ask questions
similar to those listed under systematic theology, but through the eyes
of one author, one book, and with continual reference to the setting/
purpose of the book and the culture of the day. Some of the many
broad questions with biblical theology that we might ask, *and now seek
to answer*, include the following:

What is the book's mood regarding sexual abuse? How does it
relate to the overarching redemptive theme of the book? How
does the author regard sexual abuse? How do the characters
regard sexual abuse? How does God regard sexual abuse? What
principles do I discover about sexual abuse in this book/this

author? According to this book/author, how did God design us to function sexually? How has sin marred our functioning as males and females according to this book/author? What impact does redemption have in healing from abuse according to this book/author? In this book, how do we function as relational (spiritual, social, self-aware), rational, volitional, emotional, and physical beings? According to this author, how are people sustained, healed, reconciled, and guided when abused?

As with systematic theology, in biblical theology we can study concepts, constructs, and real-life issues related to sexual abuse within the context of a book/author. When studying Genesis, for instance, we might explore issues such as these:

Why didn't Adam, who was given the command to guard the garden, guard Eve? How did Hagar experience being forced to bear a child for Sarai and Abram (Gen. 16)? How did she experience being mistreated by Sarai? Hagar was seen and heard by God. How did she find healing in being seen and heard by God, and how could that relate to sexual abuse recovery?

How does the Genesis theme of shalom, shame, nakedness, and hiding possibly relate to issues of sexual abuse recovery? Why does Genesis, among all the books of the Bible, have so many texts of terror? What are we to make of this theme in Genesis as it relates to human depravity and deprivation and to our desperate need for grace?

EXEGETICAL THEOLOGY

Exegetical theology involves examining our theme, topic, issue, and questions in key texts by using principles of hermeneutics and methods of Bible study to understand God's teaching regarding this concept. With exegetical theology and pneumatology, we might choose to do in-depth exegetical work in John 14 – 16, studying concepts such as the Spirit as the Comforter/Counselor, the guiding and teaching ministry of the Spirit, the personhood of the Spirit, the convicting ministry of the Spirit, and how all of this relates to the believer being sanctified in and by the Spirit.

With exegetical theology and sexual abuse recovery, we saturate our minds with one passage. We do the exegetical work of observation, interpretation, implication, and application. We seek to analyze the details of the passage while synthesizing the overall purpose of the passage. We ask broad questions similar to those suggested under systematic and biblical theology.

Specific questions we can raise for exegetical theology and sexual abuse recovery can be illustrated using 2 Samuel 13 and the rape of Tamar by her half brother Amnon.[2] From this text in context, what do we make of the noninvolvement of Tamar's father, David; the unhelpful, unholy involvement of her brother Absalom; the ungodly counsel of Amnon's "friend" Jonadab; the courageous, bold, wise responses of Tamar herself; the shaping of the narrative by the author; and the inspired voice of God heard in this passage? The sampling that follows is only a speck of the possible exegetical work that we could do with this one text as it relates to sexual abuse recovery.

How does the opening phrase "in the course of time" set the broader context for the purpose of this passage in this book? How does David's preceding sexual sin and murder assist in understanding the purpose for the inclusion of this passage in Scripture? How is God directing our gaze to a focus on our fallen condition? How is God directing our gaze to our desperate need for the Greater David? How are we to interpret Amnon's "falling in love"?

How is Tamar's beauty used against her and what impact might this have upon her sense of self? How should Amnon have handled his frustration and depression? How should Jonadab have counseled his friend? Why the repeated use of "love" and "do"? How does the repeated use of "my sister" and "my brother" impact our interpretation and application of this passage?

Where did Tamar, especially given the culture of her day, find the strength (find and keep her voice and power) to speak so forcefully about the foolish, wicked nature of Amnon? How did she find the bold love to force him to ponder the personal consequences of his sinfulness? How does his refusal to listen to her (repeatedly) relate to the voicelessness of sexual abuse victims?

How does his forcing her because he was stronger relate to the powerlessness of sexual abuse victims? Why did Amnon then hate her so? How did his calling her "this woman" impact her shame? How did his bolting the door against her impact her sense of shame? What does Tamar's ritual grieving suggest about helping sexual abuse victims to candidly face their grief?

How might Absalom's "counsel" to "be quiet" and "don't take this thing to heart" work against her full grieving? What, by Absalom's negative example, can we learn about sustaining and healing a sexual abuse victim? What does it mean that Tamar lived as a desolate woman, and how might this relate to sexual abuse victims today?

What do we make of David being furious but inactive? What do we make of Absalom's anger, hatred, and eventual murder in terms of family members' responses to the disgrace of sexual abuse? What do we make of David grieving the death of Amnon while never grieving the rape of Tamar?

LEXICAL THEOLOGY

Lexical theology involves examining our theme, topic, and questions by exploring the cultural and biblical meanings and uses of significant words related to this issue. With lexical theology and pneumatology, we could study key words in John 14–16. Those might include the Greek words behind "another," "Counselor," "orphans," "teach," "peace," "Spirit of truth," "testify," "grief," "convict," "guilt," "sin," "righteousness," and "judgment."

With lexical theology and sexual abuse recovery, we would want to perform studies of significant words used in the passage. We would study the meaning of the words in the culture of the day and how that author used that word in that book and section. We would examine the meaning and usage of that word by that author and other biblical authors. We could explore how the words describe God's viewpoint, the perpetrator's viewpoint, the victim's viewpoint, and the author's viewpoint. We can ponder what the words suggest about God's design for the soul, human depravity, the damage done by abuse, and *Christ's grace for our disgrace.* We could also probe what the words suggest about sustaining, healing, reconciling, and guiding for sexual abuse.

We can use 2 Samuel 13 to illustrate specific lexical work for sexual abuse counseling.

What does "fell in love with" mean and imply? Why did the author include "beautiful" in describing Tamar? What do "frustrated" and "haggard" mean relative to Amnon? How are we to interpret the author's use of "shrewd" to describe Jonadab? What is the force of "grabbed"? What is the force of "don't"? What is the meaning of "force"? Why did Tamar choose the phrase "Such a thing should not be done in Israel"?

What might the cultural context be for this phrase? What do we make of the repeated use of "don't"? What is the meaning of "wicked"? How does this meaning help us to conceptualize the evil of sexual abuse? What did Tamar mean by "What about me?" What did she mean by "Where could I get rid of my disgrace?" Culturally, what did this imply?

How can "disgrace" help us to understand the hideous consequence of sexual abuse? What did Tamar mean by "What about you?" What does "wicked fools in Israel" mean and what does it say about the evils of sexual abuse? How do these words from Tamar help us to glimpse the human author's and the divine Author's view of sexual abuse? What does "he refused to listen" mean and imply? What does "he was stronger than she, he raped her" mean and imply?

What does "he hated her with intense hatred" mean and imply? What does the curt "Get up and get out!" mean and imply? What does the repeated use of "he refused to listen to her" mean and imply? What does "weeping aloud" say about grieving sexual abuse? What does "be quiet" mean and imply? What does "Don't take this thing to heart" mean and imply? Is Absalom's word for hate the same word for Amnon's hate? Is Absalom's word for "disgrace" the same as Tamar's word for it?

TEXTUAL THEOLOGY

By textual theology, I'm describing a bridge between academic theology and spiritual theology. In textual theology, we stop. Think. Ponder. Connect the dots. Synthesize.

Too often the proverbial "missing the forest for the trees" can occur with academic theology. Textual theology helps us to relate our findings together. We connect our findings to the categories we identified in step one, to the overarching gospel theme of the Bible from step two, and to the categories we utilized in step three. What have we seen? What do we make of this? What preliminary principles and patterns are we starting to sense?

With pneumatology and textual theology, we might conclude the study of John 14–16 with a summary that the Holy Spirit is our divine counselor, mentor, and discipler. Out of that big picture, many specific interpretations and applications could begin to flow with spiritual theology and practical theology.

With sexual abuse recovery and textual theology, various big-picture conclusions might arise. For instance, with the plethora of texts of terror in Genesis, we might begin to surmise that one result of the fall is Satan's ongoing attack on Trinitarian image bearers. We are *male and female* image bearers, and sexual abuse attacks the core of our masculinity and femininity. Our sin, including sexual sin, which is sin against the body and against the soul (a soul that is a feminine or masculine soul) causes alienation from God, separation from one another, and dis-integration from self. Genesis, with its repeated portrait of men abusing women, reminds us that the fall attacked the core of our relational self—as spiritual, social, and self-aware beings. All of this reminds us of our need for *Christ's grace for our disgrace.* Out of that big picture, many specific interpretations, personal applications, and ministry implications could begin to arise with spiritual theology and practical theology.

Spiritual Theology: Formation—Transformation/ Wisdom (The "So What?" Question)

In academic theology, we ask the "What?" question. "What does the text say about this issue?" In spiritual theology, we ask the "So what?" question. "So what difference does all my work in systematic, biblical, exegetical, lexical, and textual theology make in real life as I counsel a sexual abuse victim?"

Spiritual theology is a missing step in much current theology. Theologians do at times match the stereotype of stopping at facts and missing life. They uncover truth, but fail to relate that truth to life.

Some biblical counselors might be tempted to skip academic theology and move right into spiritual theology. The frantic desire to help, to care, to speak the truth in love can motivate some to miss the rich complexity of the truth. The result is spiritualizing and psychologizing the text, and this is *not* spiritual theology. Spiritual theology builds on the foundation of academic theology. Once we lay the foundation securely, then there are some basic processes we can move through to develop a spiritual theology of any life issue.

ASK RELEVANT, RELATIONAL QUESTIONS

First, we ask relevant, relational questions of the text and of the data from the text derived from academic theology:

What was it like for Tamar to experience her brother's brutality? Hatred? Betrayal? What might have happened had Amnon's friend provided godly counsel? Why did David remain angry yet inactive? What was it like for Tamar to remain silent in Absalom's home? In her culture, what was her shame like? What might have brought her healing? How might these insights into the biblical text translate to insights for today? How does this text shout our need for redemption? What biblical counseling principles might be suggested by these insights?

USE OUR IMAGINATION: UTILIZE RELEVANT BIBLICAL LANGUAGE

Often we speak of "making the Bible relevant." However, the Bible *is* relevant. *We* make it boring and irrelevant. We need to translate our academic theology categories back into the real and raw language of Scripture. We can ask ourselves questions such as these:

What powerful images have the scriptural authors used? What effective word pictures can I use to translate those images to our times? How can I creatively capture what I have learned about this issue?

DEVELOP BIBLICAL CATEGORIES

We entered academic theology armed with some preliminary categories. By using the hermeneutical spiral, those categories morph, grow, and deepen. Some possible sexual abuse categories from our academic theology study might include the following:

Grace for disgrace. Gender. Shame. Betrayal. Silence. Voicelessness. Powerlessness. Inactivity. Revenge. Maleness. Femaleness. Ungodly counsel. Anger. Love/lust. Love/hatred. Objectification of women. Beauty for ashes. Sexual bondage.

EXPLAIN THE DATA OF PEOPLE'S LIVES USING THE BIBLICAL CATEGORIES

This final stage of spiritual theology begins to pave the way for transitioning into practical/pastoral theology. We now want to make use of our relevant, creative, real/raw biblical categories and relate them compassionately to the hurting person we are counseling.

> How does my understanding of her shame, of her sexual identity as a female, of her self-trust help me to understand her? How does my understanding of biblical gender and maleness help me to direct him to God for healing? How does my understanding of self-protective covering and hiding help me to expose any lies she is believing? How does my understanding of biblical reconciliation help me to empower him to forgive graciously and love boldly?

Practical/Pastoral Theology: Friendship—Application/ Love (The "What Now?" Question)

Practical or pastoral theology addresses the "What now?" question. It asks, "Given the truth related to life that I have uncovered in academic and spiritual theology, what do I do with it now? What difference does it make for me today as I minister to a sexual abuse victim?" Pastoral theology translates *content* to *compassionate competence*. It moves from academic and spiritual theology to spiritual friendship. It applies truth to life by speaking the truth in love through relationship informed by depth of insight.

STATE OUR PRELIMINARY THEOLOGICAL DIAGNOSIS: CREATION, FALL, REDEMPTION, AND CONSUMMATION

In this stage, we organize our academic and spiritual theology work. We can use the creation, fall, redemption, and consummation (CFRC) *theology of life* categories integrated with the relational, rational, volitional, emotional, and physical *theology of image bearers* categories. Based on our biblical findings, what preliminary biblical counseling model (creation/people, fall/problems, redemption/solutions, consummation/final hope) can we propose for sexual abuse recovery?

Consider CFRC Relationally: Spiritual, Social, Self-Aware

We now ask and begin to answer relevant life questions related to the creation, fall, redemption, and consummation of our *relational* nature as impacted by sexual abuse.

How does God's original design of the soul relate to the issue of sexual abuse? How does sexual abuse mar that design spiritually, socially, and as a self-aware being? How does our redemption in Christ and principles of progressive sanctification relate to mature responses as a spiritual, social, and self-aware victim of sexual abuse? How does the victim become a victor in Christ?

How does Christ's grace heal the disgrace of sexual abuse? How does a sexual abuse victim see God as a protective heavenly Father if their earthly father perpetrated the sexual abuse (spiritual being)? How does a sexual abuse victim begin to trust others again when betrayed by one who should have been most trustworthy (social being)? How can a sexual abuse victim begin to find shalom when they have been shamed (self-aware being)? How can our final hope of eternal healing promote Christ-centered hope today?

Consider CFRC Rationally: Images and Ideas
Next we ask and begin to answer relevant life questions related to the creation, fall, redemption, and consummation of our *rational* capacities as impacted by sexual abuse.

How does God's original design of the human mind relate to the issue of sexual abuse? How does sexual abuse mar that design as a rational being who thinks in images and ideas? How does our redemption in Christ and principles of progressive sanctification relate to mind renewal as a victim of sexual abuse?

How can victims of sexual abuse see themselves as a child of God—a saint and a son/daughter? How does Christ's truth heal the evil deceits and satanic lies associated with sexual abuse? How does a sexual abuse victim see life—past, present, and future—from God's perspective?

*Consider CFRC Volitionally: Purposes/Goals/Motivations
and Actions/Behaviors*
Then we can ask and begin to answer relevant life questions related
to the creation, fall, redemption, and consummation of our *volitional*
capacities as impacted by sexual abuse.

How does God's original design of the human will relate to the
issue of sexual abuse? How does sexual abuse mar that design as
a volitional being who purposes and acts? How does our redemption in Christ and principles of progressive sanctification relate
to mature motivations, interactions, and actions as a victim of
sexual abuse?

How does the victim of sexual abuse choose to love again, trust
again? How does the Spirit's power enable a sexual abuse victim
to love boldly and confront graciously? How does a sexual abuse
victim choose life again — choosing to live a God-sufficient,
other-centered, non-self-protective life?

Consider CFRC Emotionally: Responses and Reactions
At this point we can ask and begin to answer relevant life questions
related to the creation, fall, redemption, and consummation of our *emotional* capacities as impacted by sexual abuse.

How does God's original design of human emotions relate to the
issue of sexual abuse? How does sexual abuse mar that design as
an emotional being? How does our redemption in Christ and
principles of progressive sanctification relate to mature emotional
responses and reactions as a victim of sexual abuse? How does
the victim of sexual abuse learn to handle emotions maturely?
How does the Father's comfort transform the damaged emotions
of a sexual abuse victim?

Consider CFRC Physically
Finally, we ask and begin to answer relevant life questions related to the
creation, fall, redemption, and consummation of our *physical* nature as
impacted by sexual abuse.

How does God's original design of humans as physical beings relate to the issue of sexual abuse? How does sexual abuse mar that design as a physical being whose body and soul are united, who is one holistic "person," and whose body/soul complex has been abused? How does our redemption in Christ and principles of progressive sanctification relate to the mature yielding to God as a victim of sexual abuse? How does the victim of sexual abuse learn to be a pure sexual being? How does a victim of sexual abuse learn to be a mature male or female?

OUTLINE OUR PRELIMINARY TREATMENT PLAN: SUSTAINING, HEALING, RECONCILING, AND GUIDING

We can use the *theology of biblical counseling* as one way to organize our treatment plan. Based on our biblical findings, what preliminary biblical counseling model can we propose that relates to the issue of sexual abuse recovery?

Outline Sustaining Intervention Implications

We start by asking and beginning to answer *sustaining* questions such as the following:

How do I courageously enter the black hole of sexual abuse victims redirecting them to Christ and to the body of Christ, the church? How do I sustain the sexual abuse victim's faith, hope, and love so he/she experiences comfort from Christ and communion with Christ?

How do I empathize with the sexual abuse victim so she/he knows it's normal to experience doubts, despair, disgrace, and desolation? How do I listen to the sexual abuse victim's voice? How do I hear the sexual abuse victim's earthly story of disgrace? How do I enter the agony? How do I climb in the sexual abuse victim's casket of darkness?

Outline Healing Intervention Implications
Next we ask and begin to answer *healing* questions such as the following:

How do I help the sexual abuse victim to find grace—God's prescription for their disgrace? How do I help the sexual abuse victim to perceive that God is caring even when people are horrendous? How do I help the sexual abuse victim to experience faith, hope, love, and wholeness? How do we listen together for and to God's voice? How do we hear and apply God's eternal story of grace? How do I help the sexual abuse victim to embrace God who hears, sees, and embraces him or her? How do I help the sexual abuse victim to explore a renewed faith perspective? How can I be a champion who celebrates the resurrection with the sexual abuse victim?

Outline Reconciling Intervention Implications
Then we can ask and begin to answer *reconciling* questions such as the following:

How do I help the sexual abuse victim to ponder the holy love and justice of God as God looks at the abuser? How do I gently and lovingly expose any possible self-protective, sinful responses to sexual abuse? How do I help the sexual abuse victim to see that God is gracious and forgiving even when he or she clothes, covers, runs, and hides?

How do I provide loving wisdom that reconciles the sexual abuse victim to become a victor in Christ who faces nakedness, rejects coverings, receives God's grace-garments, and finds beauty for ashes so he or she can offer Christlike love to a desolate world? How do I help the sexual abuse victim to become a victor in Christ who confesses that it is horrible to run from God, but wonderful to return to celebrate His grace, and awesome to share His forgiveness?

Outline Guiding Intervention Implications

Finally, we ask and begin to answer *guiding* questions such as the following:

> How do I understand and describe the spiritual dynamics of shame and self-covering to expose root causes that the sexual abuse victim can put off to become a victor in Christ who puts on God-sufficiency and other-centered living? What will mature love look like for this person as he or she moves from victim to victor? How can I help the sexual abuse victim to move to victory in Christ by cooperating with God's supernatural resurrection power in creating beauty for ashes?

EXAMINE PAST AND CURRENT BIBLICAL RESEARCH ON THIS LIFE ISSUE: HOW DO WE HUMBLY RESPECT THE WISDOM OF OTHERS?

While we would be *lazy* if we avoided doing our own hard work of academic, spiritual, and pastoral theology, we would be *arrogant* if we avoided studying the contributions of others. I recommend that we examine past biblical research on sexual abuse recovery (from church history) as well as current biblical research (contemporaries in the discussion).

Historical Theology: Forebears—Validation (The "What Then?" Question)

We are not the first generation to explore the Scriptures to develop biblical models of care.[3] If our findings have *no* support in church history, then we will want to ponder why this is. While Scripture is inspired, *our interpretations and applications of Scripture are not inspired.*

As we explore the contributions of our predecessors in church history who studied this topic, we will want to analyze this data in light of our biblical interpretations. As we analyze the data, we will want to do the following:

WHAT OTHER QUESTIONS MIGHT WE TAKE BACK TO THE TEXT FOR FURTHER STUDY?

We can ask, "In light of my study of church history, what new issues do I need to study? What findings contradict my biblical interpretations? Do these suggest any faulty interpretation on my part? Their part? What findings confirm my biblical interpretations?"

DETERMINE WHAT TO ALTER IN OUR VIEWS

We can also ask, "What do I want to restudy? What might I want to change? What might I want to add?" Analyze this data in light of your biblical interpretations and evaluate your biblical interpretation in light of this data.

Current Theology: Colleagues—Validation (The "Who Else?" Question)

Just as others before us have studied matters of the soul, so also many of our colleagues are doing the same today. It would be equally arrogant for any of us to assume that we have the final word, the only word, or even the best word on how to relate truth to life. Therefore, I suggest the identical model for using the contributions of our contemporaries that I suggested for using the contributions of our predecessors.

EVALUATE DESCRIPTIVE RESEARCH REGARDING THIS LIFE AREA: HOW DO WE USE RESEARCH AS A CATALYST FOR DEEP THINKING?

The creation mandate in Genesis 1:26–28 legitimizes the role of *descriptive psychological research* that examines and quantifies human reactions and responses (see chapters 3 and 4). So I recommend that we *examine and evaluate* the descriptive psychological research being done regarding sexual abuse—frequently categorized currently under the label of post-traumatic stress disorder. I am *not*, under this header, suggesting the evaluation and examination of *prescriptive secular psychology theory* (see chapter 9).

When evaluating *descriptive* research, I suggest that we analyze this data in light of our biblical interpretations. Ask, "What further questions are suggested that I may want to take back to the text for additional study? What descriptive research findings seem to contradict my interpretations of the biblical data? Do these suggest any faulty interpretations on my part? Do they suggest any faulty research on their part?"

Then we determine what to revise in our view, asking, "What do I need to restudy? What might I want to change? Add? Improve?" We assess this data in light of our biblical interpretations and evaluate our biblical interpretation in light of this data.

SYNTHESIZE OUR FINDINGS: HOW DO WE DEVELOP A RELEVANT WORKING MODEL OF BIBLICAL COUNSELING FOR THIS LIFE ISSUE?

Now we are ready to build a working model. We likely already built a substantial preliminary model after our work in academic, spiritual, and practical/pastoral theology. Now we implement any new conclusions we have drawn after our study of church history, contemporaries, and descriptive research.

Notice that even now this is a "working" model. No conclusions we make this side of heaven are final. None constitute *the perfect model.* Still, given all the biblical work and research, we can have humble confidence in our working model. God has truly given us all things that pertain to life and godliness.

It would take a book to outline how I would synthesize my study for sexual abuse recovery—and that would be giving you a fish rather than teaching you to fish. I'll offer you instead:

• An outline suggesting final steps toward moving from your preliminary model to a working model.

- A working model—figure 11.1.
- A detailed illustration of how I used these insights to engage with Ashley and Nate, which you can find in *Sexual Abuse: Beauty for Ashes.*[4]

FIGURE 11.1.
BIBLICAL COUNSELING FOR SEXUAL ABUSE RECOVERY

Grace, God's Prescription for Our Disgrace

The Gospel for Our Suffering: The Horrors of Sexual Abuse That We Have Suffered

God Is Caring Even When People Are Evil

Biblical counselors courageously enter the black hole with sexual abuse victims, redirecting them to Christ and the body of Christ to sustain and heal their faith, hope, love, and peace so they experience comfort from Christ and communion with Christ.

Biblical Sustaining: "It's Normal to Experience Doubts, Despair, Disgrace, and Desolation"

- Listen to your friend's voice.
- Hear your friend's earthly story of disgrace.
- Enter your friend's agony.
- Explore your friend's current painful perspective.
- Be a comforter who enters the black hole / climbs into the casket—empathy.

Biblical Healing: "It's Possible to Experience Faith, Hope, Love, and Wholeness"

- Listen together to God's voice.
- Hear God's eternal story of grace.

- Encourage your friend to embrace God.
- Explore your friend's renewed faith perspective.
- Be a champion who celebrates the resurrection—encouragement.

The Gospel for Our Sin: The Sin of Our Self-Sufficient/ Self-Protective Responses to Sexual Abuse

God Is Gracious Even When We Clothe, Cover, Run, and Hide

Biblical counselors understand the spiritual dynamics of shame and self-covering and discern root causes of spiritual alienation, social separation, and self disintegration, and provide loving wisdom that reconciles and guides sexual abuse victors to face their nakedness, reject their self-made coverings, receive God's grace-garments, and find beauty for ashes so they can offer Christlike love to a desolate world.

Biblical Reconciling: "It's Horrible to Run from God, Wonderful to Return to Celebrate His Grace, and Awesome to Share His Forgiveness"

- Watch your friend's pattern of relating.
- Lovingly expose your friend's earthly story of self-covering.
- Gently explore your friend's current self-protective/self-sufficient perspective.
- Enlighten your friend to grace—received and given.
- Be a care-fronter who risks offense—exposure.

Biblical Guiding: "It's Supernatural to Love by Clinging to Christ to Create Beauty for Ashes"

- Look together for Christ's grace-focused renewal process.
- See God's eternal story of grace.
- Empower your friend to trust God.
- Equip your friend to take risks for God.
- Encourage your friend to stir up the gifts of God.
- Be a coach who trains the heart—empowerment/equipping.

Develop a Biblical Counseling Theology of This Life Issue: A Creation, Fall, Redemption, and Consummation Biblical Counseling Diagnosis

We can organize our thinking around the following categories:

- What was God's original design (creation/people) for us in this area?
- How has sin (fall/problems) marred that design for us in this area?
- How has Christ's grace returned us to dignity and brought healing (redemption/solutions) in this area?
- How can our future hope of glory impact our current journey with Christ (consummation/future hope) in this area?

Develop a Biblical Counseling Methodology for This Life Issue: A Biblical Counseling Intervention/Treatment Plan

We can also organize our thinking around these biblical counseling categories:

- What does biblical sustaining look like as I minister to people facing this life issue?
- What does biblical healing look like as I minister to people facing this life issue?
- What does biblical reconciling look like as I minister to people facing this life issue?
- What does biblical guiding look like as I minister to people facing this life issue?

WHERE WE'VE BEEN AND WHERE WE'RE HEADED

For too long we have exhorted people to counsel biblically without providing in-depth practical equipping in how to do so. My prayer is that this chapter and chapter 10, along with this entire book, will *begin* a process in all our lives where we increasingly gain *confidence* in God's

Word for life in a broken world and where we increasingly grow in our *competence* in applying Christ's changeless truth to gospel-centered life change. The rest of *Scripture and Counseling* models the richness of this biblical process as the body of Christ engages in the personal ministry of the Word to address life in a broken world.

CHAPTER 12

THE PRACTICALITY
OF THE BIBLE FOR
BECOMING A CHURCH
OF BIBLICAL COUNSELING

GARRETT HIGBEE

Having read this far, you realize that the Word of God leaves little doubt in its claim to be the supreme guide for life and godliness. The world sees that as a misplaced priority or downright foolishness. That is nothing new, but there is a more troubling problem in the local church today. Many Christians and Christian leaders don't seem to believe that the doctrine of sufficiency is relevant in a postmodern culture. For others, the Bible is preached relevantly on Sundays, but its relevant application falls woefully short in their office or in small group ministry.

One example where the practical outworking of this doctrine seems to be a platitude is when a small group just turns into rehashing of the sermon with no emphasis on application, no depth of prayer, and no compassionate and personal accountability that leads to life change. Another example is the practice of "refer and defer," where we send hurting sheep to secular counseling for help even though the Bible clearly warns against this practice (an implication of Paul's point in Col. 2:8) (see chapter 9).

Then there is the pandemic of trying to integrate psychology in our churches and our counseling in a way that dilutes truth, takes the focus off the gospel, and diminishes personal responsibility and the effects of sin in our lives. While there might be confusion on how an utter dependence on Christ and His Word works itself out practically in the church today, this is not for lack of clarity in Scripture. People don't fail for lack of content from the Bible; they fail for lack of application of God's truth in their lives. Again, the Bible makes it clear that it is a comprehensive guide and provides practical help for life and godliness (2 Peter 1:3 – 11), so isn't it time that we show this to the world by practicing what we preach?

Assuming the problem lies within us and not in Scripture, what can we do to address it? We need to reclaim soul care in the local church and thoroughly equip our people to speak the truth in love at various levels of competence. If our goal is growing into the likeness of Christ, if our ambition is to please God, then there is no reference other than the Bible that comes even close to showing us how to do it. While the Bible is so much more than a "how-to book," it is anything but ethereal in its instructions for the believer (Eph. 4:11 – 16).

To be clear, the Bible is not a cookbook or encyclopedia; it is the most amazing redemptive story ever told. We will have different stylistic approaches and contextualize our counsel to some degree. However, the power of transforming truth lies solely in the Word of God (2 Tim. 3:16 – 17), the power of conviction of sin comes only by the Spirit of God (John 16:7 – 10), and the power of authentic fellowship is found only in the people of God (1 John 1:7).

In this chapter, we are going to demonstrate just how practical the Scriptures are in giving us a *theology of caring for one another*. The mechanics of life-giving and transforming biblical counsel can be gleaned from the Word of God. We will look at the call to counsel as a job description for every believer. We will then see how the Bible lays out a model of care that is superior to anything the world has to offer. And, finally, I hope to stir your passion with the unique position the local church has in giving hope, help, and healing to a broken and fallen people.

As we go through this chapter together, I will seek to highlight relevant passages of Scripture that guide and build on one another to give us a theology of counseling in the local church. This use of Scripture is not to proof-text every point, but to clarify just how sufficient and practical Scripture is to counseling in the context of our daily lives.

WE HAVE THE CALL OF GOD: EVERY BELIEVER'S JOB DESCRIPTION (ROMANS 15:14)

Scripture is clear that disciple making and giving wise counsel are the privilege and responsibility of every believer. Think about the last time you went a whole day without giving any counsel. Counsel starts with our thoughts and self-talk (Ps. 19:7–11; Prov. 23:26–27). Naturally our counsel ripples into our family, work-life, and friendships. The question then is not, "Do I counsel?" it is, "How biblical is my counsel?"

God calls us to speak the truth in love (Eph. 4:15). He gives us clear direction through over forty imperatives in the one-another passages of Scripture. Think about these Scriptures on reconciliation and restoration as the manner of our care (2 Cor. 5:11–21; Gal. 6:1–10; Heb. 3:12–13). These Scriptures would imply urgency, purposefulness, and a gentle but courageous rescue of those entangled in sin or suffering.

While there are different skill levels that improve with training and practice (Phil. 4:9; Heb. 5:14), our core competence does not come from experience or training alone, it comes from Christ and His Word (Rom. 15:14; 2 Cor. 3:4–6). In our church, we teach that when someone needs help, it is every believer's job description to: (1) care enough to ask, (2) be wise enough to seek God's Word for answers, and (3) be humble enough to intercede in prayer. Imagine if everyone in your small group practiced this on a regular basis. Additionally, when someone attempting to help gets stuck, we have a structure in our church where they can go to the next level of church leadership for direction and support (more on this later in this chapter).

In the Scriptures, we see that churches are not just to be places *with* a biblical counseling department but a community *of* biblical counselors. To raise up a community of wise counselors, we need to look at two concepts: (1) how we equip at various levels of competency in our church so our people and leaders can counsel everything from wisdom issues to crisis care, and (2) how we develop a biblical community care plan to help those who are seeking counsel. Everything is built on a practical theology of counseling methods and starts with a strong mutual ministry ethos taken from the one-another passages of Scripture.

A comprehensive model of care for God's people cannot be exercised apart from the context that He has chosen for counsel and care — the local church community. Furthermore, God has chosen a specific way to carry out the care for His people. He calls for a structure that goes far beyond a few staff members or contractual counseling provided by a para-church ministry.

Following examples in both the Old and New Testaments, we want to offer a model that includes five levels of care on a continuum from intentional discipleship to intensive discipleship. It is easy to talk about an ideal model that is biblical, but putting it into practice is another story. Our church has tried to do that, and by God's grace we are living it with increasing effectiveness. We hope you learn from our humble efforts as we outline the challenges and rewards for you below. It starts with being serious about the Great Commission, much prayer, counting the cost, and building the right structure.

BUILDING A SUSTAINABLE STRUCTURE: ROMANS 12:4 – 8

One reason many churches don't care well for their own is the lack of an ecclesiastical structure to support a truly biblical model of care. Even solid churches find it is too hard and time consuming for a few pastors to help all the sheep. It is so overwhelming when there is a line outside the pastor's door waiting for counseling. Scripture would agree—it is hard and time consuming. Yet there are many examples and even imperatives given in Scripture to direct us on how to equip and care for the saints. Churches can never hire enough staff to meet the needs of the sheep nor should they be doing all the work of caring for God's people.

In Exodus 18:17–18, Jethro, Moses' father-in-law says to him, "What you are doing is not good. You and the people with you will certainly wear yourselves out, for the thing is too heavy for you. You are not able to do it alone." In the context of this passage, "the thing" was counseling and making decisions about God's people and their lives. Jethro went on to give Moses direction to "look for [and choose] able men ... who fear God ... are trustworthy and hate a bribe" (Ex. 18:21) to lead tens, fifties, hundreds, and thousands. This is one clear example of God saying, "This is what a biblical structure for counsel and care is."[1]

In Acts 6 we find another example of a care structure. Here deacons were raised up to handle the day-to-day care for the people so the apostles could teach and pray (Acts 6:4). God reaffirms the notion that the care for the masses is not to rest solely with the senior leaders of the church, but with "men of good repute, full of the Spirit and of wisdom" (Acts 6:3). As the church of Jesus Christ, we are to be eager and intentional about raising up those kinds of leaders.

You may say that structure is good and distribution of care necessary, but where does God speak to the how-to of equipping more leaders? In 2 Timothy 2:2 we clearly see the principle of multiplication and equipping. Paul's charge to Timothy to entrust his ministry to faithful men and women who can teach others serves as a reminder and directive for us also. In these verses there are essentially four "generations" of leaders: Paul, Timothy, "faithful men," and "others." Additionally, there is the model of Christ Himself who poured into the three (Peter, James, and John), mentored the Twelve, and sent out the seventy-two disciples in pairs (Luke 10:1). Scripture is clear on the structure and distribution of care as well as what a healthy and sustainable model for leadership multiplication looks like.

VIEWING A BIBLICAL BLUEPRINT: FIVE FLOORS IN A CHURCH OF BIBLICAL COUNSELING

What bearing do those examples have on our counseling methodology in the church today? Imagine a church building whose foundation is Jesus Christ and His Word. It has a welcoming lobby on the first floor and four floors above.

The Welcoming Lobby: Mutual One-Another Care

As you enter the building, you look around and find the mutual ministry of the one-anothers happening everywhere. People are praying together around the coffee cart, and, on some couches nearby, you overhear someone counseling a friend on purity in dating relationships — their Bibles are open. As you walk around, people are celebrating in laughter in one corner while others are consoling someone who is weeping in another corner. Suddenly, someone approaches you with a smile and welcomes you to their church. As you talk together, they ask if they can give you a tour of the church and you excitedly accept. They take you up to the second floor.

The Second Floor: Authentic Small Groups

Here you find small group meetings going on everywhere. As you listen, you see and hear people asking what the Scripture passage has to do with their everyday life. You boldly ask if you can sit in on a group. You are reminded of a need for discretion and respecting the confidential nature of what is said here. You are welcomed into what seems to be an authentic group. They acknowledge your presence and then return their focus on the moment.

You are surprised to hear a person openly confessing their struggle with lust. They say how it was going well, but that they failed in the last week. You see the others around them speak truth from God's Word into their situation. It's done with love in a way that really makes you want to be part of this group, or one like it. The leader asks them to stick around so they can pray and look at a passage together that could help them going forward. Your guide says, "Let's check out the next floor." You wonder what you'll find there.

The Third Floor: Equipping Small Group Leaders in Biblical Counseling

On the third floor, you see small group leaders meeting with their coaches or flock leaders to gain wisdom on how to help their groups grow and change. You realize the coaches seem to have more training in biblical counseling and more tools than many pastors you know.

You are encouraged by the intentionality of care and the equipping you are finding. You wonder why more churches are not like this. You ask the tour guide what's next.

The Fourth Floor: Equipping in Directive and Corrective Care

As you walk up the stairs toward the fourth floor, you ask yourself who equipped the coaches you just saw. Then, as you get to the top of what seems to be the steepest and longest set of steps yet, you find a smaller floor with trained pastors equipping other leaders in directive and corrective care. Some family pastors are consulting with small group coaches one-on-one to develop a biblical care plan for a hurting member or couple in the church. Others are meeting with lay counselors to make sure they collaborate on how to help transition a member out of formal counseling and back into the community of their small group.

You begin to see how the training and equipping reaches every level of leadership. You also see how there is a connection of care that binds each of the levels together so that the person in need doesn't wonder if the pastors know or care.

The Fifth Floor: Experiential Equipping in Intensive Soul Care

You find out there is yet another floor. Your guide tells you that this top floor is used for experiential training and intensive soul care. He cautions you not to linger by the windows in the doors of each of the rooms as people are invited to this floor only for equipping and care. He is asking you to be discreet. You agree and realize that while your paradigm of personal privacy is being stretched, in this church there seems to be no compromise to confidentiality within the circles of appropriate accountability.

As you arrive at the fifth floor, you find several seasoned staff and lay counselors in different rooms training others experientially through life counseling. Your guide tells you that here they work with the most broken and hurting people in their church. The guide explains the role of an advocate who comes into the counseling as a concerned friend. You are surprised to find the advocates are like godly mentors who are usually chosen by the person in need so that they can pray, encourage, and help the person to get the most out of the counseling experience. You realize it had to have taken years to develop all this. But you have a sense of new hope and confidence that the church can counsel and equip. Before you saw all this, you did not think it was possible.

Pondering the Biblical Blueprint at Work

Your guide takes you back downstairs. It takes a while to process what you just experienced. You wonder if this is realistic in a smaller church or with a church that has no trained counselors. You are still a bit skeptical. You wonder whether they are really competent to handle any crisis or non-organic issues (issues unrelated to physical concerns) brought to them. You ask questions about issues like psychosis and drug addictions, so your guide has you speak with a seasoned counselor. You are encouraged to find out that they work with physicians and other medical professionals and are adept in soliciting help to form a holistic care plan with a multidisciplinary perspective while holding fast to a biblical worldview.

Does this picture seem too complex? Unreachable? It is actually derived from Scripture, and although not every church has the immediate resources to build out all the "floors," there is no reason why even the smallest or newest church can't build the first four. It is not about bricks and mortar; it is about equipping God's people. It will take years to build the whole structure, but we are encouraged because it is happening more and more in churches around the country. Not all churches have all the floors, but hundreds now are on the road to building the first four and opening hearts and homes to those in crisis as well. The ability to do intensive care may mean leaning on other biblical resources, but every church is capable, with God's enabling, to build a church of biblical counselors. I hope from these examples that you can see that it is possible for the church to derive from Scripture a structure for care that is excellent and God-honoring. Wouldn't you want to be part of a church like that?[2]

The doctrine of sufficiency of Scripture calls every believer to counsel, and Scripture provides a structure for biblical care, counsel, and equipping. What about the mechanics or methods that make for a successful discipleship ministry? Even though the picture I drew is what I'm experiencing in my church, we are far from having arrived. While we do have leaders trained at all levels, we haven't trained everyone we need. It takes tremendous amounts of time and effort to build and sustain this — it is a team effort.

At first I didn't know if the leadership would embrace the vision. I struggled to make the mission clear and compelling. We ran into competing agendas and a lack of capacity. We persevered through all this, trusting the Lord to prevail. Now, four years later, we are well on our way toward the implementation of this model of one-another ministry at every level. And we firmly believe every local church can do the same.

While this model isn't "the only way" to apply biblical principles in implementing counseling methods in the local church, it is *a* way that has helped us achieve great effectiveness in transforming lives to the glory of God. To be sure, this hasn't been achieved because of who we are or what we can do. This is possible because God always empowers us to live out what He commands us to do. He has provided amazing and powerful means to build up His church. As I attempt to break down the methods behind this model, let me emphasize three things as clear means or supernatural provision from God. He has provided *His Word* as the foundation of this model; He has given *His Spirit* for discernment, encouragement, and strength in building the model; and He has called and equipped *His people* to carry out this model of care.

GOD'S MEANS FOR BUILDING THE MODEL

We have seen that the calling to counsel is truly for every believer. We have seen that the context is clearly the local church. We have outlined a possible structure to support the ministry, but, practically speaking, how do we best equip a community of believers and help those caught in sin and suffering among us? Think about it this way, what are the means God uses to help us mature into the full stature of Christ? If in fact it is the mission of every believer to "speak the truth in love,"[3] if we believe that the one-another passages of Scripture give specific instruction on how to live with each other as parts of the body that is the church, then surely God would empower us to do it, right?

In terms of caring for people, what is given to us that helps us equip those who care for others? Let me unpack the three provisions I just mentioned: God's people, God's Spirit, and God's Word. We did not list these in order of importance but, for some reason, God called people to be instruments for Him and it starts with us being willing to step up and care biblically. Brad House highlights this important fact when he says, "This we do know: God uses his people to accomplish his purposes. From the garden to Noah to Israel to the disciples, God has used his people as his primary vehicle for proclaiming his glory and working out his plan."[4]

God Gave Us Each Other: Showing Christlike Compassion (Galatians 6:1 – 3)

You may have heard the statement, "No one cares how much you know until they know how much you care." We have found that connecting with someone through sensitivity to their pain is a doorway into being able to bring help and correction. We can look to God's Word to see this lived out in Christ's life in so many ways — with the disciples, with the woman at the well, and with countless others to whom He showed compassion.

Connecting means, in part, caring enough to ask and listening to understand. We are warned not to assume (Prov. 18:13 and 17), and we are told that we are like Christ when we show mercy (Luke 10:29 – 37). People respond to Christlike compassion. Secular counselors call this a "therapeutic relationship," but God calls it "loving your neighbor as yourself." It does not involve an expert over a non-expert, called a "one-up expert," and it's not paying for a friend to help. It's a friend ministering out of love for another. This intentional care should be a part of every interaction in the culture of the local church.

Remember the lobby in the illustration of the house? At Harvest Bible Chapel in Chicago, we are taking more than six thousand people through six foundational one-anothers this year via a small group study to teach them how to care well. We have developed a social covenant, based on these one-another verses of Scripture, that spells out how we are going to treat each other in small groups. For example, "we will belong to one another" (Rom. 12:5) instructs the way we practice loving accountability; "we will forgive one another" (Eph. 4:25 – 32) instructs us to be quick to resolve conflict biblically; "we will exhort one another" (Heb. 3:12 – 14) instructs us to intentionally encourage each other in our walk in Christ; and on and on it goes. This is very relevant and practical direction from God's Word.

It all sounds good on paper, but are we living these things? As God's people we are called to it. It is simple — anything but neat and easy.

The problem is, we need to take the calling seriously and become the people of God that He is asking us to be. I want to be clear that this is more about *being* than doing. This isn't just about "knowing the Bible" and throwing around verses that may apply to someone's problem or situation. It's about living and breathing God's Word and effectively and compassionately ministering to those who are hurting—we have had to repent of being Bible thumpers in our immaturity and must try to be Christ to one another.[5]

God Gave Us His Spirit: Using Discernment and Drawing Out the Heart (Proverbs 20:5)

One reason there is hesitancy to counsel is because most people think they are just not qualified. They think it takes years of specialized training or that counseling is some kind of mystical ability to read minds. In some ways the exact opposite is true. It does not require "psychoanalyzing" a person so you can share your amazing insights to help them. Scripture says that reading into motives and thinking you know someone's heart, even your own, is a dangerous and deluded way of thinking.

As explained in earlier chapters, godly counsel in the formal sense takes competence and experience (see also chapter 15). However, if people possess godly character, the competencies can be taught. If someone is willing and ready, teaching them to connect involves building their confidence in asking good questions and compassionately listening. Godly assessment is about asking more heart revealing and clarifying questions. To be sure, we are only fruit inspectors and God alone is the "heart knower" (see Jer. 17:9–10). God does tell us, however, that the person of understanding can draw out the heart (Prov. 20:5). The question that remains then is, how do we train our leaders to do this practically?

First, we ask our leaders to do a quick assessment of severity, ownership, and support before launching into a care plan.[6] We train our people to consider their approach based on 1 Thessalonians 5:14. Is this a person who is stubborn or unruly? Are they fearful and over-whelmed? Do they need correction or encouragement? Either way, we are admonished to be patient, to restore gently, and to come alongside, not to lord over.

Second, we train all our leaders to use what we call the "fruit to root diagnostic" (named after Luke 6:45). They start at the top of the tree and work their way down from fruit (behavior) to trunk (thinking patterns) to root issues (motives). They learn to trace the heart path, helping those they serve to see why they do what they do. Our leaders have found this to be extremely helpful when ministering the truth in love in a way that exposes our heart idols (Matt. 6:21). Anything less is biblical behavior modification, when in fact God wants heart transformation.

All of the above skills take godly discernment. That is why we say that God's Spirit is a vital means of building a care ministry for His people. Without the Spirit's work in us concerning the issues at hand, discernment isn't possible. It never ceases to thrill me to watch the Spirit bring conviction as we move from fruit to root issues. The person in need often says "I never saw this before. I never connected the dots." Defensiveness drops, conviction sets in, and repentance is now possible (John 16:8 – 11).

Many of us have experienced the power of praying in the Spirit (Eph. 6:18) in a tough counseling situation. The Spirit has a way of moving the counseling interaction from a dialogue to a "trialogue."[7] It is amazing to depend on the Spirit in a way that gives insights both to the counselor and the counselee. We teach our leaders that when they need wisdom or discernment, they need to ask God directly and often (James 1:5 – 8). It is also amazing how many times the Spirit will bring to remembrance a Scripture passage that is perfect for the situation (John 14:26). We teach our people not just to pray but to take time to listen, to reflect, and to meditate on God's truth.

God Gave Us His Word: Responding in Truth and Grace (John 1:14–17)

We believe that the message of the gospel is central to good counsel. But what about the manner in which to engage the hurting? Christ engaged both the sinner and the sufferer, setting the example not only for compassion but also for speaking the truth (for example, Luke 18:18–30; John 4:1–42, 8:1–11).

Some people see themselves as truth people, and some are grace people. The problem is that these were never meant to be extremes or a perpetual compensatory pendulum swing based on our feelings. That confuses those seeking counsel and creates more work for the counselor. It is *more about a blend than a balance*. Christ was filled with grace *and* truth (John 1:14). One hundred percent grace, 100 percent truth — it is a matter of *being* more than a matter of *doing*. We have a saying around our church that goes something like this: You have to *know* Christ, to *be* like Christ, and *do* as Christ would. That is only possible with a growing love for and submission to the Word of God.

I love how 2 Timothy 3:16–17 uses several ways to describe how the Word profits us. The Word teaches us what God expects and how to live. We train our leaders to look at their own life in relationship to this passage as they ask themselves, "Have you allowed the Word to correct bad theology or sinful behavior?" They need to see it like a coach's playbook for life, training themselves and others to live in a godly way. It prepares, empowers, and inspires us to good works. We are big on not just knowing God's Word but meditating on it until it changes the way we live. That is why there is no other counsel like biblical counsel. It takes counseling to a level that surpasses symptom relief or conforming behavior.

We equip our people to trust the Bible as the final authority and to have the power to be transformative. Hebrews 4:12 says God's Word is sharper than a two-edged sword. It cuts both ways. In other words, it sanctifies or grows the counselor while they are preparing to counsel and, of course, it has the power to change the person in need.

Beyond all this, there is no other content or theory of change that supernaturally discerns the matters of the heart. I love to tell the story of how I used to practice psychology and found it helpful for rearranging symptoms or relieving some suffering, but then God showed me the power of His Word. When I became a biblical counselor, I went from rearranging fruit to watching the Word of God come alive in a way that changes hearts and lives forever. That is why we teach the leaders of our church to be students of the Word, to be familiar with Scriptures that correspond to common heart issues, and to focus all homework on getting people in God's Word.

When we speak into someone's life, we try to follow a method of counsel that is well laid out in Galatians 6:1 – 10. The person giving counsel must ask themselves if they are intentional and gentle, always keeping restoration as the goal. We coach others to be purposeful, to come up under, and to bear burdens willingly. We see it as a privilege to be used and serve the Lord in this way.

Practically speaking, there are a few very specific things Scripture guides us to do to prepare to minister to others. First, we need to consider the Scriptures that warn us to be honest with ourselves (1 Cor. 10:12 – 13). Are we too eager to confront in a way that might be judgmental, presumptive, or condemning (Rom. 8:1)? Have we prayed a humble prayer of dependence (Ps. 139:23 – 24)? We need to be careful not come up over but instead should come alongside (Mic. 6:8).

Second, we need to be sure that we are prepared by noting core Scriptures that could bring conviction and hope. We ask people to consider writing out a plan before going with questions and verses, so they are not "reacting" in the moment but "responding" in a way that is gracious and truthful.

Let God's Spirit and God's Word do the heavy lifting. We often say, "Don't get between the hammer and the work" (see Heb. 12:7 – 11). We have all wanted a counselee to change more than they themselves seemed ready to change. In my experience, this causes us to despair or get frustrated as counselors. There is no way this does not affect your manner of counseling or response to the person in need. It may cause you to present truth in a harsh way or to give up on them or the counseling process altogether. This is not to say that when we see someone who is unmotivated or unteachable, we do not address this directly. We just don't take it personally. We take it to prayer and, if needed, directly to the person, giving them a choice to "bear their own weight" or come back when they are ready.

But what about when someone is ready to live out what they have learned in counseling? In those cases, we need to talk about encouraging the people in need with hope as they begin to walk in new-found freedom.

THE WAY OUT AND FORWARD: ENCOURAGING WITH HOPE (HEBREWS 10:23–25)

A gospel-centered approach to people's problems brings two results, if done well: *conviction* and *hope*. God is so faithful to Himself and His people. The goal of our counsel is not just trying to solve problems; we are trying to help people see through a biblical lens. As they start to see and understand God's character and gain a biblically guided self-awareness, they not only handle the present situation, they also have a way forward in any circumstance.

It is immensely encouraging to remind the person in need with verses like 1 Corinthians 10:13, which teaches four great promises of Scripture: (1) they are not the only one who has been through this, (2) this is not more than they can bear, (3) they are not without a Savior who will sustain them under the weight of their burden, and (4) they are not without a way out as they walk through and wait for God in this valley.

Giving hope is a part of every encounter with a person in need, and, specifically, giving hope is a part of pointing them to their need to abide in Christ daily as they live in authentic Christian community. Helping our people to welcome counsel as a way of life is a large part of what we call *uncommon community*. If the counsel is biblical, it will lend itself to practical application—it is sufficient for everyday life. More than that, if those giving counsel are growing in competence with God's Word, they will be specific and bring clarity to what needs to be put off and put on. They will pray and call things into the light of God's grace.

There is so much hope and power when we confess and forsake our sin and see it for what it is (Prov. 28:13). We are immediately being washed over with God's mercy (1 John 1:9). This is why we encourage people to get real with God and with their friends. The Bible instructs us to confess our sins to one another (James 5:16). Not for absolution, but because, as our pastor often says, "Disclosure is the currency of intimacy" between believers. There is no place on earth that is more suited for this type of community than the local church. Let's face it, a community centered in anything but Christ is destined to morph into a cause, a cult, or chaos.

COUNSELING IN COMMUNITY: A PARADIGM SHIFT FOR THE LOCAL CHURCH (JOHN 17:20 – 23; ROMANS 12:4 – 5)

In truth, most of us don't think of the local church as the first place to look for help. No matter how crazy it sounds or how poor we have been at proving it, God has chosen only one place on earth where lasting help and hope can be found—it is in a Bible-believing and Bible-teaching church. The Bible lays out a clear ecclesiastical mandate for the church to be (1) a hospital for the most hurting and (2) a place of ongoing equipping. It is also clear that as Christians we are to look to one another, not to the world, for help and encouragement (Heb. 3:12 – 14; 10:24 – 25).

What would the world think if the church took back its rightful place in being the primary place people turn to for counsel and care? We have been a bit naive and overly deferential to the "experts" who seem to have reams of research and big words to back up their theories. Yet they don't have what we have. Their efficacy is questionable, their methodology is flawed. Our job is to show them that our means are superior and the testimonies plentiful.

The world's hyper-private-no-one-should-ever-know approach to counseling often leaves the person feeling stigmatized, isolated, and overly trusting of the therapist as the only one who can help, and it robs others of lessons learned. It is not biblical. It is not loving. It is not vulnerable in a way that breaks the snare of the fear of man (Prov. 29:25). It does not glorify God. It does not encourage others with what God is doing. Here is the bottom line: lasting change is sustained through what we call "uncommon community." We think that contained in our methodology should be a theology of friendship. Imagine a church of what Bob Kellemen calls "soul physicians and spiritual friends,"[8] the kind of friends you can say with certainty are worth their weight in gold. We call them "advocates."

Your church is full of advocates who could help a person who is in formal counseling. Imagine an advocate and the person who just finished counseling telling their story in a small group. We ask the person receiving help to share their experience with others discreetly. It's loving, it's inspiring, and it models transparency. Until you have the person in need immersed in authentic fellowship, you are not done with formal counseling.[9] The mutual encouragement from telling "God-at-work" stories is contagious and convicting in a way that brings health to the whole body of Christ.

I want to challenge you to consider the position the local church is in today. Waves of immorality and political scandal are raging, the night is dark as pitch. People are dying to be connected and are growing weary of Facebook friends. They want face-to-face authentic friendship. Here is our time to shine and for the Bible-teaching church of biblical counseling to stand as the beacon of hope in a lost and dying generation (Eph. 3:7 – 10).

If our seminaries and churches would return to the sufficiency of

Scripture and not succumb to the pressure of being culturally relevant, we might once again gain moral authority. One practice that would shut the mouths of critics is if we stop the practice of sending wounded sheep to the blind for guidance. How can we preach sufficiency from our pulpits and send our people to worldly counsel for help? How can we expect to be known for our love when we have to send our people to other Christian agencies after the crisis we could have, in many cases, prevented? Why would anyone take us seriously, including God? If we believe that Scripture lays out the right content, the right context, and a clear methodology, then we need to close the sheep gates and care for our people inside our church communities.

There are several ways to get started on this journey. The first thing we did was to pray for God's leading and His favor. We then looked at what others were doing. Faith Church in Lafayette, Indiana, set the bar for community impact, and their annual equipping conference in February has been invaluable for our formal counselors. Grace Fellowship in Florence, Kentucky, was way ahead of us in training their small group leaders in soul care skills (more on that in chapter 15). The folks at the Association of Biblical Counselors have helped us think through a balance of both philosophical and practical counseling strategies.[10] All this is to say that we are better together and we need to band together to win this war.

Don't overestimate what you can do in a year or underestimate what you can do in five years. What we thought we could build in eighteen months is still in process four years later. We are building what we hope to be a model for the local church around the world, but we could not do it without those who have been our teachers and without God guiding every step. We hope you will join us in trusting God for the competence and sufficiency to undertake an otherwise daunting task. He is sufficient, and we are hopeful that He will bring a revival in the North American church in our lifetime.

CHAPTER 13

UNCOMMON COMMUNITY: BIBLICAL COUNSELING IN SMALL GROUPS

GARRETT HIGBEE

The doctrine of the sufficiency of Scripture naturally leads to developing a personal theology of the application of the Word in everyday life. I laid out a biblical model of counseling in the local church in chapter 12. In this chapter, I want to highlight the role of the small group, and particularly the small group *leader*, in caring for the flock. I realize that not all churches have a small group model of discipleship and care. Some of the principles I am highlighting are highly transferable to Adult Bible Fellowships and other care structures. However, some are not.

G. K. Chesterton said, "The Christian ideal has not been tried and found wanting. It has been found difficult and left untried."[1] His quote speaks to the difficulty of living out what God spoke to us through Scripture. That means not only what am I doing, but what are we doing together? Elton Trueblood also understood well the condition of today's church. He explained, "Perhaps the greatest single weakness of the contemporary Christian Church is that millions of supposed members are not really involved at all and, what is worse, do not think it strange that they are not."[2] In other words, not only should we "try to live" the Christian ideal, as Chesterton said, but as Trueblood emphasized, we need to personally involve ourselves in the life of the church—not just attending church, not just being a consumer, not just being about what we get out of it. We're talking about passionate and intentional involvement in the work of God.

That's why I want to emphasize that directive soul care should and can happen in almost any context but thrives most where people are committed to doing life together with transparency, intentional love, and regularity. That usually means smaller is better; thus the small group model is the vehicle of choice. Here is where sufficiency meets the road, so to speak, because good theology is always meant to be lived out and tested on the street level. As the world looks at the church, one way we can prove the claim that the Scriptures are timeless, relevant, and authoritative is to be known by living out our faith in love even in the face of conflict, persecution, and pain. At the end of the day, it is hard to argue against the testimony of changed lives or a united community of believers truly living out God's Word for His glory.

Mahatma Gandhi reportedly told someone that he would have converted to Christianity if he could just have found someone living out the truth of God's Word.[3] It is my prayer that we would live so that no one would be able to honestly make such a statement anymore. When we encourage and counsel one another with Scripture daily, there is really nothing that compares to seeing God break through on a very real and practical level in our lives (John 13:34–35; 17:20–23; Heb. 3:12–14).

I have been part of some form of small group for over twenty years. In my formative years in Christ, a men's group was instrumental in developing my theology, encouraging my walk, and holding me accountable. I have led small groups and trained small group leaders for over fifteen years now. My wife and I joined a couples group early in our marriage, and we are still in a small group today. Few people have been more influential in my growth in Christ than small group members who have spoken truth in love. As I became a leader in the church, I saw how the unique role of a small group leader could be both that of a gatekeeper and a first responder to people in need.

As I think back over all of this, I am reminded of what Tim Lane and Paul Tripp described regarding the power of relationships. "We live with this tension between self-protective isolation and the dream for meaningful relationships. . . . Every relational decision we make is moving in one of these directions."[4] As we focus specifically on the role of a small group leader as the front lines to soul care and equipping them to be directive counselors, let's keep this quote in mind as a reminder that people need help to maintain a connection with God and with each other.

Small groups and their leaders are often the missing link between ongoing discipleship and formal counseling as a church seeks to structure its counsel and care. As we empower and equip small group leaders, there will be a lot less need for the trauma hospital at the bottom of the cliff as they function as guardrails at the top.

At Harvest Bible Chapel, we seek to be a church *of* small groups, not simply a church *with* a small group ministry. We expect our small groups to be a place where people can be devoted to the application of the Scriptures, authentic fellowship, and fervent prayer (Acts 2:42). We believe Christian community is the primary way to give God glory and show His glory to the world. We define small groups as *uncommon communities that apply God's truth in everyday life.*[5]

Small groups usually are comprised of six to eight same gender individuals or couples committed to doing life together with growing authenticity and loving accountability. We don't think that this is possible in a large group or in a classroom atmosphere. We think that small groups functionally should primarily be about two things: (1) mutual ministry and (2) multiplication of discipleship and leaders. Notice I did not say that small groups are primarily a Bible study, a social gathering, or a support group. While we firmly believe in equipping, leading, and caring for our people, an overemphasis on any of those components would be considered a failed attempt at uncommon community.

While mutual ministry is the responsibility of all members to live out the one-another imperatives of Scripture in intentional ways throughout the week, it is, first and foremost, to be modeled and led by the small group leader. That means purposeful interactions in between the small group meetings (on the phone, during a meal together, at the church focused on Christ and His Word). It means that when the group meets, there is a rich time of application-focused teaching, compassionate accountability, and a passionate and personal prayer time each week.[6] You can imagine that a lot of things get stirred up in those times, and the equipped leader catches things small and addresses things quickly. If you are a small group leader or coach, you are in a pivotal role that we want to fully utilize as we help each other grow into the likeness of Christ and solve problems biblically.

THE ROLE OF THE SMALL GROUP LEADER AS A FIRST RESPONDER

Think back to the directive level of care in the analogy of the house in chapter 12. The small group leader belongs on the first floor in our competency structure. This requires more equipping than for the small group member because leaders give more specific direction and counsel. I call these leaders "first responders" because they often are the first leader on the scene, so to speak, when a member has a problem. They are likely to see the outward evidence (fruit) of someone in sin or suffering because they intimately "do life with" this person or couple.

To equip these small group leaders, we must teach them specific skills in observation, risk assessment, asking clarifying questions, and knowing where to go next. While these skills are helpful, you don't need in-depth formal counseling training or to be ready to hang a shingle to give help and hope to others. Think of this role as more like that of a triage nurse in a MASH unit. Some things you can treat on the spot, and other things you need to identify, diagnose biblically, and get to the right level of care.

You may be wondering if a small group leader can really be qualified to step into people's problems. The answer is, "It depends." If there is no structure to support or consult with those above them, this could be a setup for failure. If they don't meet certain criteria for character (see 1 Tim. 3 and Titus 1 for some of those traits), this could be a disaster. They also need to know their limits and know when to consult or "refer up" the chain of support and care.

However, you might be surprised at how much can be handled in a mature small group. We have been surprised at times. Most of us know that leaders vary in giftedness, experience, and being equipped. Further, not every group is mature. That is why *discerning* who is ready, *developing* them with solid equipping, and *deploying* them only when they demonstrate godly *character*, a solid *commitment*, and growing *competence* are crucial to success. Before I describe some of the specific ways we equip leaders, we need to take a look at how the Bible guides us to recruit and discern the right person to pour into.

In chapter 12 we gave reference to 2 Timothy 2:2. When choosing an apprentice to train, you want to choose faithful men and women as described in that verse. For instance, do they consistently demonstrate trust in God's Word as being authoritative? Are they able to lead a discussion that is doctrinally sound and deeply penetrating with a focus on application? Do they have the ability to inspire and influence people to be followers of Christ? Do they demonstrate that they love the hurting and are serving somewhere in the church already? Our leaders are constantly watching for apprentices and spend months if not years developing them as leaders. The majority of the people who choose to stand in the gap of another believer's life are good candidates, and the best people are already serving without needing to be asked.

THE IMPACT OF TRAINING SMALL GROUP LEADERS IN SOUL CARE

In our church, we have seen a decrease of almost 50 percent of referrals to formal counseling as we have equipped our small group and flock leaders in soul care.[7] To be honest, that trend was shocking. We knew this focus on training small group leaders and their coaches with directive counseling skills was a good idea. We knew that an ounce of prevention was worth a pound of cure. What we did not know is that the small groups and their coaches were more than ready to take on more care once we equipped them. In fact, they have been pretty possessive of their people. It was quickly apparent that they wanted to provide care even if it was hard; they just needed to know how. It was not just the leaders either. We are seeing the members increasing in purposeful care and practicing the one-another commands as well.

Two great results came out of this effort. The first was the increase in the number of leaders who came to formal soul care counselors for advice on how to handle someone in their group, allowing even more hands-on equipping. Before they would have just referred the hurting person to us; now they wanted us to consult or step in for a few sessions with them to get a care plan started. The second result was the buy-in from leaders to help identify advocates (godly friends or mentors) if they did end up referring to formal counseling.[8]

At Harvest Bible Chapel we have spent four years trying to promote and encourage the inclusion of a godly friend or mentor — an advocate for the hurting person — in the formal counseling time. This is someone who cares about the person in need, who trusts God's Word, and is in good standing with the church. (See more information on advocates in chapter 12.) We had been fairly successful in getting those in need to recruit someone who could attend the formal sessions, pray with them, do the homework with them, and be there to remind them of what was taught in the sessions. But when we trained more than seven hundred small group leaders, the advocates started to come more from the small groups, and the members started to think like advocates (Prov. 17:17). While some groups are still not there, we are slowly seeing more and more soul care going on in the entire small group culture of our church.

The health of the church rests on healthy, biblical leadership. In churches that have a vital small group ministry, their commitment to the Word of God should show up in the quality of their small group leaders. Small groups are a microcosm or building blocks for the church, made of "living stones" as described in 1 Peter 2:4–5. In my experience, directive soul care is a neglected level of equipping that could lighten the load of many pastors and formal lay counselors. Think about the job description of a small group leader as not only a triage nurse but as someone who can help others to apply Scripture in the context of daily life. While directive soul care is mostly informal and conversational in nature, isn't that some of the best counsel you have ever received? It is relevant, personal, and given in real time — not three months after everything blow ups! Leaders are equipped to redirect those in sin and encourage sufferers by praying and boldly speaking the truth in love in the moment (Eph. 4:15).

THE COMPETENCIES
OF A DIRECTIVE COUNSELOR

At Harvest Bible Chapel, the competency of small group leaders is measured by how well they lead, teach, and care for people. For the purpose of this chapter, I will focus on "care." Much goes into training a leader, but our main focus in providing soul care skills for small group leaders is to equip them to (1) assess the care needed, (2) draw out the heart of those in need, (3) respond with grace and truth, and (4) develop a biblical care plan that gets them in the Word and targets the heart.[9]

The confidence of the small group leaders to step into a difficult personal situation with their members was not very high before we started training them. They cared about their people, had a reasonable knowledge of God's Word, and were good at facilitating meetings that highlighted the sermon and its connection to their personal lives. The problem was that they knew they were often on the surface level when it came to knowing their people well (unlike the directive of Prov. 27:23). We took a survey, and a significant number of people said they would not go to someone in the group if they had a problem or personal issue to work through. I am thankful for a church that has the humility to listen. Our leaders took action that included asking our counseling leaders to forge a partnership in training leaders to care more deeply. Our church will never be the same.

Assessing Care and Drawing Out the Heart

The first thing we did was to develop training that focused on the right kind of equipping for this level of care, meaning that we had to bring our assessment and response training to a fundamental level. We began by teaching them to watch, ask, and listen well. The leaders needed to know the pitfalls of presumption and the art of good listening. You might think of that as honing their gifts and skills of discernment (Prov. 18:13, 17; 20:5; James 1:19). We taught leaders to watch for incongruence between verbal and nonverbal behavior, to look for things that seemed out of character or showed distress. We then focused the teaching on how to ask clarifying questions to reveal thoughts and motives. We emphasized listening to understand, not just to respond. Then we handed out two helpful tools. The first one we call the "S.O.S. assessment tool." The other is the "fruit to root diagnostic tool."

By using the S.O.S. tool to assess the *severity* of the issues, the *ownership* of the person needing counsel, and the *support* level around them, we gave our leaders a way to start a productive conversation with their coach around developing a care plan. (I referenced S.O.S. in chapter 12.) This also gave the leaders a clear sense of knowing how quickly to refer or to move on the problem. If risk was high or teachability low, the leader would immediately consult with their flock leader or coach — or, in extreme cases, call 911. What our leaders began to understand was that if the person in need had good godly support and teachability, that actually mitigated severity in many cases, giving more time to address the issue. We found that if a hurting person didn't have to deal with a problem or trial on their own and was willing to own their part and get help and direction from their leader, a moderate or even high level of severity (in most cases) was no longer enough to make a referral to formal counseling. This was very helpful for leaders as they realized that in the past they might have been too quick to refer if severity seemed too difficult for them to handle.

We can illustrate this with a brief case scenario. Bill is in your group; you are the leader. During accountability time in the group, Bill admits he is struggling with lust. You decide to pull him aside after group to talk. You draw him out and he admits it is consuming him. The severity seems pretty high (on a scale of 1 to 10, maybe an 8). Then you find out that Bill is deeply convicted about all this and wants to work on it. He says his good friend Rick knows about this and has tried to encourage him in the Word but didn't always know how. Now that you know he's willing to receive counsel and isn't alone, you might be less likely to refer him right away to more formal counseling. Instead, you might give them both (Rick and Bill) a workbook by Steve Gallagher called *The Walk of Repentance*[10] and ask them to share progress with you on a weekly basis. You would likely talk with your flock leader or coach to confirm your plan, but unless Bill is stuck, you keep the counsel at the directive level.

Now, if you learned that Bill's wife is devastated because she found out about this, you might increase the severity to a 9 or 10 and refer them both to formal counseling because of the marriage conflict. You would have Rick join Bill as his advocate and perhaps suggest Rick's wife support Bill's spouse. We hope you see how helpful tools like S.O.S. can be in developing a simple and biblical care plan. We know that tools are just guidelines and each case is different. What we all need to learn and grow in, however, is objectively rating severity, ownership, and support because that goes a long way in making informed decisions on the urgency and kind of care needed.

The other tool is what we call the "fruit to root diagnostic tool." The S.O.S. tool is a great way to measure *who* needs to step in and *when*. The "fruit to root" diagnostic tool is great for getting to the heart of the problem and knowing *how* to help. The small group leader usually uses the diagnostic tool when the S.O.S. indicates a moderate to low severity but good ownership of the problem. The exercise of asking questions in a private interview to get to the thoughts and motives helps them discern what may be behind the behavior of the person needing help. We look forward to getting past the behavior and getting to the heart of the issue.

We can illustrate this beginning with a question: why does this person exhibit certain "symptoms," or fruit, at this time? There are three questions we need to ask to draw out the heart. First, "What is going on in your life that is hard or difficult, and how are you responding to it?" Second, "What is going on in your thinking, and how do you feel when you are in that situation?" Third, "What do you want?" Once we know someone's pattern of thinking, their pervasive attitudes, and their motives behind the behavior, we can give specific Scripture assignments out of what we call the *Soul Care Playbook*.[11]

Let's go back to Bill. If you sat down and interviewed Bill on the history and duration of his issue with pornography, you would find out a lot about him. You'd find he started to look at porn when he was ten years old. You'd find he saw his dad hide his stuff and Bill searched it out later. You might begin to see a pattern of deceit and an attitude like "what others don't know won't hurt them." You see that he received pleasure from viewing and the masturbation that followed as a daily habit. Though it was false intimacy, he fantasized about being popular and dating the best-looking girls at school without having to work through his insecurity as he became a teenager. The pattern decreased when he got married, but when under stress or when his marriage was conflicted, he readily went back to the porn.

When you ask him what he wants and what porn is doing for him, he admits he feels unappreciated and, though feeling guilty, he doesn't know how to stop. He likes the immediate gratification and feels intimacy with his wife is too much work. As you look at his life, you see *fruit* of deception, laziness, and trying to look good. His *thoughts* seem to be based on self-pity, entitlement, and loneliness. Lies like "I am hurting no one but myself, and no one understands or appreciates me" are exposed. While you immediately put some steps of radical amputation in place (Matt. 5:27–30), you are aware that this is only the beginning. You are not sure what his *motives* are completely, but when you ask what he wants, he describes wanting a life of less responsibility, more acceptance from wife and boss, and that he needs God to break this habit.

You give Bill an assignment on deception, right out of the "playbook" that has key Scriptures like Proverbs 28:13 ("Whoever conceals his transgressions will not prosper, but he who confesses and forsakes them will receive mercy"). You point out the difference between godly and worldly sorrow based on 2 Corinthians 7:10–11. You ask him to review all the Scriptures listed and fill in the questions related to hiding or deceiving God and others. You ask Rick to help Bill get a filter on his computer, to get this assignment done, and to call and pray with him daily. What you have done is this: You considered the S.O.S. tool to make a short-term plan and used the "fruit to root diagnostic tool" to find specific homework that gets to the root of Bill's issues. Now you can go to your coach to discuss the care plan going forward.

Hopefully you are beginning to see how practical the Scriptures are and how applicable they can be in the context of a small group. An emphasis of our training is to equip our people to be specific with Scripture that hits the bull's-eye. That is why we spend a fair amount of time on biblical assessment. If you don't get the assessment right, you can waste a lot of time and further complicate a difficult situation. The beauty of this process is that it is saturated with a biblical worldview that helps everyone see Bill not as an addict or even as simply someone afflicted with a besetting sin. This is an identity problem (1 Cor. 6:9–11), a worship issue at the core of who Bill is, not a disease or behavioral problem to be curbed (Col. 2:20–23).

So, because Bill has idolatry in his heart (Col. 3:5), we target his issue as an "affection issue" instead. "Put off" and "put on" is vital, but Bill needs to repent of more than behavior here. A deeper assessment helps us develop a way to target the heart. While it is essential to have a good assessment and to be as thorough as possible, the response to the problem or concern is equally important. We teach our leaders to be gracious and to provide practical and biblical solutions.

Responding with Truth and Grace

How many times have you spoken too soon or thought you had the answer before actually knowing the full picture? I think most of us have done that many times over. We have looked at not missing the heart of the problem; now we need to focus on responding with grace and truth (John 1:14). It is always easier when we can talk from experience, so let us go back to the example of how we equip our leaders. Most of our leaders did not need more head knowledge. We are fortunate to be in a strong Bible-teaching church. Granted, steadily growing in our grasp of Scripture is essential and being able to draw out the heart gives us a good place to start. However, where a lot of novice counselors fail is in the approach and response to the problem or person at hand. We teach that it is important to consider timing, testimony, and the tone of our counsel, not just the content of our counsel.

It is encouraging to watch the groaning of leaders who recognize in training that they often moved in too soon with heavy-handed truth or waited too long, thinking it was grace. The leaders gain confidence when taught how to approach care biblically. They are taught to look for people caught in sin, to restore gently, to bear up under and come alongside (Gal. 6:1 – 2). The assignments in the *Soul Care Playbook* correspond with four common heart issues that arise in all small groups. We teach case wisdom by including scenarios on how to help people who can be disruptive, impulsive, despairing, or fearful. They learn how to approach them based on 1 Thessalonians 5:14, which warns us to not fall into the trap of "one-size-fits-all" counseling. Here is where we might look to others to make sure our approach is correct. An important cultural norm for our members should be to expect compassionate accountability and leaders who consult with other leaders at their discretion.[12] Ideally, the member who is seeking help is in the loop from the beginning, but, either way, they know the counseling is always for their good and God's glory.

We have zero tolerance for gossip. Our leaders go up the ladder of supervision only for discernment or counsel on a need-to-know basis. The flock leader is part of the "family," as is the pastor who oversees them (hence we call them "family pastors"). The group understands these leaders and their role as support and wise counsel to them (Prov. 11:14; 15:22). The small group leader knows that the flock leader has been trained with more advanced skills and that the flock leader is the gatekeeper who is generally the one who makes the final decision to refer to formal care if needed. This has been a huge help. Small group leaders would hesitate to get messy if there was no plan or support. It also decreases "false positives" from people who end up coming for corrective sessions or intensive counsel when they just needed godly direction others could have given. Remember the story of Jethro advising Moses? We don't want to wear out our highest level leaders dealing with what a flock leader and a small group leader can speak into with great effectiveness. Our thinking is that they should always try to address things in community unless severity is really high or teachability is very low. In those cases a referral might be made by the flock leader to formal counseling or to a consultation so we can address risk further or consider any discipline issues.

The small group can be instrumental not only in preventive care but also in the effectiveness of formal care. The referral to formal counseling no longer means "Hey, we are stuck! Fix this person and send them back when they are better." Proverbs 18:24 says, "A man of many companions may come to ruin, but there is a friend who sticks closer than a brother." Small groups now see their role in someone's need for counsel and care. Leaders stay informed and ask questions in accountability time and advocates are chosen more frequently. As we said before, the gains from the counseling are shared discreetly in the group by the person receiving care so everyone can be encouraged and know how to pray better. Does that sound a bit idealistic or even unrealistic? For many of us who grew up in a hyper-therapeutic, autonomous Western mind-set, it is a bit of a stretch, but we think it is biblical based on Scriptures like Hebrews 12:15, Colossians 2:8, and James 5:19 – 20. It can be messy, but advocates testify over and over that it was the most rewarding and amazing privilege they have ever had to serve in this way. Groups are growing more transparent, people are gaining confidence in God's Word, and prayer is more personal and Christ-centered than ever before.

TEN LESSONS WE HAVE LEARNED ALONG THE WAY

Please understand that we have made many mistakes along the way and do not boast in who we are and what we have done. But, along with the apostle Paul, we are glad to "boast in the Lord" (2 Cor. 10:17) as we see what God has done and is continuing to do in us and in our church. While we doubted this model could actually take root in a large church, God has done what seemed highly unlikely. He is faithful. He is powerful. He has empowered us to press into uncommon community.

Wherever God is at work, we are able, if we are careful to pay attention, to learn lessons about what to do, how to do it, and when to do it. So if you are a small group leader, a coach, or a pastor over small groups, there are some things that can really help you to implement this type of care. We would like to submit to you the following ten lessons we gleaned as God refined us and our ministry.

1. Always start by praying for God's leading based on biblical vision.
2. Get buy-in from senior leaders of the church.
3. Reassess the three C's of your leaders (character, competence, and commitment).
4. Build a consulting structure to support you and your leaders. Be sure to use it too.
5. Read great equipping resources like *Instruments in the Redeemer's Hands*.[13]

6. Create assessment and response tools that are biblical and application driven.

7. Develop case scenarios so you and your leaders can practice how to respond.

8. Teach people to go to the Scriptures based on the heart, not on "fruit" issues.

9. Carefully discern, develop, and deploy new leaders to multiply this vision.

10. Develop a social covenant and expectations that drive small group culture.

ON THE ROAD TO UNCOMMON COMMUNITY

While we do believe strongly that formal biblical counseling training is needed, we do want to say that informal directive counseling training is complementary and necessary for a true culture of caring in the local church. We are on the road to taking the stigma out of counseling and redeeming the Word for the glory of God. We see the meaning of wise counsel in Scripture as helping someone to not only be a hearer of the word, but a doer also (James 1:22). We see it as applying truth to life and speaking the truth in love for someone's edification and correction when needed (Col. 3:16–17). There are no forms to fill out or big desks separating you from the person in need, and there is no one watching the clock. We have a small group contract and a social covenant that imply "informed consent." Essentially, you are saying when you join one of our small groups, "Yes, it is your business to know how I am doing. Yes, you can be intentionally intrusive as you see fit. I understand it's for my good and God's glory."

Now, to be sure, there is a difference between obnoxiousness or going on a sin hunt and being compassionately concerned. Our small group leaders know the difference and will call out self-righteousness or the sin-centric view of the person in need. If people miss the chance to focus on their identity in Christ or put less focus on the virtues of Christ, that in itself is grist for the soul care mill.[14]

We realize there is a long road to achieving uncommon community. Even those who are ahead on the road see the destination as only something to strive for until Christ returns. That is why we have patience with each other and have paved the way with clear steps for the small group leaders to move from being more authentic to being transparent and, ultimately, to being vulnerable with God and others.[15]

Uncommon community is a paradigm shift that lifts high the Word of God and looks to the Bible as the standard for best practice. No longer will we mimic the therapeutic counseling hour as the standard of care. No longer will we put ultimate privacy over uncommon community. No longer will we say we are going to pray for someone when the best ministry opportunity is right in front of us — right now. It is a long and more difficult path, but God gives us no excuses. He asks us to take the first step and trust Him for each additional step going forward.

The bottom line is that wise counsel is ours to give and receive as commended by Scripture. It is full-orbed discipleship. A church of biblical counselors fulfills the Great Commission by living out the Great Commandment. It is for every maturing believer as we make disciples and teach others in obedience. That is why in a church of around 14,000, we have a goal of training 7,000 small group members to do intentional soul care, 700 small group leaders to do directive care, 70-plus flock leaders to do informal corrective care, and 70-plus pastors and lay counselors to do formal corrective care. Finally, because of the scope of our ministry, we have endeavored to teach seven seasoned counselors to do intensive care for the most traumatic, emotionally damaged, and enslaved people in our midst.

My encouragement to you is not to be impressed with or intimidated by our vision, but to get started on this road in your church. Start with your small groups. Give your leaders a vision to be directive counselors, and then get your coaches and pastors trained in corrective care to support the directive care and mutual ministry going on in everyday life.

Few things preach to the world like changed lives, and there are few places like small groups that testify to the sufficiency of God's Word for helping us live lives of godliness. God is in the everyday interactions, and our belief is tested in everyday relationships. It would be short-sighted and sad to test the power of prayer, the gospel, or the doctrine of sufficiency only in our worst crises. I hope you now have a vision for equipping the saints at every level of care. I hope you are inspired to get equipped yourself, to equip lay leaders for ministry, and to multiply ministry through your best leaders. Finally, I hope you will join us and others in trying to create uncommon community in your local church.

CHAPTER 14

SPEAKING THE TRUTH
IN LOVE

JONATHAN HOLMES AND LILLY PARK

Paul Miller wrote, "Love moves toward people, even if that means confrontation. It doesn't leave them alone in their suffering or in their selfishness. Sometimes people are so paralyzed that unless we intrude, unless we break through both of our natural reserves, we can't love them."[1] Such words reflect the wisdom of Proverbs 27:6: "Faithful are the wounds of a friend; profuse are the kisses of an enemy."

Regardless of whether you are a biblical counselor or a professional therapist, all of us talk. Not only do we talk, but we tend to talk quite a bit. Once you stop and think about it, many of us probably wake up talking and close our day talking. "Good morning." "Good night." Words, language, conversation, and talking are such a frequent aspect of our life that it is no wonder it's also something to which we do not give much thought.

Studies and estimates have been done on the amount of words spoken by the average person. Louann Brizendine, in her book *The Female Brain*, estimates that the average woman speaks 20,000 words a day compared to 7,000 for men.[2] For women, that breaks down to a very loquacious thirteen words a minute, while men clock in at a relatively reserved five words per minute. In their book *Relationships: A Mess Worth Making*, Paul Tripp and Tim Lane wrote, "Because our talk lives in the world of the ordinary, it is easy to forget its true significance. It is easy to forget the impact our words have on every relationship. There has never been a good relationship without good communication. And there has never been a bad relationship that didn't get that way in part because of something that was said."[3]

Something that is so ubiquitous as conversation then must be given due thought. Why do we speak? To whom should we speak? How should we speak? What should we speak about? All of these questions find their ultimate *telos*, or aim, in Paul's letter to the Ephesians church, where he said, "Rather, *speaking the truth in love*, we are to grow up in every way into him who is the head, into Christ, from whom the whole body, joined and held together by every joint with which it is equipped, when each part is working properly, makes the body grow so that it builds itself up in love" (Eph. 4:15–16, emphasis added).

It is this *telos* that should guide the believer's communication and orientation. It is high time we recognize that conversation, words, quips, asides, and the like are never neutral. Rather, our body of words and communication actually constitute and reveal what we ultimately love and desire.[4] It is no overstatement when theologians Peter Gentry and Stephen Wellum comment, "If there is any way to summarize in just a few words the instructions for behavior and conduct in the new creation community, it is 'speaking the truth in love.' "[5]

If we were to pause and linger over that phrase, *speaking the truth in love*, what exactly is Paul writing about? What kind of ministry is envisioned here? Is this something just for professional counselors and therapists? Perhaps just for pastors and teachers in the local church? Or does Paul envision an every-member ministry?

If we divide up the phrase "speaking the truth in love" into its three constituent parts — speaking, truth, and love — we will be able to better understand Paul's words and goals. While these three components all might exist in part in various psychologies, together these three parts, sanctified and redeemed by Christ, form the heart and soul of Christ-centered biblical counseling. They are our mission and calling as counselors, our growth and maturity in Christlikeness.

SPEAKING

The first question that needs to be asked as we approach the Scriptures and counseling is, "Why do we even need to speak?" After all, an entire counseling paradigm of client-centered therapy founds itself on being nondirective in counseling.[6] The anecdotal scene of a client sitting on a couch free-associating is still what many people have in mind, perhaps, when they think about counseling and seeing a counselor. The counselor is simply there to listen (and to listen well and empathetically) and reflect back the client's words and thoughts.

The Bible, though, as it so often does, gives us a grander vision for our speaking and why we speak. The reason we speak and are called to speak lies in the fact that our God Himself speaks. Not only does He speak—"God *said* ..." (Gen. 1:3)—but He speaks to us—"God said *to them* ..." (Gen. 1:28). Paul Tripp wrote, "The ability to communicate is one of the things that separates us from the rest of creation. We are people and we talk."[7]

As creatures made in God's image, the unique ability to communicate in understandable language with all its accompanying nuances, syntax, and variations makes human beings distinct from all of creation. That ability is not to be understated. As image bearers of God, each and every time we speak we bear witness and testimony to God our creator.

Not only do we speak because God created us with that capacity as image bearers, but He also commands us to *talk* about specific things. Moses commanded the people in Deuteronomy 6:6–9:

> These words that I command you today shall be on your heart. You shall teach them diligently to your children, and shall *talk* of them when you sit in your house, and when you walk by the way, and when you lie down, and

when you rise. You shall bind them as a sign on your hand, and they shall be as frontlets between your eyes. You shall write them on the doorposts of your house and on your gates. (Emphasis added.)

One gets a sense from the text that not only was there to be a formal ministry and teaching of God's commands to the people, namely to love God and love others, but there was also an everyday, informal conversation that was meant to take place between parents and children about these commands. Parents were commanded to *talk* at all of the most ordinary of times: waking up, walking about, and lying down. Speaking the things of God was meant to be an ordinary, yet redemptive, mode of God's plan for His people. It should not surprise us then, as we fast-forward into history, that Paul essentially commands the same thing: speak the truth in love to build up Christ's body.

This speaking ministry in Scripture is detailed and noted in various ways, particularly through the use of words like "instruct," "admonish," and "encourage."

- Acts 20:31: "Therefore be alert, remembering that for three years I did not cease night or day to *admonish* every one with tears." (Emphasis added in all passages.)
- Romans 15:14: "I myself am satisfied about you, my brothers, that you yourselves are full of goodness, filled with all knowledge and able to *instruct* one another."
- 1 Corinthians 4:14: "I do not write these things to make you ashamed, but to *admonish* you as my beloved children."
- Ephesians 6:22: "I have sent him to you for this very purpose, that you may know how we are, and that he may *encourage* your hearts."
- Colossians 3:16: "Let the word of Christ dwell in you richly, *teaching* and *admonishing* one another in all wisdom, singing psalms and hymns and spiritual songs, with thankfulness in your hearts to God."
- 1 Thessalonians 5:11 – 15: "Therefore encourage one another and

build one another up, just as you are doing. We ask you, brothers, to respect those who labor among you and are over you in the Lord and *admonish* you, and to esteem them very highly in love because of their work. Be at peace among yourselves. And we urge you, brothers, *admonish* the idle, *encourage* the fainthearted, *help* the weak, be patient with them all."

Dietrich Bonhoeffer wrote in his now classic book *Life Together*, "What we are concerned with here is the free communication of the Word from person to person, not by the ordained ministry which is bound to a particular office, time and place. We are thinking of that unique situation in which one person bears witness in human words to another person, bespeaking the whole consolation of God, the admonition, the kindness, and severity of God."[8] This is the vision for our speaking. That in speaking we imitate our heavenly Father and carry out our missional calling to build up the body of Christ.

THE TRUTH

Examining the second part in Paul's phrase "speaking the truth in love," we find ourselves asking, "What exactly does he mean by *truth*?" Earlier in the chapter in Ephesians 4:4–6, in a very confessional declaration, Paul wrote, "There is one body and one Spirit—just as you were called to the one hope that belongs to your call—one Lord, one faith, one baptism, one God and Father of all, who is over all and through all and in all." It is this truth that the believer is called to speak: truth that affirms, encourages, and sustains one another in body and spirit, in our faith, in our baptism, in our confession as believers in Jesus Christ.

A criticism of biblical counseling has been that biblical counselors, while being well-intended, can use God's Word, the truth, in several unhelpful and harmful ways:

- *Reductionism.* In this form, counselors take a verse out of context and isolate it from the greater story line of the Bible. For example,

Philippians 4:13 is not a promise that you can do whatever you would like to do, but rather Paul's steadfast commitment in God to enable contentment in whatever circumstances he might find himself. Reductionism of the Scriptures in counseling can lead to erroneous interpretations and applications of the Scripture that often do damage to the integrity of the Word.

- *Sentimentalism.* In this form, the Bible is used in a trite and platitudinous way. We have all encountered people who, while meaning well, say things like, "God loves you and has a plan for you." Sentimentalism functions as sort of a functional Band-Aid when heart surgery is required. The prophet Jeremiah lamented: "They tried to heal my people's serious injuries as if they were small wounds. They said, 'It's all right, it's all right.' But really, it is not all right" (Jer. 8:11 NCV).

- *Moralism.* In this form, the Bible is used moralistically. The broad strokes and themes of Scripture are isolated from the larger story line of the Bible. The counselor calls the counselee to moral goodness, but disconnects it from the empowering grace of God. Moralism seeks to call people to natural virtue and goodness without telling them of a Redeemer who has lived a perfect life in their place.

- *Legalism.* In this form, the Bible is used as a rule book of dos and don'ts. The empowering work of the Holy Spirit is sidelined. Rather than emphasizing the already/not yet nature of our progressive sanctification, the legalist lobs out imperatives and commands disconnected from the truths of Scripture. It reminds us of Paul's warning in Galatians 3:3: "Are you so foolish? Having begun by the Spirit, are you now being perfected by the flesh?" Legalism lobs out imperatives of Scriptures without the indicatives of Scripture, which then leads to a set of impossibilities for the counselee to biblically live out.

We (Lilly and Jonathan) have been guilty of these. It is much easier to wield the truth of God's Word in a way that accommodates expediency than it is to "rightly divid[e] the Word of truth" (2 Tim. 2:15 KJV). The dynamic some might find is that their study of Scripture is something they have been thoroughly trained in through Bible studies, small groups, reading commentaries, etc. However, when it comes to actually speaking God's truth in conversation, many of us find ourselves overwhelmed and ill-equipped.

One caricature of biblical counseling sees the counselor as simply quoting Scripture, stringing passage to passage, and waxing eloquently from Genesis to Revelation while the counselee studiously scribbles notes and nods. This is not what we mean when we talk and write about *speaking the truth in love.* David Powlison, speaking of the role of the Bible in biblical counseling, helpfully brings clarity and balance to the conversation.

> If Bible citation were the chief methodological distinctive, how could you have a conversation with anyone?! Honest and wise conversations (like wise sermons) abound with many things: questions, comments, stories, metaphors, current events, observations, personal details, opinions, asides that double back around later, wit, emotional reactions, silences, particularizing emphases, heartfelt concerns — and the Word of Life, truth, wisdom, and mercy, shaping all. This is how Jesus converses (and preaches).
>
> The distinctive of biblical counseling is that it is shaped by the worldview and purposes of the Savior God who has given His Word — not that every sentence must contain the word "God" or refer to a text. Whether or not to quote chapter and verse is a choice (in a conversation as in a sermon), just as expressing the same truth in your own words or by a story is a choice. That choice is shaped by wise love for the particular person with whom you are now speaking. If you see with biblical eyes and intend with biblical intentions, then you are always reaching after the things that most matter.[9]

Did you see and savor that last paragraph? Powlison notes that *wise love* is what guides our expression of God's truth. Sounds familiar, right? That is exactly how the apostle Paul described our speaking of truth.

IN LOVE

As counselors, speaking the truth in love concerns not only how we speak but also how we relate to others. It tests our integrity. It says "no!" to superficial interactions or arrogant demeanors. Peter Gentry and Stephen Wellum assert that speaking the truth in love is not only concerned with obedience to God and sin (vertical relationship) but also with the reality of living in a covenant community with fellow brothers and sisters in Christ (horizontal relationships).[10] If we view people as created beings in the image of God, then we will speak the truth in love. As redeemed beings, we display the divine image when we love one another.

Have you met Christians who are zealous for biblical knowledge and know a lot about the Bible, but you hesitate to ask them for advice? Maybe their suggestions come across as ultimatums and they treat you differently if you differ with them. Or maybe they focus more on exactness rather than efforts and faithfulness.

Many years ago, a pastor discussed with a small group of leaders the danger of crushing people's spirit. He said that being right was not more important than loving others. We crush someone's spirit when we prioritize being right at all costs. This wrong desire sometimes leads to harsh words or tone (Prov. 15:4). There is a similar element and pattern of thought in Paul's teaching in 1 Corinthians 12–14 that he could be gifted in many ways, but if he did not possess love, he was "nothing" (1 Cor. 13:2).

Here's another example. Joe and Kelly are passionate about helping others with their marriages because they've experienced a renewal in their marriage through counseling. When they heard that Mary was in the process of a divorce, they tried to change her mind, sharing biblical passages on marriage and using their marriage as an example of what could happen to Mary's marriage. Sadly, Mary goes home very hurt because Joe and Kelly were so focused on convincing Mary, they didn't realize that their harsh demeanor added more weight to Mary's burdens. Instead of speaking the truth in love, they overlooked the context of Mary's marriage problems, which differed from their situation, and they focused on solutions to the problem rather than ministering to a person.

Joe and Kelly had biblical knowledge and good intentions in trying to restore Mary's marriage, but they failed to practice the two greatest commandments (Matt. 22:37 – 39).

What Love Is Not

Before discussing biblical love further, it must be distinguished from the world's perception of it. The two concepts are very different, and we often mix them in our understanding of love. In many ways, movies, TV shows, and music, to name a few, have distorted biblical love, presenting love as something that is superficial, volatile, and self-focused. In a culture that values tolerance, individualism, and pragmatism, we are confronted with endless ways to compromise biblical love, so we must be that much more discerning and intentional in loving others.

Specifically, Christians must be careful not to hold on to a one-dimensional view of love — let's just be nice to each other. In talking about biblical love, D. A. Carson says Christians face the pressure to be nice at all costs, lest they be viewed as hypocrites:

> "Niceness" means smiling a lot and never ever hinting that anyone may be wrong about anything (because that isn't nice). In the local church, it means abandoning church discipline (it isn't nice), and in many contexts it means restoring adulterers (for instance) to pastoral office at the mere hint of broken repentance. After all, isn't the church about forgiveness? Aren't we supposed to love one another? And doesn't that mean that above all we must be, well, nice?[11]

His examples are too common in how Christians avoid speaking the truth in love. As a result, some of us excel at being nice, but not at loving others. After all, being nice is easier than loving others because niceness could be superficial, but love, defined biblically, involves the whole person. It is God-centered rather than me-centered. While growing up, we probably have heard, "It isn't nice to …" more than "It isn't loving to …"

The Dynamics of Love

Love is the defining characteristic of Christians. In Colossians 3:12–14, Paul wrote that love binds the Christian qualities–such as kindness, humility, meekness, and patience–in perfect harmony. In Philippians 1:9, Paul prayed for their love to continually grow (cf. 1 Thess. 4:9–12). This love is rooted in God's truth and results in wise living, so that they are prepared for Christ's return and to glorify God (vv. 10–11).

When asked which commandment is the greatest, Jesus responded that it is loving God with our whole being (Matt. 22:37–38). But He didn't stop there. He added that the second greatest commandment is loving our neighbor as ourselves. These two commandments fulfill "all the Law and the Prophets." They emphasize the supremacy of love and its significance to God. If our focus is more on loving God and others, then we'll obey His commandments less legalistically and more naturally. For instance, we would not use God's name in vain when we love Him; we would not steal from someone we love. Ironically, the Pharisees believed they were loving God by scrupulously obeying the Law, but they missed the heart of the Law (Luke 11:42).

Following Christ means loving one another (John 13:34–35), but modeling Christ is not about being a loving therapist who merely listens. We tend to oversimplify Christ's love when we solely portray Christ as a gentle, compassionate person who is always nice. Christ was compassionate (Mark 6:34; Luke 7:11–15), but He also confronted sin and expressed righteous anger (Mark 11:15–18; Matt. 21:12–13). Likewise, the same Paul who wrote 1 Corinthians 13 also confronted Peter when the gospel was at stake (Gal. 2:11–14). We too, as counselors, should confront others in sin, but with love as our motivation. A helpful point to keep in mind is that loving others sometimes results in offending them, but they shouldn't be offended by our demeanor.

The humbling reality is that we can love others only by depending on the Holy Spirit. It's not as easy as saying "amen" to loving others. As Galatians 5:22 says, love is the fruit of the Spirit, so it grows as we meditate on and practice God's Word. Too often we try to love others by our own efforts, neglecting God's Word and the Holy Spirit, but it inevitably fails. We are also dependent on the Holy Spirit for patience, which cannot exist without love. Whether we're admonishing the idle, encouraging the fainthearted, or helping the weak, we need patience (1 Thess. 5:14) because speaking the truth in love is an ongoing process.

What if you're struggling to love someone? Maybe that person repeatedly lies to you or refuses to change. According to Jesus, we have no reason to not love someone. He knows that it is easier to love those who love us, but He says that love must be extended even to our enemies. In Luke 6:27–36 Jesus describes ways to love our enemies: bless those who curse you, pray for those who abuse you; instead of returning affliction, be generous; treat them as you would want to be treated; and be merciful, even as your Father is merciful. What challenging verses on loving people! "Jesus loved because He was a loving person, not because He found attractive qualities in those He loved. His followers are to be loving people, not simply to be drawn to attractive people."[12]

May we pray to be loving people so that we love well. And we can be loving people because we have received God's love, which makes us grateful beings. We remember that God loved us when we least deserved it (Rom. 5:8; Eph. 2:4). Our struggle changes from "Why should I love my enemy?" to "What are some ways to love my enemy?" As a result, we pursue godliness and live counterculturally by loving even our enemies (Matt. 5:47–48).

God's love is central at both the beginning of and throughout our Christian life. Truly, loving others is a defining mark of someone who knows God's love (Luke 6:36–50; 1 John 4:7–8).

TOGETHER FOR THE BETTER

Like so often happens, these three words—*speaking, truth, love*—together make up a whole that is greater than the individual parts. Like a fragmented diamond, just one piece of it apart from the whole is nice, but not as valuable, not as precious, not as beautiful. Put all the pieces together and you have a magnificent, stunning diamond. Speaking the truth in love is like that. Dissected and disconnected from the larger framework of the passage and the book, one can quickly be in danger of overemphasizing one to the harm of the other.

At times biblical counselors can bear the reputation of counseling in a manner that elevates the opportunity to speak the truth over and against to whom they are speaking and what manner they speak it in. As counselors, we're always seeking to speak the truth in love in the context of relationship. Counselor Tim Ackley wrote:

> We biblical counselors tend to be pretty good at speaking truth, but I have learned from experience that it is often hard for us to speak truth within a genuine relationship. When people come in with their sins, struggles, and sufferings, we respond with "wise" answers. But it's often a one-way process with very little give and take, where a relationship isn't *that* necessary. But, truth and relationship *together* are the fundamental ingredients of biblical counseling that "lives." Biblical counseling cannot be reduced to a few well-timed verses, a strategy for change, a prayer, and a handshake.... Scripture is so much more robust and lively than that: it is God-breathed.... As a pastor and counselor, I aim to be as personal as He is.[13]

Speaking the Truth in Love in Real Life

While working on this chapter, I (Lilly) had a very hard experience where I was tested in speaking the truth in love. Isn't God's timing perfect? It started when a brother in Christ confronted me. There was a lot of speaking but not much love.

For the next few days, I thought about the best way to handle the situation. Should I confront him or place this conflict in the "love covers a multitude of sins" category? After thinking, praying, and consulting a godly person, it seemed wise to meet with this brother in Christ and involve another person as a mediator and witness.

At the meeting, I shared my concerns about what had happened and a few Scripture verses that affected me (speaking the truth) and my motive to please God by seeking peace/unity (in love). Throughout the meeting, I continually reminded myself that this meeting was not about dissecting what had happened, but restoring our relationship, which helped me to speak less and stay focused on God's purposes. At first, progress seemed unlikely, but then something amazing happened. The atmosphere in the office changed from an icy, cold place to a warm, loving haven as reconciliation slowly thawed away misunderstandings and hurt.

By the end of the meeting, the three of us spent some time reflecting on how God used this meeting to be a blessing, and that it needs to happen more often among Christians. Prior to the meeting, I prayed for reconciliation, but God exceeded my expectations by using the meeting to strengthen our relationships and unity.

If the meeting hadn't ended well, would it have been a failure? I don't think so, because speaking the truth in love is not so much about a happy ending as it is about obedience to God (the great commandments) and furthering His kingdom (edifying one another, unity). If reconciliation hadn't happened, then I would have continued to pray for this brother in Christ and trusted God to work in both of our hearts. Speaking the truth in love was not easy, but it was worth the effort, because the gospel was displayed so powerfully and in a way that would not have been known if we had chosen to not love one another.

The conflict was a reminder of our sinful nature, and the reconciliation was a reminder of our identities in Christ. The experience was a reminder that speaking the truth in love is a serious aspect of practicing the gospel for God's glory.

As I (Jonathan) read Lilly's story, I was struck by some observations that we both believe would be helpful to you:

- We all desperately need help. We've all been in situations and times where our words have pierced like thrusts from a sword rather than brought healing to the soul. Thank God that His mercies are new every day.
- Motivation is key. Lilly's motives going into the conversation

were not framed by selfishness, but rather her desire to have unity realized in the body of Christ. When your motivation for speaking the truth in love is to build up the body of Christ rather than selfish pretext, it will enable the conversation to remain strong even if it becomes tense or uncomfortable. Your conscience will not allow an easy escape, because it's not about you.

• Lilly wisely saw that regardless of the result (success or failure), her call to speak the truth in love is not based on "happy endings." When the apostle Paul calls the church to speak the truth in love, that command is not based primarily on how others will receive it, but is an overarching command to build up the body of Christ and fulfill our calling.

PRACTICAL SUGGESTIONS

As counselors we often face ditches on two sides of the road: our counseling methodology remains firmly theoretical (orthodoxy with no orthopraxy) or our counseling methodology becomes pragmatic and disconnected from a solid Christ-centered theology. Seeking to navigate both of those guardrails, in addition to laying out the theological foundation for speaking the truth in love, we want to include some helpful suggestions and framework to actualize that process.

Prayer

Any type of conversation or movement toward another person must be prefaced and sustained by prayer. It is telling that many believers use the adverb "just" when talking of prayer. "Well, I suppose I'll *just* pray about it," as if prayer is plan B rather than our first line of communication.

Examination

If prayer is the preface, the examination allows the believer to come before God and remove the log from his own eye. Whatever the conversation might entail, thoughtful examination of the motives of the heart is crucial in moving toward one another.

Looking

Paul Miller says, "Love begins with looking."[14] It comes as no surprise, but in one of the first interactions we have recorded in Genesis 4, God sees Cain and his countenance before He moves in to speak with him. Be looking for opportunities for wise and redemptive conversations. We might be surprised by how many moments we let slide by in a day without moving toward the hurting and the struggling all because we are not looking.

Timing

Proverbs 15:23 says, "To make an apt answer is a joy to a man, and a word in season, how good it is!" Timing and setting are important. As thoughtful counselors, we should be aware of submitting our timetable to God's timetable. When is the best time to approach the person? What setting is most conducive to conversation? Is it a coffee shop, your living room, or after church on a Sunday?

Delivery

The Proverbs again are so helpful. While Proverbs definitely values wise words, Solomon also placed a high priority on *how* those words are delivered, much like we have already fleshed out in this chapter. Proverbs 16:21 says, "The wise of heart is called discerning, and sweetness of speech increases persuasiveness."

Loving

Remember who you are speaking to. You are speaking to an image bearer of God. You have an opportunity in the still small moments of your day to interact and bear God's image by speaking to this fellow image bearer. It is probably not an overstatement in some ways to say your conversation — your speaking the truth in love — is actually a form of worship.

Richard Baxter wrote, "We ourselves will take all things well from one that we know doth entirely love us. We will put up with a blow that is given us in love, sooner than with a foul word that is spoken to us in malice or in anger."[15]

These suggestions are not meant to form a linear pattern for the conversation, but rather a framework and mind-set to have as one enters into Christ-centered conversations with others. Coming full circle, Paul's words in Ephesians 4:15 – 16 serve as the clarion call for all who counsel:

> Rather, speaking the truth in love, we are to grow up in every way into him who is the head, into Christ, from whom the whole body, joined and held together by every joint with which it is equipped, when each part is working properly, makes the body grow so that it builds itself up in love.

CHAPTER 15

THE COMPETENCY
OF THE BIBLICAL
COUNSELOR

BRAD HAMBRICK

One of the classic passages that was foundational in the launch of the modern biblical counseling movement was Romans 15:14. In this verse, Paul wrote to the believers in the small house churches dotting the countryside in Rome that he was convinced that they were competent to counsel. Paul said he based his conviction about their competence on some very specific evidence — they were full of goodness (growing in Christlike character), complete in knowledge (growing in their ability to relate God's truth to their lives with wisdom and insight), and committed to one-another ministry in the body of Christ.

Like the apostle Paul and my fellow coauthors of *Scripture and Counseling*, I am committed to the robust and rich sufficiency, authority, necessity, relevancy, and profundity of Scripture. Like Paul and my coauthors, I am committed to equipping God's people so they are competent to counsel. We bring these two commitments together in this chapter as we explore the relationship between the *sufficiency of Scripture* and the *competency of the counselor.*

Practically, we can ponder the relationships between sufficiency and competency by asking, "How many things do you own that are more sufficient than you are competent?"

- Could your smartphone make life more organized and efficient if you knew how to use it better?
- Is your grill or stove capable of producing more gourmet food than you are capable of preparing?
- Could the tools in your garage build an addition to your home if you had the patience, strength, and skill?

With even this brief reflection, we can see that sufficiency and competency are distinct but related concepts.

- Sufficiency is the ability of a resource to achieve a designated task or desired result.
- Competency is the ability of a practitioner to use a resource to its full potential.
- Sufficiency of an object is measured independent from the competency of its user.
- Competency influences whether sufficiency has the opportunity to express its full potential.

We live in a day when there are a growing number of people doing biblical counseling in a variety of settings and with many different levels of training and experience. This is a special blessing to the church and a genuine expression of how God desires care for His people.

- Laypeople are caring for one another in day-to-day life; many may not consider what they do "counseling."
- Formal lay counselors are serving a defined, supervised role within a local church or para-church ministry.
- Pastors with one or more seminary classes in counseling are shepherding God's people.
- Individuals with master's or doctoral degrees in counseling plus a

larger quantity of supervised counseling experience are counseling in various settings.

This raises important questions for the church. How do these various roles and levels of training relate to competence? How should a church organize and utilize these ministries? All churches have at least two groups (people and pastors), but what advantages or opportunities exist with each group? What disadvantages or limitations exist with each group that a church would need to consider?

We will seek to provide guidance on these issues by answering three questions. First, does the Bible call us to recognize levels or layers of competence among Christians? Second, does the Bible recognize particular types or niches of ministry competence among Christians? Third, what "layers of competence" emerge from Scripture or are useful for the modern church when it comes to counseling-related ministry?

DOES THE BIBLE RECOGNIZE LAYERS OF COMPETENCE?

An early example of the Bible advocating for layers of competence is Exodus 18:21–23 (emphasis added).

> "Moreover, look for *able men* from all the people, men *who fear God*, who are trustworthy and hate a bribe, and place such men over the people *as chiefs of thousands, of hundreds, of fifties, and of tens.* And let them judge the people at all times. *Every great matter they shall bring to you, but any small matter they shall decide themselves.* So *it will be easier for you,* and they will bear the burden with you. If you do this, God will direct you, you will be able to endure, and all this people also will go to their place in peace."

Advising people on their personal and interpersonal struggles was becoming overwhelming for Moses. His father-in-law, Jethro, gave him divinely inspired advice.

- Find "able men." This means that not everyone was competent for this task.

- "Who fear God." Character was to be a key part of identifying competence.
- "Chiefs of thousands, of hundreds, of fifties, and of tens." Even among the able men there were markers of competence that differentiated their abilities.
- "Every great matter they shall bring to you." Life struggles passed through a competency hierarchy in order to provide adequate care for everyone and more experienced care for harder cases.
- "So it will be easier for you." This levels-of-competence approach was to protect the time and energy of Moses as the leader of God's people.

A similar recognition of layers of competence is found in the New Testament in Galatians 6:1–4.

> Brothers, if anyone is caught in any transgression, *you who are spiritual* should restore him in a spirit of gentleness. *Keep watch on yourself,* lest you too be tempted. *Bear one another's burdens,* and so fulfill the law of Christ. For if anyone thinks he is something, when he is nothing, he deceives himself. But let each one test his own work, and then his reason to boast will be in himself alone and not in his neighbor [emphasis added].

Here we find Paul, in the context of one-another care, offering counsel about counseling competence:

- "You who are spiritual." Paul recognized that growing spiritual maturity was a foundational requirement for effective personal ministry.
- "Keep watch on yourself." Being recognized at a higher level of competence did not remove the need for leaders to examine themselves and receive care.
- "Bear one another's burdens." The responsibility to care was not placed exclusively on the "spiritual" but spread to everyone (i.e., "one another" implies those in normal Christian community); otherwise the same problems would emerge that faced Moses in Exodus 18.

DOES THE BIBLE RECOGNIZE TYPES OF COMPETENCE?

Not only does the Bible recognize layers of competence, it also recognizes types of competence. As counselors gain experience and pass through layers of competence, it is likely that they will identify certain types of life struggles they are particularly effective at counseling.

Where do we find a biblical basis for this? The entire church leadership and mobilization structure of the New Testament is based on a recognition of various types of competence.

The distinction between deacons and elders found in Acts 6:1–7 and 1 Timothy 3:1–13 is based on a recognition of different types of competence. The emphasis on spiritual gifts in the New Testament (Rom. 12:3–8; 1 Cor. 12:1–11) is a recognition that God intentionally equips individual Christians for particular types of ministry within the church.

This does not mean that the Bible is saying that every member is to become a "counseling specialist" or that only people of high-level counseling competence should offer guidance in the church. Every believer is expected to express spiritual gifts such as evangelism, generosity, and hospitality. No Christian can simply say of these things, "That is not my gift," and be exempt. But the New Testament also recognizes that God uniquely equips certain believers to be excellent in these areas.

BEFORE PROPOSING LAYERS OF COMPETENCE

Two other issues need to be addressed before a proposal for layers of competence is made. The first relates to the strengths and weaknesses of using education and experience as the criteria of competence. There are many people who have strong giftings of discernment, life administration, relational savvy, and emotional awareness who are more helpful than a counselor with a degree who lacks these qualities. There are also examples of people who have completed a program of study, yet are ineffective counselors.

"Gifting" is very hard to measure objectively and to communicate to a stranger seeking counseling. So it is a category that is most helpful within a community with preestablished relationships and mutual trust. When counseling entails the soul care of two church members in a community small enough for mutual awareness, then gifting can be very effective for communicating competence.

Education and experience are used in this chapter for three reasons: (1) they are tangible enough to communicate with a stranger, (2) they are utilized by almost every counseling enterprise, and (3) they relate to ethical-liability issues a church should consider when creating, clarifying, or expanding a counseling ministry.

This chapter explores only the human side of the competency-sufficiency relationship. Just as a church looks at reasonable budget projections but should not doubt God's ability to provide extraordinary funds, this chapter considers the preparation necessary for a counselor for various formal and informal ministry settings, but recognizes that the Holy Spirit can provide supernatural insight and change.

Second, we need to ponder where a pastor is on this spectrum of competence. The skill set of each pastor varies — often significantly. This is true of every area of ministry competence: teaching, administration, leadership, counseling, etc.

Part of the humility of a pastor and the wisdom of a church is to know the strengths and weaknesses, giftings and limitations of their pastor(s). Related to counseling, every pastor is called to shepherd God's flock through the pulpit/teaching ministry of the Word, through the personal/counseling ministry of the Word, and through overseeing the equipping of the flock for competent one-another ministry. At the same time, it is my conviction that the office of pastor does not in and of itself endow the pastor with a particular level of counseling competence. A pastor's counseling competence develops through many means, such as training in biblical counseling, personal growth in Christlikeness, prayer, dependence on the Holy Spirit, and experience in ministering the Word personally to God's people. Thus, I advise that each person who fills the office of pastor and each church who calls a pastor should utilize the levels (or their preferred categories) developed in this chapter to identify the pastor's current competence and desired "next steps" of growth.

Since pastors bear the responsibility for the souls under their care (Heb. 13:17), this chapter can assist pastors in assessing which cases can be handled well in one-another ministry, which they should counsel, and what kind of ministries need to be created within or identified alongside the church. Pastoral responsibility for soul care requires pairing people with a helper who is a good fit for their struggle in the instructing-encouraging phases of care. And it involves serving as the leader in the authoritative disciplinary roles of care when needed.

As you read through these layers of competency, I invite you to consider two questions:

1. How do each of these layers of competence relate to counseling ethics? The largest part of counseling ethics requires knowing what you (the counselor) are *competent* to do, not just what your primary resource (the Bible) is *sufficient* to do.
2. Where am I currently on this spectrum of competence and, if desired, what are the "next steps" I would need to take to grow to the next layer of competency?

LAYERS OF COMPETENCY

"Layers of competency" are not specifically defined by Scripture. Like pastor-to-member ratios, the frequency with which a church takes the Lord's Supper, whether pastors must train in seminaries, and what worship styles to employ, the Bible leaves this open for individual churches to decide. The parameters Scripture does provide include the following:

- Pastor-teachers should be shepherds of the soul through the pulpit ministry of the Word and the personal ministry of the Word, and they should oversee the equipping of the body to speak the truth in love (Acts 20:25–38; Eph. 4:11–16; 1 Thess. 2:7–12; 5:14; 2 Tim. 2:2; 3:15–17; 4:1–2; 1 Peter 3:1–4).

- Every church member should be involved in caring competently for other church members (Rom. 15:14).
- There are unique gifts and talents that allow some to serve in unique ways (Acts 13:2).
- Those with excellent gifts and personal passion in caring for others should be equipped (Eph. 4:12), utilized (Ex. 31:1–3), and potentially compensated (1 Tim. 5:18) accordingly.

In this chapter, I am proposing five layers of competency:

1. One-another ministry
2. Lay counselor/recovery group/mentor
3. Formally educated, gaining experience (graduate intern)
4. Trained and experienced general practitioner
5. Experienced specialist

Only the first layer of competency (one-another ministry) is taken directly from Scripture. The subsequent layers seek to honor the scriptural principles established in the first two sections of this chapter in light of modern certification and education opportunities.

The latter layers and accompanying descriptions will not be agreed on by everyone inside or outside the biblical counseling movement. As with the reading competency expected of an "average second grader," there will be debate. But it is hoped that the layers provided can do two things:

1. *Start conversation.* Each church or para-church ministry must define what is competent for its setting. An ecclesiastical equivalent of the state licensing boards is unrealistic. If this proposal sparks a conversation in ministries where the definition of competence is unclear or absent, it will have served its purpose.
2. *Illustrate a team approach.* Too often distinctions breed competition and mistrust. If that is the result of this chapter, then it is a colossal failure. As each layer of competency is defined, efforts will be made to illustrate how that layer provides something

good that the other layers cannot provide and how each layer has limitations the others can strengthen.

To effectively facilitate these conversations and a team approach, each layer of competency will be examined in the same five areas: (1) scope of ministry, (2) level of training, (3) level of experience, (4) advantages and opportunities, and (5) limitations and weaknesses.

One-Another Ministry

SCOPE OF MINISTRY

Every member of a local church bears the responsibility to know others meaningfully, comfort those who are suffering, confront sin, and reinforce other believers' identity in Christ. At this layer of competency, we all do counseling every day—we hear people's struggles, make some evaluation, and offer words intended to provide encouragement and/or guidance.

One-another ministry is done predominantly through informal relationships. The reason the helpee pursues the helper has more to do with trust, respect, and availability than education or experience. The helper usually has background information about the helpee that allows the data-gathering process to feel like a natural conversation.

The hub of this type of ministry is usually small group life, mutual ministry involvement, or shared life activities. It is natural, appropriate, and beneficial for the helper and helpee to exchange phone numbers, mingle with each other's families, and have other casual social interactions.

Even when other layers of care are advisable, one-another ministry is the place where "after care" should occur. As a church strengthens the quality and quantity of one-another care between its members, these relationships fulfill God's design for "preventive care," circumventing higher layers of care from being overutilized.

LEVEL OF TRAINING

The regular preaching, teaching, and discipleship ministry of the church provides the training for one-another ministry. Whether effective or ineffective, this is where the content, tone, and culture of one-another ministry will be established for a particular church. A guiding question for every pastor-teacher in the church should be, "What do my people need to know to minister effectively at a one-another level?"

Another question each church needs to ask is, "Who supervises the one-another ministry of our church — recommending resources, debriefing conversations where the helper was uncertain, and overseeing the balance of training provided to the church?" This begins with the senior pastor and elders, but these responsibilities can be shared as a church adds more staff members.

LEVEL OF EXPERIENCE

The level of counseling experience with one-another ministry will vary widely based on age, life experience, personal history with sin or suffering struggles, number of years as a Christian, type of education, etc. A primary and irreplaceable asset that one-another ministry provides is the longevity of a relationship and accessibility. But if the individual seeking help wants (or is assessed by the church to require) help that needs expertise more than longevity, then one-another ministry should not be the only form of care provided. If it is, then an imbalance is likely to develop in this helping relationship that makes it unhealthy for the helper. This imbalance potentially makes it difficult for those equipped to provide higher levels of care to do one-another ministry. Part of good self-care for those with advanced training experience in counseling is to protect friendships from becoming helping relationships.[1]

ADVANTAGES AND OPPORTUNITIES

One-another ministry is highly replicable, readily available, and has lasting contact between the people involved. One-another ministry develops naturally without any artificial pairing. In the absence of formality, the stigma often associated with counseling can be avoided. The lack of formality also alleviates a church's liability concerns that exist with other levels of counseling. One frequent expression of this is counseling-related conferences or book studies (e.g., parenting, depression, grief, etc.) offered during the adult education hours of a church's discipleship ministries.

In the absence of a thriving one-another ministry, several negative consequences occur: (1) counselees often regress or relapse after formal counseling concludes, (2) formal counseling is extended at a cost to the counselee or lack of availability of services to others, or (3) struggles are taken on as an identity as a way to keep the individual in a community of support.

LIMITATIONS AND WEAKNESSES

It is often hard for those who do not have preexisting relationships within a church to connect to one-another ministry in a time of crisis or emotional distress. Either they wait for a friendship to develop before sharing their struggle or their struggle becomes the basis of the relationship.

In one-another care, the personal experience and favorite Bible passages and Christian books of the helper can overly influence the advice given. Anecdotal examples of "what worked for me" or "what comes to my mind" can result in a higher rate of well-intended but ineffective advice than would be provided by more experienced helpers.

Those without formal training or experience in biblical counseling will have a wide variety in their comfort level when it comes to talking about emotional or relational struggles. This discomfort can be hurtful to the person seeking help. Those who have sought formal training in biblical counseling typically gain a greater comfort level with these kinds of conversations.

IMPORTANT TRANSITION

A major transition occurs as we move from one-another ministry to other layers of care. This should be understood by churches when/if they add formal biblical counseling elements to their ministry. When counseling moves from organic, helping conversations to more formal expressions, an "artificial pairing" can occur. An artificial pairing occurs when:

- A request for counseling is made by the helpee.
- The church assigns or recommends a helper who would not otherwise be meeting with the helpee.
- The helpee comes to the helper with the expectation that counsel will be provided on the basis of the helper's training, role, or experience.

When a church facilitates a counseling-related artificial pairing, it has a responsibility to both the helper and the helpee. To the helper the church should ensure: (1) there is a reasonable opportunity for success and (2) that the helpee comes with accurate expectations of the type of counsel being provided. A church should know the scope of care possible by a given ministry or individual and refer to that ministry only individuals who are a good fit for what that ministry provides.

To the helpee the church should provide clear information about: (1) the type of care a given ministry provides; (2) the level of training a counselor or ministry leader has completed; (3) the type of curriculum or activity that will be involved in the counseling process; and (4) an estimate of the duration of the helping relationship. This requires clear information on a church's website, a well-informed receptionist who fields calls about counseling inquiries, and quality intake forms.

The question could be raised, "If one-another ministry is counseling, then why treat the next levels of care more stringently?" A parallel with missions is helpful. Every Christian should live missionally by seeking opportunities to share the gospel and advance the cause of Christ. However, almost every church or missions agency screens formal missionary candidates to make sure they are a good fit and properly equipped before sending them to do mid-term or career mission work.

In this sense, the words of Stephen Neil about missions are applicable to counseling: "When everything is mission, nothing is mission."[2] Similarly, when everything is counseling, nothing is counseling. The word "counseling" loses any meaning as an activity distinct from "doing life together." The immensely beneficial interaction of a small group to provide an experience of safe relationships is different from someone understanding how to guide a person through the traumatic effects of childhood sexual abuse.[3] Listening as a friend to the chaos of a marital argument is different from guiding a couple through a decision about separation during an ongoing affair when children are "taking sides" in order not to lose contact with the less-involved parent.

But that does not in any way downplay the essential nature of one-another ministry. The sexual abuse survivor needs a small group in which to experience healthy relationships while learning how to cultivate them. The husband and wife recovering from adultery need friends to call when they're discouraged, tempted, or confused. However, without the training and formality of higher levels of competence, the small group friends could be so overwhelmed by these situations that they begin to withdraw.

When counseling does involve an artificial pairing, the counselor should seek to return to the care or involve natural pairings in the care as early as possible. An excellent model for this is the advocate system developed by Garrett Higbee (see chapters 12 and 13). When this is not possible, then part of someone "graduating" to formal counseling should be a discussion of how to best involve the counselee's one-another relationships to solidify the progress made in counseling.[4]

Lay Counselor/Recovery Group/Mentor

SCOPE OF MINISTRY

I am defining "lay counselors" as people who have completed a designated curriculum of study tailored to serve in a particular ministry. This ministry might include meeting with individuals or couples under the supervision of a pastor, leading a subject-specific recovery group, marital and premarital mentoring, or comparable types of ministry.

If the lay counselor is conducting formal biblical counseling (i.e., defined by the utilization of intake forms, scheduled appointments, and note-taking at each session), then the church would need to have policies and protocols in place to protect confidentiality as well as a policy review of the financial policy (if applicable), philosophy of care, confidentiality statement, waiver of liability, and consent to counsel.[5]

LEVEL OF TRAINING

For those serving as formal lay counselors, their church should select the training program that best fits the church's needs and theology. Certifications in biblical counseling are offered by the Association of Biblical Counselors, the Christian Counseling and Education Foundation, the International Association of Biblical Counselors, the Institute for Biblical Counseling and Discipleship, and the Association of Certified Biblical Counselors.

Those leading a group or mentoring based on a curriculum should have clear training in the specific materials being utilized as a part of their ministry. They should have training on how to identify the most common "red flags" that would necessitate the involvement of a more experienced counselor.

LEVEL OF EXPERIENCE

The formal experience of lay counselors will be about 75 hours by the time they complete the certification process. How fast they gain experience depends on the number of hours these volunteers can devote to the ministry each week.

The quality of experience in a lay counseling ministry can be greatly enhanced by the presence of a trained and experienced general practitioner (see below) to debrief cases and answer questions from the lay counseling team. Mentors and recovery group leaders may rely heavily on their personal experiences, but their curriculum and training will help them to identify the principles and key points of assessment vital for success in their subject area.

ADVANTAGES AND OPPORTUNITIES

Ministries at this level are still able to serve the church and community free of charge. The cost of training can be paid by the church or lay counselor rather than be passed on to the counselee as a fee or donation. These ministries allow a church to utilize the strengths and experiences in their congregation and can be excellent expressions of 2 Corinthians 1:3–5, as believers share with others the comfort they have received from God.

Outreach to the community can be effective, especially in areas that are under-resourced. When built on biblical principles and when there is a clear process for assimilation into the life of the church, recovery groups and mentoring ministries can be both therapeutically and evangelistically effective.

LIMITATIONS AND WEAKNESSES

Each church will be dependent on the experience of its members to determine what subjects it can address. If the lay leaders for these ministries are not also gifted in leadership or administration, the quality of these ministries can suffer.

When a recovery group ministry grows, it can sometimes create a "church within a church" dynamic. If the level of transparency within the recovery ministry is greater than the level of transparency within the general church culture, those in recovery often begin to feel like they are the ones "really doing church."

Whenever a church begins a formal biblical counseling ministry at any level, it needs to consult with its insurance provider. Areas of consultation could include the need for increased liability insurance, coverage for volunteers, and any best practices guidelines to reduce risk.

Formally Educated, Gaining Experience (Graduate Intern)

SCOPE OF MINISTRY

I define a counselor at this level as a person who is in process of completing a master's degree with ambitions of becoming proficient as a "general practitioner." The caseload for this individual would be in formal or group counseling settings under the supervision of an experienced counselor competent in the areas being served.

This individual, in theory, should be able to manage a greater variety and complexity of counseling cases.[6] The person should have the ability and awareness to differentiate struggles with similar manifestations (i.e., generalized anxiety, mistrust, or anger outbursts from the effects of post-traumatic stress). A counselor at this level should also be growing in competence to handle communication with church leaders and medical professionals as needed.

LEVEL OF TRAINING

The training for this level of counseling is more strenuous than normal discipleship or certification. A counselor needs to be involved in a thorough master's level education that covers a full counseling curriculum.

Beginning at this level of competency, a counselee seeks a counselor on the basis of their education and growing experience. For this reason, the level of training and quality of supervision should be clearly articulated to the counselee in the counseling intake forms.

LEVEL OF EXPERIENCE

In this proposal, counselors would remain at the "gaining experience" level until their education is complete and at least 1,000 hours of supervised case experience has been attained. There is no "magic" in this number, but it represents a commitment to be excellent in one's field.

At this point, counselors are in a position to assess: (1) when a case is a good fit for their training and experience, (2) whether the counselee is rightly identifying the presenting problem, and (3) how to best assist this person based on their struggle and their unique life circumstances or resources.

ADVANTAGES AND OPPORTUNITIES

In many cases, churches can work with local seminaries or graduate schools to offer these services free of charge. In these cases, the graduate internships can be used to form or strengthen partnerships with other ministries and institutions in the community.

With this type of program, the church gains another opportunity to invest in people who will be leaders in the church, para-church ministries, or community organizations. These individuals will gain experience somewhere. When the church provides and supervises this experience, the church has an opportunity to inject a higher view of Scripture and Christian community into the counselor's lifelong practices.

Having this type of counseling in a local church can increase the quality of care for members and the community. It can also counter the stigma from the frequently held assumption, "If I were a good Christian, then I wouldn't have emotional or relational struggles." Providing counseling benefits the entire discipleship culture of a church.

LIMITATIONS AND WEAKNESSES
This level of counseling loses some of the accessibility benefits of one-another ministry. This is due to both the nature of formal counseling and the logistics of carrying a larger caseload. A strong advocate system or other means of connecting counselees to the life of the church should be developed when this type of ministry is launched.

In order for a church to have this type of ministry, it needs to have a staff position devoted to counseling. Otherwise, the liability from lack of oversight and qualified supervision would be greater than the benefit.

Each church would need to decide if it is willing to accept graduate interns from secular programs. Churches will vary on how much they value the purity of the philosophy in their program compared to the opportunity to influence Christians who will be leaders in a secular workplace.

Trained and Experienced General Practitioner
SCOPE OF MINISTRY
I define "general practitioners" as persons who have both the training and experience to serve a wide variety of counseling concerns. This

does not mean they are competent to counsel every issue that may arise; rather, general practitioners readily acknowledge their limitations. Good general practitioners will refer when their training, experience, or setting does not serve a particular counselee's struggle.

An experienced counselor can also serve as a teacher and supervisor for those at lower levels. This may be as a pastor of counseling in a local church or as a supervisor in a para-church ministry.

Most churches that hire a pastor of counseling are large and expect to hire someone with at least seven to ten years (7,000 to 10,000 hours) of counseling experience. It is difficult to gain that quantity of experience volunteering or interning in a local church. Those seeking to gain this level of experience often seek employment in a para-church setting.

LEVEL OF TRAINING

These counselors have completed at least a master's degree in counseling and are growing from 1,000 to 10,000 hours of counseling experience. General practitioners are continuing their education through discipleship, reading, conferences, and counselor consultations in order to increase the breadth and depth of their areas of competence.

LEVEL OF EXPERIENCE

At this point in a counselor's development, there is a shift in how experience is measured. Rather than tabulating one's total number of hours, a general practitioner begins to gauge how many cases or hours they have worked with particular types of cases (i.e., depression with suicidal ideations, anxiety involving panic attacks, eating disorders, etc.).

In the early stages of gaining experience, counselors grow both in comfort with the counseling process (i.e., interviewing, assessment, gauging counselee commitment, recognizing ethical dilemmas, determining the pace of counseling, etc.) and in competence with particular struggles. Now the counselor's attention can be focused predominantly on expanding their areas of competence.

ADVANTAGES AND OPPORTUNITIES

Theoretically in the counseling relationship, a well-trained and experienced counselor should be able to quickly assess the primary struggle(s), determine which approaches are likely to be most effective, and clearly explain recommendations of possible alternatives. These factors can increase the trust a counselee has with the counselor and thereby increase counseling effectiveness.

General practitioners have a level of expertise that allows their teaching and supervision of less experienced counselors to increase the quality of a church's entire counseling ministry. If desired, a general practitioner can apply to have teaching events approved for CEU credits, which allows the church to impact the level of biblical awareness among the Christian counselors in their area while educating counselors providing services offered by their church.

LIMITATIONS AND WEAKNESSES

For this level of experience, there is either a cost to the church (a paid staff position) or the counselee (a fee or donation). For many churches and individuals, these costs block access to counseling.

Some churches envision a pastor of counseling serving as a "counselor on a retainer fee." But they realize it is not sustainable. A good counselor providing free service will generate a waiting list that would create frustration in the church. Instead, the job description for that position would put the primary focus on developing and equipping a multilayered counseling ministry.

Professional counselors frequently experience "compassion fatigue" as they live in other people's crises for 20 to 30 hours per week. This, combined with the clinical categories in which personal struggles are often assessed, can result in an emotional disconnect that can decrease the effectiveness of counseling.

Experienced Specialist

SCOPE OF MINISTRY

Experienced specialists are counselors who are competent to counsel severe cases in one or more areas of specialty or are making a unique contribution to the field of biblical counseling. As supervisors, teachers, and authors, they are working to advance the ability of the church to minister effectively in these areas.

LEVEL OF TRAINING

A specialist is someone who is advancing the field in their area of expertise. Their own study and observations are becoming the curriculum for less experienced counselors. The critical feedback from peers and students within and outside the biblical counseling movement serves as a refining mechanism for their practice.

Outside of their area of expertise, a specialist should be engaging in the same types of continuing education as a general practitioner. This is vital to (1) prevent their area of expertise from unduly defining their work with other subjects and (2) strengthen their work in their area of expertise while continuing to grow in their understanding of neighboring struggles.

LEVEL OF EXPERIENCE

The number of hours selected to designate someone a "specialist" is less arbitrary than the other designations, although it is impossible to quantify a number of hours that would qualify someone to hold the title of "specialist." Ten thousand hours of experience has been noted as pivotal in many areas of study, as noted by neurologist Daniel Levitin:

> The emerging picture from such studies is that ten thousand hours of practice is required to achieve the level of mastery associated with being a world-class expert — in anything. In study after study, of composers, basketball players, fiction writers, ice skaters, concert pianists, chess players, master criminals, and what have you, this number comes up again and again.... No one has yet found a case in which true world-class expertise was accomplished in less time.[7]

ADVANTAGES AND OPPORTUNITIES

There are two major advantages and opportunities that emerge with this level of competence. First, the counselor should be able to provide an excellent quality of care for those who could otherwise receive counsel for their struggle from a more general approach (e.g., counseling religious scrupulosity—a form of OCD—as a general struggle with assurance of salvation).

Second, through writing and teaching, specialists could advance the ability of the church to minister well in their area of expertise. This advance can be for particular struggles (addiction, abusive relationships, blended families, etc.) or modes of ministry (use of advocates in formal counseling, creating excellent communities of preventive care through one-another ministry, faith-based internship opportunities to allow for effective care in under-resourced communities, etc.).

LIMITATIONS AND WEAKNESSES

The predominant weakness of any specialist is availability. This is both because of the limited number of hours any individual can counsel per week (20 to 30 hours is a typical maximum caseload for counselors) and geographic limitations. There will not be a biblical-counseling specialist for every issue in every city.

CONCLUSION

What are the major concepts you could take away from a chapter like this?

- An appreciation for the diversity in the quantity and quality of gifts that God has given to His church to accomplish everything He desires His people to do—including biblical counseling.
- An assessment of where your current level of competence resides so that you can take full advantage of your current opportunities, grow in your competence, and capitalize on the advantages and opportunities that come with a higher level of competence.

- A guide for churches to think through how to plan for and develop a counseling ministry that best suits their context and membership.

I offer one final word of encouragement on this subject: *Be excellent wherever you are.* The danger in talking about layers is the assumption that "higher is better." That is the kind of misconception that would lead us to think paid clergy are "better Christians" than laypeople.

There will never be enough "professional Christians" to change the world, and that is not God's plan. But God has called some people to be set apart for ministry based on a recognition of their gifts. He calls these people to be equipped to equip others for ministry (Eph. 4:11 – 13).

Similarly, God has called us all to use our gifts and experiences to care for one another. God will change the most lives through informal day-to-day forms of care and counseling. And some people, by God's direction, will choose to focus their career or the majority of their volunteer ministry efforts to care for others with increasing excellence and expertise.

If this chapter has accomplished its objectives, then you will have a concept of how various layers of counseling competence can work together—leveraging their unique advantages and opportunities while relying on others to balance their weaknesses and limitations—to serve God's people and advance God's kingdom in our current culture.

CHAPTER 16

RELATING TRUTH TO LIFE: GOSPEL-CENTERED COUNSELING FOR DEPRESSION

JEREMY LELEK

*D**epression* is a curious term in our day. For some, it is considered a debilitating mental disease, while for others it is a season of lowered mood that feels just a bit off from the norm. During my fifteen years of practice, ten as a licensed professional counselor, I have witnessed the vast spectrum inherent in this emotional experience we call depression. I saw the overly stressed mother of four who wants to sleep all day because she doesn't think she's doing a good job as a mom. I sat with people who subjected themselves to controversial electroshock therapy and whose very personalities have been altered, their memories severely damaged; many said they no longer feel any emotions. The gamut of emotion captured in the word "depression" is certainly vast.

The American Psychiatric Association (APA) has tried to corner this shadowy beast by formulating criteria to identify a clinical depression. Their efforts have been valiant, but their methodology of diagnosis has been anything but precise and the efficacy of treatment far from consistent.[1] In fact, the more neurologists and neuropsychologists learn about the brain, the more they realize how much they do not know. Many cite the human brain as the most complex organism in the entire universe—validating the psalmist who proclaimed, "I praise you, for I am fearfully and wonderfully made" (Ps. 139:14).

This dilemma does not end with the APA. As biblical counselors, when our etiological assumptions move from body to soul, we must admit our limitations in cornering and slaying the shadowy beast of depression. We must admit that we do not possess a magic silver bullet guaranteed to take away the weighty negative emotions experienced by those enduring melancholy. We do not possess a mechanical formula that others may utilize to ward off what feels like tormenting demons. Praying hard enough, repenting consistently enough, and diligently "putting on" the "right" thoughts are not the panaceas for depression. If we are not careful when utilizing such methods, we may inadvertently reinforce the very spirit of "wholeness" to which our secular counterparts zealously ascribe—"wholeness" captured in the experience of feeling good.

Admitting that we lack a magic bullet, in my view, forces us to realize that we have something far more glorious to offer those we serve. Although we don't have a mechanical or chemical cure to offer the emotionally debilitated in times of torment, we do have a personal, dynamic, wise, present, and faithful Person to whom we point. It is with this awareness that the course of "treatment" for depression veers off the broad path of symptom alleviation onto the divine, often very narrow, path of worship. It is the path where we are privileged to help others experience the words of our Redeemer who invited us. "Come to me, all who labor and are heavy laden, and I will give you rest. Take my yoke upon you, and learn from me, for I am gentle and lowly in heart, and you will find rest for your souls. For my yoke is easy, and my burden is light" (Matt. 11:28–30).

ENTERING IN: EXPERIENCING
THE DARKNESS

If you ever studied psychology, perhaps you came across a certain theorist named Carl Rogers. When you read Rogers, you can't help but notice he was a man who seemed to genuinely care for those he treated. His approach to counseling was known as "person-centered therapy," and it was his view that in order to help someone well, a counselor must exhibit three critical attributes: unconditional positive regard, genuineness, and empathetic understanding.[2] I do not mention Rogers to encourage us to adopt his hypothesis regarding his proposed trio of counselor qualities. His presuppositions were profoundly pagan and his worldview the epitome of Romans 1:21–25. Yet even through the fractured prism of his humanistic ideology, he was able to recognize the relevance of relationship in the process of change.

Relationship is an important variable in helping and serving others. While Rogers posited the idea of empathy (i.e., mentally experiencing the suffering of a client or thinking what it would be like to walk in their shoes) as part of his relational formula for helping others, the Bible points us to something far more captivating. It points us to a Redeemer who did not stop with mere empathy. In serving the Father for the good of His people, Jesus did not merely offer mental assent to our suffering, He entered our brokenness and suffered with us and for us.

The apostle Paul enlightens us to this marvelous reality. While instructing the Philippians in godly interpersonal ministry, he distinctly emphasized the person of Jesus: "Have this mind among yourselves, which is yours in Christ Jesus, who, though he was in the form of God, did not count equality with God a thing to be grasped, but emptied himself [made himself nothing], by taking the form of a servant, being born in the likeness of men. And being found in human form, he humbled himself by becoming obedient to the point of death, even death on a cross" (Phil. 2:5–8). Jesus' personality guides us in our attempts to enter the darkness of depression with and for others.

Making Ourselves Nothing

First, Jesus did not grasp what was rightfully His, but made Himself nothing. He left the safety and comfort of the Trinitarian relationship and subjected Himself to the harsh realities of the fall. *He made himself nothing.* What a wonderful quality to bring into the process when counseling a severely depressed individual. By so doing, we choose to leave the comforts of our rote methodologies or the elation we experience when we witness immediate results. We surrender our pat answers and oft-recited Bible verses in exchange for faith in action. We relate. Rather than tell someone Jesus will never leave or forsake her, we model the faithfulness of Jesus by exhibiting an abiding presence. Rather than offering pat answers more centered in our need to "get it right," we acknowledge our shared finitude and mutual desperation for God. Through our willingness to forget our world, our struggles, our cares and choosing instead to invest an eager ear to listen, we incarnate the qualities of the Wonderful Counselor. Therefore, we are privileged to become the very thing the Lord uses to arouse new hope and affections in an otherwise shattered heart. We enter in, not by focusing on our performance as counselors, not by having our own prepackaged biblical answer for depression, but by making ourselves nothing so that our hearts may become keenly attuned to the suffering of our neighbor.

Humility

Entering in also requires continuous humility. Jesus humbled himself to the point of death. This humility may be necessary to guard against pride. We should always give pause and examine our hearts if, when ministering to the most broken among us, we assume for one moment we could handle things far better if we were in their shoes. Humility rushes in after such arrogance and reminds us, "But for the grace of God ..."

This humility may be necessary when our favorite methods and verses don't produce the outcome we expect. Our tendency may be to blame or shame the person we are seeking to help by accusing them of having no faith or not being close enough to God or simply not yielding to the Spirit. Maybe we shame and blame ourselves for not being an effective counselor. Humility sucks the wind out of our sail of pride and reminds us of the only One with the power and authority to whisper and make good on the words "Peace! Be still!" (Mark 4:39).

Making ourselves nothing and humbling ourselves to obedience to God frees us to love and serve well. It opens the door for us to enter in. There is no need to fix. No need to produce a quick answer. No attempt to awe and inspire with our eloquence. No pressure to fulfill the expectations of the broken. No. There is simply a making nothing of self so that another may experience the full attention that God's love perpetually affords them.

EVALUATE: WISE AND COLLABORATIVE DISCERNMENT

Jesus is infinitely interpersonal. As the second person of the Trinity, it is His nature to be so. When He turned water into wine, He didn't just wave His hand and make it happen. He lovingly included those around Him in the process.

Fellowship

One means by which Jesus drew people in was through conversation. Speaking to the woman at the well, "Jesus said to her, 'Go, call your husband, and come here'" (John 4:16). Of course, Jesus knew what this woman would tell Him, but He drew her in through conversation. He asked her probing questions and responded with perfect precision. "The woman answered him, 'I have no husband.' Jesus said to her, 'You are right in saying, I have no husband; for you have had five husbands, and the one you now have is not your husband. What you have said is true'" (John 4:17–18).

And why was He drawing her in? He spoke with intentionality that would direct her, via conversation, to Himself. "The woman said to him, 'I know that Messiah is coming (he who is called Christ). When he comes, he will tell us all things.' Jesus said to her, 'I who speak to you am he'" (John 4:25 – 26). Jesus could have simply walked up, "read her mail," then walked away. But he was more discerning than that. He entered in, considered her experience, treated her as a loved human being, and talked to her. He invited her into the experience of fellowship with God. Process was important.

Intentional Conversation

Like Jesus, we are to be conversational and intentional. We need information to help us know our counselees well. We hear their story, pause in places where pertinent information may be present, probe and inquire, and seek the Lord for understanding. We ask about medical histories, family dynamics, experiences of the past. We are simply seeking to exhibit the wisdom we witness in Jesus' interaction with others as well as aspire to the stated wisdom we find in the pages of Scripture.

The author of Proverbs compels us to listen, probe, and understand. "A fool takes no pleasure in understanding, but only in expressing his opinion" (Prov. 18:2). Or "If one gives an answer before he hears, it is his folly and shame" (v. 13). And finally, "An intelligent heart acquires knowledge, and the ear of the wise seeks knowledge" (v. 15). Biblical counselors want to know the soul of those to whom they minister. We work diligently to walk in wisdom lest we imitate fools and bring shame upon ourselves and, even worse, on the name of our Lord.

Iron Sharpening Iron

Counseling is an "iron sharpen[ing] iron" process (Prov. 27:17). I don't have all the answers, and I make it a point to let those I serve know this is the case. I engage them and ask for feedback. When a counselee speaks up, it sharpens me by reminding me I'm a mere human, not the Healer of souls. It sharpens me to remember the need for sensitivity and compassion. It sharpens me by producing humility, kindness, patience, and longsuffering. It sharpens me by helping me put off fear if confrontation is necessary. As I operate from this place of love (1 Cor. 13:4 – 8), I am better prepared to serve those in my life. I am positioned to work *with* them, not *on* them.

In humility, my heart becomes open for God to reason with me as He did in Isaiah (Isa. 1:18 – 20), reminding me of the beauties of the gospel (v. 18), the bounty of wise obedience (v. 19), and the terrible consequences of rebellion (v. 20). It also opens my heart to imitate Paul by carefully reasoning with others from the Scriptures in order to minister well (Acts 17:2). This reasoning is often a "give and take" a "back and forth" reflecting two people seeking wisdom from our wise Father above. And like Paul, I am forced to trust in His eternal wisdom to work in hearts as He so chooses (Acts 17:4). I engage others in order to know them, and then we work together to press on in the journey of redemption. Together, we formulate objectives to make such "pressing on" a reasonable and wise pursuit, and we learn to trust God with any results.

PLANT: THE ART OF OFFERING MEANINGFUL HOPE

What we plant impacts what we reap. If we sow corn seed expecting to reap an apple tree, then we are in for a big surprise and disappointment. The same goes for counseling. Counselors hold an important responsibility to help those they serve plant seeds that will generate biblical hope.

Hope Is a Person

What is biblical hope? The Bible points us to a Person — God. Consider the following verses:

- "Why are you cast down, O my soul, and why are you in turmoil within me? Hope in God; for I shall again praise him, my salvation and my God." (Ps. 42:5 – 6)
- "Remember my affliction and my wanderings, the wormwood and the gall! My soul continually remembers it and is bowed down within me. But this I call to mind, and therefore I have

hope: The steadfast love of the LORD never ceases; his mercies never come to an end; they are new every morning; great is your faithfulness." (Lam. 3:19–23)

- "Though the fig tree should not blossom, nor fruit be on the vines, the produce of the olive fail and the fields yield no food, the flock be cut off from the fold and there be no herd in the stalls, yet I will rejoice in the LORD; I will take joy in the God of my salvation. God, the LORD, is my strength; he makes my feet like the deer's; he makes me tread on my high places." (Hab. 3:17–19)

The psalmist pens his cries while in the dark clutches of grief. Jeremiah writes the words of Lamentations while in a pit of his own sewage awaiting his imminent death. And Habakkuk prayed this prayer as he anticipated the desolation of his land by the very God to whom he was praying.

The paradigm of Scripture is antithetical to the paradigm of secular therapy. It is a paradigm rooted in the eternal. It is a paradigm that orients every experience, good and bad, toward worship. Genuine existential hope cannot be found in emotional states or pristine circumstances. It is not contained in a book or a pill. Hope is a spiritual reality found only in the Spirit. More specifically, genuine and abiding hope may exclusively be found in a constant, immutable, unchangeable, and loving God (James 1:17). Hope sought in anything else is guaranteed to be fleeting, sporadic, and in the end, meaningless (Eccl. 1:13–14).

I do not want to imply here that I am opposed to a good book that may be helpful, nor am I averse to medical treatment when it is needed. I do want to stress, however, that hope cannot be contained within those treatment modalities. Hope is so much more than feeling good.

Hope Is Relational

Hope is relational, not mechanical. When counseling the despairing soul, we are wise to avoid formulas and fads. We exhibit love. Instead of fixing, we walk hand in hand with the heavyhearted among us, teaching and learning from them what James meant when he encouraged us with what seems to be an impossible irony—that trials are meant to complete us so that we lack *nothing* (James 1:2–4). James attends to the attitude. He is urging the saint to be mindful of divine perspective during hardship. It is a perspective that may take rehearsing over and over and over throughout a lifetime—"When life is difficult, the great Architect of my soul is once again shaping and completing me."

I think it quite legitimate to assume depression is a trial for those enduring its unrelenting grip. Yet if we aim to counsel wisely, we cannot extract the trial from its meaning. We cannot simply diagnose a situational depression or a chemical depression and move on toward our interpretation of cure. We must consider the divine. The very nature of our interpretive task requires it. For the counselor, psychologist, or pastor, interpretation is not, according to John Frame, "the work of trying to assess for the first time the significance of uninterpreted facts. Rather, ours is a work of secondary interpretation, interpreting God's interpretation."[3]

Understanding and meaning are derived from facts that have been eternally present in the mind of God and are now ours to study, navigate, and rightly understand via the Lord choosing to express such facts in and through His creation (including trials). Within this God-centered context, the meaning and *telos* (or ultimate goal) for right thinking, right motivation, or positive emotions no longer center in subjective mental-emotional experiences (as is the case in all forms of secular therapy), but possesses a transcendent aim located in the glory of God. And by His loving grace, God has given us a glimpse of His infinite, unfathomable mind. He reveals to us that trials for the saint equate with divine healing of the soul.

Our secondary interpretation also depends on special revelation, and, based on Scripture, major depression is not simply an emotional state to overcome. It is a conduit for producing a transformed mind. This trial, depression, may in fact be an instrument to heal the mind in that it leaves no room for hope, no room for joy except in that which is found in the piercing and faithful love of Jesus Christ. And this is where James begins — remember that trials are designed to ensure that we lack nothing in our capacity and ability to imitate Jesus Christ!

Hope Is Wisdom-Oriented

After establishing the rationale for joy in trials, James prompts us to seek wisdom. This wisdom, if believed, contains the riches necessary to prevent psychological ambivalence and instability (James 1:5 – 8). It is a mind rooted in and moved by God's wisdom when trials abound. And this brings us to our perspective of healing. Are we peddling an idea of healing that parallels the construct of our secular counterparts or an idea that exceeds it? If we aim for the removal of unwanted symptoms exclusively, unfortunately we are robbing from our counselees by practicing the first. However, if our conceptualization of healing resonates with the ideas of James, then healing is displayed in our counselees becoming complete and lacking nothing (psychologically).

The perfect specimen of this condition was realized in Jesus Christ (Col. 2:9). He was wired with a perfect psyche (1 John 3:5). He possessed flawless trust in the Father (Luke 22:42). He exhibited a relentless passion to fulfill His Father's will (John 4:34). Not once did He surrender to anxiety when troubles presented themselves (Mark 4:39). His mind was consumed with loving God and others (John 17:1, 24 – 26). Jesus was complete and lacked nothing. When we are seeking a measure of psychological healing, it is embodied in Him.

Is this the construct of healing we offer those we serve?

- Healing is brought forth as you grow in your ability to think and mentally operate like Jesus (Phil. 2:5).
- Healing is realized by the power and grace offered through the Holy Spirit (Titus 2:11 – 14).
- Your healing is already actuated and finalized through the atoning power of the finished work of Jesus Christ upon the cross (Isa. 53:4 – 5; Heb. 11:14).

- Your healing is now (2 Peter 1:3–4).
- Your healing is inevitable (Phil. 1:6).

Are these the realities to which we point as we seek to impart hope? If not, then we fail to build healing on God's wisdom and are guilty of building on a foundation of sand that will not hold when our brokenness presses in (Matt. 7:24–26).

Feeling good is a precious thing. Overcoming sorrowful and despairing emotions is a worthy desire. In order for me to counsel others with compassion, I will aim for these things. That means I will seek to be as exhaustive as possible in my assessment. I will heed the words of one of my favorite authors who wrote, "The things of the body are not to be despised when compared with the soul."[4] As such, I will discuss possible physiological causes such as allergies, thyroid malfunction, hormonal imbalances, previous brain trauma, sleep apnea, or heart-related issues. I will want to assess other components that may impact the physiological such as drug or alcohol abuse or the side effects of any prescribed medications. I will send my client to a physician who may discover the etiology of the condition. If the depression is so severe that my client is literally unable to function in daily tasks or respond well to counseling, I will recommend a trusted psychiatrist.

I will also consider soul issues. Is my client harboring hidden sin, ongoing resentment, or chronic anxiety and fear? Silently angry? Coddling covetous desires that contribute to misery? Is my client making demands about life that are outside of his control? Is there hope of feeling better? Is the heart set on God's glory or on something else?

I will want to unpack the belief systems of my clients. Cognitively, what assumptions shape their understanding of God? What relationships in life may have influenced these beliefs? What are their beliefs about self, others, and their circumstances? Are these beliefs rooted in truth or distortion, grace or law, God or self? I will want to gain an understanding of whether or not they know how the gospel applies to their life and circumstances. Are past traumas continuing to grip the heart? What is their story? What events in life have impacted them most profoundly — good and bad? Have they experienced recent loss? What was their family like growing up?

These and other soul issues will consume much of my time with my counselees. I want to serve them well by rooting out potential heart struggles that are causing problems, yet not to the exclusion of emphasizing the redemptive purposes that are ever-present in whatever emotional state they may find themselves. I'm not a "problem-centered" counselor. I am a counselor seeking to center my work in God. I seek to help others grasp how Paul's words apply when he wrote that God uses "all things" to conform us to the image of Jesus — the "all things" including one's battle with severe depression (Rom. 8:28 – 29). I will take seriously the suffering being endured, I will pursue means for comfort and relief, but I will sow seeds ultimately rooted in the eternal, loving, and awe-inspiring plans of God.

We must help counselees to recognize that every square inch of their lives bears the opportunity to glorify the Creator. Their willingness to do the most mundane tasks for the glory of God when depression has sucked the emotional and mental resources from them is a beautiful thing in the eyes of our Lord. Jesus offered us a glimpse of this reasoning in Luke 21:1 – 4: "Jesus looked up and saw the rich putting their gifts into the offering box, and he saw a poor widow put in two small copper coins. And he said, 'Truly, I tell you, this poor widow has put in more than all of them. For they all contributed out of their abundance, but she out of her poverty put in all she had to live on.' "

And so it often is with the severely and chronically depressed. Their willingness to take a shower when everything within says "escape" holds the potential of glory just as much as the most passionate missionary who lives and breathes evangelism each and every day. Glorifying God is never a waste, regardless of the context.

SUBMIT: LEARNING TO TRUST GOD

Here is my most comforting thought when working with a chronically depressed person: A loving and sovereign God is presiding over the process. The Master Architect of the soul has the blueprint of my counselee's life before Him and is meticulously working to shape and frame the heart of my client precisely as He intended from before the foundations of the world! I am simply being allowed to step into a historical moment to participate, for a very brief season, in a process that has been eternally present in the mind of God.

The Lord and Shepherd of the Process

I'm elated when I read things like, "Your eyes saw my unformed substance; in your book were written, every one of them, the days that were formed for me, when as yet there was none of them" (Ps. 139:16). Or "The heart of man plans his way, but the LORD establishes his steps" (Prov. 16:9). Or "The king's heart is a stream of water in the hand of the LORD; he turns it wherever he will" (Prov. 21:1). "So then it depends not on human will or exertion, but on God, who has mercy. For the Scripture says to Pharaoh, 'For this very purpose I have raised you up, that I might show my power in you, and that my name might be proclaimed in all the earth.' So then he has mercy on whomever he wills, and he hardens whomever he wills" (Rom. 9:16–18).

If these passages are true, and they are, then there is much more going on within a counseling meeting than meets the eye. These truths do not remove volition or choice from my counselee, but they place such human actions within a larger reality governed by Another. Awareness and acceptance of this reality will require humility to something or Someone far more wise, far more loving, and far more powerful than I.

Sowing as a Patient, Hardworking Farmer

In one way, within this context, I am forced to become more like a farmer than a counselor. In my craft I must submit to the timing and nature of God's harvest. The apostle Paul's wisdom has helped me immensely here.

> Do not be deceived: God is not mocked, for whatever one sows, that will he also reap. For the one who sows to his own flesh will from the flesh reap corruption, but the one who sows to the Spirit will from the Spirit reap eternal life. And let us not grow weary of doing good, for in due season we will reap, if we do not give up. So then, as we have opportunity, let us do good to everyone, and especially to those of the household of faith.
>
> Galatians 6:7–10)

My job as a counselor is not to change people, but to sow to the Spirit. I will love, speak truth, pray for and with, listen, point to Christ, seek discernment, ask for wisdom, and pray for God's mercy. I will exhibit compassion, exude kindness, and exhort toward change. I will share Scripture. I will confront and rebuke. I will recall and remind again and again. I will exercise all of these and more as a means to sow to the Spirit. And, as the farmer is forced to wait for a budding crop, I will wait for the harvest over which God alone is sovereign. I will trust that the seeds sown will produce exactly what the Spirit intends. The harvest may consist of a lightened mood, the eradication of depression, or a new excitement for life. It may consist of an abiding hope in Jesus with an increase in depressive symptoms. It may consist of a new energy to exercise, and a renewed commitment to glorify God. I have no idea what the harvest will bring, but I am certain that it will be exactly what God knows my client needs.

I will also heed Paul's wisdom that such sowing is hard work, and I may become tempted to give up. But give up I cannot because the Lord of glory will bring His harvest, and He will do so in His perfect time. I will also seek to engender this attitude in the one I am loving and serving.

When I was a young counselor, I was very insecure and impatient. If something was not working to make my counselee feel better, I would often change my approach. While we always need to consider whether or not we are serving people well, we are also wise to keep sowing while patiently waiting. Part of the process of change resides in faithful perseverance.

Anticipate: The Hope of Exercised Faith

Biblical change is rooted in faith, and biblical faith is rooted in God. As I noted previously, God is both the author and actuator of biblical change. Change and healing center in His plans and purposes. And while we have no control over the change process, we can confidently anticipate healing and transformation in our lives. The author of Hebrews wrote, "Now faith is the assurance of things hoped for, the conviction of things not seen. For by it the people of old received their commendation" (Heb. 11:1 – 2).

Faithful Believing

By faith we believe God the Father has designed a redemptive plan for the Christian (Eph. 1:3 – 6). By faith we affirm the finished work of Christ that makes us perfect while also progressively perfecting us (Heb. 10:14). By faith we are certain that the Holy Spirit is carrying out the Father's plan in the particular lives of His people (Eph. 1:13 – 14). By faith we anticipate transformed hearts that are overwhelmingly zealous for good works in Christ Jesus (Titus 2:11 – 14).

The change process is a faith process in which we receive what already is while anticipating what is certain to come—that we would be mature and complete, lacking *nothing* (James 1:4). We hope for what we do not yet see. We are sure it is on its way. We anticipate the good gifts of a good God who is eager to give them. The entire chapter of Hebrews 11 points to people who lived this way.

It is not uncommon that the chronically depressed will have to approach their emotional healing "by faith." After years of prayer, counsel, and support, emotional relief may not come. Yet every day the Christian can anticipate that today could be the day. Whether in this life or the next, today very well may be the day when the sadness departs.

Why? Very specifically, it is because of the goodness of God. At any moment the heavy depression may evaporate from the mind, leaving a counselee overwhelmed by inexplicable peace. And we should ask for such relief. We are actually instructed to petition Him with our requests (Phil. 4:6). When I counsel, I always end sessions by praying, and when working with the heavyhearted, I always pray something like this: "Father, in your mercy please lift this burden from my sister's mind." I teach my counselees how to ask God for help, even pleading for His mercy. This is wise biblical counsel.

Trustful Waiting

Simultaneously, I echo the prayer of Christ that the Father's will be done, and I ask God to grant faith to believe and trust His will. While we wait, while we anticipate, while we hope, we also learn to feast. We learn to satisfy our souls with a nourishment that lasts. We put away the need for other foods as we bask in the bounty of God who invites the broken soul:

> Come, everyone who thirsts, come to the waters; and he who has no money, come, buy and eat! Come, buy wine and milk without money and without price. Why do you spend your money for that which is not bread, and your labor for that which does not satisfy? Listen diligently to me, and eat what is good, and delight yourselves in rich food. Incline your ear, and come to me; hear, that your soul may live; and I will make with you an everlasting covenant, my steadfast, sure love for David.
>
> Isaiah 55:1–3

As we learn to delight in the Lord, He will give us the desires of our hearts (Ps. 37:4). In our delighting, we taste and see that the Lord is good (Ps. 34:8), and our desires will fundamentally change. Our desires will long for more of Him, which He promises He will always faithfully give. It is in such tasting and delighting that healing unfolds. It is here the fractured soul learns *and accepts* that the only one in whom authentic satisfaction is found is God. Sometimes, as ironic as it may seem, a stubborn depression will serve as the most powerful aid in helping soul-healing beauty to unfold.

DEPRESSION'S DARKEST BLOW

Søren Kierkegaard wrote, "When death is the greater danger, we hope for life; but when we learn to know the even greater danger, we hope for death. When the danger is so great that death becomes the hope, then despair is the hopelessness of not even being able to die."[5] I have sat with many who have gazed into the hopeful eyes of death as a means to escape the misery of life. It is heartbreaking. It forces on me the candid realization that in the end, I am helpless to lift the burden of depression.

Even worse, sometimes, death becomes such a promising alternative that many choose to bring it upon themselves. It is a horrifying thought. Thankfully, to this point, I have not experienced losing a counselee to suicide, but I must admit there have been a few who attempted it and came within seconds of succeeding.

No one likes to imagine the possibility of suicide. This does not change the fact that at times the chronically depressed consider suicide as a viable option. So, offering some basic tips on this issue seems relevant.

The typical protocol to assess suicide is first to ask if it is something the counselee has ever considered. If yes, then the next step is to ask if there is a plan. If a person has actually formulated a "how to" of suicide, then the risk for carrying it out increases. In these circumstances, it is wise to do the following:

- Ask about the plan. Have the person describe it to you.
- Begin to formulate a counterplan. For example, if a woman says she plans to overdose on her antidepressants, then someone needs to immediately begin to manage her medications for her. The plan will offer clues that can serve the counselor, pastor, and family to help prevent the impending tragedy.
- If suicide is a risk factor, the individual should be monitored at all times until the desire to harm one's self has passed. Pastors, family, and church members will need to pull together to ensure the person is not left alone.
- Ask the person at risk to sign an agreement to seek help before they take any action that would harm them.

- When the situation is extreme and a support system is not available, hospitalization may be the only option.
- Take any threat of suicide seriously.

While these are just a few examples of what to do when suicide is a looming temptation, because we are human, we are forced to acknowledge the fact that suicide happens even in the midst of the most rigorous, loving care. We must do everything in our power to help someone press through this stubborn darkness, but the tragedy of suicide among the despairing will likely not disappear as long as any human soul is susceptible to being tormented by depression. Yet, there is hope!

Even in this darkest hour, when a loved one has taken their own life, when family and friends feel the battle has been lost, the light of Jesus' faithfulness will infinitely transcend the darkness. When He walked among us, He gave us this powerful, blessed promise that not even suicide can cancel:

> "All that the Father gives me will come to me, and whoever comes to me I will never cast out. For I have come down from heaven, not to do my own will but the will of him who sent me. And this is the will of him who sent me, that I should lose nothing of all that he has given me, but raise it up on the last day. For this is the will of my Father, that everyone who looks on the Son and believes in him should have eternal life, and I will raise him up on the last day."
>
> John 6:37–40

The hope of the depressed believer, even when suicide is the cause of death, is not the believer's faithfulness, but God's. According to Jesus, the Father's will is clear. *Everyone* He has given to Jesus *will* come to Him, *will* be accepted, and *will* be raised to eternal life in Jesus Christ. Suicide does not wield the power to void this covenant promise. So even in tragic death, even in suicide, Jesus' faithfulness and the magnificence of His gospel have the last say. His faithfulness will hold when ours desperately fails. This is faith. This is the gospel. This is the sacred story of the cross. This is biblical counseling.

CHAPTER 17

USING BIBLICAL NARRATIVE IN THE PERSONAL MINISTRY OF THE WORD

JOHN HENDERSON

Over two millennia ago, "a man from the house of Levi went and married a daughter of Levi. The woman conceived and bore a son." (Ex. 2:1 – 2).* The boy would be named Moses.

> Now it came about in those days, when Moses had grown up, that he went out to his brethren and looked on their hard labors; and he saw an Egyptian beating a Hebrew, one of his brethren. . . . He struck down the Egyptian and hid him in the sand. He went out the next day, and behold, two Hebrews were fighting with each other; and he said to the offender, "Why are you striking your companion?" But he said, "Who made you a prince or a judge over us? Are you intending to kill me as you killed the Egyptian?" Then Moses was afraid.
>
> Exodus 2:11 – 14

When Pharaoh learned of the event and sought to kill him, Moses fled east from Egypt into the wilderness.

---

* All Scripture quotations in this chapter are from the *New American Standard Bible* (NASB).

Throughout much of his life, Moses loved the acceptance and esteem of people. At times he acted from great faith and humility (as when Aaron and Miriam challenged his authority, Num. 12:1 – 13), while at other times he acted from a fear of failure and rejection (as when he prayed for God to kill him [Num. 11:10 – 15]). Typically, Moses would rather avoid conflict as he did when he refused to circumcise his son in order to circumvent conflict with his wife, who was not an Israelite (Ex. 4:24 – 26). Yet at the same time, he sacrificed everything for the task to which he was appointed. The Lord walked with him and loved him.

A man of modern times named Greg grew up in Oklahoma — generous parents, a good education, decent friends. Greg had no big complaints from childhood. After being drawn to Christ in high school, Greg committed himself to vocational ministry. Before the age of thirty, Greg was married with two young sons. A few years later, he was out of seminary and serving as a pastor in a small church. Pastoral ministry has helped Greg realize how much he hates conflict. Dealing with the disappointments and frustrations of people "makes [his] job miserable." A desire to please people has spawned an incessant craving for approval. When criticized, Greg takes days to recover. When people question his leadership or grumble about the church, Greg wants to quit ministry altogether.

To make matters worse, Greg no longer believes his wife supports him or his ministry. She complains about the time he spends away from home. In his mind, she just refuses to understand what being a pastor requires. He feels trapped between the demands of his family and the demands of everyone else. Every few weeks, he experiences a full-blown panic attack. A few mornings a week, he rolls from bed overcome with dread and worry. All his energy and passion for the day disappear ten seconds after waking up. In those moments, death seems far better to him than life. Yet the Lord walks with him and loves him.

Here's my question: Does the life and story of Moses have anything to offer the life and story of Greg? That is, *should* we even attempt to counsel Greg from Exodus or any other narrative of the Bible, and if so, *how*?

REASONS TO USE BIBLICAL NARRATIVE IN PERSONAL MINISTRY OF THE WORD

Over half of Scripture, by some estimates,[1] and approximately 40 percent of the Old Testament,[2] was written in narrative form. God chose to reveal Himself often through *a genre of writing structured in the form of a story*. Not fictional stories, but truthful stories of real people, events, and places throughout history, communicated under the Holy Spirit's inspiration, to make known God's nature, work, and pleasure, for the salvation of His people and to the praise of His glory (Eph. 1:3–14; Heb. 1:1; 2 Peter 1:20–21). The sheer amount of narrative in the Bible represents one good reason for us to learn how to counsel from it. If we don't, we risk either *ignoring* most of Scripture in the care of souls or *misusing* texts because we have failed to understand how they function, what they mean, or to what end they serve Scripture as a whole and God's mission in the world.

Like all well-told stories, the various narratives of the Bible have *characters, settings, scenes, plot, conflict, resolution*, and *closure*. The book of Genesis, for example, contains characters (e.g., God, Adam, Eve, the serpent), settings (e.g., creation as a whole, the Garden of Eden, Canaan), and scenes (e.g., Adam and Eve at the Tree of Knowledge of Good and Evil; Cain and Abel in the field). In the opening chapters, the conflict builds between Adam and Eve and the serpent, between God and mankind, between Cain and Abel, then between God and Cain. A degree of resolution is offered when God promises a future deliverance in the seed of woman (Gen. 3:15), but the moment of resolution also introduces new conflict (Gen. 3:15–19). Brief moments of closure may punctuate stories, but we must read to the end of the Bible to find any sense of final closure. This brings us to another good reason to counsel from narrative. Gordon Fee and Douglas Stuart, in *How to Read the Bible for All Its Worth*, wrote, "The essential character of the Bible, the whole Bible, is narrative."[3] It develops and follows a cohesive story line from the beginning of the world (Genesis) to its end and new beginning (Revelation). Every passage in the Bible has been divinely inspired and strategically placed to contribute something, whether big or small, to the overall theme of what Walter Kaiser calls "the redemption plan of God."[4] Each biblical narrative serves the longer, broader whole, and can only be rightly understood within the bigger story.[5] The precious doctrines, propositions, promises, and commandments of God, while valuable in and of themselves, don't stand on their own, but gain their meaning and significance inside the bigger story.

The opening scene of Exodus, for example, where we see the children of Israel enslaved in Egypt, isn't the beginning of the Bible's story. It's simply a new scene. When Moses enters, the story isn't commencing. It's *progressing*. He's becoming a part of God's story, a story that began in Genesis 1. When Moses dies in Deuteronomy 34, the story doesn't die. God continues His story through Joshua. "Just as I have been with Moses, I will be with you; I will not fail you or forsake you" (Josh. 1:5).

The Exodus narrative *continues* specific themes and truths introduced by the book of Genesis, and it *introduces* themes and truths for the rest of Scripture to build on and explain. Exodus introduces "the prototype of redemption"[6]—a smaller scale model of redemptive patterns and types that will find their ultimate fulfillment later in the Bible's narrative. The story helps frame and develop the overall story of God's glory in redeeming a people for Himself through Jesus Christ.

The main character, God, enters and exits the story. He's always there, authoring, guiding, judging, redeeming—sometimes explicitly, sometimes behind the scenes—speaking, revealing, responding, and unfolding the plotline of His righteous judgment and redemptive grace through human history; never haphazard; never out of control. God is always working all things "for good to those who love God, to those who are called according to His purpose" (Rom. 8:28).

People come and go. Kingdoms rise and fall. Yet God remains—from person to person, scene to scene, kingdom to kingdom, and epoch to epoch. A narrative portion of Daniel makes this point remarkably clear. "How great are His signs / And how mighty are His wonders! / His kingdom is an everlasting kingdom / And His dominion is from generation to generation" (Dan. 4:3). In fact, the book of Daniel show-cases God's matchless wisdom, faithfulness, and power across empires and generations. He outwits and outlasts everything. Not barely—but completely and decisively.

PURPOSES OF BIBLICAL NARRATIVE IN THE PERSONAL MINISTRY OF THE WORD

Biblical narratives are not random collections of historical facts. Rather, they create and impose *theological content, perspective, conviction, action,* and *direction*. Through the stories, God reveals Himself. Through the stories, He reveals us and provides a means to interpret our lives and experiences. "For the word of God is living and active and sharper than any two-edged sword, and piercing as far as the division of soul and spirit, of both joints and marrow, and able to judge the thoughts and intentions of the heart. And there is no creature hidden from His sight, but all things are open and laid bare to the eyes of Him with whom we have to do" (Heb. 4:12–13).

Every narrative creates and provides *theological content*, material given to reveal something about God and the created world in relation to Him. For example, Genesis 1 tells the story of God creating the world. God tells us exactly *what* He wants us to know about His activity during those days. Energy, space, and time arise from His decree. Every created thing forms at His word. Man exists because God resolved to create him in His image—to live under His care and for His display.

The narratives also create and impose *theological perspective*. This is really important! Material has been included, excluded, and organized to convey the story from a superintended point of view. Like a director inviting you to the set of a movie, putting you in a specific chair, and saying, "I want you to watch and listen from here," God's Word governs our frame of reference. When we read the plain language of Scripture, we can safely say, "Here is what He wants me to see and *how* He wants me to see it."

Consider Acts 2 for a moment. The apostles were accused of being drunk because they were declaring "the mighty deeds of God" (v. 11) in foreign languages. So Peter stood up to explain. The whole scene, according to him, fulfilled God's promise through the prophet Joel: "'And it shall be in the last days,' God says, 'That I will pour forth of My Spirit on all mankind" (Acts 2:17).

Peter went on to preach from the Psalms and the story of David to prove Jesus Christ was the promised Messiah. The passage delivers rich theological content from Old Testament prophecy, poetry, and narrative and gives us theological perspective for interpreting the events being witnessed. It was not drunkenness, Peter argued, but the Holy Spirit filling His church. Jesus was not an insignificant figure, but the promised Davidic Messiah. Certain words and moments from Joel's life and David's life were included, and much was excluded, to fix and clarify our view. Like a spotlight focused on a stage, Peter preached in such a way and Luke recorded and organized the material in such a way to show *what* God wants us to see and *how* He wants us to see it.

The narratives of the Bible do even more. They personally engage and challenge us! They create *theological conviction*. They alert us to God and our standing before Him. Peter's sermon seriously affected those who listened. "Now when they heard this, they were pierced to the heart, and said to Peter and the rest of the apostles, 'Brethren, what shall we do?'" (Acts 2:37). Like an earthquake sending tremors through the ground beneath their feet, Peter's words forced them to evaluate the quality of their footing before God. It alarmed them. It should alarm everyone!

At the same time his words provoked *theological action*. After being pierced to the heart by Peter's sermon, the audience cried, "What shall we do?" This should be our cry in response to the Bible's story: *How now shall we believe and live?* Biblical narratives force us to do something with God, for better or for worse. They leave us to believe or disbelieve, to obey or disobey. They draw us near to the Lord or repel us. Either way, we're forced to think, feel, say, and do something in relation to God.

Thankfully we're never left to figure it out on our own. Biblical narratives give *theological direction*. They lead us to God. Right after the people cried out to Peter for help, he said, "Repent, and each of you be baptized in the name of Jesus Christ for the forgiveness of your sins; and you will receive the gift of the Holy Spirit. For the promise is for you and your children and for all who are far off, as many as the LORD our God will call to Himself" (Acts 2:38–39). Right when we need it, the story delivers grace and hope. It gives clear, concrete direction. Using a carefully recorded story of a Jewish festival, a miraculous outpouring of the Holy Spirit, a sermon, and a conversation, Luke's account guides us to the Creator, Lord, and Savior of life. Not only did Peter guide the crowd to the throne of God's grace in Jesus Christ, but Luke, in the way he tells the story, leads us to the same place.

BIBLICAL NARRATIVE SPEAKS TO INDIVIDUAL PEOPLE

Scripture speaks to individual souls because God the Creator and Redeemer actively pursues specific people. The narratives of the Bible clearly illustrate the idea. Moses was a real person the Lord sought, loved, gifted, and guided in life and ministry. We can relate to him. We can learn from everything the Lord spoke to him. While Moses acted as a type of Jesus Christ, bearing various qualities of Him to come (Deut. 18:15), Moses also acted as a fearful, needy-of-grace, frustrated, forgiven, and in-the-process-of-sanctification human being, bearing resemblance to each of us.

A similar conclusion could be drawn from Adam, "who is a type of Him who was to come" (Rom. 5:14). At the same time, he is personally familiar to each of us. The patterns of temptation he faced resemble the patterns of temptation we face (Gen. 3:1–7). The curse he lived under happens to be the same curse we live under (Gen. 3:16–19). The need for a Redeemer he carried is the need we carry (Gen. 3:15). We may not be the hero of his story, or any other story, but we tend to relive various scenes from his story and a great many other scenes from Scripture. We're definitely not *the* focus of the Bible, but we are, nonetheless, *a* focus of the Bible.

The many narratives of Scripture contribute to the redemptive story of Scripture and point to the Redeemer, but in a way that calls you by name and meets you right where you stand, or sit, or kneel, or lie. It says, "You there, Greg, whose hairs I have numbered, whose body I knit together, whose steps I ordained before you could walk, whose name I have written in my book, whose fears I see and understand, whose sins I will not count against you, whose troubles I bear, whom I called from afar, whom I have loved and adopted as my child, whose soul I am refining, I have something important and personal to say to you." We want to hear and help others hear the important and personal things God has to say.

So how might we do this? How do we faithfully and graciously counsel people from the biblical narratives? I want to answer these questions by proposing *nine basic elements, or steps, for using biblical narrative in the personal ministry of the Word*. While much more could be said, I think these can serve as starting points.

ELEMENT ONE: KNOW THE BIBLICAL NARRATIVES AND THEIR PEOPLE WELL

While I realize I am about to state the obvious, I have to say it. If we are to counsel biblically, then we must know the Word of God—deeply, broadly, personally, keenly, perhaps instinctively. When people convey their stories, dilemmas, ideas, emotions, relationships, trials, and desires, then passages and verses and themes of Scripture should flood into our minds. I realize this takes great time and energy to develop, as well as the ongoing ministry of the Holy Spirit. Yet surely it deserves our devotion and commitment.

Good surgeons spend years in training before they put someone under the knife. They spend their entire working lives learning and practicing their craft. They keep growing and refining in their work. The same can be said for us. Good ministers of the Word are, first, good students of the Word. I'm not saying we must be near perfect in our grasp of the Bible before we serve others from it. Rather, we need to know enough about the map and compass to carefully lead others according to Scripture through the complex terrains of human life.

I think we learn by *prayerfully* and *humbly* reading the narratives *over and over and over* again. I can think of no substitute for this part of the process—faithful, personal, and joyfully repetitious reading of Scripture. "For everyone who partakes only of milk is not accustomed to the word of righteousness, for he is an infant. But solid food is for the mature, who because of practice have their senses trained to discern good and evil" (Heb. 5:13–14).

After reading the narratives of Scripture, we should study them. We should dig into the exact meaning of words and the many details of the stories. We should ask questions of the text that drive us toward their meaning and significance. Why did God say and do that? Why are the people responding to Him this way? What is God trying to show them and us through these situations and troubles? Here's where I would encourage good Bible study resources to help you understand basic grammar and various keys to interpreting biblical narrative.[7] It helps to know how to arrive at the main point or points of a biblical story in order to apply it to different areas of modern life.

At the same time, we should learn the narratives of the Scripture in a way that transforms us, in a way that draws us to the Lord Jesus Christ and feeds our communion with Him. They should be no less than the active voice of God in our lives—governing, guiding, feeding, and compelling us. When passages invade and shape our thoughts, emotions, passions, and activities, we will be better prepared to apply them wisely and graciously to others. Surely we must dine each day at His table and drink each day from His cup if we actually intend to help others find nourishment there.

ELEMENT TWO: HEAR PEOPLE AND THEIR NARRATIVES WELL

If we want to counsel people biblically, then we must come to know *them* well. That is, hear enough of their history, relationships, thoughts, activities, motivations, and desires to understand and respond to them with prudence and love. "He who gives an answer before he hears, it is folly and shame to him" (Prov. 18:13). Paul told us to speak "only such a word as is good for edification according to the need of the moment, so that it will give grace to those who hear" (Eph. 4:29). Good listening guides us to the need of the moment. I hope to never forget what Dietrich Bonhoeffer said, "Brotherly pastoral care is essentially distinguished from preaching by the fact that, added to the task of speaking the Word, there is the obligation of listening."[8]

Think back to Greg for a minute. The more he shares his burdens and concerns, relevant experiences from childhood, lifelong passions and desires, key relationships, fears, obsessions, joys, and disappointments, the more insight we gain into who he is and where he needs help. What motivates him? Who does he live for, bank on, look to? By whose power, and to what end, and by what means does he seek change? All these questions start finding their answers in the atmosphere of warm, attentive, and transparent conversation.

This step in the process is dependent on and shaped by the previous step. Wise, careful listening depends on a biblical understanding of people. Humble, discerning questions arise from a broad, personal, and perceptive understanding of Scripture. The clearer we see people from God's point of view, the better we can filter and organize their stories, know what to notice, when to clarify, and where to dig deeper.

In Numbers 11, Moses asked God to end his life. "So if You are going to deal thus with me, please kill me at once, if I have favor in Your sight, and do not let me see my wretchedness" (v. 15). What a remarkable request! Where did it come from? How did he get there?

The Scripture shows us. Earlier in the passage, the people cried out and wept over food. It wasn't the first time! Because of their complaining, "the anger of the LORD was kindled greatly, and Moses was displeased" (Num. 11:10). Moses felt the burden of providing for the people and saw no conceivable way to satisfy their demands. Worst of all, he felt totally alone and unable to escape. In no uncertain terms Moses said, "If this is what I have to expect for the rest of the journey, LORD, just kill me now!"

I think the account can shape the way we respond to someone who expresses dejection and hopelessness. When Greg says, "Some days I get out of bed and just pray for death," we could ask, "Where do you feel trapped in life?" "What are you trying to escape?" "In what ways are you trying to please people and/or God to no avail?" Or maybe, "Talk about where you feel most alone." In my mind, these questions and prompts *arise from* Numbers 11. A prior awareness of the passage can organize what we hear from Greg and guide our next steps in the conversation.

Of course, the reasons for Greg's dejection may not mirror Moses' reasons. Perhaps his reasons sound more like Jonah's (Jonah 4), or Elijah's (1 Kings 19:1–4), or Ahab's (1 Kings 21:1–5). Any and all of these passages can provide a framework for hearing, understanding, and loving Greg with the Lord's wisdom and care.

ELEMENT THREE: SEE THE PARALLELS AND CONNECTIONS

According to Alistair Begg, "Expository preaching seeks to fuse the two horizons of the biblical text and the contemporary world."[9] His perspective on the public ministry of the Word can help us think rightly about the personal ministry of the Word. Biblical counseling aims to *fuse the two horizons of the biblical text and the person at hand.* The fusing begins by seeing the parallels and connections between the people of Scripture and the person we serve.

The *people* of the Bible talk, feel, and act like us. We talk, feel, and act like them. We all see and know this! Every one of us can read an account in the Bible and say, "Yes, that's how I am too!" Or "I know what he's talking about." The words, attitudes, and actions we observe in the biblical characters resemble our own—all of us being made by the same Creator, living in the same world, under the same curse, and in need of the same redemption.

At other times the characters of Scripture display attitudes and actions unlike our own, whether righteous or unrighteous. When on his way to Jerusalem, knowing prison and pain awaited him, the apostle Paul said, "But I do not consider my life of any account as dear to myself, so that I may finish my course and the ministry which I received from the Lord Jesus, to testify solemnly of the gospel of the grace of God" (Acts 20:24). I think we're meant to say, "Mercy! I need to think and live that way." We could say to Greg, "If you want to learn how to deal with fear and anxiety in your life, then just watch Paul in action. Learn from him." In fact, Paul tells us to. "The things you have learned and received and heard and seen in me, practice these things, and the God of peace will be with you" (Phil. 4:9).

The *situations* people face in the stories of Scripture resemble our own—the trials, relationships, and personal histories. Moses and Greg faced adversity in relationships. They felt exhaustion and despair. Tension in their marriages, hardships in ministry, encouragement and discouragement with the Lord, confusion about His works and timing—all these circumstances they bear in common.

The *themes and truths* of the biblical narratives parallel the themes and truths of our lives as well: marriage, child-rearing, anxiety, anger, salvation, hope, love, war, reconciliation, sexual assault, perseverance, and money. A thousand themes and topics have been woven into and emerge from the stories of Adam, Abraham, Jacob, Joseph, the judges, the kings, the exile, and the book of Acts. As we sit and listen to Greg describe and explain the themes and topics of his life, we can pray for the Spirit to show us the innumerable points of intersection in Scripture.

ELEMENT FOUR: ENTER THE STORY TOGETHER

Once we see enough parallels and connections between the stories of the people in front of us and the stories of Scripture, we pick one of those stories and enter it. We enter by turning to the narrative and reading together. Of course, this step depends on the previous three. And we will take this step only if we believe the Word of God—and thoughts or truths arising from it, when used by the Spirit of God—has the power to explain and transform us.

At some point during my meetings with Greg, we would open the Scripture to Exodus 1 and begin to read. Perhaps we would read every verse of the first two chapters. Or we might hit a few verses from every paragraph. I might paraphrase parts of the narrative, but not too much of it, since I want Greg to hear, primarily, God's voice, not mine. The text itself can guide our questions, ideas, and discussion. We may cover a lot of ground in the passage, or we may not. Maybe I have Greg read the first dozen chapters of Exodus between our meetings and share the highlights. It could be done a great many ways. My goal would be to enter the story with Greg in order to get our affections and thoughts into and around what God has spoken.

ELEMENT FIVE: STAY INSIDE THE STORY TOGETHER

Once inside the story, we ought to stay there for a little while. This means paying attention to God and people in the story, considering what God is revealing about Himself and His works, considering what the people must have been wanting, thinking, feeling, and pursuing.

Let's go back to Exodus. The narrative slows down in chapter 3 when God reveals Himself to Moses at the burning bush. I think we're meant to notice the change of pace. Centuries of time were covered in the opening verses of Exodus, and forty years passed during chapter 2. But when God reveals Himself and speaks to Moses in chapter 3, their encounter spans several pages of text. It's one of those conversations we're meant to hear and soak in.

Given Greg's wrestling with anxiety, panic, and approval seeking, I might try to help him notice the same patterns in Moses. "But Moses said to God, 'Who am I, that I should go to Pharaoh?'" (Ex. 3:11). If we jump further into the interaction, "Then Moses said, 'What if they will not believe me or listen to what I say?'" (Ex. 4:1). And later, "Then Moses said to the LORD, 'Please, LORD, I have never been eloquent, neither recently nor in time past, nor since You have spoken to Your servant; for I am slow of speech and slow of tongue'" (Ex. 4:10). At every turn God comforts Moses with promises of His presence, power, and purpose. "Who has made man's mouth? Or who makes him mute or deaf, or seeing or blind? Is it not I, the LORD?" (Ex. 4:11). Finally, Moses pleads, "Please, LORD, now send the message by whomever You will." (Ex. 4:13). That is, "LORD, please send someone else!"

By staying inside the story, Greg and I can absorb far more than a single, static principle. We can witness *a relational dynamic* between God and Moses that explains Moses's fear, anxiety, and disobedience at multiple levels (thoughts, emotions, actions, desires) and across multiple relationships (with God, with snakes, with his wife, with Pharaoh, with the people). The story exposes the weakness of Moses' faith and his self-centeredness and how these affect every aspect of his life. The drama shows God trying to shift the focus of attention back to His power, provision, and glorious purposes. God invites Moses to a mission far bigger than his own social standing and success. The question that truly strikes and convicts me from their conversation is not *what* are you going to think and do? But rather, *upon whom* are you going to focus, look, trust, rest, rejoice, hope, and cast your obedience?

The text never explicitly says, "Moses is anxious and afraid because he thinks about himself, trusts in himself, and leans on his own understanding, no matter what God says or promises." But the text, quite decisively, forces this conclusion. It forces us to evaluate our way of relating to our God. It urges us to ask ourselves, "When facing a scary or painful situation, to whom do I run and in whom do I trust?" The passage offers a powerful diagnostic. We can almost hear God asking each of us, "Exactly who do you want to talk about right now, you or Me? Who will consume your thoughts? Around whom will this conversation, and your whole life, revolve?"

Staying inside the story also helps us see the story unfold in a divinely ordered sequence. Over time we get to watch God transform Moses. The narrative actually answers the question, How do people change? — though indirectly. The story never says Moses changed because he spent time in the presence of God looking upon His glory and learning from His Word, but the content and flow of the story definitely proves it. By the end of the Exodus story, Moses approached God with a new agenda. "I pray You, show me Your glory!" (Ex. 33:18). Not less pain, but *more of God* — that's what Moses wanted in the end. The story chronicles the supernatural transformation of a man.

ELEMENT SIX: EXTRACT A FEW RELEVANT TRUTHS

It may be possible to draw out fifty relevant points for Greg from the opening four chapters of Exodus, let alone the rest of the story. But I think we should avoid that. Pouring a flood of truths and ideas onto Greg probably would leave him overwhelmed and unsure of what to think or do next. Better to settle on a few ideas for him to take home.

Perhaps we extract the truth that Moses was created, called, and equipped for a mission bigger than himself, just like all of us. Moses does not exist to help people think highly of him, but to help people think highly of God. With Greg we might say, "Like Moses, you exist to serve a purpose greater than you, and to fix upon a Person greater than you." Much discussion can flow from this single, relevant truth.

When the narrative warrants it, I would highlight truths about Jesus Christ and the gospel for Greg's daily life, since "the gospel … is the power of God for salvation" (Rom. 1:16). If we're talking the Passover lamb in Exodus 12, then a connection to the life, death, and resurrection of Jesus Christ makes perfect sense. It makes sense to emphasize and celebrate our justification before God because of Jesus Christ, our perfect substitute and righteousness, and the effects His work for our redemption should render in our lives.

Images and events stand out from Exodus that reveal the nature and work of our God with His people *and* foreshadow Jesus Christ. The bitter water made sweet declared something critical about God to the Israelites: "I, the LORD, am your healer" (Ex. 15:22–26). It also declared something about the Christ to come, who would be our healer (John 5). The provision of manna (Ex. 16:1–21), the Sabbath (Ex. 16:22–30), and water from a rock (Ex. 17:1–7) taught something about God in relation to His people at the time *and* looked to a future Redeemer. Jesus Christ is our bread of life (John 6:29–35), the Lord of the Sabbath and our rest (Luke 6:5), and our living water (John 4:10, 14; John 7:37–39). At any given moment, one or more of these realities could be something for Greg to consider, believe, and apply. Greg and I could spend hours discussing and enjoying these life-changing truths.

ELEMENT SEVEN: ENHANCE THE NARRATIVE INTERPRETATION AND APPLICATION FROM THE REST OF SCRIPTURE

When counseling from biblical narrative, especially a lengthy narrative, hundreds of cross-references might come to mind. This is good. We must interpret and apply biblical narrative in the context of the whole Bible. There always exists the danger of making the story mean what we want or missing the main point of it altogether. The rest of Scripture can help us stay true to the meaning of the narrative, then help us drive the points of the text home.

Say we want Greg to realize that lasting heart and life change happens by spending time in the presence of the Lord and beholding His glory through the Word. Moses changed because he beheld the glory of God. Change won't happen, we believe, by Greg simply looking more carefully at himself in order to fix himself. With this goal in mind, we should offer other passages of Scripture that support the idea. Perhaps we could start with 2 Corinthians 3:18: "But we all, with unveiled face, beholding as in a mirror the glory of the Lord, are being transformed into the same image from glory to glory, just as from the Lord, the Spirit."

In this passage, Paul is saying that lasting and good change in the Christian life doesn't actually happen by beholding self, but by beholding Christ. We look into the mirror of the Word of God and the gospel to see Him and His work. And the more we see, enjoy, honor, and worship Him, the more the Holy Spirit changes us into His glorious image. That's incredible. If we really want to be transformed in beautiful and eternal ways, then we need to stop looking so often at ourselves. We need to begin looking more intently at the glory of Jesus Christ revealed and exalted in the Scriptures (Heb. 12:2–3; 1 John 3:2–3). The life of Moses teaches this reality and other passages from Scripture confirm it.

ELEMENT EIGHT: APPLY THE NARRATIVE TRUTH TO HERE-AND-NOW PERSONAL LIFE

All fruitful time in the Word of God leaves us with something to *believe* and something to *obey*. These two outcomes are closely related — they are the two legs of walking with God. We could say *knowing* and *practicing*, or *trusting* and *following*. Each pair of words offers a way to think about the believing and obeying parts of life with Christ. Good biblical counseling tries to get *who we are in Christ* and *what we do in Christ* harmonized and cooperating in daily life.

Perhaps Greg could go home and spend more time beholding, enjoying, and worshiping Jesus Christ through the Word of God. Maybe Greg needs to cry out from his affliction more often and honestly with God. Perhaps Greg needs to develop a daily posture of repentance from self-focus and concern for his own glory and think more often of God and His glory. If he doesn't rest in the sufficient grace of God forgiving his sin through Jesus Christ our Passover Lamb, then he may need to sit and reflect on the truth of it. I think counseling ministry builds in excitement and fascination at this stage because there are endless possibilities for application.

The key, therefore, rests in narrowing the endless possibilities down to a few—a few truths to believe and obey. Greg doesn't need to bite, chew, swallow, and digest the whole meal at one time. It will never be a one-time-fix-all. In fact, this idea brings us to our final point.

ELEMENT NINE: ENCOURAGE OVER TIME

The sometimes slow-moving nature of biblical narrative, and especially the gradual transformation of the people presented in them, can offer comfort to our stubborn souls. We are each, in our own way, by divine decree and providence, a work in progress. We must not forget this. The earthly lives of Moses, David, Abraham, Peter, and so many others force us to remember the truth. People sanctify slowly, at least from an earthly point of view. The promise of change we have been given does not guarantee a great velocity, but a great destination. The destination will come quickly only because death comes quickly. "Behold, I tell you a mystery; we will not all sleep, but we will all be changed, in a moment, in the twinkling of an eye, at the last trumpet; for the trumpet will sound, and the dead will be raised imperishable, and we will be changed" (1 Cor. 15:51–52).

In the meantime, we must accept with patience the time it takes for us to learn and grow. Counseling from biblical narrative, I have often found, thrusts this perspective into our minds and onto our conversations. We simply cannot cover the whole story in a single sitting. We cannot digest and apply every truth in one conversation. The only way to joyfully persevere in this work is to accept the smallness and temporariness of our part. The part matters, we are assured, but as a humble and joyful representative of a God who is eternally wise and supreme. God changes people, and what a privilege we have been given to be used by God in such a glorious work!

CONCLUSION

Since the Lord delivered a large portion of His Word in narrative forms and shaped the basic character of His Word into a grand redemptive story, the personal ministry of the Word must include the proper and timely use of narrative passages. They offer something wonderful for us today. They offer the theological content, perspective, conviction, action, and direction we need for daily life. They offer food for our souls and light for our paths. Through the stories of Scripture, God reveals Himself, and us, and how we can live with Him and one another fruitfully in the present age.

This chapter proposed a nine-step process for the use of biblical narrative in personal ministry. Using parts of Moses' life and the Exodus story in ministry to Greg, we considered the importance of (1) knowing the biblical narratives well, (2) hearing people and their narratives well, and (3) seeing the parallels and connections between the two horizons of Scripture and the person at hand. After (4) entering the story together, (5) staying inside it, (6) extracting the relevant truths, and (7) enhancing them from the rest of Scripture, we can move to (8) applying the biblical truths to personal life and (9) encouraging one another in the truth over time.

These steps can serve as a starting point for using any narrative of Scripture in serving someone facing any range of troubles in human life. At a minimum, the process can help us deal faithfully with the Bible as a whole and lessen the risk of ignoring or misusing those parts of Scripture our Lord intentionally and carefully included for our consumption — to serve His glory, to work for our true good, and to build His church.

CHAPTER 18

USING WISDOM LITERATURE IN THE PERSONAL MINISTRY OF THE WORD

DEEPAK REJU

I can't do this anymore." "Jill" sat on my couch, tears in her eyes, heartache and bitterness ruling her heart. Her marriage was in bad shape, and she was exhausted.

"John," her husband, was a workaholic. Early in their marriage, John liked his job, but not enough to keep him away from his new bride. As marriage became hard over the last few years, and as the pressure to perform at work grew with his ever-increasing responsibilities, John's work became a good excuse to avoid the troubles at home. Jill's "nagging and complaining" were just the start of their troubles. Her high expectations, his preoccupation with climbing the corporate ladder, and his passive leadership at home all combined to slowly degrade their relationship. Not surprisingly, when I asked John how he felt about their marriage, he said things like: "I don't want to go home because we're both miserable," or "She must hate me because she is so belittling to me when we argue," or "Jill just doesn't meet my needs."

In a messy situation like this, questions abound: How do we (as pastors, friends, family, counselors, or fellow church members) help them? How do Jill and John face their disintegrating marriage with hope? What does God's Word have to say to both of them? Does faith matter to them, and if so, what difference does it make? Is it possible to save their marriage and rebuild it on a better foundation, namely, Christ?

Our goal for this chapter is to consider how the genre of Wisdom Literature can be used in marital counseling. To do so, we will give attention to Psalms, Proverbs, Ecclesiastes, Song of Songs, and Job. A central question we want to consider is this: *How does Wisdom Literature help us to deal with the suffering, futility, and confusion that often arise in bad marriages?*

This is our bridge question. It spans the chasm that goes from the biblical text into real life, showing how biblical poetry and Wisdom Literature are relevant to what we do and how we counsel. Too many Christians today are stuck in the ravine between the biblical text and real life, not knowing how to cross over from one to the other.

Why take an interest in Wisdom Literature? Sadly, many Christians are biblically illiterate, spending very little time in Scripture, especially neglecting the Old Testament. So it is imperative for biblical counselors to show the relevance of the whole Bible to daily life. A counselor who is genuinely biblical won't be satisfied with a lazy knowledge of just a few texts. Wise counselors will want to know *all* of God's Word because they understand the vast treasure trove it contains. Wisdom Literature offers riches and wisdom beyond compare — gold, silver, rubies, and diamonds that can enrich the counselor's work and provide deep insight into the counselee's heart and life.

Apart from the rapturous descriptions of love in Song of Songs and the adulterous women in Proverbs 5 to 9, there is not much that (on the surface of things) we commonly associate with marriage in this part of the Bible. Because sex is such a vital part of marriage, it is obvious how Song of Songs is relevant for marriage, but how are Psalms, Proverbs, Ecclesiastes, and Job useful in marital counseling?

A BRIEF INTRODUCTION
TO WISDOM LITERATURE

Let's do a quick review of Wisdom Literature. Our desire is to understand the genre so that we can faithfully apply the Scriptures in counseling.[1]

A major component of biblical literature is *poetry*. After narrative, poetry is the most common genre in the Bible.[2] It covers well over one-third of the Old Testament and includes both individual poems (Psalms) and sections where it is interwoven into other genres. Biblical poetry should be read and understood as poetry, which means its lines are compressed and rich with biblical imagery. Unlike English poetry, biblical poetry doesn't exhibit distinct rhythm or rhyme, but uses other literary devices.[3] There is a lot that does not translate from Hebrew to English, like Hebrew sounds or syntax, so some of the beauty of biblical poetry is lost in translation. But the most important element of biblical poetry—the meaning of words—is faithfully translated by modern-day scholars. Jesus, the greatest teacher that ever lived, used poetry in his teaching, and, understandably so, poetry creates memorable content and form for the hearers.

Not only does biblical poetry communicate facts about a situation (e.g., Job's anger at God or his friends; the lover's affection and attraction for his beloved in Song of Songs), but it also reveals the emotions wrapped up in this content. You not only know David's plight as he is chased by his enemies, you also feel his despair. You not only know Job's problems as he loses everything, but you experience his anger at God. You not only hear about Solomon's experimentation as he tries to find purpose and meaning, but you experience his deep disappointment as he describes the futility of finding hope or happiness through worldly things.

Wisdom Literature is a broad genre that encompasses the writings of the wise.[4] Its goal is to encourage the reader to pursue godliness and flee from foolishness. The wisdom books can be categorized in two ways. *Speculative wisdom* is contemplative in nature. It includes disputations and dialogues (Job) or self-reflective monologues (Ecclesiastes) and attempts to consider topics such as the injustice of evil, the meaning of human existence, and the futility of being attached to worldly things. Rather than being theoretical philosophy, these deep questions about life are considered with the concrete examples of Job and Solomon. *Proverbial wisdom* is in the short, pithy sayings that give us guidelines for how to live life successfully and in the fear of God. These are recorded observations of God's created order that help one to live in harmony with God's ordering of His world.

POETRY FOR YOUR MARRIAGE

The book of the Bible most commonly associated with biblical poetry is the Psalms.[5] Psalms is one of the most beloved parts of Scripture. Trial, suffering, a cursing of one's enemies, thanksgiving, intrigue, and, most importantly, hope in God are all present and provide the rich content that makes this some of the most engaging and enriching poetry ever written. The book of Psalms is a collection of 150 separate poetic songs written by various authors over the course of a thousand years, from the 1400s BC to 450 BC. The Psalms are often an oasis for those who are suffering. As one of my grieving counselees said recently, "The psalms put into words my experience of suffering, especially when I don't know how to describe what I'm going through."

Each psalm was written as a complete unit, with a specific background and context. Some questions to consider as you read the psalms: What was the psalm's function in Israel's life? Was it a liturgy for worship, a wedding song for a ceremony, a dirge for a funeral, or something else? What information is given to us by the superscription? The best and most reliable ancient manuscripts of the psalms provide superscriptions, so while the superscriptions are not inspired like the biblical text, they are helpful.[6] As we study the different literary devices used in poetry, we see that an author's flow of thought is not always clear, so the reader needs a "disciplined imagination" to follow the progression.[7] The psalms often employ images rather than abstractions, the figurative rather than the literal. One useful way to study Psalms is to think about the different types of psalms throughout the book—praise, lament, thanksgiving, penitence, confidence, remembrance, and many more. Each type of psalm has certain common elements.

One of the bridges we can construct from the psalms into marital counseling is *suffering*. The psalms are well known as a treatise on suffering. Most marital struggles are not as bad as the graphic experiences of many of the psalmists. (You normally don't have your spouse chasing you on horseback with spears, right?) Yet marital difficulties are often hard, frustrating, and, at times, unbearable, so they rightfully can be labeled as a form of suffering.

While all the psalms are useful, *psalms of lament* can be especially helpful in counseling struggling couples. Jill wanted to give up and couldn't bear the marriage anymore. She was grieved over the state of her marriage. As her counselor, I wanted Jill to see that Scripture speaks to her difficulties. So, toward the end of our first meeting, we read Psalm 13 together. King David, the author of Psalm 13, starts out with questions that resonated with her experience: "How long, O LORD? Will you forget me forever? How long will you hide your face from me? How long must I take counsel in my soul and have sorrow in my heart all the day? How long shall my enemy be exalted over me?" (Ps. 13:1–2).

Jill's struggle was not just with her husband, but with God who put her in this marriage. To come to terms with her marital difficulties, she had to come to terms with what God was doing. A good first step was to ask God hard questions that put her suffering into words. "How long, O LORD?" was often on the tip of her tongue, though it came out in various expressions, such as "I'm exhausted" or "I can't do this anymore." I asked Jill to articulate what hard question she would ask God. After a few minutes of thinking, she said, "I want to know why God is punishing me with this bad marriage. What did I do wrong?" That's a very honest question from someone who is struggling.

Jill was scared that she was all alone in this battle. Characteristic of many biblical laments, there is a plea to God for help. "Consider and answer me, O LORD my God; light up my eyes, lest I sleep the sleep of death" (Ps. 13:3).

As a second step in applying the psalm, I asked Jill to follow King David's example and ask something of God based on her hard question. My hope was to embolden Jill to ask something of God rather than isolate herself (which was her normal habit). Her petition was quite simple: "God, don't abandon me in my time of need. Love me, please."

"But I have trusted in your steadfast love; my heart shall rejoice in your salvation. I will sing to the LORD, because he has dealt bountifully with me" (Ps. 13:5 – 6). Jill was not ready to trust God. She was not at all confident in His character. "Maybe God just doesn't love me." So owning the last two verses was much more difficult compared to the first three, but it gave her something to strive for. "I know I need to trust God, but I can't right now." As a third step I asked her to write out in her journal (as a homework assignment) what it would take to fight for faith and trust in God while she struggles in her marriage.

Because marriage difficulties so often focus couples on their own selfish desires and marital fights (James 4:1 – 2), a husband and wife become blind to God and His providential working in their lives. Can Psalm 13 give Jill greater insight into her marital struggles? Can David's words help her to see how to relate to the God she professes to love? Can it begin to define her suffering? Absolutely. Psalm 13 helps her to ask the hard questions, to turn to God in her dark moments, and to begin to trust Him despite the circumstances.

Counselors will be well served to make use of the psalms of lament to build a bridge into marital suffering. Psalm 13 is just one of a host of individual laments found in the Psalter; others include Psalms 3 – 7, 17, 22, 25 – 28, 31, 35, 39, 42 – 43, 54 – 57, 59, 61 – 64, 70 – 71, 77, 86, 88, 102, 120, 130, and 140 – 43.[8] Knowing a particular type of psalm and its key elements helps us to cross over from the biblical text to real life. In Jill's case, we used our knowledge about the different parts of a lament (e.g., complaints, a plea to God for help, an expression of trust, and confidence in God's response) to sort through her difficult marriage.

Another practical suggestion for using psalms in marital counseling relates to *penitential psalms* (Pss. 32, 38, 51). An important step in all marital counseling is helping a spouse come to terms with their own sin (Matt. 7:1–5). In John's life, confession of sin was nonexistent, so helping him to own his sin, especially his passive leadership and avoidance of his wife, was key to moving the marriage forward. While recognition of sin (2 Peter 1:9) and verbal confession (James 5:16) are important, conviction of sin, sorrow over sin, and genuine repentance are gifts of the Holy Spirit (2 Cor. 7:9–11; 2 Tim. 2:25). Helping John see his sin and acknowledge it using penitential psalms was a first step in moving the marriage forward.

After some time of reflection in the biblical texts, another useful homework assignment is to ask the counselee to use the psalms of lament as a model to *write their own psalm*. The goal is to put their marital difficulties in their own words using key elements from the psalms of lament (asking hard questions to God; complaints; pleas to God for help; a trust and confidence in God's response). The key to making this assignment helpful is to not allow the counselee to just vent their frustrations, but to try to model the psalms of lament, which commonly add an expression of trust in God. Real life is most often a strange and wonderful mixture of both sorrow and joy, so that should be reflected in the counselee's writing.

WISDOM FOR YOUR MARRIAGE

Ecclesiastes, Job, and Proverbs are the three books most commonly associated with Wisdom Literature. I will briefly introduce each book, consider a few hermeneutical principles, and see how each book can be applied to marital counseling.

Ecclesiastes

Ecclesiastes[9] was written by King Solomon, David's son, who was world renowned for his great wisdom.[10] This book is an autobiographical account by Solomon, looking back on his years and reflecting on the meaning of life. The main point is that finding purpose in life apart from God is futile (Ecc. 12:13–14). The things of this world—pleasure, work, achievement, possessions, friends, etc.—are all meaningless when pursued as ends unto themselves. True purpose and joy in life is found in God. Solomon writes in order to alert the reader to the many mistakes he made, hoping to warn those who are younger to not follow the same path. The reader gets to peek into his journal, witnessing the misguided path of a king who had everything that life had to offer: "And I applied my heart to seek and to search out by wisdom all that is done under heaven" (Ecc. 1:13).

Ecclesiastes is composed of Solomon's personal reflections (1:12–12:7), with an introductory and concluding frame (1:1–11; 12:8–14) that puts Solomon's journal in proper perspective. The book includes opening formulas ("I have seen ..." or "I saw ... " in 1:14; 3:16; 4:1; 5:13; 6:1; et al.), example stories and proverbs, poetry (1:2–11; 3:1–8; 7:1–13), and concluding morals drawn from Solomon's observations (2:24–25; 3:22; 4:12; 5:18–20; et al.). The key to understanding Ecclesiastes is to interpret the different elements (reflections, stories, poetry, proverbs) in light of the concluding moral observations and the frames on the front and the back of the book.

When I started to help John, one of the first things we needed to sort out was his obsession with work. John used his job as a way to escape his marriage. He couldn't stand the daily nagging and the self-righteous disposition that Jill took in arguments. At his job, life was filled with nothing but praise. His boss loved him. His personal assistant worked really well with him ("We both seem to be 'in sync' with one another."). He got a lot of satisfaction from the job. So why go home? He would often remark, "Why leave paradise just to walk into a war zone?"

The bridge I tried to construct between the biblical text and John's job was *exposing the vanity of his work*. John worshiped his job. He was suffering from a worship disorder—he had reoriented his entire life around his job. My goal was to help him see that in order for his life to function properly, his work could no longer be ultimate. In order for his marriage to be restored, he had to reorder his priorities. God had to come first, and only then could marriage and work be reprioritized in his life.

A typical strategy I employ is to use the biblical text to shed light on any idolatry (success, friends, pleasure, achievement, work, etc.) that distracts from the marriage. This would be the first step in helping John face up to his worship disorder. Because King Solomon's catalog of vanities are not just problems for his own day but are common temptations for modern-day readers, we can learn from Solomon's mistakes. In our initial conversation, John and I read Ecclesiastes 2:17–26; 4:4–12; and 5:1–20. Because John took great pride in his work as a financial planner, he was intrigued by Ecclesiastes 2:20–21:

> So I turned about and gave my heart up to despair over all the toil of my labors under the sun, because sometimes a person who has toiled with wisdom and knowledge and skill must leave everything to be enjoyed by someone who did not toil for it. This also is vanity and a great evil.

The thought of putting so much effort into building financial portfolios, only to see it all given away to someone who is less capable, was depressing to him. This was the first chink in his protective armor. But the portion of Scripture that really began to rearrange the furniture in John's heart was Ecclesiastes 2:24–25: "There is nothing better for a person than that he should eat and drink and find enjoyment in his toil. This also, I saw, is from the hand of God, for apart from him who can eat or who can have enjoyment?" (cf. also 5:18–20).

At first John didn't buy into it. Often counseling moves slowly because of the blinding effects of sin. John loved his job and hated his marriage—end of story. His plan was to spend very little time at home in order to avoid his wife. A few months later, he got the biggest promotion that he could ever anticipate, and not long afterward, he began to reflect on how it didn't add any joy to his life, but actually had made things harder because it brought a lot more pressure to his job. His idol had finally slipped off of its pedestal. He said, "I had dreamed of this promotion for years, and when I finally got it, it just wasn't as meaningful as I thought it would be. In fact, I almost regret taking it."

Ultimately, to enjoy his work and find satisfaction in it, John had to understand it as a gift from God. That was Solomon's concluding moral for his journal entries about work (Eccl. 2:24–26; 5:18–20). So when work wasn't enjoyable anymore, John started to wonder what else he had to turn to, and the only thing that seemed to be left was God.

Now that his idol of work was beginning to weaken, I had John write his own Solomonic journal entry about work.[11] This was part two of my strategy to expose John's vanities and help him reprioritize his life. One week later, John came to me with the following entry in his journal:

> I am starting to hate my job. I don't want to do this anymore. I don't know what to do. What are you doing to me, God? Don't you like me? You must not because my life sucks. My marriage is bad, and now the one thing I liked (my job) is no good. I thought this promotion would be much more glorious, but it's not. What else do I have to look forward to? Nothing. Absolutely nothing.

I asked John to rewrite his journal in light of Ecclesiastes 2:24–26; 5:18–20; 12:13–14. He came back with this: "I hate my job, but I have to acknowledge that God gave it to me. It's better than being unemployed like my brother. Maybe if I was scared of God more, I wouldn't be so fixated on my job." Not exactly a glowing praise of God, but it was a start.

Another practical suggestion for using Ecclesiastes in marital counseling involves *writing an Ecclesiastes journal entry to expose any kind of vanity in life.* Solomon's list of vanities is very applicable to modern-day readers (2 Cor. 10:13), but does not exhaust every possibility. There are some modern-day vanities that Solomon probably would have never conceived of despite all of his wisdom (smartphones, destination weddings, etc.). So, one suggestion is to get counselees to read the entire book of Ecclesiastes and write a Solomon-like journal entry based on their own personal vanities. The entry can be written as a personal narrative or even poetry. Similar to the Psalms exercise, the key is to not just let the counselees vent, but to make sure they write in light of Solomon's epilogue in 12:13–14. Earthly vanities need to be viewed in light of our fear of the Lord and His final judgment.

Proverbs[12]

The book of Proverbs contains 513 proverbs written by a Davidic king from Israel (1:1), likely Solomon, and compiled with the work of other authors ("the wise" in 22:17–24:34, Agur in 30:1–33, and Lemuel in 31:1–9). Solomon's interest in proverbs is well documented in 1 Kings 4:29–34: "Solomon's wisdom surpassed the wisdom of all people of the east and all the wisdom of Egypt.... He also spoke 3,000 proverbs, and his songs were 1,005" (vv. 30, 32).

The purpose of Proverbs is set out in the very first chapter: "To know wisdom and instruction, to understand words of insight, to receive instruction in wise dealing, in righteousness, justice, and equity; to give prudence to the simple, knowledge and discretion to the youth—Let the wise hear and increase in learning, and the one who understands obtain guidance" (Prov. 1:2–5).

Solomon wanted the reader to gain wisdom, which begins with a fear of the Lord and moves out from there into all of life. Folly, in contrast, is more than just ignorance; "fools despise wisdom and instruction" (Prov. 1:7). Folly is described as done by one who despises the godly path.[13]

The first nine chapters set up the context for the entire book. King Solomon, as a father, is addressing his son and invites him to a decision—to choose a life that follows the path of wisdom and spurns folly. What follows are two kinds of conversations with the son—pleas and warnings (1:8 – 19; 2:1 – 3:12; 3:21 – 7:27), and descriptions of wisdom and folly, which are both personified as women trying to lure the son into their ways (1:20 – 33; 8:1 – 9:18). While the father stands in front of his son, instructing him, wisdom and folly sit on each shoulder (like a little devil and angel whispering in each ear), trying to convince the son of their individual merits. Which path will the son choose? Will he listen to the wise warnings of his loving, God-fearing father? Or will he choose the path of folly? The later chapters of the book (chapters 10 – 30) are filled with rich proverbial sayings that should be read in light of the first nine chapters.[14] With each proverb, the reader is confronted with a central question: will you choose wisdom or folly?

The proverbial sayings are moral guidelines and wise observations that give basic instructions in how to live a God-fearing life (Prov. 29:25). They offer practical guidance. These sayings are meant to describe the way life normally works, but there are exceptions.[15] Proverbs are not meant to be foolproof promises that guarantee an outcome if one follows them. Most proverbs are relevant to a specific situation or occasion. Because each proverb is circumstantially relevant, its natural range of application is limited.[16]

The bridge into John and Jill's marriage was using Proverbs as a way to highlight and clear up *the confusion in their marital communication.* Often in marital conflict, communication breaks down. Couples need help sorting through their practical, tactical, and foolish habits in communication. As a homework assignment, I gave John and Jill a catalog of proverbs related to communication.[17]

I asked them each to pick out three weaknesses, three strengths, and three ideals in their communication. In other words, tell me three things wrong in your communication, three things right, and three things you hope to learn.

Simply reading proverbs does not make problems go away. Rather, the proverbs provide insight into foolish communication patterns. But without any understanding (Prov. 18:2), there is little hope of change.

John picked proverbs related to anger as a more obvious

communication problem (Prov. 29:11), but the one that surprised him was Proverbs 10:18: "The one who conceals hatred has lying lips." Rather than deal with his marital difficulties, for months John would just avoid his wife and stay at work. His workaholism was really a cover-up for his hatred of his marriage. He thought he was just avoiding Jill, but when he came to see that as a form of lying, the moral connotation was unavoidable.

Another practical suggestion for using Proverbs in marital counseling involves *using specific proverbs for specific marital problems*. Most proverbs are situationally specific. While there are many proverbs specific to marriage (Prov. 5:18; 12:4; 18:22; 19:13; 21:9; 25:24; 27:15; 30:23; 31:10, 11, 23, 28), most deal with the merits of a good wife and the problems of a bad one. And there is a lot more to marriage than just choosing or tolerating your wife. In order to apply the proverbs, one needs to understand which ones are most relevant for marriage. If you are like me, you probably have a few proverbs tucked away for certain situations, but many elude your memory.[18] So, as a counselor, it is useful to have a topically organized catalog of proverbs that address issues in marital counseling—see this note for one such list.[19]

As you come to know the specific issues of a couple, you may return to this catalog and pick a range of proverbs that relate to their circumstances. Keep a topical list of proverbs right next to your counseling chair so you can easily pick a few proverbs for each spouse to meditate on during the week (maybe one for each day of the week). Pick them out during the session or at the end of the session so you can assign *specific* proverbs relevant to a *specific* person and the *specific* issues discussed in that day's session. I won't ask a couple to just read them; I ask them to draw out the relevance for their marriage by considering: What is the general principle behind the proverb? Have them write out the point of the proverb in just one sentence. Is this proverb relevant for your marriage, and if so, why? What do you need to think, feel, commit to, say, or do that will help you to follow this wisdom and reject folly? As you begin to use Proverbs for homework assignments or in your sessions, you might be surprised at how much the wisdom of the proverbs has to say about marital problems!

Job[20]

The book of Job is an extended treatise on the problem of suffering. Job, the main character, is described at the outset as an upright and blameless man (1:1). After Satan and God enter into a debate about Job, God offers up Job as one who has exemplary faith (1:8). Satan takes God up on His offer, convincing God to allow him to inflict great suffering on Job. Despite his overwhelming plight, Job refuses to curse God (2:10). What follows are thirty-five chapters of debate between Job and his friends, who accuse Job of sin because they assume such great suffering must have been brought on by an evil life (Job 3–37). Job gets caught up in the debate, wishing for his own misery to end (3:1–26; 6:8–9; 7:12–21), decrying his friends (13:4), defending himself (12:2–3; 13:2), demanding a mediator (9:32–35), and asking God for his day in court to vindicate himself (13:3, 14–23). In the end, God responds to this debate by cross-examining Job, showing God's greatness (38:1–40:2; 40:6–41:34) and Job's foolishness in insisting on an answer. Job finally recognizes that he demanded answers to things he could not understand, and the only proper response to God is repentance and faith (42:1–6).

The book of Job is a timeless classic because it asks universal questions about the problem of evil and suffering that resound across time. Central to the book are the questions "Can mortal man be in the right before God?" (Job 4:17) and "Who is ultimately wise?" Job is the hero of the book, with God commending him in the prologue and, in the epilogue, confronting him and restoring him doubly. As with Ecclesiastes, the frame of the book is important in interpretation. The main content of the book (chaps. 3–37) should be viewed in light of the frame (chaps. 1–2 and 38–42). God's vindication of Job should be seen as a refutation of the friends' advice and a validation of Job's faith.

Jill was angry with God for her bad marriage. Though marital communication had gradually improved, and John started to confront his idolatry of work and become more engaged at home, Jill still was confused. She asked me one day, "Why did God put us through this? What did I ever do to deserve this? Did I do something wrong?" She sounded a little like Job asking for his day in court (Job 13:3, 15–16).

The bridge we built from the biblical text to Jill's life was *her suffering*. She didn't understand why God would allow her marriage to be such a struggle for so long. She asked theodicy questions, though the word "theodicy" never came out of her mouth. She struggled with how she could go through such a rough season of marriage and believe at the same time that God is still good. On many of her days, the two seemed diametrically opposed. Jill assumed that God owed her an answer. She was entitled to it. She didn't deserve a lousy husband, so God needed to give her a day in court and He would need to vindicate Himself.

I asked her to set aside a whole day and to read the book of Job in just one sitting. The climax of the book is in chapters 38 through 41, where in four glorious chapters, the wonders of God's wisdom, might, and power are extolled as God cross-examines Job. Job is left almost speechless, and his only response is to acknowledge God's wonder and to repent (42:3, 6). After some initial reluctance, Jill set aside an afternoon and was very moved by reading the whole account of Job at one time. She said, "I was fixated on my own difficulties, but by the time I got to the end of the book, I had to say, 'Of course, the point is God, not me.'" And she said that with a smile on her face. Her problems weren't solved. In the days that followed, Jill slipped back into questioning God's goodness, but for that one moment, she was able to see with greater clarity. She saw that the point of her suffering was to grow in greater faith in God and to not assume she is entitled to answers for all of her questions.

Another practical suggestion for using Job in marital counseling involves *articulating honest suffering*. Believers are often reluctant to ask God hard questions about their suffering. This is where Job can serve us because he is a great picture of honest suffering. In his worst moments,

Job was brutally honest with God, crying out in the bitterness of his own soul, complaining about his plight, and asking piercing questions. Ask your counselee to read the texts where Job addresses God directly (7:7, 11; 10:1–22; 13:20–14:22) and then write out their own honest statements or direct questions to God about suffering.

One more practical suggestion involves *contemplating God's character*. Use Job 38–41 to help your counselee to consider God's attributes. Suffering distorts a sinner's perceptions of who God is and what He has done, so God's Word can rectify those false perceptions and help a person view Him rightly.

THE END OF THE MATTER: JESUS CHRIST

While biblical poetry and Wisdom Literature provide a wonderful lens to view and rectify marital difficulties, the wisdom that transforms marriage can ultimately be found in only one place—Christ. The apostle Paul wrote in Colossians 2:3 that in Jesus are hidden all the treasures of wisdom and knowledge. He said elsewhere that Christ not only encompasses wisdom but actually "became to us wisdom from God" (1 Cor. 1:30).

On the road to Emmaus, Jesus walked through the Old Testament Scriptures with two of His disciples, showing them how all of Scripture pointed to one great Savior—to Him (Luke 24:27). Can you imagine being there, Jesus explaining to His disciples Old Testament poetry and the Wisdom books, and how clear it would have been that the Scriptures are ultimately fulfilled in Jesus?

CHAPTER 19

USING THE GOSPELS IN THE PERSONAL MINISTRY OF THE WORD

ROB GREEN

John just turned sixteen years old. In many ways, it is an exciting time in his life. John is active in sports, reasonably popular, and a decent student. John is active in church and in the youth group. By all appearances, it seems as if he is doing quite well. However, behind closed doors in the Joneses' family home, John regularly struggles with his parents. He finds them legalistic and at times hypocritical. He questions their authority and occasionally chooses the path of disobedience. The conflict in the home does not result in violence even if it is stifling and at times explosive. Conflict is not daily, but under normal conditions, one could anticipate three instances in a given week of conflict between John and his parents. When one factors in their busy schedules, conflicts occur most evenings that the family is home together.

Tommy is John's little brother. Tommy is eleven. While he does not idolize John, he is following in his brother's footsteps with regard to his parents. Tommy is a good student and he has many friends. At home, he is becoming ambivalent to his parents, especially his mother.

Tommy agrees with John's assessment that their parents are legalistic and hypocritical.

Craig and Karen are struggling with what to do. They are faithful members of their church, even if they do not attend every Sunday. They try to be good parents to both John and Tommy by providing for them, supporting their various activities, and giving them what they themselves never had during their childhood years. However, Craig and Karen admit that conflict is a regular part of the home and that the frequency of conflict is proportional to the amount of time they spend together—the more they are together, the more conflict. The family wants help.

While Scripture has much to say about the needs and concerns of this family, the purpose of this chapter is to use this case study of parent-child conflict to show how the Gospels can be used to provide hope and help to the Jones family. Working a case study from a particular section of Scripture is what John Henderson did in his chapter on the use of biblical narrative to help a person struggling with anxiety (see chap. 17). It's the format that Deepak Reju used to discuss the value of Wisdom Literature—focusing on the matter of marital struggles (see chap. 18). The point of these chapters is not simply to show that narratives speak to anxiety or that Wisdom Literature applies only to marriage, but rather to help all of us be convinced of the robustness of Scripture to speak directly to the issues that people face.

Before we rush into the use of the Gospels for parent-child conflict, let's pause to acknowledge a few facts about counseling training in general. For many of us, our counseling training helped us learn how to minister in a personal context.[1] We have learned to ask good questions, to listen carefully, to write homework that encourages our friends to apply truth to the daily situations in life. Our training has also given us a commitment to the Scriptures themselves. We are deeply persuaded by the necessity of Scripture to all issues in life. But our training has not necessarily made us experts in understanding the Bible.[2] Many counselors learn a few dozen "go-to" verses or passages and counsel virtually every case from them. But this book is encouraging us to go beyond our go-to passages and think more deeply about the use of all of Scripture.

A reading of the Gospels reveals a few important facts about them. First, it is easy to see that each gospel is a biography of Jesus, but not like the ones we Americans are used to reading. Instead of a standard biography, each of the four gospels is a *theological* biography about Jesus.[3] As professor Richard Burridge explained, "The Gospels are nothing less than Christology in narrative form."[4] It sounds simple; the focus of the Gospels is on Jesus. The apostle Paul stresses our identity *in* Christ, but the gospel writers are far more concerned with the identity *of* Christ. The Gospels force us and our counselees to think deeply about Jesus — the promised Messiah.

Second, none of the gospel writers provide us with a full picture of the life of Christ. In fact, only about fifty days of Jesus' life are narrated in gospel literature.[5] In addition, each gospel writer includes stories and episodes that are found in other gospel material.[6] In fact, almost 25 percent of all gospel material is focused on the final week of Christ in Jerusalem. The Gospels are selective in the material they include, and in that selection, there is great care and thought.[7] In other words, each episode is included to contribute to the purpose of that gospel. Thus, each gospel writer had at least one purpose for writing what he did.[8]

Third, the Gospels were written decades after the events they record actually occurred. While the dating of the Gospels is not known for certain, a rough estimate is that Matthew, Mark, and Luke were written in the late AD 50s and early 60s, while the gospel of John was not completed until around AD 80. If Jesus died in the early 30s that suggests that three gospels were not written until twenty-five to thirty years after the death, burial, and resurrection of Jesus, and the remaining gospel was not completed until forty-five to fifty years after Christ ascended to heaven.[9] With these issues in mind, let us now consider how the Gospels speak into the lives of parents Craig and Karen and children John and Tommy, given the conflict between them.

JESUS IS THE SUFFERING SERVANT
WHO CALLS PEOPLE TO FOLLOW HIM

One of the most prominent elements of Jesus' identity is that He is the suffering servant predicted by Isaiah. His mission led to the suffering of the cross. Every gospel writer emphasizes this point, but it is the gospel of Mark that focuses on it most. Mark 1 – 8 asks the question of Jesus' identity. Mark explains that Jesus is the Son of God come as the fulfillment to the promises given by Isaiah and Malachi (Mark 1:1 – 8; Isa. 40:3; Mal. 3:1). He narrates Jesus performing miracles — making those who were sick well and giving freedom to those who were demon-possessed (Mark 1:32 – 34). Jesus healed a paralyzed man (2:1 – 12), even forgiving his sins. Mark shows that Jesus is an authority over Mosaic law (2:23 – 3:6). Jesus has power over the natural elements (4:35 – 41) and over the most captive man (5:1 – 20). Jesus is able to provide food for thousands from a small lunch (6:33 – 44), and He can walk on the water (6:45 – 52). Amazingly enough, Jesus is able to make the deaf hear and the mute speak (7:37). So the question becomes, "Who is Jesus? Is Jesus John the Baptist? What about Elijah? A different prophet?" Jesus pressures His disciples by asking, "Who do you say that I am?" (Mark 8:29).

The tension is thick enough to cut. Peter boldly proclaims that Jesus is the Christ. One might expect celebration, expectation, and excitement. What one finds is that Mark immediately records a prediction of Jesus' death and suffering. In fact, Mark records three times that Jesus predicts His upcoming death and resurrection (8:31; 9:31 – 32; 10:32 – 34). And chapters 11 – 16 explain the fulfillment of Jesus' prediction as He willingly dies on the cross, is buried, and rises on the third day. Mark explained that all the acts of power by Jesus are constrained within the bounds of His role as the suffering servant. Yes, Jesus is the promised Messiah who gives sight to the blind, hearing to the deaf, and release to the captives, but He is also the suffering servant come to die so that others may go free.

There is application to our family situation, but before we get to the family, let's consider one more element about Jesus' role as suffering servant. After Jesus predicts His suffering, the disciples respond (Mark 8:32 – 33; 9:32; 10:35 – 40) with varying degrees of understanding. But after each response, Jesus teaches the importance of humility and service. Jesus being the suffering servant is not simply a blessing for His disciples, it is a call to response. Jesus expects His disciples to follow Him. He expects them to approach life with a similar sense of self-denial by taking up their cross and following Jesus (Mark 8:34 – 38). He expects a compassionate and service-oriented attitude toward others (9:33 – 37), especially those who could be subject to abuse. He explained to them that the greatest is actually the servant of all (10:41 – 45) that even He came to serve and to give His life as a random for many (10:45). In other words, every time Jesus predicted His death, He immediately taught His disciples the importance of being a servant.

We have two very powerful truths from the gospel of Mark that need to be applied to the Jones family. First, Jesus is Himself the suffering servant who gave His life. Second, that Jesus calls His followers to a "servant and self-denial" approach to life. For every member of the family, there is the possibility of a reorientation in their thinking. They are used to thinking about prior or even potential conflicts. John comes home from practice, and it is not thirty minutes before someone says something unkind, and the cycle begins. Karen begins to stress about four in the afternoon, knowing that John will be home in another hour or so. Craig wonders on his way home what the conflict will be about today. It is easy to think about the conflicts from yesterday or the week before or how annoying a child, sibling, or parent can be.

But Jesus offers a reorientation for all of them. There is Jesus the suffering servant. Without Him they could not have been freed from the power and penalty of sin. Without Him they would have no hope for a home in heaven. Without Him they would not have the indwelling presence of the Holy Spirit. Without Him they would not be blessed with all spiritual blessings in the heavenly places. In other words, it is time for Craig, Karen, John, and Tommy to pray, thank, and think about the wonderful Savior who suffered and rose for them. So life now is centered on Jesus, who is the perfect suffering servant.

Remembering the sufferings of Jesus also helps put some of our own suffering in perspective. Craig, Karen, John, and Tommy have been sufferers in the home. Conflict normally creates "winners" and "losers." But in due time, they realize that the "winners" of the disagreement were actually "losers" in the sphere of relationships. Therefore, in the wake of conflict, we find a bunch of sufferers. If allowed to fester, suffering easily transfers to self-pity.

No such action occurs with our Savior. His suffering results in the ransom of souls because He entrusted His suffering to the Father. The Jones family needs to do the same. The rich history of God's Word that Jesus draws on in His own teaching reminds us that God's people needed to run to the Lord in the midst of their suffering. He is the one who can provide the grace and strength to endure suffering properly. It is easy to see how each Jones family member loses in the conflicts, even if they did not take an active part, and how the suffering of each person could help them grow closer to the Lord or more bitter toward one another.

In addition to reorienting their thinking to the greatness of Jesus and to the need to run to Him to handle their suffering, there is also the call to radically follow Jesus. Conflicts occur over individuals demanding, possibly to the point of sin, their own way. Instead of living in a home where each person fights for control, they can follow the example of Jesus and seek to serve. Imagine if John applied this to his life so that (1) he keeps his room clean because he knows his mom appreciates that, (2) he cleans up after himself and others whether that involves dishes after supper or clothes left in the bathroom, (3) he regularly cuts the grass because he wants to serve his dad, and (4) he regularly thanks his parents for providing for him, for attending his sporting events, and for seeking to help him mature into a godly man.

These same thoughts could be applied to Karen, who at this point may think she is being taken advantage of. Thus, rather than clamoring for appreciation, she serves the suffering servant who ransomed her soul.

John, as the father, would no longer think of everyone in the home as people to command, but as people to serve. Thus, he works hard at serving Karen. He also weighs his comments and demands of his boys against the grid of how important his demands are for the spiritual, physical, and emotional development of his sons. In other words, he listens carefully to the charge of hypocrisy and legalism and evaluates whether it is true.

One simple truth regarding the identity of Jesus provides an opportunity for thought reorientation and behavioral realignment. The suffering servant aspect and the work of Jesus provide an avenue to focus on Jesus rather than conflict, to properly look to Jesus when faced with moments of suffering, and to follow Jesus by choosing self-denial and being a servant of all.

JESUS IS CONCERNED ABOUT TRUE RIGHTEOUSNESS

We know that the conflicts between John, Tommy, and their parents originate in their hearts. James 4:1–2 teaches that the source of quarrels and conflicts comes from the desires in our hearts. James's teaching did not arise out of a vacuum, but rather came from the teaching of his older half-brother. For Jesus on numerous occasions emphasized the importance of the heart in all of behavior.[10] Jesus' focus on the inside of a person may be embodied best in His Sermon on the Mount (Matt. 5–7). It is this sermon that gives readers of Matthew's gospel an opportunity to read Jesus' explanation of the meaning of true righteousness. It is not a standard of requirements to be met, but of a heart solely fixed on the Lord God that results in behavior that is holy.[11]

Once armed with this hermeneutical approach to the Sermon, it is not long before text and application meet the lives of our family in conflict. One wonders, for example, whether John's tongue or the heart that motivated it ever said anything close to the words found in Matthew 5:21–22. Have John, Tommy, and their parents resorted to the godless activity of name calling? Have they failed to see the murder in their heart by looking solely at their own interests? Have they developed telescopic vision that has fooled them into believing they were right or justified in what they said? Have they focused on others around them, like John's or Tommy's friends, and compared? When John, Tommy, or either of their parents justify their actions by the worst actions of someone else, they have completely abandoned the Lord in both behavior and heart. Jesus and His Word stand on the sidelines while they shell one another with their words, looking for the definitive hit.

This sermon in Matthew is calling the family to a new level of self-evaluation. If each member of the family will take the time to think deeply about the text, then each one will realize just how dependent they are on a vibrant and personal relationship with Jesus in order for any of this to come about. As believers living on this side of the cross work of Jesus, John, Tommy, and their parents will more appropriately see the significance of their new birth (John 3) and the promise of the Holy Spirit, who profoundly works in the lives of believers until the return of Christ or their death.[12] Not only will the family have panoramic vision, but they will also understand that sometimes it is simply best to remain quiet.

The Sermon on the Mount certainly has not finished its work on this family, for Matthew 5:43–48 exhorts this family to love one another. As counselors, we have served many families like the Joneses in our ministry careers. They have given example after example of how challenging it is to live with one another. John can think of twenty reasons why Tommy annoys him. He can find fifteen examples in the last three weeks how, in his mind, his parents have been hypocritical. That ability is not limited to John alone, for Tommy, Craig, and Karen are equally skilled at providing examples of their own. In other words, if pushed, there are times when they all feel as if they are enemies of one another. Not surprising, once this thought is allowed to set up camp, the worse they treat each other. Jesus, however, calls them to love each other. He calls them to a willing self-sacrifice that gives rather than takes, that believes the best rather than the worst, that is patient rather than quick-tempered, that is kind rather than harsh, and that sets things aside as opposed to piling on perceived wrongs.

The applications of the sermon on the family are practically boundless, but one other deserves mention.[13] There is an ethic in the sermon that calls for building treasure in heaven (Matt. 6:19–21, 33). Conflict is an incredibly time-consuming affair. When one considers the time of the conflict itself, the mental energy used in the aftermath of the conflict, the potential preparation for the next conflict, and the cycle repeating, it should not surprise us to realize that the family is wasting incredible amounts of time that could be invested in kingdom work. Maybe this family needs a series of service projects so they can invest their time in something productive rather than waste it in petty arguments. It is clear that if their conflicts are not viewed differently, then one day each member of this family will realize that stewardship of time, energy, and giftedness were wasted trying to settle what, in many cases, were meaningless conflicts.

JESUS IS THE KING

To this point, Craig, Karen, John, and Tommy have learned from the Gospels (primarily Mark) that Jesus is the suffering servant who calls His disciples to follow Him. They also discovered that these truths have helped them to think about their own suffering in a biblical fashion and to hear Jesus' call for them to be servants. In addition, Jesus' concern for true righteousness (from the Sermon on the Mount recorded in Matthew) has helped them focus on the condition of their heart. Jesus is not merely after behavioral modification or conformity to a series of rules; Jesus is concerned that each member of this family be pure in heart. Despite the robustness of the material already covered, we have only begun to drink from the Gospels' springs. Jesus taught His disciples that the greatest was the servant of all. They needed to look no further than their Master to see this idea in living color. For Jesus is not simply a suffering servant, He is also the King. Matthew's gospel is rich with kingly imagery.[14]

Jesus' royalty is brought out in the first verse of Matthew, where Jesus is declared the "son of David, the son of Abraham." Just one chapter later the wise men ask Herod where is the baby who is born "king of the Jews?"[15] Jesus' teaching was done with authority (Matt. 7:28–29). His miracles of healing and casting out demons were further authentications that Jesus was the Promised One. While Matthew's gospel chooses not to make the feeding of the five thousand an issue of royalty, John's gospel states the matter plainly. After the crowd enjoyed the amazing miracles, Jesus withdrew because He knew they were planning to make Him king by force (John 6:15). In Matthew, Jesus accepts the reality that He is the king of Jews in His trial before Pilate (Matt. 27:11). Even the ironies of the cross rally around the concept that Jesus is, in fact, the king.[16] The sign above His head proclaimed that Jesus is the king of the Jews (Matt. 27:36). Prior to the finished cross work of Jesus, we see His kingship combined with His mission as a suffering servant. Since Jesus' mission involved reconciling the world to Himself, His kingly authority was exercised to accomplish that mission.[17] After His resurrection, Jesus explained that all authority has been given to Him (Matt. 28:18). As D. A. Carson said, "He is king of the universe. He is king over the soldiers who mock Him. He is king over you and me. And one day, Paul assures us, every knee will bow, and every tongue will confess that Jesus is Lord."[18]

The Jones family can see the implications. Conflicts occur as little kings vie for control. John wants freedom and believes that in his little kingdom, freedom should reign. Craig, on the other hand, paid for his kingdom, and John enjoys many of the benefits of his father's kingdom—a warm home, a room, a bed, laundry and meal services, and even concierge services. Craig is absolutely convinced that his subjects (John and Tommy) should be grateful for all these benefits and respond with unquestioned loyalty and civility. Karen is the family equivalent to the Peace Corps, Red Cross, Save the Whales, and the UN wrapped into one peace-loving package. She rushes into the battles looking to help the wounded. She negotiates contracts, offers dramatic speeches over dinner, and occasionally protests the skirmishes. One can see that as long as John and Craig remain as builders of their own kingdoms where they can each be king, and as long as Karen tries to deal with behavior as it arises, everyone loses. Fundamentally, the problem is that no one seems to be functioning under the true King—Jesus. They are not viewing their roles and responsibilities to one another first through the grid of their relationship to their Savior.

In my years of counseling, I have never seen, in my office, the full-scale version of the conflicts that occur in the home. I understand why. Our setting is not conducive to full-scale attacks. I am in the room, as are advocates, cocounselors, and/or observers. Thus, what happens in my office is the tame version of what occurs at home. I have often asked counselees why the fact that Jesus is with them as their King has not had a dampening effect on their conflicts. Why has the presence of the King of the universe, who died for each one of them, not influenced the way they think, speak, or act? When John understands that Jesus is King, he will be more grateful for the father the King gave him. He will be more respectful of the authority lines that exist between a father and his children. He will be more appreciative of his father's correction, knowing that correction is designed to help him become wise. Equally, when Craig appreciates Jesus as his King, he will think more carefully about his parenting. Is he trying to control, to exercise authority, or to demonstrate power? Or is Craig seeking to follow the instruction of his King and bring up his son in the nurture and admonition of the Lord? Will Craig pursue his King and ask for his King's grace, strength, wisdom, and help in order to accomplish the mission his King has given him?

Equally important, when Karen understands that Jesus is King, she will be encouraging her husband and her son to look to the King. She no longer has to be the moderator or the peace keeper. Instead, Karen can have the joy of being a peacemaker by encouraging her family members to serve the King. Imagine the hope for Karen, and for each member of the family, if only they will serve their King instead of trying to set up their own little kingdoms.

JESUS IS THE ONLY PATH TO ETERNAL LIFE

One could not leave a chapter on the Gospels without considering the evangelistic focus of the Gospels, especially regarding the gospel of John. John explained his purpose in John 20:30–31: "Now Jesus did many other signs in the presence of the disciples, which are not written in this book; but these are written so that you may believe that Jesus is the Christ, the Son of God, and that by believing you may have life in his name." Thus, the book of John proves that Jesus is the Christ. John's evidence is overwhelming. He records a few of Jesus' miracles, including the time Jesus turned water into wine (2:1–11), healed the official's son (4:46–54), healed the man at the Bethesda pool (5:1–17), fed the five thousand (6:1–15), walked on water (6:16–21); healed the blind man (9:1–34), and raised Lazarus from the dead (11:1–45). John also records the identity statements of Jesus, including "I am the bread of life" (6:35), "I am the light of the world" (8:12), "I am the door of the sheep" (10:7), "I am the good shepherd" (10:11), "I am the resurrection and the life" (11:25), and "I am the way, and the truth, and the life" (14:6). John was interested in his readers understanding that the long-awaited Messiah predicted in the Old Testament came in the person of Jesus. Then, and most importantly, John wanted his readers to have life in Jesus' name. It is more than a simple intellectual assent to a few ideas. The gospel of Jesus Christ is life transforming. It is reaching the place where a person understands there is no way, no path to God without the death, burial, and resurrection of Jesus.

In many instances, we have counselees or possibly one counselee who seeks biblical help, but has yet to experience new birth. In our family case, it is very possible that Tommy, as the youngest and only eleven, has not heard a clear presentation of the gospel. His home may have centered on conflict for a sizable portion of his short life. Thus, counseling may be the opportunity the Lord provides to help Tommy see that part of his challenge is that he has yet to experience the saving grace of Jesus, he has yet to be indwelled with the Holy Spirit, and he has yet to see meaning in anything other than "eat, sleep, and play sports." It might also be the case that Craig, John, or Karen may have a form of godliness but lack the power thereof. It is possible that conflict is the tool that God will use to show every member of this family how desperate they are for Christ. If each member of this family has a saving relationship with Jesus, then the very least a careful consideration of the gospel of John will result in is a growing belief in the identity of Jesus. Jesus' miracles and identity statements would remind this family yet again of the loving, gracious, compassionate, caring, and powerful Savior they call their own.

CONCLUSION

The Gospels can be used in very practical ways in the personal ministry of the Word. But as is the case with every portion of God's Word, our first task is to understand the content of the Word.[19] Following are several important hermeneutical concepts that I would now like to make explicit.[20]

1. Every gospel writer has a theological reason for writing.[21] We do well to remember each one's theological concerns as we read and apply the Gospels to our own lives first and then to the lives of our counselees.
2. Every gospel writer tells the story of Jesus. Thus, time in the Gospels should focus our attention on the risen Christ. Hopefully, our time spent in the Gospels will remind us and help our counselees to conclude that Jesus is awesome.[22]
3. The Sermon on the Mount is an ethic for the here and now. It has application for all those whose citizenship is in heaven. It even serves to remind us that the Mosaic law, as an accurate

expression of the moral law of God, was not simply behavioristic. God has been concerned about the heart of His people from the very beginning. The sermon even serves an evangelistic purpose. Its requirements are so high, no one could ever meet them on their own. Having a heart so godly can only come through the work of Christ.

It is from these hermeneutic concepts that we discovered that Mark's gospel emphasizes Jesus as the suffering servant who calls His followers to be servants as well. We also saw, primarily from Matthew's account of the Sermon on the Mount, that Jesus is not solely interested in behavior, but also in the heart that motivates that behavior. The gospel of Matthew shows us that Jesus is the King, and He is the only way for a person to be right with God.

These truths were practically applied to the needs of the Jones family who, like many counselees, were experiencing regular conflict.

My hope is that this chapter encourages you to read, study, and know the Gospels better. I hope that it encourages you to sit often at the feet of Jesus and learn afresh His identity, miracles, majesty, and His suffering. After all, he is *the Wonderful Counselor.* Then, as God allows, teach these same truths to the people God has led to you. May the Lord bless you and your efforts to lift high the name of Jesus through the use of the Gospels.

CHAPTER 20

USING THE EPISTLES IN THE PERSONAL MINISTRY OF THE WORD

HEATH LAMBERT

I come to the topic of using the Epistles in counseling with a heavy heart. The reality is that the majority of counseling practitioners do not focus on the relevance of the Epistles for helping people with their problems. The dominant counseling models used today see the New Testament letters as valuable resources for personal Bible study and devotions and as appropriate subject matter for sermons or adult education classes, but not useful or helpful in counseling. This is tragic. Some of the most helpful, pertinent, and relevant material for counseling is found in the Epistles. If the Epistles are overlooked, then our counseling will be worldly, lifeless, irrelevant, and ineffective.

The biblical counseling movement has focused on understanding the relevance of particular passages to the many problems that vex people as they live life in a shattered world. To my knowledge, there has not been a concentrated effort to show how various literary forms are uniquely helpful in doing this. Thus, I have two tasks in this chapter: first, to show what we can learn about ministry from God's decision to communicate in the form of letters; and second, to show the practical benefits of this genre for the specific problem of obsessive-compulsive disorder (OCD).

A person who struggles with OCD feels trapped between a problem on which they fixate (obsessions) and their attempts at managing that problem (compulsions). For example, a person may obsess over a fear of germs collecting on their hands as they do normal activities — opening doors, shaking hands, touching staircase banisters. They attempt to manage their obsessive fear by compulsively washing their hands (maybe until they are raw) in order to find the elusive sense of cleanliness. People with OCD struggle with various fears, or obsessions, some the fear of germs, others a fear of leaving a door unlocked, a stove burner on, objects not in line. But the common theme in attempting to manage their obsession is a specific compulsion that is always present in a way that dominates the person's life. The problem with OCD is not only that it is a life-dominating problem but that people *experience* it as such. The personal pain they experience is real, and their deep desire is to be free. They feel imprisoned by their personal obsession and compulsion.[1]

Considering the complex, challenging, and unique problems of OCD, some counselors wonder how God's revelation in the Epistles can have any relevance for such a difficult and debilitating problem. The Epistles are a fairly straightforward genre in biblical literature, each a letter to a person or group that addresses a specific situation or set of issues.[2] These New Testament letters offer fairly clear-cut instruction. This does not mean that there are no interpretive challenges in the Epistles, because there certainly are. In fact, the biggest challenge concerns how we bridge the different historical contexts. The difficulty here is in ascertaining how first-century instruction applies to the present day. Yet the obvious instructive nature of the Epistles that applies universally makes us feel comfortable with them.[3]

My five observations about the Epistles show how they are relevant in counseling for a problem like OCD.

THE EPISTLES DEMONSTRATE MINISTRY THAT IS OCCASIONAL

New Testament scholars tell us that one of the unique characteristics of letters is that they are *occasional*. Letters are sent occasionally, as the need arises. The letters of the Epistles deal in a timely manner with specific situations in the lives of those to whom they are addressed. The Epistles *are* counseling. Reading these letters is like reading the counselor half of a counseling session verbatim. Though we do not hear the voice of the congregational counselees, we are able to listen in on the inspired counsel of the apostolic authors.

The occasional nature of these letters fits the needs of those who receive them. They also demonstrate that the counseling contained in them is built on a relationship with the receivers, a mutual love. The apostles were not just dropping abstract truths on a congregation of strangers. They were well acquainted with the concerns and difficulties the individual recipients faced, the growth and development of their faith, the questions they had. And the apostles responded to all of this with specific details. The book of Philippians is one example of this relational connection between the apostle Paul and his people. Paul repeatedly reveals his love for the believers at Philippi (Phil. 1:8, 21–26; 2:2, 19–20; 4:10). In the Epistles we find loving ministers of the gospel connecting with the lives and problems of individuals. The Epistles don't just communicate truth in a vacuum; they convey truth through a loving ministry where concerns of the people are heard and addressed.

In the Epistles, the counseling does not just communicate generalized or technical truth; it addresses specific problems, and it is done at the lay level. While it is wonderful to have counseling students pursuing advanced education at Bible colleges and seminaries, there is a danger that in learning the language of scholarship, they will begin speaking like a professionally trained theologian. They will begin to use big words like *infralapsarianism* and *inaugurated eschatology*. The writers of the Epistles did not use such high-flying language. They were writing to a broad audience that included pastors, day workers, house-wives, and children. They used everyday speech, understandable to all. While they discussed matters of theology, hermeneutics, and biblical studies, they did not require their readers to learn a new vocab-ulary. Instead, they met the people where they were. The Epistles model counseling instruction that is accessible and relevant to all people.

This model of counseling with its clear communication explodes with relevance in the lives of people who are struggling with OCD. The pain, trauma, and turmoil of this enslaving problem is debilitating and isolating. The Epistles model for us how to draw near to the people, to listen to them, and to understand them. As you listen well to what a counselee is saying and gain understanding, you are giving the kind of help that God loves to see us use when He changes His people in the midst of a painful situation like OCD.

THE EPISTLES DEMONSTRATE COUNSELING THAT IS ENCOURAGING

Epistles in the ancient world in general, and in the New Testament in particular, all have a similar structure. There is typically a greeting, fol-lowed by a thanksgiving and prayer, a body, an exhortation and instruc-tion, and a conclusion. Though there are some exceptions to this pattern, the letters in the New Testament almost always conform to this structure.

One of the most predictable elements of the Pauline Epistles is the way the body of the letters is foreshadowed by the thanksgiving sec-tion. We see this in Paul's letter to the Roman church. In Romans 1, Paul thanked God for the faith of the Romans and then proceeded to expound an absolutely magisterial series of chapters on the impor-tance of faith. In Philippians 1, Paul thanked God and the Philippians for their participation in the gospel, and then he structured his letter around examples of servants who were partnering in the gospel, and he urged the church to grow more and more in their own partnership. The most famous example of this pattern is found in Paul's first letter to the Corinthians, where Paul thanked God and the church for their spiritual gifts before he initiated a period of extended instruction and correction on their use of spiritual gifts.

These examples show us that Paul worked hard to look for reasons to praise those to whom he was ministering. He often found things worthy of praise in the precise areas where people were struggling and needed corrective instruction. This example models for us the importance of being counselors who encourage those we are trying to help. It is easy to blame, criticize, and have a list of problems that we will address, one by one. Instead, the Epistles teach us to take a tender look at the person who is hurting and find reasons to be thankful for them and for what God is doing in their life.

As we seek to help those who are struggling with OCD, we need to see them as more than one big problem. If a person senses that you view them only as a big problematic knot that needs to be untangled, your counseling will be less effective. They will become discouraged. And seeing a problem rather than a person made in the image of God puts you, the counselor, in a spiritually dangerous position. We must never define the people we counsel solely by their problems. Instead, look for things that are praiseworthy and talk about them. Look for ways to encourage a counselee, as Paul did in his epistles.

Expressing words of encouragement has strategic benefits in counseling. People respond with trust that builds relationship. A person struggling with OCD — or any other difficult problem — will begin to trust you, the counselor, as you let them know that you see them as a person with both strengths and weaknesses. When counselees with OCD learn early on in counseling that you see more than just their obsessions and compulsions, they will be more willing to listen to you.

In the New Testament letters, the authors tackled real problems of real people. The secret here for counselors is to engage difficulties in ways that are full of biblical wisdom, love, and prudence. How do those you are counseling know you? Do they know you as someone who is focused only on their problems? Or do they know you as a person who has built a loving relationship with them, who has earned the right to say things that may be difficult for them to hear?

THE EPISTLES DEMONSTRATE COUNSELING THAT IS DIVERSE

The Epistles are a complex genre of literature in Scripture. God is communicating His truth to people in the early church — and to us — in these letters. God is never formulaic in how He communicates His truth. Instead He uses varied ways to reveal His will to us, and the Epistles offer strong examples of this variety.

Biblical counselors have, at times, been known for communicating in ways that are overly formulaic. Some of our contemporary efforts turn biblical counseling into a fixed and rigid form of counseling. This is at odds with the diversity we find in the Bible.

One current debate among counselors concerns the use of indicative and imperative statements in Scripture. Indicative statements in Scripture refer to who we are in Christ. Imperative statements refer to what we do in Christ. Some biblical counselors focus on the indicatives because they want to emphasize who we are in Christ. They wish to correct a perceived overemphasis in past years on the imperatives in the Bible. Other counselors go in the other direction, emphasizing the imperative statements of the Epistles because they believe that proper doctrine leads to proper behavior. They want their counseling to be practical. What the Epistles show us is that if you try to pick one group of statements over the other, you unnecessarily and unwisely restrict the diversity that is present in the Epistles.

The Epistles provide several corrective approaches to this ongoing debate. Trying to decide whether indicative statements are more important than imperative statements is like trying to decide whether you prefer the left wing of an airplane or the right wing. You need both, just as you need both types of statements found in the New Testament letters. This is not an either/or choice.

Think of the interplay between the imperatives (what we do) and the indicatives (who we are) like the wheels on a bicycle. The indicatives, in their role of telling us who we are in Christ, work like the back wheel of the bicycle. They propel and power the bicycle forward. The front wheel guides and steers the forward progress of the bike. We all need the power that the indicatives provide in life, but if we have no direction for where we going, that power is useless. The imperatives (what we do) guide and steer the indicatives (who we are) so we know where all the power we have in Christ is directing us.

How does this help the individual struggling with OCD who is distracted by the stifling realities of life in a dangerous world? They need to be reminded that as a Christian, they are raised up with Christ and seated with Him in the heavenly places (Eph. 2:6). This is an indicative statement that reorients our perspective on all of life, whether we struggle with obsessions, compulsions, or any other difficult problems.

And yet, as true and wonderful as this statement is, people with OCD need to do more than just come to grips with this reality. In his letter to the Ephesians, Paul did not stop writing when he completed the indicative portions of his letters. He kept writing. In fact after he wrote those words, he wrote chapter after chapter of imperative statements that flow out of his indicative statements. People who struggle with OCD need the reorienting truth that they are seated with Christ. They also need to learn how to have wise and loving conversations with other believers; how to avoid harmful behaviors; how to foster godly behaviors; how to serve others in love; how to work hard in a job; and how to confess their sin, forgive others, and participate as responsible members of their families. But most important is for them to pray. All of these imperative statements describe what a person should do as they live, occupying the exalted status of being seated with Christ as described in indicative statements. We will not help people with OCD if we make them choose between the front wheel or the back wheel of the bicycle, or the left wing or right wing of an airplane. We need to show them that they need both.

The Epistles help us to see that both indicative and imperative statements are related to the gospel of grace, but in different senses. Some biblical counselors say they counsel with only indicative statements of Scripture because they want to be a gospel-centered counselor. But this reveals a fundamental misunderstanding of the gospel of grace. Both indicative and imperative statements are related to the gospel of grace. Indicative statements are *true* because of what Jesus has done for us in the gospel. Imperative statements are *possible* because of what Jesus has done for us in the gospel. We must not make the mistake of equating indicatives with the gospel while disconnecting imperative statements. They are both related to the gospel and depend on the gospel to accomplish their purpose.

A person with OCD needs to understand that every indicative statement (who we are in Christ) in the Epistles is *true* for them because of Jesus' work of extending gospel grace by His life, death, and resurrection. A person with OCD must also know that every imperative statement (what we do in Christ) is *possible* for them because of that same gospel grace from Jesus.

Another way the Epistles inform the current debate on indicatives and imperatives is by containing many other kinds of statements. If you were to cut out every indicative and imperative statement in the New Testament, most of the language of the letters of the Epistles would still remain. That means that these indicative and imperative statements occupy just a small portion of the Bible. This fact does not mean that indicatives and imperatives are not important. It means biblical writers had a lot more to say.

When you read the Epistles, you will find instruction about God in Christ, descriptions of the attributes of God, statements about who human beings are apart from Christ and the consequences of sin, exhortations about who you should spend time with, explanations about how to understand the Old Testament in light of the New Testament. There also are details about how to organize the church, about prayers, wise statements, expressions of gratitude, praise for individuals and the good work they have done, personal statements by the writers, benedictions, doxologies, ministry strategies, greetings, farewells, personal instructions, warnings, ministry updates, descriptions of how things work, quotes of hymns and ancient confessions, defenses of authority—and these are just a sample of what we find! With so many topics to choose from, biblical counselors should not be having debates about only two kinds of counsel. Those who counsel people with OCD need to offer more than just two kinds of statements in their counseling sessions— or just one kind of statement. They need to select from all the advice that God has provided in the Bible.

Deciding in an arbitrary way which kind of statements we prefer and limiting our reliance on God's Word to either indicative or imperative statements in Scripture hampers the effectiveness of our counseling. We should, instead, pay careful attention to counselees as they tell us why they are seeking our help. We need to listen so we can understand their problems. Only then can we offer the wisdom from Scripture to help them. When we read passages of Scripture in a counseling session, we are teaching how a particular passage applies to their needs. We are giving our counselees God's Word.

There will be times when our counseling sounds very indicative, times when it sounds very imperative, times when our counseling is prayerful, encouraging, exhorting, and on, and on. This is as it should be. God gave us diversity in the Bible because He wants to avoid limiting our counseling. God desires rich diversity in the advice we provide from the Bible to help those who seek our counsel. We must be careful that our desire to be a certain kind of counselor or to do a certain kind of counseling does not get bigger than our desire to counsel according to the model presented in Scripture.

THE EPISTLES DEMONSTRATE COUNSELING THAT IS FOUNDED ON GOD'S POWER

The writers of the Epistles began their letters with encouraging words and descriptions of spiritual power. Have you ever noticed how regularly the Epistles open with a prayer for power for believers (e.g., Col. 1:11; 1 Peter 1:3–5; 2 Peter 1:3)? The Epistles then go on to explain the power that is available to us through Jesus Christ.

In Ephesians 1:15–23, Paul wanted Christians to know the immeasurable greatness of God's power for those who believe. Paul explained that this power is the same as the power God used when He raised Jesus from the dead and when He raised Jesus up to heaven and seated Him at His right hand. Believers have been given that same kind of amazing and overwhelming power. That power is at work within us (Eph. 3:20).

Think of the implications of having this power working in those who struggle constantly with the demands of OCD, not knowing what is wrong with them, how their problem started, or how to make it stop. Can you imagine what it is like to believe you must constantly wash your hands to get rid of germs? Can you imagine going out to your car for the twentieth time to check to see if you locked the doors? Can you imagine checking the stove dozens of times to be sure it is turned off? Now imagine dealing with this problem for years, not knowing how to stop doing what is an overwhelming and constant struggle.

Where can a person with OCD turn for help? When the Epistles unpack God's power, they answer that question. It takes more power than we can comprehend to bring a dead man to life, to raise Him up into heaven, and to place all things under His feet (Eph. 1:19–22). But God has that power. And Ephesians 1 says that God gives that power to all believers (see Eph 3:20; Acts 1:8; Col. 1:29). In Paul's letter to the Ephesians, he was trying to alert them to the power they had already received so they would use it.

This power is available to those who struggle with OCD. Imagine learning for the first time that God's great power can be working in you to help you. This power has everything to do with the sufficiency of Scripture for counseling. Only the Bible points to this power, and only the Bible tells us how we can make use of this power. No other source of counseling wisdom understands how to access this power or even refers to it. People who rely on other approaches to counseling believe that the biblical counseling movement exists because of what we are *against*. They see us as anti-science, anti-drug, and anti-psychiatry.

But biblical counseling has never been motivated by what we are *against*, but what we are *for*. Biblical counseling is motivated by a conviction that people need God's power. It understands in a way that no other approach to counseling has grasped that when people are weighed down with sin, Jesus brings change through His death on their behalf—once for all. When people are broken by pain, Jesus brings comfort through the power of His resurrection.

The Epistles point to God's all-sufficient power that can overwhelm any struggle—even OCD—no matter how deep it has become ingrained in a person's life. Scripture points us to the power in Jesus that brings true change. It is through Jesus alone that we receive this power. Only the Bible shows you how to access it, understand it, and use it. The most dangerous thing you can do in your counseling ministry is to disregard Scripture. A disregard of Scripture is a disregard of God's power.[4]

THE EPISTLES DEMONSTRATE COUNSELING THAT IS FOCUSED ON PRAYER

One of the standard parts of the Epistles is a section on prayer. In the Pauline Epistles, this prayer typically happens in the midst of Paul's expression of gratitude for the church to whom he is writing. The writers of the Epistles did more than express gratitude, they *prayed* prayers of thanks. It is a mark of the ministry of the apostles not only to pray for people but to also tell the people of the prayers and to write down those prayers. The Epistles teach us to pray. They model for us a counseling ministry that is anchored in prayer.

Prayer should be a vibrant part of our ministry—not merely something we do at the beginning and end of a counseling session because that is what Christians are supposed to do. Prayer should drive and motivate our ministry to troubled people. In fact, a biblical understanding of prayer is essential for our belief in the sufficiency of Scripture. Although the biblical counseling movement is based on the sufficiency of Scripture, nobody believes the Bible is effective by merely reading and hearing the words. Salvation is not automatic. Not every person who hears the Bible read or reads the Bible becomes a Christian. The mere hearing of God's Word does not immediately sanctify us. Instead, God fixes His Word in the hearts of His people through the work of the Spirit, and the Spirit works in response to our prayers.

In Ephesians 1:3 – 14, Paul gave an authoritative presentation to the Ephesians of the grace of God, how they were included in Christ and received the Holy Spirit "when [they] heard the word of truth, the gospel of [their] salvation ... and believed in [Christ]" (v. 13). Immediately after that exalted presentation of divine grace, Paul said that because of their faith in God's grace, he had been praying for them and thanking God for them. Paul prayed not just that the Ephesians would *hear* the words, but that they would *know* the hope they had in Christ (v. 18). Paul knew that it is possible to hear about God's grace, even read about it, yet miss it entirely. He prayed that God would also give them "the Spirit of wisdom and of revelation" so that they might know Him better (v. 17).

Just as Paul continued to pray for the Ephesians, we need to pray for those we counsel, asking God to open their eyes so they will understand and embrace the biblical counsel offered to them. When counselors do not pray for those who seek their help, they show that deep down they believe it is their efforts, their words, and their wisdom that bring change. The apostle Paul was inspired by the Holy Spirit as he wrote these epistles. Yet he believed he also needed to pray for those who would receive his letters. If the inspired apostle would not do ministry of the Word without praying, then we as counselors should not either. If we are counselors who aren't praying, then we aren't good at our counseling—regardless of how scriptural our words sound.

When counseling someone who has OCD, prayer brings power. People who struggle with this affliction have serious problems that are deeply ingrained in their lives. To change, they need the kind of power we have just talked about. The ministry of prayer modeled by the apostles in their epistles reminds us that we cannot help troubled people to access the power of God by our own efforts and winsomeness. To aid people with difficulties as serious as OCD to know God's power, we must earnestly plead with God to give them confidence in the power they received as believers so they will use that power. I do not doubt that many of us, upon meeting Christ in heaven, will discover that one of the reasons we were not more effective in counseling was because we were not more diligent in prayer.

CONCLUSION

The Bible offers people with OCD the means to be able to change and live in a way that honors Christ. Much more could be said about counseling people with persistent problems like OCD. But the model of counseling found in the New Testament Epistles teaches us that the effective ministry in these letters offers counseling when needed, with clear instruction and encouragement that demonstrate God's power. But most important is counseling anchored in prayer. Only then can the Holy Spirit work in answer to our prayers.

LESSONS LEARNED THROUGH COUNSELING EXPERIENCE

RANDY PATTEN

Some aspects of the Scriptures *and* counseling are best learned by using the Scriptures *in* counseling. Dozens of books and hundreds of conference sessions have enriched my understanding of God, His Word, and how to minister effectively using the Scriptures. However, some of the most meaningful lessons have been learned apart from books and conferences.

I have had the privilege of serving God in vocational Christian ministry for nearly forty years. Biblical counseling has always been a prominent part of my spiritual leadership, whether I was a local church pastor, a consultant to pastors and churches, or the executive director of the National Association of Nouthetic Counselors (NANC) (now known as the Association of Certified Biblical Counselors).

Over the years I have done several thousand hours of counseling, and God has deepened and broadened my understanding of the process of scriptural counseling in four central categories:

- The Nature of Spiritual Ministry

- Counseling Methodology
- Developing Skill as a Biblical Counselor
- Training and Supervising Counselors

THE NATURE OF SPIRITUAL MINISTRY

First, I've come to learn that *God and His Word are strong and effective even when you as a counselor are weak and needy.* There have been times when I have gone to counseling sessions with my own heart breaking, struggling in key relationships, tired, discouraged, and hoping the counselees don't show up. There was no wind in my spiritual sail. I kept the appointments out of a sense of duty, not out of love for God and my counselee. Amazingly, God often used those times to show Himself strong in bringing needed understanding, repentance, and hope to counselees. Several times those became "turn-around sessions" for them and an "in-your-face" reminder to me that God, using His Holy Spirit–energized Scripture, is the one who changes people.

Be encouraged that Hebrews 4:12 is true regardless of how you feel. "For the word of God is living and active, sharper than any two-edged sword, piercing to the division of soul and of spirit, of joints and of marrow, and discerning the thoughts and intentions of the heart." Note that Psalm 19:7 – 8 lists four synonyms for God's Word and tells us what it effectively accomplishes, regardless of the one ministering it. "The law of the LORD is perfect, reviving the soul; the testimony of the LORD is sure, making wise the simple; the precepts of the LORD are right, rejoicing the heart; the commandment of the LORD is pure, enlightening the eyes."

Second, I have learned that *you will never hurt someone when you compassionately point them toward Jesus Christ and His Word as the source of long-term solutions.* Consider this wonderful invitation of Jesus Christ recorded in Matthew 11:28 – 30: "Come to me, all who labor and are heavy laden, and I will give you rest. Take my yoke upon you, and learn from me, for I am gentle and lowly in heart, and you will find rest for your souls. For my yoke is easy, and my burden is light."

A yoke was an implement used to connect animals for the purpose of accomplishing a task. It speaks of responsibility. Knowing and following the Lord Jesus Christ requires effort, but the burden or responsibility of following His ways is lighter than the way of the transgressor (Proverbs 13:15 KJV). Christ is the one who provides rest for troubled souls — not loving, well-intended counselors.

Are you a newcomer to Scripture-based counseling? Know that while you may not be able to help an individual as quickly as a seasoned veteran, you will not hurt someone if you simply listen carefully to their struggles and then lovingly and tenderly point them toward Christ and His Word.

COUNSELING METHODOLOGY

Over the years, I've also learned several lessons about using Scripture *in* counseling. *How you start a counseling case influences how you finish.* An awkward, stumbling beginning frequently hinders the counselor's effectiveness. It adds to the pressure and nervousness the counselee may already be experiencing, and it may raise questions about our competence in the mind of the counselee.

Good starts are usually the result of good planning, especially for a novice counselor. Prior to the scheduled counseling session, it is wise to plan a tentative agenda. Anticipate key questions you will ask, how you intend to give hope, what Scriptures might be most helpful, and what homework assignments might be appropriate. Information gained in the actual counseling session will influence what parts of the plan are followed and when you deviate from it. Good starts do not guarantee good finishes, but they certainly increase the likelihood of it happening.

I've also come to understand that *a question pricks the conscience; an accusation hardens the will.* God confronted Adam and Eve after they sinned (Genesis 3) by asking four probing, convicting questions. As God, He was certainly not seeking information, but was leading

Adam and Eve to face what they had done. The book of Malachi, the final prophecy recorded in the Old Testament, is four chapters long. The prophet rebuked the people of Israel for their neglect of the true worship of the Lord and called them to repentance. How? Through no fewer than 23 questions in a book of 55 verses! Christ also used questions many times in His dealings with people, most notably with Peter. Three times He asked him, "Do you love me?" (John 21:15–17).

There are times when it is appropriate to state that a particular action was sinful. Some counselors, however, have a tendency to do that far too often. It is wiser to address these behaviors in the form of good questions. For example, instead of saying, "Jack, you sure were a lousy father and a poor example of a Christian last Thursday evening in the way you spoke to your son with such sinful anger," you could consider asking him a question about his behavior. "Jack, if we could ask God to evaluate your behavior last Thursday evening with your son, what do you think the Lord would say?" "How do you think God would want you to act and speak if a similar situation were to arise this week?"

I've also come to see that *selective silence can be powerful.* Sometimes a counselee will ask or say something particularly incriminating, and the wisest response is to remain silent for a few moments. Let the question or statement hang in the air for the purpose of thoughtful evaluation. Christ did this when the scribes and Pharisees brought Him a woman caught in adultery (John 8:1–11).

Another lesson I've learned about counseling methodology is that *robust, focused homework, if used well, can help you get much more done in less time.* "Homework" is simply the application of God's truth to one's life. It is taking scriptural truth taught in the counseling session and discussing with the counselee how to apply it to their thinking and behavior patterns. The purpose is to help counselees grow spiritually in the areas you are dealing with in the counseling sessions.

I have found it fruitful to usually include the following in my homework assignments:

A. Strategic, systematic Scripture reading

B. Meaningful Scripture memory

C. Reading in theologically sound and pertinent literature

D. Acts of loving, humble service to others

E. Church service attendance and note taking

F. Fervent, focused prayer

The assignments in each area would be tailored with sensitivity to each individual's spiritual state, load in life, and learning abilities. I customarily discuss each of these areas in the subsequent session, seeking to squeeze all the good possible from each growth project. It is not enough that we teach the truths of the Scriptures, we must also emphasize the understanding and application to life.

I'm also discovering that many of us have *a tendency to be general and long; and that it takes discipline to be precise and short.* The Scriptures are silent on how long a counseling session should be. This is a wisdom issue and godly counselors can and do differ on the matter. I seek to have my "normal" counseling sessions go about 60 to 75 minutes. On occasion I have had sessions that went a few hours. In one of my jobs, we regularly had Christian leaders in our home overnight for intensive counseling.

I have seen in my own life and in the ministry of counselors I supervise that counseling effectiveness is not determined by session length. Longer sessions do not necessarily equate to better sessions. Instead, effectiveness is more influenced by the counselor directing the session so as to move toward specific goals to benefit the counselee. The goal is to make it a spiritually productive session, regardless of length.

Some sessions go longer than needed because the counselor is just not aware of the time, or doesn't guide a talkative counselee, or doesn't know what to do regarding the matters presented and, therefore, just keeps talking, hoping something he says will be helpful. There are three strategies that have helped many counselors control session length. First, to place a small clock right in front of you that you can look at frequently and inconspicuously. This aids in becoming aware of time passing. Second, explain to your counselee that if you interrupt them it is because you have enough detail on the matter they are discussing, and you want to move the conversation forward toward the other vital matters. Third, narrow the focus of your scriptural teaching so that you are more like a laser than a floodlight.

I've also learned that *it is easy to have a counseling session talking about the counselee's circumstances, assigned homework, pleasing God, changing and growing, etc., but the Bible is never opened.* Don't ask me how I know that statement is true! I am embarrassed to say it, but there have been times when I spent time talking about the Bible but failed to use the Bible in the counseling session. I have since determined that whenever I am doing formal counseling, the Scriptures will be opened and used.

It is important to distinguish between God's wisdom and our wisdom. Counselors can do that by carefully explaining the meaning of appropriate passages of Scripture and then offering insights on application of those truths to the counselee's life circumstances. The goal is to demonstrate that your advice grows out of understanding and seeking to apply the Scriptures. We must always remember that "Thus says the Lord" and "Here's my ideas on how to apply it" are in two very different categories. Demonstrate the authority of the Scriptures by the attention given it in the session.

DEVELOPING SKILL AS A BIBLICAL COUNSELOR

I've also learned several lessons about using Scripture *in* counseling that have helped me to develop my skill as a counselor. First, *the hard cases are the ones you grow on.* I can still vividly remember a man sitting in my office many years ago confessing that he had lived a homosexual lifestyle. He was a new believer in Christ who wanted to do right, but was struggling to resist the friends and other allurements of his former life. Would I help him? I said, "Yes," even though I did not have the foggiest idea of what I was going to do.

That man was the first individual I had counseled who was struggling with homosexual sin. My ignorance of how to help him was overcome by my confidence that the Scriptures had answers and by my love for him that motivated me to find those answers. Nothing will motivate your study, prayer, seeking wisdom from more experienced counselors, and careful consideration of theological truths quite like wanting to help someone you care about but for whom you do not have scriptural solutions. Let the challenging cases motivate your own growth.

I'm learning that *seat time precedes skill.* There is a difference between being "book wise" and "case wise." Thank God for the wonderful literature that is available today to help us understand God's Word and how to use it effectively in ministry to hurting individuals. Yet despite these rich resources, knowing the what, when, where, and how of expressing God's truth is something learned primarily from sitting across from people and trying to help them. To quote Nike's motto, "Just do it!"

Proverbs 15:2 says, "The tongue of the wise makes knowledge acceptable" (NASB). Listening to individuals' circumstances and seeking to help them session after session, week after week, year after year contributes to gaining that kind of wisdom. I'm also finding that *thoughtfully reading an average of ten pages per day in theologically solid counseling literature will change your life and level of counseling insight.* The good news is that as our culture devolves, becoming less godly, God is blessing us with more theologically solid, well-written, helpful counseling resources than ever before. The bad news is that unless you read regularly, you will not be aware of materials that could be very helpful to your counselees.

Did you know that if you read an average of ten pages a day you could finish a book about every month? I know that there are some days when you can't read any, but consider that there are other days when you could read 20, 30, or 40 pages or more. The key is to keep reading and to be selective. There is so much available, and it is impossible for one person to read it all. I have found it helpful to note the book reviews provided by the Biblical Counseling Coalition on their website as a guide to my reading (see www.biblicalcounselingcoalition.org).

The supervision phase of the ACBC certification process *taught me skills I could not have learned from a book.* The Association of Certified Biblical Counselors (ACBC) certifies both individual counselors and training centers. Many years ago, after meeting the training requirements and successfully completing the theological and counseling exam, I was cleared for the supervision phase. I reported on 50 of my own counseling cases over a period of several months to Dr. Robert Smith, M.D., a leader in ACBC (called NANC at the time — the National Association of Nouthetic Counselors). His insightful challenges to my analysis of the issues, Scripture chosen to address those issues, how I ministered the Word, the homework assigned, the words I used to address matters, and even time management of sessions were unbelievably helpful. He also provided significant encouragement. As a result of his careful coaching, my counseling skills grew and developed. I will be forever grateful for his influence in my life.

Submitting to the ACBC certification process requires humility to allow someone to evaluate what you believe and how you communicate it, to evaluate your understanding of counseling procedures and how well you can communicate it, and to look over your shoulder as you conduct at least 50 counseling sessions. But we know that God gives grace to the humble (James 4:6) and exalts them "at the proper time" (1 Peter 5:6, NASB). You can learn more about ACBC certification at www.biblicalcounseling.com.

TRAINING AND SUPERVISING COUNSELORS

Regarding training and supervising counselors, I've learned that *too much of a strength can make it a weakness.* Many biblical counselors are skilled teachers, either because of training, spiritual gifting, or both.

This is a wonderful positive. The negative is that teachers tend to view every problem as calling for another lesson.

Oftentimes counselees already know more spiritual truth than they are obeying. What they need in such cases are not more Bible lessons, but guidance and accountability in developing a lifestyle of obedience to the truth. Every strength can potentially become a weakness if not balanced with other important aspects of counseling.

Second, *our tendency is to dispense rather than to minister the Word.* Dispensing the Word involves several verses, short explanations, surface application, and little review, if any, in following sessions. It seems to grow out of the philosophy that if one verse is good, then five verses is five times more powerful. Some counselors do this because this is primarily the style of preaching and teaching to which they have been exposed. But ministering the Word involves a key verse or passage, careful exposition of the text, asking the counselee to explain the passage back to you, and specific application to life circumstances with counselee interaction, assigned as homework and then reviewed in multiple future sessions.

A question that has helped a number of counselors move from dispensing to ministering the Word is, "What verse or passage could I teach my counselee, which if understood and obeyed, would help this individual in multiple areas of life?" All the Scriptures are inspired and profitable, but determining which passage would be most profitable for your counselee right now is the key.

Third, *listening to a recorded counseling session can be painfully profitable.* Many counselors find it uncomfortable listening to themselves counseling, just like a pastor listening to his own message. There are the inevitable groans and head shakes as your mistakes are brought to your attention in stereo. There are usually some approving nods also as you realize that God used you for His glory to help someone. Listening to a digital recording allows you to easily note the amount of time given to various segments, such as data gathering, homework review, teaching, etc. You will also get insight into who did the most talking and who controlled the session.

Feeling brave? Ask a biblical counselor more experienced than you to listen to a few sessions and discuss his observations with you. It will be even more helpful than your private review of the session.

THANK YOU, LORD

The authors of this book have demonstrated the rich, robust superiority of Christ and His Word to any of the world's theories on how to genuinely help hurting individuals. Scriptural counselors are given a front-row seat to watch God change people's lives. It is a great privilege and brings with it a great responsibility not only to God but to the people we influence. May we all, like the writer of Psalm 119, say:

"I am your servant; give me understanding that I may know your testimonies!" (v. 125).

"Therefore I consider all your precepts to be right; I hate every false way" (v. 128).

"The unfolding of your words gives light; it imparts understanding to the simple" (v. 130).

"Keep steady my steps according to your promise and let no iniquity get dominion over me" (v. 133).

ACKNOWLEDGMENTS

The Biblical Counseling Coalition (BCC) seeks to advance the ministry of the biblical counseling movement through *collaborative relationships* and *robust resources*. *Scripture and Counseling* certainly fits that mission. We're thankful for the leadership of the BCC's board of directors: Nicolas Ellen, John Henderson, Garrett Higbee, Bob Kellemen, Randy Patten, David Powlison, Deepak Reju, and Steve Viars. It is because of their vision and commitment that *Scripture and Counseling* came to fruition.

We're also thankful for all the coauthors of *Scripture and Counseling*. Each man and woman contributed their chapter in the midst of a heavy load as pastors, counselors, professors, and ministry leaders. And each coauthor contributed all payments back to the BCC to further advance our mission. Thank you!

We'd like to express a special thanks to Ryan Pazdur of Zondervan for his vision for this project and for his commitment to it. Thank you, Ryan, for the work you and your team have done to shape *Scripture and Counseling*.

Our agent, Andrew Wolgemuth, of Wolgemuth & Associates, Inc., has a rare blend of a sharp mind, business acumen, and a loving heart. He understands biblical counseling and is passionate about advancing the ministry of the BCC. Thanks, Andrew!

THE MISSION, VISION, AND PASSION STATEMENT OF THE BIBLICAL COUNSELING COALITION

OUR MISSION

The BCC exists to *multiply the ministry of the biblical counseling movement* by strengthening churches, para-church organizations, and educational institutions through promoting unity and excellence in biblical counseling. Our mission is to foster collaborative relationships and to provide robust, relevant biblical resources that equip the Body of Christ to change lives with Christ's changeless truth through the personal ministry of the Word. All that we do flows from our calling to empower the biblical counseling movement to equip people to love God and one another in Christ-centered ways. We pursue this purpose by organizing our thinking around one central question: "What does it mean to counsel in the grace and truth of Christ?"

OUR VISION

More than counseling, our vision is for the entire church to speak God's truth in love. Our vision is to unite, advance, and multiply the biblical counseling movement in Christ-centered cooperation by relating in ways that are loving and wise, pursuing the unity of the Spirit in the bond of peace. We are dedicated to developing the theology and practice of the personal ministry of the Word, whether described as biblical counseling, personal discipleship, one-another ministry, small group ministry, the cure of soul, soul care, spiritual friendship, or spiritual direction. We seek to promote the strengthening and multiplication of these ministries by ministering to people who offer care, people who are seeking care, and people who train caregivers.

OUR PASSION

It is our passion to promote personal change centered on the person of Christ through the personal ministry of the Word.

BE EQUIPPED

To fulfill our mission, vision, and passion, the Biblical Counseling Coalition maintains a robust website designed to equip you to change lives with Christ's changeless truth. We invite you to visit us at www. biblicalcounselingcoalition.org. You will enjoy daily blogs, weekly book reviews, thousands of free resources, training videos, links to dozens of other equipping websites, and much more.

THE CONFESSIONAL STATEMENT OF THE BIBLICAL COUNSELING COALITION

PREAMBLE: SPEAKING THE TRUTH IN LOVE — A VISION FOR THE ENTIRE CHURCH

We are a fellowship of Christians committed to promoting excellence and unity in biblical counseling. Our goal is to foster collaborative relationships and to provide robust, relevant biblical resources that equip the Body of Christ to change lives with Christ's changeless truth. We desire to advance the biblical counseling movement in Christ-centered cooperation by relating in ways that are loving and wise, pursuing the unity of the Spirit in the bond of peace (Eph. 4:3).

We pursue this purpose by organizing our thinking around one central question: What does it mean to counsel in the grace and truth of Christ? All that we do flows from our calling to equip people to love God and others in Christ-centered ways (Matt. 22:35–40).

More than counseling, our vision is for the entire church to speak the truth in love (Eph. 4:11–16). We are dedicated to developing the theology and practice of the personal ministry of the Word, whether described as biblical counseling, pastoral counseling, personal discipleship, one-another ministry, small group ministry, cure of souls, soul care, spiritual friendship, or spiritual direction. We seek to promote the strengthening of these ministries in churches, para-church organizations, and educational institutions by ministering to people who offer care, people who are seeking care, and people who train care-givers.

INTRODUCTION: IN CHRIST ALONE

The goal of biblical counseling is spiritual, relational, and personal maturity as evidenced in desires, thoughts, motives, actions, and emotions that increasingly reflect Jesus (Eph. 4:17 – 5:2). We believe that such personal change must be centered on the person of Christ. We are convinced that personal ministry centered on Christ and anchored in Scripture offers the only lasting hope and loving help to a fallen and broken world.

We confess that we have not arrived. We comfort and counsel others only as we continue to receive ongoing comfort and counsel from Christ and the Body of Christ (2 Cor. 1:3 – 11). We admit that we struggle to apply consistently all that we believe. We who counsel live in process, just like those we counsel, so we want to learn and grow in the wisdom and mercies of Christ.

All Christian ministry arises from and is anchored in God's revelation — which is both the written Word (Scripture) and the living Word (Christ). This is true for the personal ministry of the Word (conversational and relational ministry, which our culture calls "counseling") and for the various public ministries of the Word. In light of this core conviction about Christ-centered, Word-based ministry, we affirm the following central commitments as biblical counselors.

BIBLICAL COUNSELING MUST BE ANCHORED IN SCRIPTURE

We believe that God's Word is authoritative, sufficient, and relevant (Isa. 55:11; Matt. 4:4; Heb. 4:12 – 13). The inspired and inerrant Scriptures, rightly interpreted and carefully applied, offer us God's comprehensive wisdom. We learn to understand who God is, who we are, the problems we face, how people change, and God's provision for that change in the Gospel (John 8:31 – 32; 10:10; 17:17). No other source of knowledge thoroughly equips us to counsel in ways that transform the human heart (Ps. 19:7 – 14; 2 Tim. 3:16 – 17; 2 Peter 1:3). Other systems of counseling aim for other goals and assume a different dynamic of change. The wisdom given by God in His Word is distinctive and robust. He comprehensively addresses the sin and suffering of all people in all situations.

Wise counseling is an insightful application of God's all-embracing truth to our complex lives (Rom. 15:4; 1 Cor. 10:6; Phil. 1:9 – 11). It does not merely collect proof-texts from the Bible. Wise counseling requires ongoing practical theological labor in order to understand Scripture, people, and situations (2 Tim. 2:15). We must continually develop our personal character, case-wise understanding of people, and pastoral skills (Rom. 15:14; Col. 1:28 – 29).

When we say that Scripture is comprehensive in wisdom, we mean that the Bible makes sense of all things, not that it contains all the information people could ever know about all topics. God's common grace brings many good things to human life. However, common grace cannot save us from our struggles with sin or from the troubles that beset us. Common grace cannot sanctify or cure the soul of all that ails the human condition. We affirm that numerous sources (such as scientific research, organized observations about human behavior, those we counsel, reflection on our own life experience, literature, film, and history) can contribute to our knowledge of people, and many sources can contribute some relief for the troubles of life. However, none can constitute a comprehensive system of counseling principles and practices. When systems of thought and practice claim to prescribe a cure for the human condition, they compete with Christ (Col. 2:1 – 15). Scripture alone teaches a perspective and way of looking at life by which we can think biblically about and critically evaluate information and actions from any source (Col. 2:2 – 10; 2 Tim. 3:16 – 17).

BIBLICAL COUNSELING MUST BE CENTERED ON CHRIST AND THE GOSPEL

We believe that wise counseling centers on Jesus Christ—His sinless life, death on the cross, burial, resurrection, present reign, and promised return. Through the Gospel, God reveals the depths of sin, the scope of suffering, and the breadth, length, height, and depth of grace. Wise counseling gets to the heart of personal and interpersonal problems by bringing to bear the truth, mercy, and power of Christ's grace (John 1:14). There is no true restoration of the soul and there are no truly God-honoring relationships without understanding the desperate condition we are in without Christ and apart from experiencing the joy of progressive deliverance from that condition through God's mercies.

We point people to a person, Jesus our Redeemer, and not to a program, theory, or experience. We place our trust in the transforming power of the Redeemer as the only hope to change people's hearts, not in any human system of change. People need a personal and dynamic relationship with Jesus, not a system of self-salvation, self-management, or self-actualization (John 14:6). Wise counselors seek to lead struggling, hurting, sinning, and confused people to the hope, resources, strength, and life that are available only in Christ.

BIBLICAL COUNSELING MUST BE GROUNDED IN SOUND THEOLOGY

We believe that biblical counseling is fundamentally a practical theological discipline because every aspect of life is related to God. God intends that we care for one another in ways that relate human struggles to His person, purposes, promises, and will. Wise counseling arises from a theological way of looking at life—a mind-set, a worldview—that informs how we understand people, problems, and solutions. The best biblical counselors are wise, balanced, caring, experienced practical theologians (Phil. 1:9–11).

Biblical counselors relate the Scriptures relevantly to people's lives

(Heb. 3:12–19). All wise counseling understands particular passages and a person's unique life experience within the context of the Bible's larger story line: God's creation, our fall into sin, His redemptive plan, and the consummation of all things. Thus we engage in person-specific conversations that flow naturally out of a comprehensive biblical theology of life.

BIBLICAL COUNSELING MUST BE DEPENDENT UPON THE HOLY SPIRIT AND PRAYER

We believe that both genuine change of heart and transformation of lifestyle depend upon the ministry of the Holy Spirit (John 14:15–16:16; 2 Cor. 3:17–18). Biblical counselors know that it is impossible to speak wisely and lovingly to bring about true and lasting change apart from the decisive, compassionate, and convicting work of the Spirit in the counselor and the counselee. We acknowledge the Holy Spirit as the One who illuminates our understanding of the Word and empowers its application in everyday life.

Wise counselors serve in the truth that God reveals and by the strength that God supplies. By the Spirit's work, God receives glory in all the good that takes place in people's lives. Biblical counselors affirm the absolute necessity of the work of the Holy Spirit to guide and empower the counselor, the counselee, and the counseling relationship. Dependent prayer is essential to the work of biblical counseling (Eph. 6:18–20). Wise counselors humbly request God's intervention and direction, praise God for His work in people's lives, and intercede for people that they would experience genuine life change to the glory of God (Phil. 4:6).

BIBLICAL COUNSELING MUST BE DIRECTED TOWARD SANCTIFICATION

We believe that wise counseling should be transformative, change-oriented, and grounded in the doctrine of sanctification (2 Cor. 3:16–18; Phil. 2:12–13). The lifelong change process begins at salvation (justification, regeneration, redemption, reconciliation) and continues until we see Jesus face-to-face (1 John 3:1 – 3). The aim of wise counseling is intentional and intensive discipleship. The fruit of wise counseling is spiritually mature people who increasingly reflect Christ (relationally, rationally, volitionally, and emotionally) by enjoying and exalting God and by loving others well and wisely (Gal. 5:22 – 6:10).

Wise counseling seeks to embrace the Bible's teaching regarding God's role and human responsibility in spiritual growth. God's strength and mercy call for our response of faith and obedience. A comprehensive theology of the spiritual life provides the basis for applying relevant biblical methods of spiritual growth. Biblical counseling helps believers to understand what it means to be in Christ (Rom. 6:3 – 14). It equips them to apply the principles of progressive sanctification through renewing their minds and actions based on Scripture with a motive of love for God and others (Rom. 12:1 – 2).

BIBLICAL COUNSELING MUST BE ROOTED IN THE LIFE OF THE CHURCH

We believe that we best reflect the Trinity as we live and grow in community (John 17; Eph. 4). Sanctification is not a self-improvement project, but a process of learning to love and serve God and others. Wise counseling embeds personal change within God's community — the church — with all God's rich resources of corporate and interpersonal means of grace (1 Cor. 12:12 – 27). We believe that the church should be both the center and the sender of gospel-centered counseling (Rom. 15:14).

By example and exhortation the New Testament commends the personal, face-to-face, one-another ministry of the Word — whether in one-to-one or small group relationships (Heb. 3:12 – 19; 10:19 – 25). God calls the church to mutual wise counseling just as He calls the church to public ministries of the Word in preaching, teaching, worship, and observing the ordinances of baptism and the Lord's Supper. God desires His people to love and serve each other by speaking His truth in love to one another (Eph. 4:15–16). The primary and fullest expression of counseling ministry is meant to occur in local church communities where pastors effectively shepherd souls while equipping and overseeing diverse forms of every-member ministry (Eph. 4:11–14). Other like-minded counseling institutions and organizations are beneficial insofar as they serve alongside the church, encourage Christians to counsel biblically, and purpose to impact the world for Christ.

BIBLICAL COUNSELING MUST BE FOUNDED IN LOVE

We believe that Christ's incarnation is not just the basis for care but also the model for how we care (Heb. 4:14–16; John 13:34–35). We seek to enter into a person's story, listening well, expressing thoughtful love, and engaging the person with compassion (1 Thess. 2:8). The wise and loving personal ministry of the Word takes many appropriate forms, from caring comfort to loving rebuke, from careful listening to relevant scriptural exploration, all while building trusting, authentic relationships (1 Thess. 5:14–15; 1 John 4:7–21).

Wise counseling takes into account all that people experience (desires, thoughts, goals, actions, words, emotions, struggles, situational pressure, physical suffering, abuse, injustice, etc.). All of human experience is the context for understanding how God's Word relates to life. Such awareness not only shapes the content of counseling but also shapes the way counselors interact so that everything said is constructive, according to the need of the moment, that it may give grace to the hearer (Eph. 4:29).

BIBLICAL COUNSELING MUST BE ATTENTIVE TO HEART ISSUES

We believe that human behavior is tied to thoughts, intentions, and affections of the heart. All our actions arise from hearts that are worshiping either God or something else, therefore we emphasize the importance of the heart and address the inner person. God fully understands and rightly weighs who we are, what we do, and why we do it. While we cannot completely understand a person's heart (even our own), God's Word reveals and penetrates the heart's core beliefs and intentions (Heb. 4:12–13).

Wise counseling seeks to address both the inward and outward aspects of human life to bring thorough and lasting change into the image of Christ. The Bible is clear that human behavior is not mechanical, but grows out of a heart that desires, longs, thinks, chooses, and feels in ways that are oriented either toward or against Christ. Wise counsel appropriately focuses on the vertical and the horizontal dimensions, on the inner and the outer person, on observable behavior and underlying issues of the heart (Matt. 23:23–28). Biblical counselors work to help struggling people to learn wisdom; to love God with heart, soul, mind, and strength; to love one's neighbor as oneself; and to endure suffering in hope.

BIBLICAL COUNSELING MUST BE COMPREHENSIVE IN UNDERSTANDING

We believe that biblical counseling should focus on the full range of human nature created in the image of God (Gen. 1:26–28). A comprehensive biblical understanding sees human beings as relational (spiritual and social), rational, volitional, emotional, and physical. Wise counseling takes the whole person seriously in his or her whole life context. It helps people to embrace all of life face-to-face with Christ so they become more like Christ in their relationships, thoughts, motivations, behaviors, and emotions.

We recognize the complexity of the relationship between the body and soul (Gen. 2:7). Because of this, we seek to remain sensitive to physical factors and organic issues that affect people's lives. In our desire to help people comprehensively, we seek to apply God's Word to people's lives amid bodily strengths and weaknesses. We encourage a thorough assessment and sound treatment for any suspected physical problems.

We recognize the complexity of the connection between people and their social environment. Thus we seek to remain sensitive to the impact of suffering and of the great variety of significant social-cultural factors (1 Peter 3:8–22). In our desire to help people comprehensively, we seek to apply God's Word to people's lives amid both positive and negative social experiences. We encourage people to seek appropriate practical aid when their problems have a component that involves education, work life, finances, legal matters, criminality (either as a victim or a perpetrator), and other social matters.

BIBLICAL COUNSELING MUST BE THOROUGH IN CARE

We believe that God's Word is profitable for dealing thoroughly with the evils we suffer as well as with the sins we commit. Since struggling people usually experience some combination of besetting sin and personal suffering, wise counselors seek to discern the differences and connections between sin and suffering, and to minister appropriately to both (1 Thess. 5:14).

Biblical counseling addresses suffering and engages sufferers in many compassionate ways. It offers God's encouragement, comfort, and hope for the hurting (Rom. 8:17–18; 2 Cor. 1:3–8). It encourages mercy ministry (Acts 6:1–7) and seeks to promote justice. Biblical counseling addresses sin and engages sinners in numerous caring ways. It offers God's confrontation of sins, encourages repentance of sins, presents God's gracious forgiveness in Christ, and shares God's powerful path for progressive victory over sin (1 John 1:8–2:2; 2 Cor. 2:5–11; Col. 3:1–17; 2 Tim. 2:24–26).

BIBLICAL COUNSELING MUST BE PRACTICAL AND RELEVANT

We believe that a commitment to the sufficiency of God's Word results in counseling that demonstrates the relevancy of God's Word. Biblical counseling offers a practical approach to daily life that is uniquely effective in the real world where people live and relate (1 John 3:11–24). By instruction and example, the Bible teaches foundational methodological principles for wise interaction and intervention (Acts 20:26–37; Gal. 6:1–5; Col. 1:24–2:1).

Within the Bible's overall guidelines for the personal ministry of the Word, there is room for a variety of practical methods of change, all anchored in applying scriptural truth to people's lives and relationships. The Bible calls us to use wise methods that minister in Christ-centered ways to the unique life situations of specific people (Prov. 15:23; 25:11). We are to speak what is helpful for building others up according to the need of the moment, that it may benefit those who listen (Eph. 4:29).

BIBLICAL COUNSELING MUST BE ORIENTED TOWARD OUTREACH

We believe that Christianity is missionary-minded by its very nature. Biblical counseling should be a powerful evangelistic and apologetic force in our world. We want to bring the good news of Jesus and His Word to the world that only God can redeem. We seek to speak in relevant ways to Christians and non-Christians, to draw them to the Savior and the distinctive wisdom that comes only from His Word (Titus 2:10–15).

We want to present the claims, mercies, hope, and relevance of Christ in a positive, loving, Christlike spirit (1 Peter 3:15). We seek to engage the broad spectrum of counseling models and approaches. We want to affirm what is biblical and wise. Where we believe models and methods fall short of Christ's call, we want to critique clearly and charitably. When interacting with people with whom we differ, we want to communicate in ways that are respectful, firm, gracious, fair-minded, and clear. When we perceive error, we want to humbly point people forward toward the way of truth so that we all become truer, wiser, more loving counselors. We want to listen well to those who disagree with us and learn from their critiques. Our mission to spread the truth and fame of Jesus Christ includes a desire that all counselors appreciate and embrace the beauty of a Christ-centered and Word-based approach to people, problems, and solutions.

CONCLUSION: UNITY IN TRUTH AND LOVE

We are committed to generating a unified effort among God's people to glorify Christ and multiply disciples through the personal ministry of the Word (Matt. 28:18–20). We trust in Jesus Christ in whom grace and truth are perfectly joined (John 1:14). We cling to His Word, in which truth and love live in perfect union (Eph. 4:15; Phil. 1:9; 1 Thess. 2:8). We love His church—living and speaking the truth in love, growing up in Him who is the Head, and building itself up in love as each part does its work (Eph. 4:15–16).

We desire to encourage this unity in truth and love through a fresh vision for biblical counseling. When people ask, "What makes biblical counseling truly biblical?" we unite to affirm:

> Biblical counseling occurs whenever and wherever God's people engage in conversations that are anchored in Scripture, centered on Christ and the Gospel, grounded in sound theology, dependent upon the Holy Spirit and prayer, directed toward sanctification, rooted in the life of the church, founded in love, attentive to heart issues, comprehensive in understanding, thorough in care, practical and relevant, and oriented toward outreach.

We invite you to join us on this journey of promoting excellence and unity in biblical counseling. Join us as we seek to equip one another to promote personal change, centered on the person of Christ through the personal ministry of the Word.

THE DOCTRINAL
STATEMENT OF THE
BIBLICAL COUNSELING
COALITION

The following statement summarizes the core doctrinal beliefs of the Biblical Counseling Coalition. It is not an exhaustive statement, but a theological framework concerning our core affirmations regarding the central doctrines of the Christian faith.

ABOUT THE BIBLE

We believe that God has given the Bible as His inspired, infallible, inerrant, and living revelatory Word. We affirm the verbal, plenary inspiration of the Bible and are therefore committed to the complete trustworthiness and primacy of Scripture. The Bible is God's relevant, profound, deeply personal communication to us that invites us to intimate fellowship with Him. The Scriptures consist of the sixty-six books of the Old and New Testaments. They are the totally sufficient, authoritative, and normative rule and guide of all Christian life, practice, and doctrine, and are profitable for glorifying God through growth in likeness to Christ, which is our life purpose.

The Bible is complete in its revelation of Who God is, His person, character, promises, commandments, and will for the salvation of a people for His own possession. The Bible reveals who we are: created in God's image, accountable to God, fallen into sin against God, judged and justly condemned by God, redeemed by Jesus Christ, and transformed by the Holy Spirit. The Bible reveals the meaning of our total life situation in each and all its aspects—all the blessings of this life, the variety of sufferings and hardships, Satan, the influence of other human beings, etc. The Bible also reveals the nature of the Christian life and the ministries of the church, showing the content, the functions, and the goals that express the image of Christ.

ABOUT THE TRIUNE GOD

We believe in one God, eternally existing in three equally divine Persons: the Father, the Son, and the Holy Spirit, Who know, love, and glorify one another. They are forever equal in nature, attributes, and perfection, yet forever distinct in Their relations to one another and distinct in Their particular relationships both to the creation and to the actions and processes of redemption. They are equally worthy of our worship, love, and obedience. This one true and living God is infinitely perfect both in His love and in His holiness. The Triune God, in affectionate sovereignty, sustains and rules over all things, providentially bringing about His eternal good purpose to redeem a people for Himself—to the praise of the glory of His grace.

ABOUT GOD THE FATHER

We believe that God, as the Father, reigns over His entire universe with providential care, holy justice, and saving mercy, to His own glory. In His holy love, the Father is all-powerful, all-loving, all-knowing, and all-wise. He is fatherly in attitude toward all men, but Father, indeed, to those who have been made children of God through salvation in Christ.

ABOUT GOD THE SON, JESUS CHRIST

We believe in the deity of our Lord Jesus Christ, the eternal Son of God, Who humbled Himself by taking on the form of a man by means of His virgin birth, becoming forever both fully human without ceasing to be fully God. We affirm that He lived a sinless life of active love and perfect wisdom. He died by crucifixion on the cross, by His shed blood and death making a vicarious, substitutionary atonement for our sins. After three days, He was resurrected bodily from the dead, unto an indestructible life. After appearing to His disciples and instructing them for forty days, He ascended to heaven. He is now seated at the right hand of the Father, interceding for believers, reigning as King over all creation, and working in and through His church. He will personally return in power and glory to judge the living and the dead, and to raise to immortality those who eagerly await Him, perfecting them in His image.

ABOUT GOD THE HOLY SPIRIT

We believe that God the Holy Spirit, sent by the Father and the Son, has come into the world to reveal and glorify Christ and to convict and draw sinners to Christ. From the moment of spiritual birth, He indwells believers, individually and corporately, as their Helper. By the Spirit's agency, believers are renewed, sanctified, and adopted into God's family. He imparts new life to believers, placing them into the Body of Christ, transforming and empowering them for Christlike living, and sealing them until the day of redemption. He is the source of power for all acceptable worship and ministry as He imparts a diversity of enabling gifts that equip God's people for service. He provides the power to understand and apply God's truth in love.

ABOUT HUMANITY — CREATION

We believe that God created Adam and Eve in His image, male and female, and declared them "very good," granting them all the capacities of image bearers. God created them to reflect and to enjoy His glory. They were created material and immaterial, physical body and spiritual soul, these qualities united and inseparably interdependent. They were created with a conscience able to discern good and evil; with the capacity to relate, think, choose, and feel in all the fruitfulness of wisdom. They were designed and commissioned to love God and one another, living in holy and devoted fellowship with God, and in loving, complementary relationship with each other. They were designed and commissioned to care for and govern His creation, working in and ruling over all creation as God's faithful servants and stewards.

ABOUT HUMANITY — FALL

We believe that because of voluntary sin against God, Adam and Eve fell from the actively good, sinless, and innocent state in which they were first created. They became self-willed, perverse, and transgressive against God and each other. Immediately they died spiritually and also began to die physically. Consequently, for them and all their progeny, the image of God was distorted and their nature depraved and corrupted in every aspect of their being (spiritually, socially, mentally, volitionally, and emotionally). While human beings are corrupted in every aspect of their being and functioning, because of God's common grace the image of God has not been totally eradicated, and evil is not given full reign. God preserves and enables many common goods. All people have true dignity, a conscience in which clarity coexists with distortion, and many powers of mind, action, and feeling. All humanity is separated and alienated from God and thus spiritually dead — until God's own gracious intervention. The supreme need of all human beings is to be reconciled to God; and the only hope of all human beings is to receive the undeserved grace of God in Christ. God alone can rescue us and restore sinners to Himself.

ABOUT SALVATION — REDEMPTION

We believe that salvation is the gift of God by grace alone and is received through faith alone in the Lord Jesus Christ. Salvation is wholly conceived, accomplished, and applied by God's sovereign grace. It is not, in whole or in part, conceived or accomplished by human will or works. We believe that salvation refers comprehensively to the entire work of God that redeems His people from the penalty, power, and eventual presence of sin while imputing to His people the righteousness of Jesus Christ and all the benefits of adoption into His family. This salvation overthrows the dominion of darkness and creates a new people who enter Christ's Body of light, truth, and love.

We affirm that salvation is only through Christ, for there is no other name given under heaven by which we must be saved. Christ voluntarily took upon Himself the form of a man, was tempted in all points as we are, yet was without sin in nature, word, or deed. He honored the Divine Law by His personal obedience, and by His death made a full and vicarious atonement for our sins. Jesus, having risen bodily from the dead, is now enthroned in heaven serving as the suitable, compassionate, all-sufficient Savior and the Mediator for His believer-priests.

We believe that all the blessings of salvation are free gifts of God, and that each is a glorious facet of union with Christ. In Christ, persons once justly condemned are now forgiven and justified because Christ died bearing our sins, because He was raised for our justification, and because God imputes to His people the righteousness of Jesus Christ. In Christ, persons once dead in trespasses and sins are now made spiritually alive in the new birth, receive the Holy Spirit, and receive eternal life. In Christ, persons whose father and master was the devil are now adopted by God the Father into His family and become citizens and servants in God's kingdom. In Christ, persons who were estranged from God are now reconciled forever. God gives all these gifts, and more, by the Holy Spirit, and we receive all these gifts by faith.

We believe that by His incarnation, life, death, resurrection, and ascension, Jesus Christ acted as our representative and substitute. He did this so that in Him we might become the righteousness of God. On the cross He canceled sin, satisfied by His sacrifice the wrath of God, and, by bearing the full penalty of our sins, reconciled to God all who believe. We believe that by His resurrection, Christ Jesus was vindicated by His Father, broke the power of death, defeated Satan who once had power over it, and brought everlasting life to all His people. We believe that by His ascension, Jesus Christ has been forever exalted as Lord and has prepared a place for us to be with Him. We believe that at His return, Jesus Christ will wipe away all tears, will remove all sin and suffering, will establish forever His kingdom of love, joy, and peace, and will perfect His holy Bride. We believe that all whom God regenerates are made at once children of God, justified in His sight through faith alone in Christ's atoning work, and brought into His family. We believe that believers are kept by the power of God through faith in a state of grace, and are eternally secure apart from any human works. We believe that we who are Christ's Body will see Him face-to-face and that we will live with Him and with one another forever.

ABOUT SANCTIFICATION

We believe that sanctification is the process by which believers, each one and all together — as set apart from sin and united in Christ — are increasingly conformed to the image of Christ. Sanctification has past, present, and future aspects. First, believers are "chosen, holy and beloved" in Christ, set apart for God in union with Christ, and are actually made new by regeneration (positional or definitive sanctification). Second, believers begin to mature in their new life, set apart day by day through growth in grace into the likeness of Christ. This process (progressive sanctification) takes place by the power of the Holy Spirit, through the Word of God, in the communion of the saints, by the continual use of God's appointed means of growth in grace, each member contributing to the growth of the whole unto maturity in Christ.

Third, believers will be set apart from the very presence of sin when sanctification is completed (glorification) at the coming of Christ for the church. Definitive sanctification in the past and glorification in the future provide anchors that sustain hope and bring encouragement amidst the failures and sufferings that make progressive sanctification a long and arduous pilgrimage.

ABOUT THE CHURCH

We believe that the church, the Body of Christ, is composed of all persons living and dead who have been joined to Christ and one another by the power of the Holy Spirit. Every true believer is baptized by the Holy Spirit into the Body of Christ and thus united in Christ to one another in unity and love across social, economic, and ethnic lines. We affirm that the local church is God's primary instrument and context for His work today; that every believer should be an active member in a local assembly; and that the Christian community is the context where believers are mutually encouraged, equipped, and empowered to conform to the image of Christ through worship, fellowship, discipleship, stewardship, and ambassadorship (evangelism). The sanctification of an individual is not a personal self-improvement project, but is the formation of a constructive, fruitful member of the Body of Christ. We believe it is every believer's privilege and obligation to be an instrument in the Redeemer's hands. This requires an intentional involvement in the lives of others: learning to speak and to live the truth in love, learning humility, and learning to forgive and to give, so that we all grow in unity and maturity into Christ Who is the Head. The true mission of the church is to bring God glory, as believers (individually and corporately) live consistent with the Great Commandment and the Great Commission. We believe that baptism and the Lord's Supper are ordained by the Lord Jesus Himself. They are our public vows of submission to the once crucified and now resurrected Christ, and anticipations of His return and of the consummation of all things.

ABOUT THE ETERNAL STATE AND THE RESTORATION OF ALL THINGS

We believe in the personal, glorious, and bodily return of our Lord Jesus Christ when His kingdom will be consummated. We believe in the bodily resurrection of both the just and the unjust—the unjust to judgment and eternal conscious punishment in hell, and the just to eternal blessedness in the presence of Him Who sits on the throne and of the Lamb, in the new heaven and the new earth, the eternal home of righteousness. On that day, the church will be presented faultless before God by the obedience, suffering, and triumph of Christ; all sin will be purged and its wretched effects forever banished. God will be all in all, His people will be enthralled with Him, and everything will be done to the praise of His glorious grace.

NOTES

INTRODUCTION – THE PREACHER, THE COUNSELOR, AND THE CONGREGATION

1. From unpublished University Reformed Church biblical counseling training material: Pat Quinn, "Theology and Practice: CRUCIS Counseling," 2013.
2. Names and some details have been changed in these stories.
3. Timothy Keller, *The Prodigal God* (New York: Penguin, 2008).

CHAPTER 1: THE RICHNESS AND RELEVANCE OF GOD'S WORD

1. Peter O'Brien, *The Epistle to the Philippians* (Grand Rapids, MI: Eerdmans, 1991), 76.
2. Ibid., 77 (emphasis added).
3. Some might concur with what has been written thus far, yet conclude, "Yes, God's Word is richly relevant for 'spiritual matters,' *but not* for the type of issues brought to counselors and pastors today." Throughout *Scripture and Counseling* we demonstrate that *all* of life is "spiritual" and that, thus, the Bible provides wisdom for living for the types of issues counselors and pastors address today — for the hard cases like depression, anxiety, sexual abuse, eating disorders, enslavement to pornography, marriage and family discord, OCD, etc. — for life in a broken world.

4. Wayne Grudem prefers the term "God-breathed," which is the literal meaning for Θεόπνευστος; see Wayne Grudem, *Systematic Theology* (Grand Rapids, MI: Zondervan, 1994), 75. For further information regarding the doctrine of the Word of God, refer to Grudem, *Systematic Theology*, 47–138 (chaps. 2–8). See also John M. Frame, *The Doctrine of the Word of God* (Phillipsburg, NJ: P&R, 2010).

5. Grudem, *Systematic Theology*, 73.

6. Frame, *Doctrine of the Word of God*, 169.

CHAPTER 2: SUFFICIENT FOR LIFE AND GODLINESS

1. *English Standard Version Study Bible* (Wheaton, IL: Crossway Bibles, 2008), 961.

2. For a comprehensive exposition of the argument that Scripture is "the mind of God in written form," see chapter 7 in Paul Tautges, *Counsel One Another* (Leominster, UK: Day One, 2009), 129–51.

3. Wayne Grudem, *Systematic Theology* (Grand Rapids, MI: Zondervan, 1994), 74–75.

4. Fritz Rienecker and Cleon Rogers, *A Linguistic Key to the Greek New Testament* (Grand Rapids, MI: Zondervan, 1976), 647.

5. Richard Trench, *Synonyms of the New Testament* (Grand Rapids, MI: Baker, 1989), 125–26.

6. Ibid., 91.

7. A. W. Tozer, *The Pursuit of God* (Camp Hill, PA: Christian Publications, 1982), 74.

8. James Strong, *Strong's Exhaustive Concordance of the Bible* (Peabody, MA: Hendrickson, n.d.), #5114.

9. A. W. Pink, *The Attributes of God* (Grand Rapids, MI: Baker, 1975), 23.

10. Quoted in Iain Murray, *Spurgeon v. Hyper-Calvinism* (Edinburgh: Banner of Truth, 1995), 7.

11. Westminster Confession of Faith, art. 1.6, accessed September 2, 2013, http://www.reformed.org/documents/wcf_with_proofs.

CHAPTER 3: WHERE DO WE FIND TRUTH?

1. Phrases quoted are from Peter C. Craigie, *Psalms 1–50, Word Biblical Commentary.* Vol. 19. (Waco, TX: Word, 1983), 180.

2. Paul G. Hiebert, *Anthropological Insights for Missionaries* (Grand Rapids, MI: Baker, 1985), 21–22.

3. The verb used for "keep" in Genesis 2:15 is used of the cherubim's activity in 3:24. The cherubim *"guarded* the way to the tree of life." See Kenneth A. Matthews, *The New American Commentary: Genesis 1–11:26* (Nashville: Broadman & Holman, 1996), 210.

4. Genesis 2:5 seems to highlight humanly cultivated plants as distinct from the more general creation of plants by God (outside the Garden of Eden?) in Genesis 1:11–12.

5. Albert M. Wolters, *Creation Regained* (Grand Rapids, MI: Eerdmans, 1985), 35.

6. The term "Covenant of Preservation" is from O. Palmer Robertson, *The Christ of the Covenants* (Phillipsburg: P&R, 1980), 109–125. See 2 Peter 3:4–7.

7. Gary Collins, quoted in Jay E. Adams, *Is All Truth God's Truth?* (Stanley, NC: Timeless Texts, 2003), 30–31. Of course, different Christian psychologists will have slightly different ways of articulating their positions, but this quote is sufficient to represent a common way of thinking about the nature of psychology by many Christian counselors.

8. This effect of sin on the mind is often labeled the "noetic effect." See the discussion in Jay E. Adams, *A Theology of Christian Counseling* (Grand Rapids, MI: Zondervan, 1979), chapter 11.

9. From the lyrics to "Joy to the World" by Isaac Watts, 1719, an English hymn writer.

CHAPTER 4: WHAT IS PSYCHOLOGY?

1. See chapter 3, "Where Do We Find Truth?" on page 62.
2. Saundra K. Ciccarelli and J. Noland White, *Psychology*, 3rd ed. (Upper Saddle River, NJ: Prentice Hall, 2012), 5–6.
3. The example is from Tremper Longman III, *How to Read Proverbs* (Downers Grove, IL: InterVarsity, 2002), 71.
4. John M. Gottman and Joan DeClaire, *The Relationship Cure* (New York: Three Rivers, 2001).
5. Ibid., 27.
6. Ibid., 28.
7. Ibid., 16.
8. Ibid., 40.
9. Ibid., 17.
10. Ibid., 53.
11. Ibid., 17.
12. Ibid., 45.
13. Ibid., 37.
14. Ibid., 47.
15. Ibid., 47.
16. Jay E. Adams, *Marriage, Divorce, and Remarriage in the Bible* (Grand Rapids, MI: Zondervan, 1980), 11–16.

CHAPTER 5: SCRIPTURE IS SUFFICIENT, BUT TO DO WHAT?

1. See, e.g., the excellent historical treatment of this doctrine in Michael Horton, *The Christian Faith* (Grand Rapids, MI: Zondervan, 2011), 186–98.
2. Gregg Allison, *Historical Theology* (Grand Rapids, MI: Zondervan, 2011), 155.
3. Timothy Ward offers a helpful iteration of speech act theory to explain in a postmodern context how Scripture is sufficient to accomplish what God intends with His action (illocutions) to be

the effect on the receiver (perlocution). "Whatever 'God is now using scripture to do' he does precisely by means of the intrinsic features of the text, in the act of bringing about in believers by the Holy Spirit the perlocutionary effect appropriate to the illocutionary act represented by the text.... The Holy Spirit acts first to enable understanding and discernment of the Christ so conveyed to us in Scripture, and supremely to stir up in us faithful and active response to him." Timothy Ward, *Word and Supplement* (Oxford: Oxford University Press, 2002), 301.

4. Timothy Ward, *Words of Life* (Downers Grove, IL: IVP Academic, 2009), 113.

5. John Owen, quoted in Allison, *Historical Theology*, 157. Original source: John Owen, *Causes, Ways, and Means of Understanding the Mind of God*, chapter 6 in William Goold, *Works of John Owen* (Carlyle, PA: Banner of Truth, 1966), 4:196.

6. John Frame, *The Doctrine of God* (Phillipsburg, NJ: P&R, 2002), 81 (emphasis added).

7. Ibid., 92 (emphasis added).

8. Frame expresses something similar when he says, "Sufficiency in the present context is not sufficiency of information but sufficiency of divine words. Scripture contains divine words sufficient for all of life. It has all the divine words that the plumber needs, and all the divine words that the theologian needs. So this is just as sufficient for plumbing as it is for theology. In that sense it is sufficient for science and ethics as well." In other words, a plumber sufficiently knows from Scripture how the knowledge he gains in the practice of his trade relates to God's expectations and promised direction of his life. John Frame, *The Doctrine of the Christian Life* (Phillipsburg, NJ: P&R, 2008), 157.

9. The illustration of a grandfather's story also gives the advantage of highlighting the relational aspect of the emphatic authority of Scripture as well. In the study of any given topic, God calls individuals to personally submit to His priorities and main concerns.

J. I. Packer points out that receiving God's instruction from the Word "is to comprehend, not just the public facts but also the personal thoughts and feelings concerning them." We primarily care about what God cares about, and this takes epistemological priority over all other concerns. In this way, sufficiency is not merely a theoretical matter, but a relational one. I am forced to ask myself: Does my view of the human experience follow along God's main trajectory of concerns? J. I. Packer, "Infallible Scripture and the Role of Hermeneutics," in *Scripture and Truth*, edited by D. A. Carson and John Woodbridge (Grand Rapids, MI: Baker Academic, 1983), 336.

10. The nature of theology itself demands this interpretive authority of God's words over our own. "Theology is the sustained effort to know the character, will, and acts of the triune God as he has disclosed and interpreted these for his people in Scripture, to formulate these in a systematic way in order that we might know him, learn to think our thoughts after him, live our lives in this world on his terms, and by our thought and action project his truth into our time and culture." David Wells, "The Theologian's Craft," in *Doing Theology in Today's World*, edited by John Woodbridge and Thomas McComiskey (Grand Rapids, MI: Zondervan, 1994), 172.

11. "The Christian gospel calls us not only to a well-formed theistic matrix but also to make conscious connections between that matrix and the other matrices of our lives. What we believe about God ought to influence how I view my own identity, my vocation, my family, my leisure pursuits, and so on.... Theology involves not just the study of God (the theistic matrix) but also the influence of that study on the rest of one's life." Richard Lints, *The Fabric of Theology* (Grand Rapids, MI: Eerdmans, 1993), 18–19.

12. Ibid., 269.

13. The parallels between the concern of this chapter and the issue of contextualization are remarkably strong. Grant Osborne, *The*

Hermeneutical Spiral, rev. ed. (Downers Grove, IL: IVP Academic, 2006), 411.

14. David K. Clark, *To Know and Love God* (Wheaton, IL: Crossway, 2003), 355–57.

15. David Powlison, *The Biblical Counseling Movement* (Greensboro, NC: New Growth, 2010), 276.

16. "The working assumption in much of contemporary evangelicalism seems to be that modern culture, whether identified with academic disciplines or with popular fashion, exegetes human identity and the ideals of proper human flourishing. According to this assumption, the culture shapes the vision of our experience, expectations, and felt needs — determining what is relevant — and the Christian task is to apply the Bible to this already-defined 'life' in relevant ways." Horton, *Christian Faith*, 200.

17. Powlison, *Biblical Counseling Movement*, 281.

18. Ibid., 284 (emphasis added).

19. A more detailed way of saying this would be the following: *Scripture is sufficient to provide all the ultimate norms regarding the nature, function, and purpose of humanity—in other words, all of the normative premises—that we need to explore human experience.* Discussing *what* the Bible says about the nature, function, and purpose of humanity would take another chapter (or book, or library). Here I have simply argued that the Bible's vision of these things is sufficient for framing a psychology. The italicized statement I just made mimics Frame's application of sufficiency to the field of ethics (which is closely related, though different in significant ways). Frame says, "We may state the sufficiency of Scripture for ethics as follows: Scripture is sufficient to provide all the ultimate norms, all the normative premises, that we need to make any ethical decision. It contains all the divine words we need to make our ethical decisions, and all ultimate ethical norms come from the mouth of God." Frame, *Doctrine of the Christian Life*, 166.

20. "The gospel is the event (or the proclamation of the event) of

Jesus Christ that begins with his incarnation and earthly life, and concludes with his death, resurrection and ascension to the right hand of the father. This historical event is interpreted by God as his preordained program for the salvation of the world." "The Bible makes a very radical idea inescapable: not only is the gospel the interpretive norm for the whole Bible, but there is an important sense in which Jesus Christ is the mediator of the meaning of everything that exists. In other words, *the gospel is the hermeneutical norm for the whole of reality*. All reality was created by Christ, through Christ, and for Christ (Col. 1:15–16). God's plan is to sum up all things in Christ (Eph. 1:9–10). In him are all the treasures of wisdom and understanding (Col. 2:2–3). As a consequence, the ultimate significance of all nonbiblical literature can be summed up in biblical-gospel terms." Graeme Goldsworthy, *Gospel-Centered Hermeneutics* (Downers Grove, IL: IVP Academic, 2006), 58, 63.

21. Horton, *Christian Faith*, 200.

CHAPTER 6: THE CHRIST-CENTEREDNESS OF BIBLICAL COUNSELING

1. Merriam-Webster.com, s.v., "driven," accessed August 28, 2013, http://www.merriam-webster.com/dictionary/driven. Unfortunately, in our day, the term "Christian" is sometimes broadly applied to counseling approaches that do not emerge from God's Word and do not center on Christ.

2. The list is not exhaustive. I selected five areas that I believe are both vital and sometimes neglected by biblical counselors.

3. See Jay Adams, "Change Them?... Into What?" *Journal of Biblical Counseling* 13:2 (Winter 1995), 15.

4. Ibid., 16.

5. Ibid. Author's note: The Biblical Counseling Coalition (http://

biblicalcc.org) explicitly aims to encourage this "consensus" among all Christ-centered biblical counselors, churches, and organizations.

6. J. Murray Harris, *The Second Epistle to the Corinthians* (Grand Rapids, MI: Eerdmans, 2005), 418.

7. Paul Tripp, *Instruments in the Redeemer's Hands* (Phillipsburg, NJ: P&R, 2002), 8.

8. "Confessional Statement," Biblical Counseling Coalition, accessed August 30, 2013, http://biblicalcounselingcoalition.org/about/confessional-statement.

9. John Piper, "Toward a Definition of the Essence of Biblical Counseling," December 12, 2001, accessed August 27, 2013, http://www.desiringgod.org/resource-library/articles/toward-a-definition-of-the-essence-of-biblical-counseling.

CHAPTER 7: A COUNSELING PRIMER FROM THE GREAT CLOUD OF WITNESSES

1. For the fruit of that research, see Robert Kellemen, "Spiritual Care in Historical Perspective: Martin Luther as a Case Study in Christian Sustaining, Healing, Reconciling, and Guiding" (PhD dissertation, Kent, OH: Kent State University, 1997); Robert Kellemen and Karole Edwards, *Beyond the Suffering* (Grand Rapids, MI: Baker, 2007); Robert Kellemen and Susan Ellis, *Sacred Friendships* (Winona Lake, IN: BMH, 2009).

2. G. K. Chesterton, *Orthodoxy* (Whitefish, MT: Kessinger, 2004), 3 (emphasis added).

3. See E. Holifield, *A History of Pastoral Care in America* (Nashville: Abingdon, 1983); John McNeil, *A History of the Cure of Souls* (New York: Harper, 1951); William Clebsch and Charles Jaekle, *Pastoral Care in Historical Perspective* (New York, Harper, 1964).

4. See Thomas Oden, *Classical Pastoral Care.* Vol. 3. (Grand Rapids, MI: Baker, 1987); Charles Kemp, *Physicians of the Soul* (New York: Macmillan, 1947).

5. Oden, *Classical Pastoral Care*, 4–5 (emphasis added).
6. Wayne Oates, *Protestant Pastoral Counseling* (Philadelphia: Westminster, 1962), 11.
7. Thomas Oden, "Whatever Happened to History?" *Good News* (January–February 1993), 7.
8. Clebsch and Jaekle, *Pastoral Care*, xii.
9. McNeil, *Cure of Souls*, 39.
10. Kemp, *Physicians of the Soul*, 3.
11. Clebsch and Jaekle, *Pastoral Care*, 1.
12. Holifield, *Pastoral Care in America*, 15 (emphasis added).
13. Oden, *Classical Pastoral Care*, 1 (emphasis added).
14. Cited in Ian Jones, "Counselor Preparation in Evangelical Seminaries: Reclaiming the Pastoral Counseling Identity" (paper presented to the annual meeting of the Evangelical Theological Society, Milwaukee, 2012); from Thomas Oden, "Recovering Lost Identity," *The Journal of Pastoral Care* 34, no. 1 (March 1980), 4–19.
15. Seward Hiltner, *Preface to Pastoral Theology* (Nashville: Abingdon, 1958), 70.
16. Ibid., 71.
17. F. F. Bruce, *The Epistles to the Ephesians and Colossians* (Grand Rapids, MI: Eerdmans, 1979), 167.
18. Edmond Hiebert, *An Introduction to the New Testament* (Chicago: Moody, 1977), 222–28.
19. William Hendriksen, *Philippians, Colossians, and Philemon* (Grand Rapids, MI: Baker, 1979), 17.
20. Martha Nussbaum, *The Therapy of Desire* (Princeton, NJ: Princeton University Press, 1994), 13–28.
21. Consider the following additional historical insights into the connection between ancient philosophy and modern psychology. "The philosophers in ancient Greece took over from religion the moral direction of daily life.... In ancient times the healer of the soul who emerges in advancing cultures is not typically a member of the medical guild. In Greece he belongs instead to *the fraternity*

of philosophers. Socrates was, and wished to be, *iastros tes psuches*, a healer of the soul. These Greek syllables have been recast to form the word 'psychiatrist.' ... Socrates understood himself as a religious doctor of the soul. It is primarily as the *physician of the soul* that Socrates regarded himself. ... Socrates was a great forerunner of the many who have searched out and sifted the thoughts of men for the healing and well-being of their souls" (McNeil, *Cure of Souls*, 17, viii, 20, 41). Epicurus wrote: "Empty is that philosopher's argument by which no human suffering is therapeutically treated. For just as there is no use in a medical art that does not cast out the sicknesses of bodies, so too there is no use in philosophy, unless it casts out the suffering of the soul." Quoted in Nussbaum, *Therapy of Desire*, 13. Speaking of first-century culture, Oden wrote, "The study of psychology was included in what Clement called philosophy—for it included the study of motivation, perception, passion, habit, and behavior modification" (Oden, *Classical Pastoral Care*, 228).

22. Bruce, *Epistles to the Ephesians and Colossians*, 166–67.
23. Ibid., 219.
24. Hendriksen, *Philippians, Colossians, and Philemon*, 17.
25. Bruce, *Epistles to the Ephesians and Colossians*, 166–67.
26. Nussbaum, *Therapy of Desire*, 102–39.
27. Ibid., 115–26. These first-century secular counselors even practiced their own brand of secular nouthetic counseling—often using the word *nouthetein* for their need to share strong reproof and correction to express passionate disapproval of their counselees' beliefs and conduct (Ibid., 126).
28. For detailed examinations of the history of Christian soul care, see the books previously referenced in this chapter: Clebsch and Jaekle, *Pastoral Care*, 1964; Hiltner, *Pastoral Theology*, 1958; Holifield, *Pastoral Care in America*, 1983; Kellemen, "Spiritual Care in Historical Perspective," PhD dissertation, 1997; Kellemen and Edwards, *Beyond the Suffering*, 2007; Kellemen and Ellis, *Sacred Friendships*, 2009; Kemp, *Physicians of the Soul*, 1947;

McNeil, *Cure of Souls*, 1951; Oates, *Protestant Pastoral Counseling*, 1962; Oden, *Classical Pastoral Care*, 1987.

29. Robert Kellemen, *Soul Physicians* (Winona Lake, IN: BMH, 2007), 131–39.
30. Wayne Rollins, *Soul and Psyche* (Minneapolis: Fortress, 1999), 4.
31. Franz Delitzsch, *A System of Biblical Psychology*, 2nd ed. (Eugene, OR: Wipf & Stock, 1855, 1861, 2003), 3.
32. Morton Hunt, *The Story of Psychology* (Sioux City, IA: Anchor, 1994), 128.
33. Delitzsch, *System of Biblical Psychology*, 5.
34. Rollins, *Soul and Psyche*, 4.
35. Oden, *Classical Pastoral Care*, 103.
36. Westminster Confession, chap. 1, CC, 195, quoted in Oden, *Classical Pastoral Care*, 103.
37. Cyril of Jerusalem, *Catechetical Lectures*, IV, 17, LCC, IV, 108–10, quoted in Oden, *Classical Pastoral Care*, 106.
38. Tertullian, *Prescription against Heretics* 7, *ANF* 3, quoted in Roger Olson, *The Story of Christian Theology* (Downers Grove, IL: InterVarsity, 1999), 93.
39. Olson, *Story of Christian Theology*, 91.
40. Tertullian, *Prescription against Heretics* 7, *ANF* 13, quoted in Olson, *Story of Christian Theology*, 94.
41. Olson, *Story of Christian Theology*, 94.
42. Delitzsch, *System of Biblical Psychology*, 3.
43. Clement of Alexandria, *Christ the Educator*, bk. 1, chap. 12, FC 23, 99, quoted in Oden, *Classical Pastoral Care*, 111 (emphasis added).
44. Oden, *Classical Pastoral Care*, 111.
45. Gregory the Great, *Pastoral Care*, part 3, chap. 2, ACW 11, 90, 93; quoted in Oden, *Classical Pastoral Care*, 111 (emphasis added).
46. Robert Kolb, "Luther as *Seelsorger*," *Concordia Journal* 2 (1985), 2.
47. Martin Luther, *Luther's Works, Volume 54: Table Talk* (Philadelphia: Fortress, 1967), 157.
48. J. P. Burns, *Theological Anthropology* (Philadelphia, Fortress, 1981).

49. Kellemen, "Spiritual Care," 153–54.
50. Holifield, *Pastoral Care in America*, 16.
51. Ibid., 22–24.
52. Rollins, *Soul and Psyche*, 23.
53. Delitzsch, *System of Biblical Psychology*, 7–8.
54. Richard Baxter, *The Reformed Pastor* (Carlyle, PA: Banner of Truth, 1656, 1979).
55. Oden, *Classical Pastoral Care*, 50.
56. Ibid., 96.
57. Timothy Keller, "Puritan Resources for Biblical Counseling," *The Journal of Pastoral Practice*, no. 3 (1988): 11–44. See also Mark Deckard, *Helpful Truths in Past Places: The Puritan Practice of Biblical Counseling* (Ross-shire, Scotland: Christian Focus, 2010).
58. Delitzsch, *System of Biblical Psychology*, 8.
59. Delitzsch, *System of Biblical Psychology*, 8; see Jones, "Counselor Preparation," 20.
60. Delitzsch, *System of Biblical Psychology*, 12.
61. Ibid., 16.
62. Ibid., 15.
63. Ibid., 16.
64. Ibid., xiv.
65. Ibid., 384, 18.

CHAPTER 8: WHAT ABOUT THE BODY?

1. Brian Wren, "Good Is the Flesh," *Bring Many Names: 35 New Hymns* (Carol Stream, IL: Hope, 1989), 16.
2. John Cooper, *Body, Soul, and Life Everlasting* (Grand Rapids, MI: Eerdmans, 2000), 161–64.
3. Michael W. Otto and Jasper A. J. Smits, *Exercise for Mood and Anxiety* (New York: Oxford, 2011); John J. Ratey, *Spark: The Revolutionary New Science of Exercise and the Brain* (New York: Little, Brown, 2008).

4. The annual turning of seasons and the amount of sunlight a person is exposed to can have a marked impact on some persons with recurrent mood problems. For example, major depressive episodes peak in the spring and in the fall. Suicides follow this same pattern. This may be because during the spring and fall, light conditions are changing most rapidly, probably negatively affecting people with sensitive biological clocks and resulting in precipitous mood shifts. On the other hand, manic episodes tend to peak in the summer.

5. Edward T. Welch, *Blame It on the Brain: Distinguishing Chemical Imbalances, Brain Disorders, and Disobedience* (Phillipsburg, NJ: P&R, 1998), 127.

6. Currently, the American Psychiatric Association's *Diagnostic and Statistical Manual of Mental Disorders, Fifth Edition* (DSM-5, 2013), defines mental disorder as "a syndrome characterized by clinically significant disturbance in an individual's cognition, emotion regulation, or behavior that reflects a dysfunction in the psychological, biological, or developmental processes underlying mental functioning. Mental disorders are usually associated with significant distress in social, occupational, or other important activities. An expectable or culturally approved response to a common stressor or loss, such as the death of a loved one, is not a mental disorder. Socially deviant behavior (e.g., political, religious, or sexual) and conflicts that are primarily between the individual and society are not mental disorders unless the deviance or conflict results from a dysfunction in the individual, as described above" (p. 20).

7. Joel Paris, *The Intelligent Clinician's Guide to the DSM-5* (New York: Oxford, 2013), xvi.

8. *My Blog*, Tom Insel, "Transforming Diagnosis," April 29, 2013 (accessed September 9, 2013) http://www.nimh.nih.gov/about/director/2013/transforming-diagnosis.shtml.

9. A good example of this type of work is Cathy Wiseman's booklet *Borderline Personality: A Scriptural Perspective* (Phillipsburg, NJ: P&R, 2012).

10. Welch, *Blame It on the Brain*, 106–7.

11. Jeremy Pierre, *Psychiatric Medication and the Image of God*, October 10, 2012 accessed September 2, 2013, http://biblicalcounseling coalition.org/blogs/2012/10/10/psychiatric-medication-and-the-image-of-god/.

12. Brian Richardson, "The Teenage Brain: Surprising New Findings," *Living with Teenagers* (March 2004): 12.

13. Ed Welch, *Depression: A Stubborn Darkness* (Greensboro, NC: New Growth, 2004).

14. Robert Jones, a clinical psychologist and Christian life coach, from an unpublished manuscript.

CHAPTER 9: CAUTION: COUNSELING SYSTEMS ARE BELIEF SYSTEMS

1. Alfred Adler (1870–1937) was an Austrian physician best known for the concept of "inferiority complex." Family systems theory helps change to take place by giving an understanding of the systems of interaction between family members.

2. *Oxford On-Line Dictionary*, s.v. "syncretism," (accessed August 31, 2013), http://oxforddictionaries.com.

3. This chapter is not specifically addressing scientific research or descriptive research. Chapters 3 and 4 address those matters. This chapter focuses on *psychology as theory building*—a way of thinking about people, problems, and solutions.

4. David Powlison, "Is There Value in Biblical Counselors Pursuing a PhD at Secular Institutions?" Biblical Counseling Coalition, accessed September 3, 2013, http://biblicalcounselingcoalition.org/resources/is-there-value-in-biblical-counselors-pursuing-a-phd-at-secular-institution.

5. Most scholars believe that full-blown Gnosticism was a later development, thus the term proto-Gnosticism or incipient-Gnosticism.

6. Edward Goodrick and John Kohlenberger III, *The Strongest NIV*

Exhaustive Concordance (Grand Rapids, MI: Zondervan, 2004), #4747.

7. Heath Lambert, "Explaining the Difference between Nouthetic and Biblical Counseling: Two Sides of the Counseling Coin," quoting Jay Adams, *Competent to Counsel: Introduction to Nouthetic Counseling* (Grand Rapids, MI: Zondervan, 1970); .Biblical Counseling Coalition, accessed August 9, 2013, http:// biblicalcounselingcoalition.org/blogs/2012/10/30/explaining-the-difference-between-nouthetic-and-biblical-counseling-two-sides-of-the-counseling-coin/.

8. Stuart Scott and Heath Lambert, *Counseling the Hard Cases* (Nashville: B&H Academic, 2012).

9. Paul Vitz, *Psychology as Religion*, 2nd ed. (Grand Rapids, MI: Eerdmans, 1994), 2 (emphasis added).

10. Charles Barber, *Comfortably Numb: How Psychiatry Is Medicating a Nation* (New York, Random House, 2009), 164.

11. I am thankful for Dr. David Powlison of the Christian Counseling and Education Foundation (CCEF) for teaching this framework for evaluating counseling systems.

12. It is beyond the scope of this chapter to talk about scientific studies, but the authors would urge readers to think through issues related to how easy it is for scientific studies to become "scientism." That is, science *as a form of inquiry* becomes the authority, instead of God's Word.

13. John MacArthur, "Foreword," in Nathan Buzenitz, *Reasons We Believe* (Wheaton, IL: Crossway, 2008), 9.

14. Carl Rogers, "Notes on Rollo May," *The Journal of Humanistic Psychology*, 22 (Summer 1982), 4.

15. Ibid.

16. *The Psychology of C. G. Jung* (New Haven, CT: Yale University Press, 1973); Jolande Jacobi quoted in Vitz, *Psychology as Religion*, 3 (emphasis added).

17. Douglas Bernstein and Peggy Nash, *Essentials of Psychology*, 4th ed. (New York: Houghton Mifflin, 2008), 4.
18. Barber, *Comfortably Numb*, 179.
19. For a fuller view of Howard's perspective, see Ed Hindson and Howard Eyrich, *Totally Sufficient* (Edinburgh: Christian Focus), 11–24, 265–77.

CHAPTER 10: THE BIBLE IS RELEVANT FOR THAT?

1. I develop Ashley's story and a biblical counseling response in Robert Kellemen, *Sexual Abuse: Beauty for Ashes* (Phillipsburg, NJ: P&R, 2013).
2. Robert Kellemen, *Soul Physicians* (Winona Lake, IN: BMH, 2007), 29–57.
3. Walter C. Kaiser, *Toward an Exegetical Theology* (Grand Rapids, MI: Baker, 1981).
4. Grant Osborne, *The Hermeneutical Spiral*, rev. and exp. ed. (Downers Grove, IL: IVP Academic, 2006); Anthony Thiselton, *Hermeneutics of Doctrine* (Grand Rapids, MI: Eerdmans, 2007); Kevin Vanhoozer, *The Drama of Doctrine* (Louisville: Westminster John Knox, 2005); Kevin Vanhoozer, *First Theology* (Downers Grove, IL: InterVarsity, 2002).
5. For an example of past Christian responses to sexual abuse, see Robert Kellemen, *Beyond the Suffering* (Grand Rapids, MI: Baker, 2007), 92–95.
6. See Kellemen, *Soul Physicians*.
7. Ibid.
8. See Robert Kellemen, *Spiritual Friends* (Winona Lake, IN: BMH, 2007).

CHAPTER 11: THE RICH RELEVANCE OF GOD'S WORD

1. The Biblical Counseling Coalition Confessional Statement, accessed September 6, 2013, http://biblicalcounselingcoalition. org/about/confessional-statement/.

2. For a detailed examination of 2 Samuel 13 and sexual abuse recovery, see Robert Kellemen, *Sexual Abuse: Beauty for Ashes* (Phillipsburg, NJ: P&R, 2013).

3. See chapter 7, "A Counseling Primer from the Great Cloud of Witnesses," 126.

4. Kellemen, *Sexual Abuse.*

CHAPTER 12: THE PRACTICALITY OF THE BIBLE FOR BECOMING A CHURCH OF BIBLICAL COUNSELING

1. Brad House does a great job explaining this passage and principle in more detail. See Brad House, *Community: Taking Your Small Group Off Life Support* (Wheaton, IL: Crossway, 2011), 172–75.

2. On how to get started through equipping your leaders, visit www. harvestbiblechapel.org/bsc-resources for information.

3. Speaking the truth in love is more than reciting applicable Scriptures when someone shares a problem. In C. J. Mahaney, *Why Small Groups* (Gaithersburg, MD: PDI Communications, 1996), 68, Mahaney reminds us that "once sin is exposed, God gives us others who help us deal with our sin through confrontation, counseling, encouragement, accountability, and prayer."

4. House, *Community,* 48.

5. Jerry Bridges, *Crisis of Caring* (Colorado Springs: NavPress, 1985), 20, 34–35, helps shed light on this issue when he talks about fellowship and the importance of having the right focus. First, he explains that "we cannot have meaningful fellowship with one another unless we are individually experiencing vital fellowship

with God" (p. 20). He then explains, "It is not the Word of God itself or even prayer that supplies the power and grace to live the Christian life; it is Christ who is our life (Col. 3:4). The Word of God and prayer are the primary means by which the Holy Spirit mediates Christ's life to us. We must never so emphasize the spokes of the Wheel, which is God's channels of grace, that we lose sight of the hub, Jesus Christ, who is the source of our life" (pp. 34–35).

6. More on discerning someone's severity, ownership, and support (S.O.S.) in chapter 13, "Uncommon Community: Biblical Counseling in Small Groups," 252ff.

7. Justin Holcomb and Mike Wilkerson in *Christ-Centered Biblical Counseling*, edited by James MacDonald, Robert Kellemen, and Steve Viars (Eugene, OR: Harvest House, 2013), 52.

8. Robert Kellemen, *Soul Physicians* (Winona Lake, IN: BMH, 2007); Robert Kellemen, *Spiritual Friends* (Winona Lake, IN: BMH, 2007).

9. One of the activities we started in our church is creating "God at Work" stories for our people to be reminded what God is doing in our midst. They are videotaped and shown in the services and are available online. For an example of such a testimony see http://www.harvestbiblechapel.org/10780/content/content_id/307673/God-at-Work-Anthony-Acevedo.

10. I want to commend to you the Biblical Counseling Coalition (www.biblicalcounselingcoalition.org), which provides the reader with a website full of resources and places for further equipping.

CHAPTER 13: UNCOMMON COMMUNITY: BIBLICAL COUNSELING IN SMALL GROUPS

1. G. K. Chesterton, *What's Wrong with the World?* (New York: Dodd, Mead, 1910), 48.

2. Elton Trueblood, quoted in Bill Hull, *The Disciple-Making Pastor* (Old Tappan, NJ: Revell, 1988), 19.

3. It's disputed whether Gandhi actually spoke the words "I like your Christ; I do not like your Christians. Your Christians are so unlike your Christ." ("Mahatma Gandhi," last modified September 9, 2013, http://en.wikiquote.org/wiki/Mohandas_Karamchand_Gandhi.) While I do not want to put words in his mouth, it seems that from some of his own writing, it could at least be deduced that the quote could have been something he said. While this may certainly have been some of his contention with the faith, his non-conversion seems to be more focused on the issue of Jesus Christ being the only way to be redeemed completely from your sins.

4. Tim Lane and Paul Tripp, *Relationships: A Mess Worth Making* (Greensboro, NC: New Growth, 2008), 17.

5. What serves as a constant reminder for us is the example of the Trinity for what uncommon community really is. Lane and Tripp explain in *Relationships*, "The biblical teaching of the Trinity is very practical for relationships since God himself is a model of loving, cooperative, unified community where diversity is an asset, not a liability. If God is making us into his likeness, we can be encouraged that he will give us the grace to live like this in community with one another" (p. 22).

6. Brad House helps us to remember that small groups will thrive only when "they become the place where we experience life-giving transformation." Brad House, *Community: Taking Your Small Group Off Life Support* (Wheaton, IL: Crossway, 2011), 18–19.

7. This is exactly the kind of thing Grace Fellowship Church in Florence, Kentucky, experienced. See Brad Bigney and Ken Long, "The Transformational Tie between Small Group Ministry and Biblical Counseling" in *Christ-Centered Biblical Counseling*, edited by James MacDonald, Robert Kellemen, and Steve Viars (Eugene, OR: Harvest House, 2013), 283. The context was a bit different, but the lessons learned were the same — discipleship

and counseling go hand in hand, and if the church does its job well, people will be more involved, more passionate, and more intentional in discipling one another than if we leave it to our "expert counselors" to "fix" the hurting while everyone else continues working on their "discipleship silo."

8. You can find more about advocacy by checking out our advocate manual at www.harvestbiblechapel.org/bsc-advocate-manual.

9. You can find heart-targeting homework assignments at www.harvestbiblechapel.org/bsc-resources2.

10. Steven Gallagher, *The Walk of Repentance* (Dry Ridge, KY: Pure Life Ministries, 1993).

11. The *Soul Care Playbook* we developed is "low-hanging fruit" for the small group leader needing a quick reference. There are ten assignments that contain specific Scriptures to memorize and meditate on as well as questions related to the person's situation, their thinking, and their motives and desires. It is a helpful way to give the small group leader a tool to get people into the Word of God and get a clear sense of their teachability and heart attitude as the leader considers more ways to help. When the person in need is struggling with a stronghold or suffering deeply, the flock leader or coach might step in to help or decide with the small group leader to fill out a leader referral form to begin the formal counseling care process depending on the assessment of the S.O.S.

12. By discretion we don't just mean randomly talking to leaders who are wise, but talking specifically only with leaders who belong to the care structure for this individual. Furthermore, we would always ask our small group leaders to let their people know that they are about to talk to their leaders so they are not caught off guard. Plus, this gives the opportunity to remind the person in need how much the leaders care and that it is about discretion over privacy and giving hope versus condemning people.

13. Paul Tripp, *Instruments in the Redeemer's Hands* (Phillipsburg, NJ: P&R, 2002). This isn't the only resource of its kind, but it is a

solid one. You are looking for materials that are biblical, practical, and known as a solid resource. The website of the Biblical Counseling Coalition (www.biblicalcounselingcoalition.org) is a great place to look for such resources.

14. We need to keep in mind that we won't see true change and cannot have true community if we don't understand, as Dietrich Bonhoeffer put it, that *"Christianity* means *community through* Jesus Christ *and in* Jesus Christ. No Christian community is more or less than this" (emphasis added). Dietrich Bonhoeffer, *Life Together* (New York: HarperCollins, 1954), 21.

15. Again, Bonhoeffer wisely said, "The more genuine and the deeper our community becomes, the more will everything else between us recede, the more clearly and purely will Jesus Christ and his work become the one and only thing that is vital between us. We have one another only through Christ, but through Christ we do have one another, wholly, and for all eternity." Bonhoeffer, *Life Together*, 26.

CHAPTER 14: SPEAKING THE TRUTH IN LOVE

1. Paul Miller, *Love Walked Among Us* (Colorado Springs: NavPress, 2001), 148.

2. Louann Brizendine, *The Female Brain* (New York: Broadway, 2006); Boston Globe, boston.com, accessed July 8, 2013, http://www.boston.com/news/globe/ideas/articles/2006/09/24/sex_on_the_brain/.

3. Paul Tripp and Tim Lane, *Relationships: A Mess Worth Making* (Greensboro, NC: New Growth, 2006), 70.

4. James K. A. Smith's book *Desiring the Kingdom* (Grand Rapids, MI: Baker Academic, 2009) is of particular help here in thinking through the human being primarily as a lover directed toward a particular aim, *telos*.

5. Peter Gentry and Stephen Wellum, *Kingdom through Covenant* (Wheaton, IL: Crossway, 2012), 570.

6. Jay Adams, *Competent to Counsel* (Grand Rapids, MI: Zondervan, 1970) devotes chapter 6 to critiquing Carl Rogers and his system of counseling.

7. Paul Tripp, *War of Words* (Phillipsburg, NJ: P&R, 2000), 3.

8. Dietrich Bonhoeffer, *Life Together* (San Francisco: Harper & Row, 1954), 103–4.

9. David Powlison, *Speaking Truth in Love* (Winston-Salem, NC: Punch, 2005), 107.

10. Gentry and Wellum, *Kingdom through Covenant*, 570–87. For a more detailed understanding of the Old Testament background on speaking the truth in love, refer to these pages. The authors show that speaking the truth in love is closely related to the Old Testament concepts of faithfulness and loving-kindness.

11. D. A. Carson, *Love in Hard Places* (Wheaton, IL: Crossway, 2002), 12.

12. Leon Morris, s.v. "love," in *The Dictionary of Jesus and Gospels*, edited by Joel B. Green and Scot McKnight (Downers Grove, IL: InterVarsity, 1992), 492.

13. Tim Ackley, "Real Counsel for Real People," *Journal of Biblical Counseling* (Winter 2003), 37.

14. Miller, *Love Walked Among Us*, 33.

15. Richard Baxter, *The Reformed Pastor* (Carlisle, PA: Banner of Truth Trust, 1974), 118.

CHAPTER 15: THE COMPETENCY OF THE BIBLICAL COUNSELOR

1. In my own life, I am indebted to the counsel of Paul Tripp to be in a small group you do not lead to help me see the importance of this (now emphasized in his *Dangerous Calling* curriculums).

2. Stephen Neill, *Creative Tension* (London: Edinburgh House, 1959), 81.

3. Small group relationships can facilitate significant progress even in hard cases. This is especially true when the small group members and the individual with a particular struggle are willing to do the work to understand the issue being faced. Chapter 13, "Uncommon Community: Biblical Counseling in Small Groups," by Garrett Higbee, provides an excellent example of the high-functioning small group ministry. Mike Wilkerson's Redemption Groups model provides a fine resource for processing a variety of intense struggles within the biblical narrative of redemption. See Mike Wilkerson, *Redemption* (Wheaton, IL: Crossway, 2011). As Higbee's chapter illustrates, even with a high-functioning, well-trained small group, additional layers of biblical counseling help can be made available to assist with these "hard cases."

4. An excellent resource to help churches pair formal care with informal care to allow for this transition is Garrett Higbee, *Uncommon Community* (available at www.store.harvestbiblechapel.org).

5. Robert Kellemen, *Equipping Counselors for Your Church* (Philipsburg, NJ: P&R, 2011) provides an excellent and thorough process for developing a lay counseling ministry and legal forms for churches to use.

6. We must recognize that degrees alone are no guarantee of counselor efficacy. As noted at the outset of this chapter, Romans 15:14, among many passages, indicates that the believer's biblical knowledge, Christlike character, relational competency, and connection to a strong Christian community are essential for growth as a "competent counselor." For research into effectiveness, or at times the lack thereof, of professional counseling/psychology training, see J. S. Berman and N. C. Norton, "Does Professional Training Make a Therapist More Effective?" *Psychology Bulletin* 98, no. 2 (1985): 401–7; J. Durlak, "Comparative Effectiveness of Paraprofessional and Professional Helpers," *Psychological Bulletin* 86, no.

1 (1979): 80–92; J. A. Hattie, C. F. Sharpley, and H. J. Rogers, "Comparative Effectiveness of Professional and Paraprofessional Helpers," *Psychological Bulletin* 95, no. 3 (1984): 534–41; Keith Herman, "Reassessing Predictors of Therapist Competence," *Journal of Counseling and Development* 72 (September–October 1993): 29–32.

7. Daniel Levitin, *This Is Your Brain on Music* (New York: Penguin, 2007), 193. See also Malcolm Gladwell, *Outliers* (New York: Little Brown, 2008).

CHAPTER 16: RELATING TRUTH TO LIFE: GOSPEL-CENTERED COUNSELING FOR DEPRESSION

1. Allen Frances, *Saving Normal: An Insider's Revolt against Out-of-Control Psychiatric Diagnosis, DSM-5, Big Pharma, and the Medicalization of Ordinary Life* (New York: HarperCollins, 2013).
2. Carl Rogers, *On Becoming a Person* (New York: Houghton Mifflin, 1995).
3. John Frame, *The Doctrine of God* (Philipsburg, NJ: P&R, 2002), 217.
4. Francis Schaeffer, *Escape from Reason* (Downers Grove, IL: InterVarsity, 1968), 10.
5. H. V. Hong and E. D. Hong, trans., *The Essential Kierkegaard* (Princeton, NJ: Princeton University Press, 2000), 354.

CHAPTER 17: USING BIBLICAL NARRATIVE IN THE PERSONAL MINISTRY OF THE WORD

1. Walter Kaiser, *Preaching and Teaching from the Old Testament* (Grand Rapids, MI: Baker Academic, 2003), 63.
2. Gordon D. Fee and Douglas Stuart, *How to Read the Bible for All Its Worth*, 2nd ed. (Grand Rapids, MI: Zondervan, 1993), 78.
3. Ibid., 21.

4. Kaiser, *Preaching and Teaching*, 63.
5. For resources in the area of biblical theology, consider: Peter Gentry and Stephen Wellum, *Kingdom through Covenant* (Wheaton, IL: Crossway, 2012); James Hamilton, *God's Glory in Salvation through Judgment* (Wheaton, IL: Crossway, 2010); and Michael Lawrence, *Biblical Theology in the Life of the Church* (Wheaton, IL: Crossway, 2010).
6. Mike Wilkerson, *Redemption* (Wheaton, IL: Crossway, 2011), 33.
7. Howard Hendricks and William Hendricks, *Living by the Book*, 2nd ed. (Chicago: Moody, 2007). Fee and Stuart, *Read the Bible for All Its Worth*.
8. Dietrich Bonhoeffer, *Life Together* (New York: Harper & Row, 1954), 98.
9. Alistair Begg, *Preaching for God's Glory* (Wheaton, IL: Crossway, 2010), 36.

CHAPTER 18: USING WISDOM LITERATURE IN THE PERSONAL MINISTRY OF THE WORD

1. An underlying principle for this chapter is: A better understanding of the genre should affect the way we teach and should shape our homework assignments. We obviously want to avoid proof-texting and taking verses out of context while we apply the Bible to our counselee's life.
2. Some useful references that I used to write this section on biblical poetry include: Michael Lawrence, *Biblical Theology in the Life of the Church* (Wheaton, IL: Crossway, 2010), 46–47; Rob Plummer, *40 Questions about Interpreting the Bible* (Grand Rapids, MI: Kregel, 2010), 243–48; "Introduction to Poetic and Wisdom Literature," *English Standard Version Study Bible* (Wheaton, IL: Crossway Bibles, 2008), 864–68.
3. Literary devices in biblical poetry include things like parallelism, alphabetic acrostics, metonymy, chiasm, and an "X, X+1" form.

4. Dallas Hubbard, s.v. "Wisdom Literature," in *The New Bible Dictionary*, 3rd ed. (Downers Grove, IL: InterVarsity, 1997), 1245–46; Plummer, *40 Questions*, 235–42.

5. Raymond Dillard and Tremper Longman III, *An Introduction to the Old Testament* (Grand Rapids, MI: Zondervan, 1994), 211–33; Michael Lawrence, *Biblical Theology in the Life of the Church* (Wheaton, IL: Crossway, 2010), 46–47; John MacArthur, *MacArthur's Quick Reference Guide to the Bible* (Carol Stream, IL: Word, 2001), 86–90; Plummer, *40 Questions*, 249–255; Robert Stein, *A Basic Guide to Interpreting the Bible* (Grand Rapids, MI: Baker, 1994), 1999–2002; "Introduction to the Psalms," *English Standard Version Study Bible*, (Wheaton, IL: Crossway Bibles, 2008), 937–41.

6. Plummer adds that the New Testament authors seem to approach the Psalms as if the superscriptions are true. While the superscriptions may not be authentic to the original author, they reflect a reliable tradition that has passed them down to us. See Plummer's "How Do We Interpret the Psalms?" in Plummer, *40 Questions*, 257.

7. "Introduction to the Psalms," ESV, 940.

8. This is in contrast to national psalms of lament that involved the whole nation of Israel (Psalms 44, 74, 79–80, 83, 85, 90, 94, 137) and so would be less directly relevant to marital counseling.

9. Dillard and Longman, *Introduction to the Old Testament*, 247–256; MacArthur, *MacArthur's Quick Reference Guide*, 96–100; Plummer, *40 Questions*, 239–40; William Klein, Craig Blomberg, and Robert Hubbard, *Introduction to Biblical Interpretation* (Dallas: Word, 1993), 316–17.

10. An alternative view of authorship is that another wise man wrote the prologue and epilogue in order to create a frame for Solomon's journal reflections. In either case, the interpretative point remains the same — the different elements of the book should be read in light of the prologue (Ecc. 1:1–2) and epilogue (Ecc. 12:9–14).

11. The reason why I didn't have John write his lament earlier is because his idolatry of work was too strong. If I had asked him to do it initially, his journal entry would have come out something like this: "Meaningful! Meaningful! How meaningful and wonderful is my job!"

12. Dillard and Longman, *Introduction to the Old Testament*, 235–246; Klein, Blomberg, and Hubbard, *Introduction to Biblical Interpretation*, 313–317; MacArthur, *MacArthur's Quick Reference Guide*, 91–95; Plummer, *40 Questions*, 235–242.

13. William LaSor, David Hubbard, and Frederic Bush, *Old Testament Survey: The Message, Form, and Background of the Old Testament*, 2nd ed. (Grand Rapids, MI: Eerdmans, 1996), 461–62.

14. Tremper Longman III, *Proverbs* (Grand Rapids, MI: Baker Academic, 2006), 58.

15. A good example of an exception: Solomon wrote, "Plans fail for lack of counsel, but with many advisers they succeed" (Prov. 15:22 NIV). While it is true that plans are generally much more successful if a number of different people think through the logistics and goals prior to execution (the principle), that doesn't mean that if one person thinks up something on his own, it can't be successful (the exception).

16. In no sense does a person need to be perfect in following the proverb. Solomon wrote, "Trust in the Lord *with all your heart* and lean not on your own understanding; *in all your ways*, [follow] him, and he will make your paths straight" (Prov. 3:5–6 NIV, emphasis added). There is no one who can follow God's Word with *all your heart*, and *in all your ways*, but partial obedience, no matter how little, is rewarded.

17. Proverbs 10:8, 10, 11, 14, 18, 19, 21, 31, 32; 11:9, 11, 12, 16, 17; 12:6, 13–19, 22, 25; 13:2–3; 14:3, 5, 7, 9–10, 17, 25, 29; 15:1–2, 4, 7, 12, 18; 16:5, 13, 18, 19, 21, 23, 24, 28, 32; 17:7, 9–10, 14, 19, 20, 27, 28; 18:2, 4, 6–8, 13, 15; 19:11; 20:3; 21:9, 19, 23, 24; 22:10, 11, 24, 25; 23:9; 24:17, 26; 25:11, 12, 14, 15;

26:4, 5, 21, 24, 25, 26, 28; 27:2, 5, 14, 15, 19; 28:23, 26; 29:1, 8, 11, 19, 20, 22.

18. I use Proverbs 28:13–14 for those who need to grow in confession; 15:4 to exhort people to communicate with gentleness and not harshness; 25:11 to think about the timing of speech, etc.

19. Accountability, Prov. 27:17; adultery, 5:1–14; 6:20–7:27; 23:24–25; 30:20; adversity, 17:17 (persevering through it); **advice**, 15:22 (seeking it out), 15:12 (not seeking it); **anger**, 14:17 (results in foolishness), 15:18 (stirs up conflict), 16:32 (controls it), 19:19 (don't rescue, lest you repeat), 22:24–25 (don't associate), 29:11, 22; 30:32–33; annoyance, 12:16; betrayal, unfaithful, traitor, 22:12; 23:24–25; 25:19 (unreliable); bitterness, 14:10; boasting, 27:1; commands, the law, 28:4; concealing, hiding, 28:13; confession, 28:13; **conflict, dispute**, 16:28 (stirring it up), 17:14 (stop it quickly), 17:19 (whoever loves sin, loves conflict), 18:6 (creates strife; cf. 26:21), 18:19 (creates resistance), 20:3 (avoid it), 26:17 (jumping into someone else's fight); **consequences** 11:17 (for foolishness), 28:10 (for deceiving the righteous); covering over/overlooking an offense 17:9; 19:11; cruelty, 11:17; danger, 22:3; 27:12; diligence, 21:5; dishonesty, 20:23; 29:27; envy vs. peace, 14:30; **evil, wrongdoing**, 16:12; 24:1–2 (don't envy it), 8–9 (plotting it), 29:6; faithfulness, trustworthiness, 20:6; false pretenses, 20:14; 23:6–8; 24:11–12; favor, 22:1; fear of the Lord, 14:26–27; 19:23; 23:17–18; fear of man, 29:25; flattery, 26:28; 28:23; 29:5; **fools or foolishness**, 11:17 (consequences), 13:16 (exposed), 17:12 (avoided), 19:3 (ruins your life, yet rages against God), 23:9 (spurns insight), 24:7 (wisdom is inaccessible), 26:1 (doesn't deserve honor), 26:3–11; 27:3, 22; fraud, 20:17; friendship, 27:9; gentleness, 25:15; graciousness, kindness, 11:16–17; gossip, 16:28; 17:9; 20:19; 26:20, 22; guilt, 21:8; 30:20 (denying it); hardening, 28:14; hastiness, 19:2; healing talk, 12:18; honesty, 12:17, 19; 16:11, 13; 24:26; hope deferred, 13:12; humility, 22:4; 27:2; 29:23; innocence, blameless, integrity, 21:8; 28:18; isolation,

18:1; jealousy, 27:4; judging, 25:7–8 (don't rush to judgment); laziness vs. hard work, 12:11, 14, 24; 13:4; 14:23; 18:9; 19:24; 20:4, 12; 24:30–34; 26:13–16; listening, 12:15; **loving**, 17:17 (at all times), 21:21 (pursuing it), 25:21–22 (loving your enemy); lying, 12:17, 19; 19:5, 9; 20:14; 21:6; 26:28; mocking, 21:24; 22:10; 24:8–9; **motives**, 16:2; 21:2, 27 (evil), 22:11 (pure); nagging, 21:9, 19; obedience to God's commands, 19:16; offensive, 17:19 (leads to strife); offended, 18:19; overlooking insults, 12:16; patience, slow to anger, 15:18; 16:32; 19:11; 25:15; **peace**, 12:20 (promoting it), 14:30 (peace as life giving); perseverance, 17:17; planning, being thoughtful about decisions, 14:8, 15; 16:3, 9; 21:9; pleasure, 21:17; pride, arrogance, 16:5, 18, 19; 21:4, 24; 29:23; punishment, 21:11 (learning from it); quarrelsomeness, 21:9, 19; 25:24; 27:15–16; rebelliousness, sinful talk, 12:13; rebuke, correction—accepting it, 15:31; 17:10; 19:25; 25:12; 27:5–6; 28:23; rebuke, correction—rejecting it, 15:10, 12; 29:1; reckless or rash speech, 12:18; reputation, 22:1; rescue, 24:10–12; revenge, 20:22; 24:28–29; righteousness, 21:21 (pursuing it); ruthlessness, 11:16; silence, holding your tongue, 17:28; **speech, talk**, 12:13 (rebellious, sinful), 12:18 (reckless), 12:18; 16:24 (healing), 16:23 (persuasive, instructive), 16:24; 22:11 (gracious), 18:2, 13 (talking before listening), 18:7 (ruins his life), 21:23 (guarded), 25:11 (aptly spoken; fits the occasion), 25:15 (gentleness), 26:2 (undeserved curse), 26:23–26 (deceptive speech that disguises an evil heart), 26:28 (flattery; cf. 28:23; 29:5), 29:20 (hasty); strengthening one another, 27:17; testing, 17:3; 27:21 (by praise); thinks before answering, 15:28; timely words, 15:23; **trusting**, 3:5–6 (God), 28:26 (self); understanding, insight, 16:16, 22; 18:2; 19:8; 20:5; 23:9 (spurned); violence, 16:29; 21:7; wise-in-his-own-eyes or being right, 12:15; 14:12; 16:25; 26:12; work, 21:25 (refusing to work), 28:19; zeal without knowledge, 19:2.

20. Dillard and Longman, *Introduction to the Old Testament*, 199–210; Klein, Blomberg, and Hubbard, *Introduction to Biblical*

Interpretation, 319–22; MacArthur, *MacArthur's Quick Reference Guide*, 81–55; Plummer, *40 Questions*, 239–40.

CHAPTER 19: USING THE GOSPELS IN THE PERSONAL MINISTRY OF THE WORD

1. Some have read books like Paul Tripp, *Instruments in the Redeemer's Hands* (Phillipsburg, NJ: P&R, 2002), or James MacDonald, Robert Kellemen, and Steve Viars, eds., *Christ-Centered Biblical Counseling* (Eugene, OR: Harvest House, 2013), or attended training offered through the ministries at Faith Church in Lafayette, Indiana, or through ACBC, CCEF, or one of the many others who have worked to train others in counseling.

2. The Southern Baptist seminaries are among those schools leading the way in helping to train students in both areas. Their rigorous MDiv, DMin, and PhD programs are training students in biblical and people exposition.

3. For a helpful introduction to the literary genre of "gospel," see the outstanding work of Richard A. Burridge, *What Are the Gospels?*, 2nd ed. (Grand Rapids, MI: Eerdmans, 2004).

4. Burridge, *What Are the Gospels?*, 289. The most basic definition of narrative is story. We need to be reminded that calling the Gospels a story is not an attempt to remove their veracity. Instead, we would hold firmly to the fact that the gospel writers were historically accurate. For more information, see Craig Blomberg, *The Historical Reliability of the Gospels* (Downers Grove, IL: InterVarsity, 1987).

5. Scholars have long debated how much of Jesus' life is contained in the Gospels. The differences of opinion often center on the decision of whether certain stories recorded in the different gospels narrate the same event or whether two separate instances of a very similar event occurred. In the end, however, scholars agree that the Gospels record a very small percentage of Jesus' life and ministry. A helpful

volume on the life of Jesus as well as a detailed timeline for the major events is Harold W. Hoehner, *Chronological Aspects of the Life of Christ* (Grand Rapids, MI: Zondervan, 1977).

6. This is particularly true with the so-called Synoptic Gospels (i.e., Matthew, Mark, and Luke). My point is that reading the Gospels reveals that some of the same episodes are recorded in multiple gospels. I make no reference here to the synoptic problem, but for those who want to think more about that discussion, see Robert Stein, *Studying the Synoptic Gospel*, 2nd ed. (Grand Rapids, MI: Baker, 2001) and David Black and David Beck, *Rethinking the Synoptic Problem* (Grand Rapids, MI: Baker, 2001).

7. For more helpful advice on reading the Gospels, see Gordon D. Fee and Douglas Stuart, *How to Read the Bible for All Its Worth*, 3rd ed. (Grand Rapids, MI: Zondervan, 2003), esp. 127–62.

8. Two additional helpful introductions to the Gospels are Darrell L. Bock, *Jesus According to Scripture* (Grand Rapids, MI: Baker, 2002) and Craig L. Blomberg, *Jesus and the Gospels* (Nashville: Broadman & Holman, 1997).

9. It would be well worth one's time to carefully read the chapters on the Gospels in D. A. Carson and Douglas J. Moo, *An Introduction to the New Testament*, 2nd ed. (Grand Rapids, MI: Zondervan, 2005), 134–284. It should be noted that the Gospels were written for people living twenty to forty years after Christ. That helps us recognize that the Gospels were not mere history; they were careful theological biographies meant to impact the daily lives of believers and to confront unbelievers with the claims of Christ.

10. Some of Jesus' most well-known statements on the heart include Matthew 15:15–20 and Mark 7:14–23. However, He addresses the heart on a plethora of occasions (everything from the disciples' desire to be greatest to the rich young ruler).

11. Carson reminds us that the divisions of law and grace are not always helpful or even biblical. He wrote, "To pit law, righteousness, and peace as kingdom concepts against grace and belief as

salvation concepts is to create an antithesis that the New Testament writers will not tolerate. According to Paul, for example, salvation has always been by grace, even when God's people were under the Mosaic legislation. And salvation, however construed, has always demanded conformity to the will of God portrayed in Matthew 5–7." D. A. Carson, *Jesus' Sermon on the Mount and His Confrontation with the World: An Exposition of Matthew 5–10* (Grand Rapids, MI: Global Christian, 1999), 298.

12. The Holy Spirit has a very active role in the life of a believer, including but not limited to: (1) His role in conviction, (2) His role in rebirth, (3) His role in prayer, (4) His role in placing the believer into the body of Christ, (5) His role in guidance, and (6) His role in gifting.

13. I chose not to discuss Matthew 7:3–5 because I was convinced that many of my readers would immediately think of this text. Indeed, it is a powerful text to use when working with those in conflict. However, since it is already a common place to visit, I wanted to spend my time in gospel passages that may not have been equally obvious.

14. See Stanley D. Toussaint, *Behold the King* (Grand Rapids, MI: Kregel, 1980).

15. Immediately after the question is asked, Herod gathers the chief priests and elders together in order to understand the OT prophecies regarding the coming of Messiah—which they envisioned as solely a military ruler. Such Old Testament evidence was not difficult to find (Matt. 2:6 and the quotation of Mic. 5:2).

16. One of the great ironies occurs prior to Jesus' crucifixion. He is taken by the soldiers and forced to endure some barracks humor. The soldiers mockingly hail Him, dress Him, and crown Him. Yet, the One they are mocking as king really is! See D. A. Carson, *Scandalous* (Wheaton, IL: Crossway, 2010), 13–37.

17. We often read in gospel literature that the leaders are unable to arrest Jesus because His hour had not yet come. He enters the

temple despite the fact that they were looking to arrest Him. He leaves crowds that look like they are turning into riot mobs. His sovereign control is exercised in His miracles, in His travels, in His escapes from His enemies, in His arrest by His enemies, and by His death.

18. Carson, *Scandalous*, 18.

19. Jay Adams is known for saying that the best preparation for a counselor is a seminary education. While that may be a bit of an overstatement, I think we do well to consider carefully his point. Biblical counseling is Word-centered counseling. Thus, one of the requirements to do biblical counseling well is to know the Word well.

20. There were two additional areas that I, regrettably, was unable to discuss and apply that I would like to highlight here. First, I was unable to illustrate an appropriate hermeneutic to the parables found in the Gospels, despite the fact there are dozens of them. One of the most helpful resources is Craig L. Blomberg, *Interpreting the Parables* (Downers Grove: InterVarsity, 1990). Second, I also failed in my attempt to incorporate some background studies into this work, at least in the endnotes, not only due to the tumultuous four centuries that occurred before the arrival of Jesus but also because of the vast literature that illumines the way people were thinking at the time of Christ. Thus, I am left with offering the encouragement that Bock and Herrick's work will serve as a nice introduction (Darrell L. Bock and Gregory J. Herrick, eds., *Jesus in Context* [Grand Rapids, MI: Baker, 2005]).

21. Matthew focuses on Jesus as King. Mark focuses on Jesus as the suffering servant. Luke focuses on telling the story of Jesus so that readers could have a discerning ear regarding the oral stories circulating thirty years after Jesus' death and resurrection. John focuses on Jesus as the only pathway to eternal life. There is, of course, overlap since all the Gospels are about the same person. My statements are also a bit simplistic in that Matthew's

theology is not *only* that Jesus is the King. However, I find these four points generally helpful. If you would like to do some additional study on the theological concerns of the gospel writers, see Frank Thielman, *Theology of the New Testament* (Grand Rapids, MI: Zondervan, 2005) and I. Howard Marshall, *New Testament Theology* (Downers Grove, IL: InterVarsity, 2004).

22. I gave two talks regarding gospel literature in the last twelve months. The first was at the 2012 annual conference of the National Association of Nouthetic Counselors in Indianapolis, Indiana, where I organized my time around the phrase "Jesus is awesome," trying to show how the Gospels could be used in the counseling room. The second occurred at my home church, Faith Church in Lafayette, Indiana, where I was given the pulpit to explain the place of the Gospels in the story line of Scripture. While the content of the second talk was modified from the first, I still used the phrase "Jesus is awesome" as a controlling thought. My point is not to provide a juvenile spin on the profundity of the gospel narratives, but rather to see the overwhelming presentation for more than two hundred pages in our Bibles of our great God and Savior—Jesus Christ!

CHAPTER 20: USING THE EPISTLES IN THE PERSONAL MINISTRY OF THE WORD

1. A description of OCD behavior is cataloged in *Diagnostic and Statistical Manual of Mental Disorders*, 4th ed. (Washington, DC: American Psychiatric Association, 2000), 456–63.

2. Most of the Epistles were written to churches (Romans, Ephesians, Colossians, etc.), but some were written to individuals (1 and 2 Timothy, Philemon, et al.).

3. There are many places where one can find information about the nature of the epistolary genre. Consider, for example, Thomas R. Schreiner, *Interpreting the Pauline Epistles* (Grand Rapids, MI:

Baker, 1990); Gordon D. Fee and Douglas Stuart, *How to Read the Bible for All Its Worth* (Grand Rapids, MI: Zondervan, 1981), 45–77; William W. Klein, Craig L. Blomberg, and Robert L. Hubbard Jr., *Introduction to Biblical Interpretation* (Nashville: Word, 1993), 352–56; Robert L. Plummer, *40 Questions about Interpreting the Bible* (Grand Rapids, MI: Kregel, 2010), 185–90, 279–92; and Robert H. Stein, *A Basic Guide to Interpreting the Bible* (Grand Rapids, MI: Baker, 1994), 169–86.

4. Such statements do not mean that there is no role for certain types of medical interventions in counseling. It does mean that medical interventions will never solve the most significant difficulties that people experience. It also means that as counselors, we are not medical practitioners called to traffic in the business of psychopharmacology. We are ministers of the gospel who are called to traffic in spiritual power.

REFERENCES

Ackley, Tim. "Real Counsel for Real People." *Journal of Biblical Counseling* 1, no. 2 (Winter 2003): 34–39.

Adams, Jay E. "Change Them?... Into What?" *Journal of Biblical Counseling* 13, no. 2 (Winter 1995): 14–21.

——. *Competent to Counsel: Introduction to Nouthetic Counseling.* Grand Rapids, MI: Zondervan, 1970.

——. *Is All Truth God's Truth?* Stanley, NC: Timeless Texts, 2003.

——. *Marriage, Divorce, and Remarriage in the Bible: A Fresh Look at What Scripture Teaches.* Grand Rapids, MI: Zondervan, 1980.

——. *A Theology of Christian Counseling: More Than Redemption.* Grand Rapids, MI: Zondervan, 1979.

Allison, Gregg. *Historical Theology: An Introduction to Christian Doctrine.* Grand Rapids, MI: Zondervan, 2011.

American Psychiatric Association. *Diagnostic and Statistical Manual of Mental Disorders.* 4th ed. Arlington, VA: American Psychiatric Association, 2000.

American Psychiatric Association. *Diagnostic and Statistical Manual of Mental Disorders.* 5th ed. Arlington, VA: American Psychiatric Association, 2013.

Barber, Charles. *Comfortably Numb: How Psychiatry Is Medicating a Nation.* New York: Random House, 2009.

Baxter, Richard. *The Reformed Pastor*. Carlyle, PA: Banner of Truth, 1656, 1979.

Begg, Alistair. *Preaching for God's Glory*. Wheaton, IL: Crossway, 2010.

Berman, J. S., and N. C. Norton. "Does Professional Training Make a Therapist More Effective?" *Psychology Bulletin* 98, no. 2 (1985): 401–7.

Bernstein, Douglas, and Peggy Nash. *Essentials of Psychology*, 4th ed. New York: Houghton Mifflin, 2008.

Black, David A., and David R. Beck. *Rethinking the Synoptic Problem*. Grand Rapids, MI: Baker, 2001.

Blomberg, Craig L. *The Historical Reliability of the Gospels*. Downers Grove, IL: InterVarsity, 1987.

———. *Interpreting the Parables*. Downers Grove, IL: InterVarsity, 1990.

———. *Jesus and the Gospels*. Nashville: Broadman & Holman, 1997.

Bock, Darrell L. *Jesus According to Scripture*. Grand Rapids, MI: Baker, 2002.

Bock, Darrell L., and Gregory J. Herrick, eds. *Jesus in Context: Background Readings for Gospel Study*. Grand Rapids, MI: Baker, 2005.

Bonhoeffer, Dietrich. *Life Together: The Classic Exploration of Christian Community*. New York: HarperCollins, 1954.

Bookman, Douglas. "The Scriptures and Biblical Counseling." In *Introduction to Biblical Counseling: A Basic Guide to the Principles and Practices of Counseling*. Edited by John MacArthur and Wayne Mack, 63–97. Nashville: Thomas Nelson, 1994.

Bridges, Jerry. *Crisis of Caring: Recovering the Meaning of True Fellowship*. Colorado Springs: NavPress, 1985.

Bruce, F. F. *The Epistles to the Ephesians and Colossians*. Grand Rapids, MI: Eerdmans, 1979.

Burns, J. P. *Theological Anthropology*. Philadelphia: Fortress, 1981.

Burridge, Richard A. *What Are the Gospels?: A Comparison with Graeco-Roman Biography*. 2nd ed. Grand Rapids, MI: Eerdmans, 2004.

Busenitz, Nathan. *Reasons We Believe: 50 Lines of Evidence That Confirm the Christian Faith.* Wheaton, IL: Crossway, 2008.

Carson, D. A. *Jesus' Sermon on the Mount and His Confrontation with the World: An Exposition of Matthew 5–10.* Grand Rapids, MI: Global Christian, 1999.

_____. *Love in Hard Places.* Wheaton, IL: Crossway, 2002.

_____. *Scandalous: The Cross and Resurrection of Jesus.* Wheaton, IL: Crossway, 2010.

Carson, D. A., and Douglas J. Moo. *An Introduction to the New Testament.* 2nd ed. Grand Rapids, MI: Zondervan, 2005.

Chesterton, G. K. *Orthodoxy.* Whitefish, MT: Kessinger, 2004.

Ciccarelli, Saundra K., and J. Noland White. *Psychology.* 3rd ed. Upper Saddle River, NJ: Prentice Hall, 2012.

Clark, David K. *To Know and Love God: Method for Theology.* Wheaton, IL: Crossway, 2003.

Clebsch, William, and Charles Jaekle. *Pastoral Care in Historical Perspective.* New York: Harper, 1964.

Cooper, John. *Body, Soul, and Life Everlasting.* Grand Rapids, MI: Eerdmans, 2000.

Craigie, Peter C. *Psalms 1–50.* Nashville: Thomas Nelson, 1983.

Deckard, Mark. *Helpful Truths in Past Places: The Puritan Practice of Biblical Counseling.* Ross-shire, Scotland: Christian Focus, 2010.

Delitzsch, Franz. *A System of Biblical Psychology.* 2nd ed. Eugene, OR: Wipf & Stock, 1855, 1861, 2003.

Dillard, Raymond, and Tremper Longman III. *An Introduction to the Old Testament.* Grand Rapids, MI: Zondervan, 1994.

Durlak, J. "Comparative Effectiveness of Paraprofessional and Professional Helpers." *Psychological Bulletin* 86, no. 1 (1979): 80–92.

Fee, Gordon D., and Douglas Stuart. *How to Read the Bible Book by Book.* Grand Rapids, MI: Zondervan, 2002.

_____. *How to Read the Bible for All Its Worth.* 3rd ed. Grand Rapids, MI: Zondervan, 2003.

Frame, John M. *The Doctrine of the Christian Life: A Theology of Lordship*. Phillipsburg, NJ: P&R, 2008.

———. *The Doctrine of the Word of God: Theology of Lordship*. Phillipsburg, NJ: P&R, 2010.

Frances, Allen. *Saving Normal: An Insider's Revolt against Out-of-Control Psychiatric Diagnosis, DSM-5, Big Pharma, and the Medicalization of Ordinary Life*. New York: HarperCollins, 2013.

Gallagher, Steven. *The Walk of Repentance: A 24-Week Guide to Personal Transformation*. Dry Ridge, KY: Pure Life Ministries, 1993.

Gentry, Peter J., and Stephen J. Wellum. *Kingdom through Covenant: A Biblical-Theological Understanding of the Covenants*. Wheaton, IL: Crossway, 2012.

Gladwell, Malcolm. *Outliers: The Stories of Success*. New York: Little, Brown, 2008.

Goldsworthy, Graeme. *Gospel-Centered Hermeneutics: Foundations and Principles of Evangelical Biblical Interpretations*. Downers Grove, IL: InterVarsity, 2006.

Goodrick, Edward, and John Kohlenberger III. *The Strongest NIV Exhaustive Concordance*. Grand Rapids, MI: Zondervan, 2004.

Gottman, John M., and Joan DeClaire. *The Relationship Cure*. New York: Three Rivers, 2001.

Grudem, Wayne. *Systematic Theology: An Introduction to Biblical Doctrine*. Grand Rapids, MI: Zondervan, 1994.

Hamilton, James M. *God's Glory in Salvation through Judgment: A Biblical Theology*. Wheaton, IL: Crossway, 2010.

Harris, J. Murray. *The Second Epistle to the Corinthians*. Grand Rapids, MI: Eerdmans, 2005.

Hattie, J. A., C. F. Sharpley, and H. J. Rogers. "Comparative Effectiveness of Professional and Paraprofessional Helpers." *Psychological Bulletin* 95, no. 3 (1984): 534–41.

Hendricks, Howard, and William Hendricks. *Living by the Book: The Art and Science of Reading the Bible*. 2nd ed. Chicago: Moody, 2007.

Hendriksen, William. *Philippians, Colossians, and Philemon.* Grand Rapids, MI: Baker, 1979.

Herman, Keith. "Reassessing Predictors of Therapist Competence." *Journal of Counseling and Development* 72 (September–October 1993): 29–32.

Hiebert, Edmond. *An Introduction to the New Testament: Volume Two—The Pauline Epistles.* Chicago: Moody, 1977.

Hiebert, Paul G. *Anthropological Insights for Missionaries.* Grand Rapids, MI: Baker, 1985.

Hiltner, Seward. *Preface to Pastoral Theology.* Nashville: Abingdon, 1958.

Hindson, Ed, and Howard Eyrich. *Totally Sufficient.* Edinburgh: Christian Focus, 1997.

Hoehner, Harold W. *Chronological Aspects of the Life of Christ.* Grand Rapids, MI: Zondervan, 1977.

Holcomb, Justin, and Mike Wilkerson. "The Ministry of the Holy Spirit." In *Christ-Centered Biblical Counseling: Changing Lives with God's Changeless Truth.* Edited by James MacDonald, Robert Kellemen, and Steve Viars, 49–61. Eugene, OR: Harvest House, 2013.

Holifield, E. Brooks. *A History of Pastoral Care in America: From Salvation to Self-Realization.* Nashville: Abingdon, 1983.

Horton, Michael. *The Christian Faith: A Systematic Theology for Pilgrims on the Way.* Grand Rapids, MI: Zondervan, 2011.

House, Brad. *Community: Taking Your Small Group Off Life Support.* Wheaton, IL: Crossway, 2011.

Hubbard, Dallas. "Wisdom Literature." In *The New Bible Dictionary.* 3rd ed. Edited by I. Howard Marshall, A. R. Millard, J. I. Packer, and D. J. Wiseman. Downers Grove, IL: InterVarsity, 1997.

Hull, Bill. *The Disciple-Making Pastor.* Old Tappan, NJ: Revell, 1988.

Hunt, Morton. *The Story of Psychology.* Sioux City, IA: Anchor, 1994.

Insel, Tom. *Transforming Diagnosis.* Accessed September 2, 2013. http://www.nimh.nih.gov/about/director/2013/transforming-diagnosis.shtml.

Jones, Ian. "Counselor Preparation in Evangelical Seminaries: Reclaiming the Pastoral Counseling Identity." Paper presented to the annual meeting of the Evangelical Theological Society, Milwaukee, 2012.

Kaiser, Walter C. *Preaching and Teaching from the Old Testament: A Guide for the Church.* Grand Rapids, MI: Baker Academic, 2003.

_____. *Toward an Exegetical Theology: Biblical Exegesis for Preaching and Teaching.* Grand Rapids, MI: Baker, 1981.

Kellemen, Robert. *Equipping Counselors for Your Church: The 4E Ministry Training Strategy.* Phillipsburg, NJ: P&R, 2011.

_____. *Sexual Abuse: Beauty for Ashes.* Phillipsburg, NJ: P&R, 2013.

_____. *Soul Physicians: A Theology of Soul Care and Spiritual Direction.* Winona Lake, IN: BMH, 2007.

_____. "Spiritual Care in Historical Perspective: Martin Luther as a Case Study in Christian Sustaining, Healing, Reconciling, and Guiding." PhD dissertation, Kent State University, 1997.

_____. *Spiritual Friends: A Methodology of Soul Care and Spiritual Direction.* Winona Lake, IN: BMH, 2007.

Kellemen, Robert, and Karole Edwards. *Beyond the Suffering: Embracing the Legacy of African American Soul Care and Spiritual Direction.* Grand Rapids, MI: Baker, 2007.

Kellemen, Robert, and Susan Ellis. *Sacred Friendships: Celebrating the Legacy of Women Heroes of the Faith.* Winona Lake, IN: BMH, 2009.

Keller, Timothy. "Puritan Resources for Biblical Counseling." *The Journal of Pastoral Practice* 9, no. 3 (1988): 11–44.

Kemp, Charles. *Physicians of the Soul.* New York, MacMillan, 1947.

Klein, William, Craig Blomberg, and Robert Hubbard. *Introduction to Biblical Interpretation.* Dallas: Word, 1993.

Kolb, Robert. "Luther as *Seelsorger.*" *Concordia Journal* 2 (1985): 2–9.

Lambert, Heath. "Explaining the Difference between Nouthetic and Biblical Counseling: Two Sides of the Counseling Coin." Accessed August 9, 2013. http://biblicalcounselingcoalition.org/blogs/2012/

10/30/explaining-the-difference-between-nouthetic-and-biblical-counseling-two-sides-of-the-counseling-coin/.

Lane, Tim, and Paul Tripp. *Relationships: A Mess Worth Making.* Greensboro, NC: New Growth, 2008.

LaSor, William, David Hubbard, and Frederic Bush. *Old Testament Survey: The Message, Form, and Background of the Old Testament.* 2nd ed. Grand Rapids, MI: Eerdmans, 1996.

Lawrence, Michael. *Biblical Theology in the Life of the Church: A Guide for Ministry.* Wheaton, IL: Crossway, 2010.

Levitin, Daniel. *This Is Your Brain on Music: The Science of Human Obsession.* New York: Penguin, 2007.

Lints, Richard. *The Fabric of Theology: A Prolegomenon to Evangelical Theology.* Grand Rapids, MI: Eerdmans, 1993.

Longman, III, Tremper. *How to Read Proverbs.* Downers Grove, IL: InterVarsity, 2002.

———. *Proverbs.* Grand Rapids, MI: Baker Academic, 2006.

Luther, Martin. *Luther's Works, Volume 54: Table Talk.* Edited by Theodore G. Tappert and Helmut T. Lehmann. Philadelphia: Fortress, 1967.

MacArthur, John. *MacArthur's Quick Reference Guide to the Bible.* Carol Stream, IL: Word, 2001.

MacDonald, James, Robert Kellemen, and Steve Viars, eds. *Christ-Centered Biblical Counseling: Changing Lives with God's Changeless Truth.* Eugene, OR: Harvest House, 2013.

Mahaney, C. J. *Why Small Groups?* Gaithersburg, MD: PDI Communications, 1996.

Marshall, I. Howard. *New Testament Theology: Many Witnesses, One Gospel.* Downers Grove, IL: InterVarsity, 2004.

Mathews, Kenneth A. *The New American Commentary: Genesis 1–11:26.* Nashville: Broadman & Holman, 1996.

McNeil, John. *A History of the Cure of Souls.* New York: Harper, 1951.

Miller, Paul. *Love Walked among Us: Learning to Love Like Jesus.* Colorado Springs: NavPress, 2001.

Morris, Leon. s.v. "love." In *The Dictionary of Jesus and Gospels.* Edited by Joel B. Green and Scot McKnight, 492. Downers Grove, IL: InterVarsity, 1992.

Murray, Iain. *Spurgeon v. Hyper-Calvinism: The Battle for Gospel Preaching.* Edinburgh: Banner of Truth, 1995.

Neill, Stephen. *Creative Tension: The Duff Lectures, 1958.* London: Edinburgh House, 1959.

Nussbaum, Martha. *The Therapy of Desire: Theory and Practice in Hellenistic Ethics.* Princeton, NJ: Princeton University Press, 1994.

Oates, Wayne. *Protestant Pastoral Counseling.* Philadelphia: Westminster, 1962.

O'Brien, Peter. *The Epistle to the Philippians.* Grand Rapids, MI: Eerdmans, 1991.

Oden, Thomas. *Classical Pastoral Care.* Vol. 3. Grand Rapids, MI: Baker, 1987.

————. "Recovering Lost Identity." *The Journal of Pastoral Care* 34, no. 1 (March 1980): 4–19.

Olson, Roger. *The Story of Christian Theology: Twenty Centuries of Tradition and Reform.* Downers Grove, IL: InterVarsity, 1999.

Osborne, Grant. *The Hermeneutical Spiral: A Comprehensive Introduction to Biblical Interpretation.* Rev. ed. Downers Grove, IL: InterVarsity, 2006.

Otto, Michael, and Jasper Smits, *Exercise for Mood and Anxiety* (New York: Oxford, 2011).

Packer, J. I. "Infallible Scripture and the Role of Hermeneutics." In *Scripture and Truth.* Edited by D. A. Carson and John Woodbridge, 325–50. Grand Rapids, MI: Baker Academic, 1983.

Paris, Joel. *The Intelligent Clinician's Guide to the DSM-5.* New York: Oxford University Press, 2013.

Pierre, Jeremy. *Psychiatric Medication and the Image of God.* Accessed

September 2, 2013. http://biblicalcounselingcoalition.org/
blogs/2012/10/10/psychiatric-medication-and-the-image-of-god.

Pink, A. W. *The Attributes of God.* Grand Rapids, MI: Baker, 1975.

Piper, John. "Toward a Definition of the Essence of Biblical Counseling." Accessed August 27, 2013. http://www.desiringgod.org/
resource-library/articles/toward-a-definition-of-the-essence-of-
biblical-counseling.

Plummer, Robert L. *40 Questions about Interpreting the Bible.* Grand
Rapids, MI: Kregel, 2010.

Powlison, David. *The Biblical Counseling Movement: History and Context.* Greensboro, NC: New Growth, 2010.

———. "Is There Value in Biblical Counselors Pursuing a PhD at
Secular Institutions?" Accessed September 3, 2013. http://biblical
counselingcoalition.org/resources/is-there-value-in-biblical-coun
selors-pursuing-a-phd-at-secular-institution.

———. *Speaking Truth in Love: Counsel in Community.* Winston-
Salem, NC: Punch, 2005.

Ratey, J. Spark: *The Revolutionary New Science of Exercise and the
Brain.* New York: Little, Brown, 2008.

Rienecker, Fritz, and Cleon Rogers. *A Linguistic Key to the Greek New
Testament.* Grand Rapids, MI: Zondervan, 1976.

Rogers, Carl. "Notes on Rollo May." *The Journal of Humanistic Psychology* 22 (Summer 1982): 3–7.

Robertson, O. Palmer. *The Christ of the Covenants.* Phillipsburg, NJ:
P&R, 1980.

Rollins, Wayne. *Soul and Psyche: The Bible in Psychological Perspective.*
Minneapolis: Fortress, 1999.

Schreiner, Thomas R. *Interpreting the Pauline Epistles.* Grand Rapids,
MI: Baker, 1990.

Scott, Stuart, and Heath Lambert. *Counseling the Hard Cases: True
Stories Illustrating the Sufficiency of God's Resources in Scripture.*
Nashville: B&H Academic, 2012.

Smith, James K. A. *Desiring the Kingdom: Worship, Worldview, and Cultural Formation.* Grand Rapids, MI: Baker Academic, 2009.

Stein, Robert. *A Basic Guide to Interpreting the Bible: Playing by the Rules.* Grand Rapids, MI: Baker, 1994.

————. *Studying the Synoptic Gospels: Origin and Interpretation.* 2nd ed. Grand Rapids, MI: Baker, 2001.

Strong, James. *Strong's Exhaustive Concordance of the Bible.* Peabody, MA: Hendricksen, n.d.

Tautges, Paul. *Counsel One Another: A Theology of Personal Discipleship.* Leominster, UK: Day One, 2009.

Thielman, Frank. *Theology of the New Testament: A Canonical and Synthetic Approach.* Grand Rapids, MI: Zondervan, 2005.

Thiselton, Anthony. *Hermeneutics of Doctrine.* Grand Rapids, MI: Eerdmans, 2007.

Toussaint, Stanley D. *Behold the King: A Study of Matthew.* Grand Rapids, MI: Kregel, 1980.

Tozer, A. W. *The Pursuit of God.* Camp Hill, PA: Christian Publications, 1982.

Trench, Richard. *Synonyms of the New Testament.* Grand Rapids, MI: Baker, 1989.

Tripp, Paul. *Instruments in the Redeemer's Hands: People in Need of Change Helping People in Need of Change.* Phillipsburg, NJ: P&R, 2002.

————. *War of Words: Getting to the Heart of Your Communication Struggles.* Phillipsburg, NJ: P&R, 2000.

Vanhoozer, Kevin. *The Drama of Doctrine: A Canonical Linguistic Approach to Christian Doctrine.* Louisville: Westminster John Knox, 2005.

————. *First Theology: God, Scripture & Hermeneutics.* Downers Grove, IL: InterVarsity, 2002.

Vitz, Paul. *Psychology as Religion: The Cult of Self-Worship.* 2nd ed. Grand Rapids, MI: Eerdmans, 1994.

Ward, Timothy. *Word and Supplement: Speech Acts, Biblical Texts, and the Sufficiency of Scripture.* Oxford: Oxford University Press, 2002.

————. *Words of Life: Scripture as the Living and Active Word of God.* Downers Grove, IL: InterVarsity, 2009.

Welch, Edward T. *Blame It on the Brain: Distinguishing Chemical Imbalances, Brain Disorders, and Disobedience.* Phillipsburg, NJ: P&R, 1998.

————. *Depression: A Stubborn Darkness.* Greensboro, NC: New Growth, 2004.

Wells, David. "The Theologian's Craft." In *Doing Theology in Today's World.* Edited by John Woodbridge and Thomas McComiskey, 171–94. Grand Rapids, MI: Zondervan, 1994.

Wilkerson, Mike. *Redemption: Freed by Jesus from the Idols We Worship and the Wounds We Carry.* Wheaton, IL: Crossway, 2011.

Wiseman, Cathy. *Borderline Personality: A Scriptural Perspective.* Phillipsburg, NJ: P&R, 2012.

Wolters, Albert M. *Creation Regained: Biblical Basics for a Reformational Worldview.* Grand Rapids, MI: Eerdmans, 1985.

Wren, Brian. *Bring Many Names: 35 New Hymns.* Carol Stream, IL: Hope, 1989.

ABOUT THE
CONTRIBUTORS

Ernie Baker, MDiv, DMin. Ernie Baker joined the Master's College in 2005 as a faculty member in the college's biblical counseling department. He received his MDiv from Capital Bible Seminary and his DMin from Westminster Theological Seminary. Baker has been in ministry since 1980 with twenty-five years' experience as a pastor and in training and equipping pastors and laypeople in the skills of biblical counseling and conciliation. He is a certified conciliator with Peacemaker Ministries, teaching a number of conflict resolution courses and doing conciliation. He is certified as a biblical counselor with the Association of Certified Biblical Counselors and a council board member of the Biblical Counseling Coalition. At the Master's College, Baker is responsible for teaching a wide range of the biblical counseling courses in both the bachelor's and master's degree programs. He is married to Rose, and they have three sons and three daughters. He enjoys reading, studying the American Civil War, hunting, and gardening.

Kevin Carson, MDiv, DMin. Kevin Carson serves as pastor of Sonrise Baptist Church in Ozark, Missouri, and also serves as professor and department chair of biblical counseling at Baptist Bible College and Theological Seminary in Springfield, Missouri. He earned his MDiv from Baptist Bible Graduate School, Springfield, Missouri, and his

DMin from Westminster Theological Seminary. He is certified by the Association of Certified Biblical Counselors (ACBC) and travels with ACBC as a teacher-trainer. Carson also serves as an adjunct faculty member at several institutions. He and his wife have four children.

Kevin DeYoung, MDiv. Kevin DeYoung has been the senior pastor at University Reformed Church in East Lansing, Michigan, since 2004. Prior to serving at University Reformed Church, he was the associate pastor at First Reformed Church in Orange City, Iowa. He and his wife, Trisha, have five children: Ian, Jacob, Elizabeth, Paul, and Mary. DeYoung is the author of eight books, including *Crazy Busy*. He is a graduate of Hope College and Gordon-Conwell Theological Seminary and is currently enrolled in a doctoral program in early modern history at the University of Leicester (United Kingdom).

Howard Eyrich, DMin. Howard Eyrich serves as pastor of counseling ministries at Briarwood Presbyterian Church in Birmingham, Alabama. He is also the director of the DMin program in biblical counseling at Birmingham Theological Seminary, where he is president emeritus. In forty-nine years of ministry, he has been privileged to teach at three seminaries and two colleges. In addition, he has worked in four churches, directing the counseling ministries. He has had the joy of seeing three booklets and five books published, with one remaining in print for more than twenty-five years. Eyrich writes a weekly blog on marriage and family issues. He has been married to his wife, Pamela Jayne, for almost fifty-one years. They have two adult children and eight grandchildren. Eyrich's hobbies are hunting, shooting, model railroading, and building projects.

Jeffery Forrey, PhD. Jeffery Forrey has been involved in counseling and training counselors since 1992. Most recently he has taught at Trinity College of the Bible and Theological Seminary and Westminster Theological Seminary. Previously he worked at the Center for Biblical Counseling and Education in St. Louis, Missouri, as a counselor, teacher, and interim director. He also served as a counselor, teacher, and academic administrator at the Biblical Counseling Center in suburban Chicago. Forrey is a graduate of Delaware Valley College (BA, biology), Westminster Theological Seminary (MAR, counseling/theology), the University of Alabama (MSPH, health behavior), and Trinity Evangelical Divinity School (PhD, educational studies). He and his wife, Debbie, have two children.

Rob Green, MDiv, PhD. Rob Green serves as the pastor of counseling and seminary ministries at Faith Church in Lafayette, Indiana. He and his wife, Stephanie, have three children. Green earned his MDiv degree and his PhD in New Testament from Baptist Bible Seminary in Clarks Summit, Pennsylvania, after having completed a bachelor's degree in engineering physics.

Brad Hambrick, ThM. Brad Hambrick is pastor of counseling at the Summit Church in Durham, North Carolina. Hambrick also serves as a council board member with the Biblical Counseling Coalition and as an adjunct professor of biblical counseling at Southeastern Baptist Theological Seminary. Hambrick has been married to his wife, Sallie, since 1999 and has two wonderful boys.

John Henderson, PhD. John Henderson is a counseling pastor at Denton Bible Church in Denton, Texas. He serves on the board of the Biblical Counseling Coalition as well as the board of the Association of Biblical Counselors (ABC). Henderson has written *Equipped to Counsel*, a three-volume biblical counseling curriculum for the ABC, and *Catching Foxes*, a resource for marriage preparation. His prayerful desire is to see the gospel of Jesus Christ redeem and transform the hearts and lives of people in real and practical ways. Henderson married his wife, Ruth, in 2000, and they have five children.

Garrett Higbee, PsyD. Garrett Higbee is the executive director of Harvest Bible Chapel's Biblical Soul Care Ministries in Chicago, Illinois. He serves on the board of directors of the Biblical Counseling

Coalition. He is also the cofounder of Twelve Stones Ministries, located in Brown County, Indiana. Higbee was trained as a clinical psychologist, but in 1992 came to know Christ as Lord and Savior. He was quickly convinced that Christ and His Word are sufficient for even the most difficult issues encountered in counseling. Higbee is an author and frequent conference speaker around the country. He and his wife, Tammy, have three children and live near the Harvest Bible Chapel campus in Elgin, Illinois.

Jonathan Holmes, MA. Jonathan Holmes serves as the counseling pastor at Parkside Church in Cleveland, Ohio, as well as campus pastor at their Green Campus. Holmes graduated from the Master's College with degrees in biblical counseling and history, and received his MA from Trinity Evangelical Divinity School. He and his wife, Jennifer, have three daughters, Ava, Riley, and Ruby. In his spare time, Holmes enjoys traveling, reading, and politics.

Robert Jones, MDiv, DMin. Robert Jones is a biblical counseling professor at Southeastern Baptist Theological Seminary, having served previously for nineteen years as a lead pastor. He is also the pastor of biblical counseling at Open Door Church in Raleigh, North Carolina, and a visiting professor at several seminaries. Jones graduated from the King's College, Trinity Evangelical Divinity School (MDiv), and Westminster Theological Seminary (DMin, pastoral counseling). He is a certified Christian conciliator and a church reconciliation trainer with Peacemaker Ministries, a certified counselor with the Association of Certified Biblical Counselors, and the author of *Pursuing Peace, Uprooting Anger,* and numerous booklets, articles, and chapters. Jones and Lauren, his wife of thirty-one years, have two adult sons.

Bob Kellemen, ThM, PhD. Bob Kellemen is the executive director of the Biblical Counseling Coalition and serves on the board of directors. He is the founder and CEO of RPM Ministries. For seventeen years, Kellemen served as the founding chairman of and professor in the MA in Christian counseling and discipleship department at Capital Bible Seminary in Lanham, Maryland. He now is an adjunct professor at half a dozen seminaries. Kellemen has pastored three churches and equipped biblical counselors in each church. He is a teaching/leading elder at Cornerstone Community Church in Hobart, Indiana. He and his wife, Shirley, have been married for thirty-three years; they have two adult children, Josh and Marie, one daughter-in-law, Andi, and two granddaughters, Naomi and Penny. Kellemen is the author of twelve books, including *Equipping Counselors for Your Church*.

Heath Lambert, PhD. Heath Lambert serves as the executive director of the Association of Certified Biblical Counselors (ACBC). He also serves as assistant professor of biblical counseling at the Southern Baptist Theological Seminary and at its undergraduate institution, Boyce College. He has been teaching at Southern for the last six years. He also serves as the pastor of biblical living at Crossing Church in Louisville, Kentucky, overseeing counseling and marriage ministries. Before coming to Southern/Boyce, Lambert was a pastor for six years. Heath is thrilled to be married to Lauren and loves life with their three children, Carson, Chloe, and Conner.

Jeremy Lelek, PhD. Jeremy Lelek is president of both the Association of Biblical Counselors and Metroplex Counseling (a local center for biblical soul care in Dallas/Fort Worth). He is a licensed professional counselor in the state of Texas, having earned his master's degree in counseling and a bachelor's degree in psychology. He earned his PhD at Regent University. Lelek is an adjunct professor at Redeemer Seminary and lectures frequently in area churches, training believers with ABC's *Equipped to Counsel* curriculum. Lelek and his wife, Lynne, have four children and are active members of Fort Worth Presbyterian Church (PCA).

Lilly Park, MA, MDiv, PhD Candidate. Lilly Park is assistant professor of biblical counseling at Crossroads Bible College in Indianapolis, Indiana. She enjoys discipling women and serves on the biblical counseling staff at her church. She completed her MA in biblical counseling at the Master's College and her MDiv at the Southern Baptist Theological Seminary, where she is completing her PhD in family ministry.

Randy Patten, MDiv. Randy Patten served for seventeen years as the executive director of the National Association of Nouthetic Counselors (now the Association of Certified Biblical Counselors) and now serves as the ACBC's director of training and development. Patten also serves on the board of directors of the Biblical Counseling Coalition. He served as a senior pastor for twelve years, followed by twelve years as a pastor to pastors and consultant to churches. Patten served as a trainer and counselor at Faith Biblical Counseling Ministries in Lafayette, Indiana, for more than twenty-four years. Patten has been married to his wife, Cindy, for forty-two years, and they have two adult married children and six grandchildren. They all live in the Indianapolis area and are members of College Park Church.

Jeremy Pierre, PhD. Jeremy Pierre is dean of students and assistant professor of biblical counseling at the Southern Baptist Theological Seminary, where he chairs the Department of Biblical Counseling and Biblical Spirituality. He currently serves as a pastor at Clifton Baptist Church and is a speaker at various engagements in the United States and overseas. Pierre is coauthor of the forthcoming *A Primer for Pastoral Counseling* and is a council board member of the Biblical Counseling Coalition. He and his wife, Sarah, raise their five children in Louisville, Kentucky.

Pat Quinn, MAT. Pat Quinn is the director of counseling ministries at University Reformed Church in East Lansing, Michigan, where he applies his love for the gospel to counseling, training counselors, serving as an elder, worship leading, and teaching. He has degrees from Michigan State University and Calvin College and received counseling training from the Christian Counseling and Educational Foundation.

Quinn has been married to his wife, Judie, since 1976. She is a teacher at Lansing Christian High School, where Pat taught Bible for thirty years. Pat and Judie have two grown children and a granddaughter. Quinn is a council board member of the Biblical Counseling Coalition and a part of the blogging team.

Deepak Reju, MDiv, PhD. Deepak Reju serves as the pastor of biblical counseling and families at Capitol Hill Baptist Church in Washington, DC. In this role, he provides individual and couples counseling, leads groups, develops the vision for the counseling ministry, and supervises the counseling team. He also serves as the president of the board of directors for the Biblical Counseling Coalition. Reju did his theological training at the Southern Baptist Theological Seminary (MDiv, PhD). He is the author of three books, including *On Guard: Preventing and Responding to Child Abuse at Church*. Reju and his wife, Sarah, have been married for thirteen years and have five children.

Paul Tautges, DMin. Paul Tautges has served Immanuel Bible Church in Sheboygan, Wisconsin, as pastor since 1992. He is also an adjunct professor of biblical counseling in the United States and overseas. Paul has authored eight books, including *Delight in the Word, Counsel One Another, Comfort Those Who Grieve*, and *Brass Heavens*. He is also the editor of the Help! counseling booklet series. Tautges is an ACBC fellow. He and his wife, Karen, are the parents of ten children. Tautges blogs at Counseling One Another.

Steve Viars, DMin. Steve Viars has served as a pastor and biblical counselor for more than twenty-five years at Faith Church and Faith Biblical Counseling Ministries in Lafayette, Indiana. He serves on several boards, including as vice president of the Biblical Counseling Coalition; Vision of Hope, a faith-based residential treatment center for at-risk girls; and the Association of Certified Biblical Counselors. Viars is a frequent speaker at conferences, colleges, and seminaries in the

United States and abroad. He and his wife, Kris, have three children, Bethany, Karis, and Andrew.

Sam Williams, PhD. Sam Williams went to school at the University of Arizona and then to California School of Professional Psychology in San Diego for graduate school in clinical psychology. He went into private practice for ten years as a licensed clinical psychologist in Lake Charles, Louisiana. Williams has now taught for over a dozen years at Southeastern Baptist Theological Seminary (SEBTS) and in Brazil (as coordinator of SEBTS's Global Theological Initiative). He and his wife, Mindy, and their children attend North Wake Church.

Scripture Index

SUBJECT INDEX

A

academic theology, 204–12
Ackley, Tim, 273
Adams, Jay, 93, 114, 164, 387
Against Heresies, 135
Ambrose, 129
American Psychiatric Association, 151, 173, 300–301
American Psychological Association, 102, 173
Ames, William, 139
ancient philosophy, 132–34
apologetics, 169, 173–74
Aristotle, 138, 140
asceticism, 163–64
Association of Biblical Counselors, 244, 291
Association of Certified Biblical Counselors, 291, 380, 387
Athens, 136–38
Augustine, 130
authoritative revelation, 59–60
authority
    of Bible, 11, 103
    emphatic authority, 98–104
    encyclopedic authority, 98–104
    of God, 10–11, 21, 44–45, 97–98
    psychology and, 100–104
    of Scripture, 96–98, 103, 161, 165
    source of, 169–70

B

Baker, Ernie, 18, 159, 168, 174
Barber, Charles, 168–69, 173–74
Bartholinus, Casper, 139–40
Baxter, Richard, 130, 139, 140, 277
Beck, Aaron, 168

Beck, Johann T., 141
Begg, Alistair, 328
belief systems
    counseling systems and, 159–76
    evaluating, 169–74
    philosophical belief systems, 167–68
Bible
    authority of, 11, 103
    character of, 43–44
    as discerning book, 58–59
    as divine book, 56–57
    as energizing book, 57
    as God's Word, 43–44
    inspiration of, 43–44
    for life issues, 202–25
    as living book, 57
    necessity of, 34–35
    as penetrating book, 57–58
    practicality of, 226–44
    profundity of, 43
    relevance of, 39, 177–97, 338
    theme of, 194–96
    trajectory of, 194–96
    trustworthiness of, 44–45
    unique character of, 43–45
    unique content of, 31–43
biblical blueprint, 231–35
biblical categories, 214
biblical counseling. See also counseling
    beauty of, 124–25
    belief systems and, 159–76
    Christ-centeredness of, 109–25
    church and, 226–44
    in community, 242–43
    contextual observations for, 162–67
    hermeneutical spiral of, 184–85

textual theology, 211–12
theology
  academic theology, 204–5
  of biblical counseling, 138–39, 178–84,
    199–200, 204, 218
  biblical theology, 206–8
  of body, 18, 139, 145–47
  current theology, 221
  exegetical theology, 208–10
  of God's word, 17–18
  historical theology, 220–21
  lexical theology, 210–11
  for life issues, 206–8
  pastoral theology, 215–20
  practical theology, 215–20
  psychology and, 161–62
  of Scripture, 17–18
  spiritual theology, 212–14
  systematic theology, 204–6
  textual theology, 211–12
theory building, 161–64, 167
Thiselton, Anthony, 184
Toward an Exegetical Theology, 184
Tozer, A. W., 57
Trench, Richard, 55
Tripp, Paul, 122, 247, 263–64
Trueblood, Elton, 245–46
trust, 44–45, 312–15
truth
  explanation of, 266–68
  finding, 62–76
  in love, 262–77
  questions for, 178
  relating to life, 300–317
  speaking, 264–77
  suggestions for, 275–77

U
unfaithfulness, 25–27

V
Vanhoozer, Kevin, 184
Viars, Steve, 17, 47
Vitz, Paul, 168

W
Walk of Repentance, The, 253
walking with God, 35–40, 52–53, 92, 334
Welch, Ed, 149, 153, 156
Wellum, Stephen, 263, 269
Westminster Confession, 136
Williams, Sam, 18, 144
wisdom
  competing sources of, 133–34
  formation/transformation of, 212–14
  knowledge from, 40–41
  for life, 40
  literature for, 337–52
  man of, 113
  for marriage, 343–52
  of others, 220–21
  pastoral wisdom, 136
  proverbial wisdom, 340
  psychological wisdom, 127, 136
  relational wisdom, 181
  results from, 42–43
  from Scripture, 50
  speculative wisdom, 340
  understanding from, 41–42
  wise discernment, 304–5
Wisdom Literature
  introduction to, 339–40
  in personal ministry, 337–52
  poetry, 339–43
  value of, 354
Wolters, Albert, 68
Word of God
  authority of, 10–11, 21, 44–45, 97–98
  Bible as, 43–44
  implications of, 45–46
  importance of, 20–22
  ministry of, 131–34
  relevance of, 21–22, 29–46, 202–25
  richness of, 29–46
Word of Life, 28, 268
Wren, Brian, 146
Wundt, Wilhelm, 135